Inside the
Arab World

Other books by the author

A Hundred Million Dollars a Day – Inside the World of
Middle East Money

The Merchants – The Big Business Families of Arabia

Inside the
Arab World

MICHAEL FIELD

HARVARD UNIVERSITY PRESS
Cambridge, Massachusetts
1995

This book is printed on acid-free paper, and its binding materials
have been chosen for strength and durability.

Library of Congress Cataloging-in-Publication Data

Field, Michael, 1949–
    Inside the Arab world / Michael Field.
        p.   cm.
    Includes bibliographical references and index.
    ISBN 0-674-45520-7 (alk. paper)
    1. Arab countries—Politics and government—1945–   2. Arab
countries—Economic conditions.   I. Title
DS63.1.F54   1995
909'.0974927–dc20   94-25822
                                                                        CIP

CONTENTS

To my godchildren and their brothers and sisters

Oliver and Peter
Alexander, Anne-Marie and Lydia
Christopher and Katherine
Georgina and Victoria
Mungo, Theodora and Lydia

Preface

This book has its origins in two articles I wrote for the *Financial Times* in November 1987 and January 1990. The first, headlined 'The Agony of the Arab World', dealt with the reasons for the Arabs' political and economic failure during the previous seventy years, and the other, 'Living in Fear of the Mosque', discussed economic reform and its political consequences. In this book I follow roughly the sequence of logic of those articles, but I also discuss Arab-Israeli peacemaking, the political and economic problems of Saudi Arabia and the changes there have been in the relations of Arab countries with each other and with the West since the end of the Gulf war.

My research was done in three visits I made to the region specifically for the book, in the trips I made before I wrote the *Financial Times* articles and in many other trips during the past twenty-seven years. Hundreds of people have helped me during this time and here I should like to thank some of them. I am leaving out the names of all those to whom I have spoken in Iraq, Syria, Sudan and Iran because I believe that many, or all, of those who are not in government would rather they were not mentioned. Otherwise, working from west to east, I should like to thank:

In Morocco: Rachid Cherkaoui, Karim Bin Brahim, Abdelghani Sbihi, Fouad Akalay, Aziz Bideh, Nadia Salah, Pierre Sala, Khalid Belyazid, Abdelmounaim Dilami, Jack Aubert, Nicholas Hopton.

In Algeria: Yusuf Salmane, Mili Badr Eddine, Miloud Brahimi, Kamal and Anissa Bouslama, Omar Belhouchet, Taher Djaout, Ahmed Bedjaoui, Christopher Battiscombe, John Baggeley, Leila Hamoutene, Ali Lakdari, Christopher Webster, Francis Ghilès.

In Tunisia: Haseeb Ben Ammar, Abdul-Baki Hermassi, Moncef Murad, Ismail Boulahia, Salah Hanachi, Moncef Kaouach, Moncef Cheikh-Rouhou, Fatma Felah, Harold Cool, Robert Glass.

In Egypt: Hazem Beblawi, Mansour Hassan, Dr Ali Dessouki, Saad Ibrahim, Mohammad Sid Ahmed, Yousuf Boutros Ghali, Ismail Sabri Abdullah, Mohammad Fayek, Ahmed Fouda, Paul Balabanis, Sam Skogstad, Sven Burmester, Alan Goulty, Ahmed El-Gindi, Ibrahim Zaki Kinawy, Marc Schwarz, Mohammad Hafez.

In Israel and the occupied West Bank: Ibrahim Dakkak, Radwan Abu Ayyash, Daoud Kattab, Hugh Carnegy, Alex Brodie, David Winn, Daoud Abu Ghazaleh, Shlomo Avineri, Ariye Naor, Reuven Merhav, Dore Gold, Ehud Yaari, Tom Phillips, John Herbst, David Kimche, Nimrod Novik.

In Jordan: Dr. Jamal Shaer, Adnan Abu Odeh, Ahmed Mango, Kamal Abu Jaber, Touma and Ginny Hazou, Rami and Ellan Khoury, Patrick Eyers, Jonathan Owen, Dr Sari Nasr, Jafar Salem, Michel Marto, Jawad Anani, Maher Shukri, Raja Halazon, Hosni Shiyab, Leith Eshbeilat, Bassam Saket, George Hawatmeh, Fahd Fanek.

In Saudi Arabia: Teymour Alireza, Omar Aggad, Abdullah Dabbagh, Ibrahim Touq, Abdel-Aziz Al-Orayer, Prince Fahd bin Salman, Prince Sultan bin Salman, Prince Abdel-Aziz bin Salman, Prince Abdullah bin Faisal bin Turki, Prince Bandar bin Abdullah bin Abdel-Rahman, Turki Khaled Sudairi, Daham Al-Shammary, Abdel-Rahman Zamil, Dr. Ali Namlah, Jafar Askari, Tarek Al-Malki, Khaled Maeena, Dr Abdullah Nassier, Mohammad Salahuddin, Aidarous Kazmi, Ismail Nawwab, Abdullah Mouallimi, Jim Williams, Ahmed Al-Malek, Andrew Thompson.

In Yemen: Abdel-Aziz Al-Saqqaf, Ahmed Al-Gemozi, Dominic Simpson, David Katz, Eric Watkins, Omar Bazara, Allan Furman, Yahya Al-Qassim, Sultan Al-Sha'ibi, Tamam Bashraheel, Abdel-Wahad Sharaf, Abdullah Said Abadan.

In Kuwait: Saleh Al-Falah, Ismail Shati, Sheikh Khaled Nasser Al-Sabah, Siraj Al-Baker, Abdlatif Al-Hamad, Sulaiman Mutawa, Anwar Mulla, Abdullah Nibari, Jasim Al-Qatami, Isa Majid Shaheen, Shaker Madooh, Abdullah Alghanim.

In the United Arab Emirates: David and Frauke Heard, Faraj Bin Hamoodah, Muncif Bin Hamida, Abdullah Mazrui, Zaki Nusseibeh, Sheikh Nahayyan bin Mubarak Al-Nahayyan, Hussein Nowais, Khalaf Otaiba, Anwar Sher, Abdel-Khaleq Abdullah, Khalaf Habtoor, Mohammad Shams, Mahdi Tajir, Abdullah Saleh, Sulaiman Mazrui, Anwar Gargash, Robin Allen, Mahdi Sajjad.

In Oman: Kamal Sultan, Nigel Harris, Deepak Attal, Saad Al-Jenaibi, Ahmed Farid Al-Aulaqi.

In London: Fouad Jaffar, Abdullah Alireza, Dr Ghazi Algosaibi, Sinclair Road, Jamie Bowden, George Joffé, Charles Gurdon, George Kanaan, Mohammad Ramady, Tim Smith, Abdelwahab El-Affendi, Said Sukkar, Jameel Al-Sanea, Keith McLachlan.

1

Failure

1

The Arab World

Failure and reform – the Arab peoples – minorities – Sunnis and Shias – Arab economies – oil states

The Arab world has not been a happy or successful place in the last fifty years, and the misery and disenchantment of the people has recently become acute. As one of the Arab ambassadors in London put it to me, 'the people have lost faith in their governments. There is a sense of failure, which has opened a gap between the rulers and the ruled. It has led to a lack of self-confidence in Arab culture, and hostility to foreign influences. For years the Arab world has not been at ease with itself'.

When he made these remarks the ambassador, who represented Algeria, had particularly in mind the disastrous recent events in his own country. The obvious corruption of Algeria's political system in the 1980s had led the mass of the people to reject the Government and embrace the revolutionary Islamic Salvation Front, not because they were necessarily devoutly religious but because the Islamists were the only powerful and organized opposition party. The results during the years since 1988 had been that the Government's belated but genuine attempt to introduce democracy had led to riots, mass arrests, the cancellation of elections, the assassination of the President and the imposition of what amounted to military rule. For the Algerian establishment, the people associated with the Front de Liberation Nationale, which had won the country's independence from France, the whole experience was politically (and financially) threatening, and also disillusioning. The ambassador and many like him wanted to believe that they were creating a new, just, powerful and successful society and it hurt them to be told by their people that they had failed.

Algeria's experience of hope being destroyed by corruption, and corruption breeding violence, has been the experience of the Arab world as a whole since the end of the Second World War. This book is about exactly this theme. It is about failure and the reaction to it. It deals first with the rise and fall of the Arabs' political and economic hopes, and with the unhappiness and soul-searching that has gone with the fall. Then it discusses the change that is happening. In all Arab societies there is a feeling among a large part of the middle classes – not just the intelligentsia but small businessmen and traders – that they have been badly ruled. There is a debate on how government should be improved, on how it should be made 'legitimate'. Legitimacy is an important topic in the Arab world at present. Coinciding with this debate the huge indebtedness of the poor countries, which make up most of the Arab states and contain almost all of the region's population, has led the creditors, namely the Western governments, the International Monetary Fund and the World Bank, to demand economic reforms. These have involved devaluations, the reduction of the food and energy subsidies given to the people and the privatization of state corporations – all measures designed to stop the countries consuming more than they produce. In return for seeing these reforms put in place the creditors have been prepared to grant new credit or reschedule the repayment of loans, and in one case they have actually forgiven debt.

Any government which cuts its spending and tells its people that they can no longer have the subsidies and guaranteed jobs they have been used to for the last twenty years, is going to have to give something in return. This has taken the form of steps towards democracy: it is here that the economic pressures and the intellectual ferment of recent years have come together. Since 1988 there have been democratic reforms, or moves in a democratic direction, in Jordan, Egypt, Tunisia, Algeria and even in Morocco, Yemen and Saudi Arabia. In Algeria the reforms were radical. A totally free press was allowed, the Ministry of Information was abolished, all sorts of political parties were licensed and elections were being held in December 1991 and January 1992 when the Government panicked at the prospect of an Islamic victory, cancelled the second round of the contest, imprisoned thousands of Islamic political activists and banned their party. Algeria's problem was that it had gone too fast. As a Palestinian columnist writing a few months later observed, 'Arab democracy is like a medicine which if taken all in one dose kills the patient and embarrasses the doctor'. The more successful countries so far have been those where reform has been slow. At times this has led to the process coming to a halt, or even taking a few steps backwards.

In every case the reason for the governments' hesitation has been the challenge of the Islamists, the only body ready and waiting to step into the vacuum created when opposition has suddenly been made legal. While new secular political parties have had to build themselves from scratch, the Islamic politicians have had an established network of contacts through the links between mosques, the religious faculties at the universities and charitable societies. Some of the Islamic politicians have been genuinely idealistic and even Godly people, but most are using religion simply as a means of gaining power. Their supporters are backing them for a mixture of reasons: disenchantment with the corruption of the existing regimes, dislike of the way Western influence has been undermining the family, which is at the very centre of a Muslim's sense of values, and a general objection to what a journalist in Jordan described as 'spivs, BMW drivers and women in mini-skirts'. A few people believe they can re-establish the perfect Islamic society that the Prophet Mohammad created in Medina in the seventh century. In socialist countries the small shopkeeper class likes the sense of strength it gets from belonging to a militant organization and looks forward to the bigger profits it might make from a more free enterprise Islamic economy. All of the supporters of the Islamists are reacting to a feeling that their countries have failed in the last half century. They see political Islam as a philosophy that comes from their own culture, rather than being an imported Western ideology, such as socialism, and because it has its roots in their own society they believe it will bring out their hidden strengths and make them great again.

While the Arab countries, or some of them, have been changing internally their relations with each other and with Israel have changed. Since the late 1970s, the Arab world has been edging towards making peace with Israel. Egypt agreed a peace treaty in 1978, which left the other Arab states knowing that there was no longer any possibility of their being able to confront Israel militarily. But none of them dared follow Egypt in making peace because they knew that they would be accused by their brethren of betraying the national cause. Then the Palestinian leadership and a large part of its guerilla force was evicted from Lebanon in 1982 and 1983, having been thrown out of Jordan in 1970 and 1971. The leadership went to Tunis, a thousand miles from its homeland. Although a majority of the Palestinian fighters stayed in Lebanon and others trickled back in the mid-1980s, they were embroiled in that country's civil war and since 1990, when the Syrians were able to impose peace on Lebanon, they have been firmly under Syrian control. For the last ten years the Palestinian Liberation Organization and its guerilla forces have not been able even to pretend to wage war on Israel. They have had no base from which to operate. After 1987, when an uprising against Israel, the *intifadah*, was begun by the Palestinians living in the occupied territories, the leadership in exile realized that if it did not get involved in the American-sponsored 'peace process' it could be ignored, and excluded from any deal that emerged between the Israelis and the Palestinians in the territories. It risked being forgotten. Therefore in late 1988 Yasser Arafat, the PLO Chairman, prodded by the Americans, finally, awkwardly recognized Israel. The Israelis, meanwhile, were slowly coming to realize that their occupation of the West Bank and Gaza entailed economic and security costs, as well as giving them a buffer between their state and Arab countries which looked far less threatening than they had twenty years earlier. From late 1988 the Palestinians and Israelis began intermittent talks, and in September 1993 the Israeli Foreign Minister and Mahmoud Abbas signed the first stage of a peace settlement between them.

The peace process has been speeded up by the change in the global balance of power that has occurred with the collapse of the Soviet Union, which was the principal backer of the Arab radicals, Syria, Iraq and Libya, the countries which used to work hardest to embarrass or undermine any Arab state or Palestinian group which might have recognized Israel – while making sure that they were not sucked into war with Israel themselves. The departure of the Soviets has left America as the dominant power in the Middle East, able to put pressure both on the Arab radicals and on Israel, which is no longer seen as such a vital ally in 'the fight against Communism'. American power has been enhanced by the easy victory of the allied coalition over Iraq in the Gulf war of 1991. That war and the crisis which led to it also had the effect of splitting the Arab world in a way which will take many years to heal. The immediate effect of this for the Arab nationalists, particularly the Palestinians, was traumatic. Previously the Arabs had tried always to maintain a veneer of unity, however bad their disagreements, because they found it emotionally necessary to do so. The Gulf crisis, however, forced the different governments to admit to themselves that they had fundamentally different interests. The Gulf states and Saudi Arabia acknowledged that the Western powers were closer friends and better allies than other Arab countries. I was in Saudi Arabia during the Gulf war and I noticed in the early stages, when Iraqi missiles were landing on Riyadh every night, how the Saudis were becoming steadily more pro-Western and anti-Palestinian, and they were on the verge of being quite sympathetic to the Israelis who were also under attack, when the missile raids stopped.

After the war several of the poor Arab countries, which had

sympathized with the Iraqis, realized that they would be getting little
aid from the oil states in future and should redouble their efforts to
live within their means. The countries of the Maghreb, Algeria,
Morocco and Tunisia, decided there was no point in looking to the
future in pan-Arab terms and they had better look directly to their own
interests and try to develop their relations with Europe. This type of idea
has become general in the Arab world. People are no longer thinking of
unity, or joint Arab action as a means of solving their problems and
achieving prosperity and greatness. They are no longer looking to their
brothers to help their cause, and so giving themselves somebody else
to blame when things go wrong. Each country is having to fend for
itself. The pressing economic problems of the poor countries – debt,
fast expanding populations, huge unemployment, worries about a
shortage of water – are pushing in the same direction. Arab politicians
are becoming more pragmatic – not in a smooth and steady fashion,
but in a difficult and erratic way with steps backwards as well as
forwards. The result may be disappointing for the nationalists, but
in practical terms of peace and prosperity it should be beneficial for
everybody, inside the Arab world and outside.

Before going on to discuss these themes of economic and political
change in more detail, it may be useful to give some introductory information on the Arab world, to explain what it is, who are its people
and what its resources are.

A simple political definition is that the Arab world is composed of
the twenty-one members of the Arab League, an institution promoted
by the British at the end of the Second World War and based in Cairo.
During its first thirty years Arab states joined the League as they became
independent, which by 1973 gave it the following eighteen members,
working from west to east: Morocco, Algeria, Tunisia, Libya, Egypt,
Sudan, Lebanon, Syria, Jordan, Iraq, Saudi Arabia, North and South
Yemen, which merged in 1990, Kuwait, Bahrain, Qatar, the United
Arab Emirates (principally Abu Dhabi and Dubai) and Oman. During
the 1970s three further states, Mauritania, Somalia and Djibouti, were
admitted, though it was muttered that these new members had rather
doubtful Arab credentials and had joined in part to benefit from the
flow of aid that might result from the rise in oil prices in 1973–4. A final
member, admitted in 1976, was the Palestine Liberation Organization,
representative of the Palestinian state in exile.

What the Arab League members, with the exception of Somalia and
Djibouti, have in common is that most of their inhabitants speak Arabic
as their mother tongue. It is this rather than any physical or ethnic trait

that makes them Arab. A language brings with it a way of thinking and a culture, and in the Arabs' case it also brings a religion. Not all Arabs are Muslim – a minority of about 5 per cent is Christian – and certainly not all Muslims are Arabs – together the Turks, Iranians, Pakistanis, Indian Muslims, Bangladeshis and Indonesians greatly out-number the Arabs – but, even so, Islam is a particularly Arab religion. It was revealed by God to the Prophet Mohammad in Arabic and its laws were suited to the structure of society in seventh-century Arabia. Muslims are called to prayer five times a day in Arabic, the prayers themselves are in Arabic and anyone who aspires to be an Islamic scholar has to speak Arabic. For most Arabs the senses of being Arab and being Muslim are closely bound together.

The Arabs, therefore, define themselves as a collection of peoples who speak Arabic and are mainly Muslim, and they are bound together in a broad emotional and cultural sense not just by these two character-istics but by a sense of being heirs of a shared history. This history begins with God's revelation of the Koran to the Prophet – anything before this is regarded as being rather obscure and of minority academic interest. Then it runs through the early conquests, which spread Islam and Arabic as the language of religion, law and government, out of the Arabian Peninsula to Egypt, North Africa, Spain, Syria, Iraq, Persia and central Asia. The two centuries after the conquests were a time of cultural and scientific prosperity. Arab scholars developed the system of counting that uses zeros, they invented algebra, advanced the Greeks' and Romans' discoveries in astronomy and medicine, and, assisted by Greeks and Persians, built some magnificent and spacious buildings of beautiful proportions. Modern Arabs, who are much more conscious of their history than Westerners are of theirs, like to remind foreigners of how far they were in advance of Europe in the eighth and ninth centuries. It is fair to say that Arab schools today represent the golden days of Arab civilization in a religious and uncritically glowing fashion, without stressing the contributions of the conquered peoples, or the political turbulence of the early caliphate, or the relatively short time, two hundred years, that elapsed between the initial conquests and the Arab empire beginning to fall under the control of the Turks. These shortcomings of teaching, of course, do nothing to alter the relevance of history to the people's feeling of themselves as being Arab. An Arab in Morocco and an Arab in Oman can learn the same lessons in school or watch the same Egyptian-produced historical drama on television, and each can say to himself 'ah, that invention, those buildings, that victory, that civilization, were the works of my ancestors'. And the more the story is glamorized the stronger its influence may be. The knowledge that when the Arab world was very briefly under one rule it was rich, sophisticated and powerful has inevitably acted as a strong force pushing twentieth-century Arabs towards the idea of unity.

The definition of 'Arabs' in terms of their language, religion and history is made necessary by their being so varied racially. The Arab armies which came out of the Arabian Peninsula in the mid-seventh century numbered only a few tens of thousands at the most. A few of the people they conquered, in Yemen, the Syrian desert and the Sahara, were Arab, but the rest were not. They were Persians and the descendants of the Sumarians and Assyrians in Iraq, Greeks and Syrians on the east Mediterranean coast, Eygptians and, further south, black African tribes on the Nile, and Berbers, Vandals and whatever settlers had arrived in Roman times along the coast of North Africa. The descendants of these people now regard themselves in a broad sense as being Arab. But they may be very different from each other physically. The Sudanese are black and many of the Syrians, who must have much Crusader blood, are quite fair. The people of the Maghreb, who by origin are mainly Berber, tend to have a slimmer, more angular physique than the thick-set, swarthy Iraqis. None of this means that anybody can tell where an Arab comes from just by looking at him – most Arabs look just generally Arab, Middle Eastern or Mediterranean – but it does mean that sometimes one can say of a particular person 'he looks typically Egyptian, or Nejdi (central Saudi Arabian) or Yemeni'.

Along with the physical differences goes people's sense of belonging to a particular place. The inhabitants of the Arab world feel themselves to be both Arabs and citizens of individual countries. A hundred years ago, when the broad concept of Arabism hardly existed, people thought of themselves, and were thought of by foreigners, only as inhabitants of countries or regions. The idea of the 'Arab world' did not begin to be developed by nationalists until early this century, and it did not become common in Western countries until the Egyptian President, Gamal Abdel-Nasser, made it popular in the 1950s and 1960s.

The temperaments of Arab peoples differ. Arabs and the other nations of the Middle East readily make sweeping and often disdainful generalizations about each other. The Iraqis are said to have a streak of violence and brutality running through their character, and it is certainly true that their country has had an appallingly violent history both recently and in past centuries. Another characteristic of the Iraqis is that in business and government they are forceful and energetic. They are said to be 'effective' people. The Syrians have a reputation for being cunning and commercial. The Kuwaitis are 'arrogant' – or have become arrogant since they became rich in the 1950s – though this is a trait that seems to be much more apparent to Arabs than to Westerners. Algerians are secretive and suspicious. And the Egyptians are tolerant and easy-going, with a relaxed confidence that comes from having 5,000 years of history behind them. They are the one Arab people for whom history does not begin with the Muslim conquests. Another characteristic of the Egyptians is that they have a fatalistic and submissive streak, which makes them liable to be mistreated when abroad. An Egyptian once complained to me in a surprised and hurt tone, 'the other Arabs, they are not nice to us'.

These sorts of generalizations may not be easily accepted by the more sensitive members of the Western liberal intelligentsia. And the decision of an Iranian newspaper a few years ago to run a daily series of jokes – albeit very innocent and quite affectionate jokes – that were meant to represent the characters of different Middle Eastern peoples (including the Iranians themselves) would seem extraordinary to most Westerners. But the fact is that an awareness of racial differences and discrimination based on this is part of life in the Middle East, and anyone who looks at the area through Western eyes and pretends that these prejudices do not exist is likely to misunderstand it. The Arabs – and the Iranians and Turks – believe in racial differences and are not embarrassed about discussing them. Middle Eastern society, and for that matter society in most developing countries, is coarser than that in the industrialized West.

The ethnic mixture of the Arab world is complicated further by the existence of distinct minorities of non-Arab peoples, and by religious minorities, some Arab and some non-Arab. In some countries the minorities together make up more than half of the population. The classic case is Iraq, a country created after the First World War out of the three Ottoman provinces of Basra, Baghdad and Mosul. In the south, including the marsh areas between the Tigris and Euphrates rivers, the population is composed of Arabs of the non-conformist Shia sect of Islam. In the centre it is mainly orthodox Sunni Arab and in the north it is Kurd. The exact origin of the Kurds, who are spread between Turkey, Iran and Iraq, is uncertain. They are one of the Iranian peoples, who live to the east of the Arab world in Iran, Afghanistan, Tadjikistan and Pakistan. They may be descendants of the Medes, who are mentioned in the Old Testament, particularly in the context of King Darius, 'the Mede and Persian', who was one of the monarchs who built the Persian empire. In smaller communities spread around Iraq are groups of Assyrian and Armenian Christians, Iranians, Turkomans and Christian Arabs.

Lebanon and Syria have similar mixtures of peoples, with Lebanon having a particularly large proportion of Christians making about 30 per cent of the population. The biggest Lebanese Christian group is the Maronites, who belong to a church that was founded by a monk named Maron in the fifth century. The church acknowledges the supremacy of the Pope in Rome but has its own liturgy. In Algeria and Morocco there are Berber communities which are quite distinct from the Arab population, which is itself, by origin, of largely Berber stock. In these two countries the distinction between Arab and Berber today is less a matter of blood, or genes, than of the cultures the two peoples have retained, or of what people consider themselves to be. Even in the Gulf states, which have indigenous populations of less than a million, the 'nationals' are a mixture of people of central Arabian, Iranian and Iraqi origin – and in Kuwait, Qatar and the United Arab Emirates the nationals are greatly outnumbered by recently arrived expatriate workers from all parts of the Arab world and Asia.

Only Egypt and Tunisia are blessed by populations that are racially homogenous – and in Egypt the homogeneity is made incomplete by the existence of a Christian minority, made up mostly of members of the Orthodox church, which accounts for about 8 per cent of the population. These people, known as Copts, take their name from the same Greek word that produced the name 'Egypt'; in Arabic the country is called 'Misr'. They are descended from the Egyptian Christians who were overrun by the Arab conquests in the seventh century. They consider themselves to have at least as good a claim to their country as the Muslim Egyptians and even when they have come under pressure from Islamic extremists, as has happened in Upper Egypt in the last ten years, they have not shown any inclination to emigrate, as minorities sometimes do.

In most cases Copts and Egyptian Muslims live side by side in harmony. In all the secular aspects of life their cultures are the same. Even their religious beliefs have become entwined in minor ways, partly through both religions having absorbed some pharonic practices, notably a respect for the dead. Some Egyptians acknowledge both Christian and Muslim saints, and pray at their tombs. The leaders of the two religions attend each other's major festivals. In Ramadan, the month when Muslims fast during the daylight hours, the Coptic Pope gives an Iftah banquet at sunset one evening for the senior members of the Muslim clergy. And the Muslims have adopted the day after the Coptic Easter Sunday as a national holiday called Sham en-Neseem, which means 'smelling the breezes'. These practices, the Egyptians like to say, show their 'genius for tolerance'.

Among the religious minorities of the Middle East the most conspicuous in Western eyes in recent years have been the Shias. The beliefs of these people have their origin in the seventh century, in the early years of the caliphate, the government of the Prophet Mohammad's successors. For almost fifty years, from soon after the Prophet's death in 632 until 680 when his cousin's son, Hussain, was killed, at the same time as the Arabs were making their great conquests, in the Arab heartland a very bloody dispute was waged over who should rule. It saw several battles and the murder of three out of the first four caliphs. It revolved around the principle of the succession in an Islamic state. One party, espoused by the Prophet's three immediate successors, maintained that it should go to whomever was most fitted to the task, this being some-body chosen by the previous leader and the other best-regarded men of the new community. The other party, led by the Prophet's greatly respected cousin and son in law, Ali, said that the succession should stay in the Prophet's family. In due course the first faction's supporters became known as Sunnis, after the Arabic word, *sunna*, tradition, denoting their belief in the established tribal principle of a leader being selected by consensus, while Ali's faction became known as the 'Shia Ali', the 'party of Ali'. There was merit in the Shia claim as well as in that of its opponents, because although the election of a leader is certainly part of the Arab tradition, the choice is nor-mally made from those quite closely related to the previous ruler. In practice both parties were interested in more than legal principles. Although the first four caliphs were themselves men of dignity and Godliness, many of the people around them had scarcely absorbed the beliefs and moral code of the new religion and were still more concerned by traditional matters of personal ambition and tribal and family jealousy.

The outcome of the feud was a victory for the establishment faction, which was centred on the Umaiyid family of Mecca. In 661 this family established the Umaiyid Caliphate in Damascus, where it ruled for ninety years. Ali was defeated in battle and then murdered in Kufa, in modern Iraq, in the first year of Umaiyid rule. His son, Hussain, was surrounded by Umaiyid forces near the Iraqi town of Kerbela when he was travelling from Mecca to Kufa in 680, possibly to lead a revolt. He and his small party, which included all the members of his immedi-ate family, were massacred.

Both Ali and Hussain were orthodox in their religious beliefs – in so far as one can say there was such a thing as orthodoxy at this early stage when Islamic law had not yet been codified. But it was not long before the two men's supporters began to acquire elements of other beliefs. This happened because their party was one of opposition. It attracted elements of the original God-fearing and puritan Arab armies who were not relations of the Umaiyids and who were shocked by the Graeco-Syrian luxury and the nepotism which characterized Umaiyid rule. It also attracted some of the new non-Arab converts – Syrians, Greeks and Persians – who had embraced Islam after the conquests. In theory these people were equal to all other Muslims, but in practice in the early days they remained subjects of the Arabs and continued to pay the taxes which were supposed to be the lot only of infidels. These foreigners adopted the Arabic language and Arab dress, but introduced into the Shias' Islam elements of their own previous religions, so giving it a mystical character. Messianic notions of a Mahdi, a deliverer, became established, saints were created, and places of pilgrimage, above all Kerbela, appeared. Thus within a century Shiism evolved from a family political party into a distinctive religious cult with a strong anti-establishment bias. The Shias' leaders, the imams, remained, or were supposed to remain, direct descendants of Ali, until the late ninth century AD. At this point the twelfth of their line, a semi-mythical figure who happened to be called Mahdi, went into hiding, where he allegedly remains to this day. Other elements of Ali's family achieved power in the year 750. They overthrew the Umaiyids and established the Abbasid Caliphate in Baghdad – named after their ancestor, Abbas, an uncle of the Prophet. These men were not closely related to Ali and not connected to the imams. They won their victory over the Umaiyids with Shia support, but thereafter turned on the Shias and suppressed their frequent rebellions.

Since the seventh century the two major theological differences between the Sunnis and Shias have remained those which appeared at the beginning. The Shias retain their view that Ali and his family should have succeeded to the Caliphate, and they invest their leaders with spiritual authority, to the extent that particularly Godly leaders and all the early imams have the status of saints. The Sunni *ulema* (religious leaders), in contrast, are no closer to God than the ordinary man in the street. They are simply well-educated teachers and judges able to interpret the Koran and the Hadith, the compilation of the sayings and actions of the Prophet, which together are the basis of Islamic (Shariah) law. The Sunni *ulema* can give helpful guidance to their congregations, but their opinions are purely those of lawyers. This is logical, given that Islam, for Sunnis especially, is as much a law, setting out rules for every aspect of life, from how to wash to how to govern an Islamic community, as it is a religion, in the sense that Christians understand the idea. Compared with Christianity there is more emphasis on carrying out God's instructions in daily life and less on understanding and believing spiritual mysteries.

The fundamentals of Islamic belief are the same for both Sunnis and Shias. God has the same personality and Mohammad has the same role as His messenger. The sects have the same Koran, the word of God as memorized by the Prophet. Their differences in the Shariah law are minor, being mostly concerned with matters of family law and inheritance. Sunnis and Shias share the basic obligations of Muslims to pray five times a day, give taxes to the poor, fast during the month of Ramadan, and go on pilgrimage to Mecca if they can afford it.

Where there are big differences between the sects are in matters of ritual. This is seen most strikingly in Moharram, the first month of the Muslim year, when the Shias commemorate in public (or, in Saudi Arabia, in private) the martyrdoms of Ali, Hussein and Hussein's older brother, Hassan. The centrepiece of the processions they hold is a form of passion play, representing the events that took place in Kerbela in 680. There are 'corpses' carried upright in their biers, Hussein on a magnificent white horse and troops of sinister black riders. At either end of the processions are troops of chest beaters and back-flagellants, who scourge themselves in unison with steel whips as they chant the name of Ali. When the processions stop, professional sermonizers tell the story of the martyrdom. They describe how Hussein's little party is surrounded by thousands of its enemies. Entreaties for mercy to be shown to the women and children fall on deaf ears and so Hussein draws up his seventy-two retainers for battle. The Umaiyids stand back and shoot down the party with arrows until there is only Hussein left, wounded and exhausted, cradling his little son dead in his arms. He sinks down beside his tent to drink some water, and in the act of drinking he is shot through the mouth by an arrow. As they hear this heart-rending tale punctuated by the preachers' calling on God to bless the souls of Hussein and his relatives, the listeners weep at the pity of it.

The Moharram processions show in a theatrical way the Shia concern with sainthood, martyrdom, and death. Related to these ideas are an interest in tombs, pilgrimages to tombs, and the decoration of tombs and the mosques associated with them. There is nothing of a formal religious or architectural nature which separates a Sunni from a Shia mosque – adherents of either sect can pray in any mosque. But Shia mosques in Iran and Iraq tend to be much more elaborately decorated, with gold domes and blue tiles covered with designs of flowers and arabesques. To Muslims in Egypt and Morocco, both countries with strong artistic traditions and long-established popular habits of reverence for holy men, the decoration of the Shia mosques and the pilgrimages do not seem exceptional, though neither Egypt nor Morocco, nor any other Sunni country has anything like the Moharram processions. To see the contrast between Sunni and Shia decoration and ritual at its starkest one has to consider Saudi Arabia, where since the eighteenth century the ruling Saud family and the *ulema* have had a partnership whose specific intention has been to purge Islam of superstitious practices. According to the pure, legalistic, Saudi doctrine any respect given to saints detracts from the fundamental concept that there is only one God. The declaration that 'There is no God but God and Mohammad is the Messenger of God' is a Muslim's basic statement of his belief. To emphasize the importance they attach to this the followers of the austere Saudi doctrine call themselves Muwahiddin, Unitarians. The Muwahiddin believe that people who decorate a religious building will quickly begin to worship the decoration rather than God. Likewise they think that to pay respect to a tomb, a mere lump of stone with a skeleton beneath it, is weak-minded sentimentality. Even Saudi kings are buried in unmarked graves in the desert, and soon after their deaths nobody can remember where they have been laid. As to the Moharram processions, the standard Saudi belief is that they are quite simply mad. One year, a day before the processions were due to take place, a young Saudi prince told me he could not understand why the Shias had to scourge themselves. 'The events they are remembering took place long before they were born, and there's no reason for them to blame themselves now because there's nothing they can do to stop what happened,' he remarked with a sublime lack of sensitivity.

Because the rituals and the decoration of mosques are visible, whereas legal issues such as the succession to the Caliphate or the question of whether God will be visible to souls on judgement day (which provokes occasional correspondence between the Saudi and Omani *ulema*) are not, it is these relatively unimportant external differences that provoke anti-Shia prejudice. In most cases the Muslims who are prejudiced against Shias are the ill-educated; the exceptions are the Saudis, who, given their commitment to promoting a very pure form of Islam, have to be considered a case apart. Among educated people of goodwill in the Muslim world little attention is paid to the differences in religious custom.

Even the most tolerant people, though, are aware of the social and economic differences that separate the Sunnis from most of the Shia communities. As the story of Shiism's early evolution shows, from the beginning Shiism has been associated with the underprivileged and oppressed. In one country, Iran, Shiism became the religion of the establishment but the circumstances were contrived. In the sixteenth century the Safavid shahs forced the conversion of the majority of their subjects, who were not Shia, with the specific intention of generating a stronger Iranian national consciousness and feeling of separateness from the neighbouring Turks and Arabs. Everywhere else the Shias remained at the bottom of society. In southern Iraq, Bahrain, southern Lebanon and the Saudi Arabian Eastern Province Shias make up majorities or large minorities of the population, but they have always been under foreign ruling classes. Occasionally they have been persecuted; more often they have been ignored and left to do the most menial jobs, irrigating the fields and cultivating the date palms. It has only been under the influence of the Iranian revolution and the judgements of Ayatollah Khomeini, who believed that rather than wait for deliverance by Mahdi, whenever he might reappear, the Shias should rise and try themselves to improve their lot, that some of them, particularly those in Lebanon, have become militant. During the 1980s the Shia militias were the most important forces in Lebanon after the Syrian and Israeli armies. What impressed both the Christian and Sunni Lebanese, and foreigners, about the Shias' violence was how it was aimed against everybody. It did not matter to Hizbollah and its associate, Islamic Jihad, their most militant organizations, that many of the Westerners they kidnapped were known to be friends of the Arab world. Nor did they care anything for Lebanon's tradition of tolerance, strained as this was by the early 1980s, and the profitable mixing of cultures which had produced the comfortable, sophisticated and highly commercial Levantine way of life. The Shias made their entry into Lebanese politics as exactly what they were, embittered outsiders.

It is the economic differences between the Sunni establishments and the Shias that are important, not the religious differences. Nobody in Lebanon in the 1980s cared about the theological differences that separated the Shias from the Sunnis. The Shias had been thought of not as heretics but as the poor, unimportant farmers who lived in the rocky hill country of the south, cultivating infertile ground and having their villages shelled, bombed and periodically occupied by Palestinians and Israelis, who treated them as if they did not exist. What led the Shias to assert themselves after the Israeli invasions of 1978 and 1982 were political and economic grievances, the destruction of their villages and the miserable lives they lived as refugees on the outskirts of Beirut. They realized that they had become the biggest single section of the population. They were spurred into action, and trained and armed, by the Iranian revolution. Their religious beliefs did nothing to cause them suddenly to become militant – the thrust of Shia culture with its acceptance of suffering is rather in the opposite direction. Where the Shia religious tradition was influential was in adding a willingness to be martyred to a militancy that stemmed from secular sources.

This basic principle, that religion is not the cause of conflicts but provides a rallying point for conflicts that are basically economic and/ or political, is valid in almost every case where religion surfaces in Middle Eastern politics – which is why I have devoted some space here to the differences between Sunnis and Shias. The rebellion of Shias in southern Iraq after the Gulf war in 1991 was political – it was concerned with overthrowing a brutal system of government that subjected people to the rule of cruel, petty Baath Party officials, many of whom happened to come from the Sunni centre of the country. But it was not in itself a rebellion of Shias against Sunnis. Likewise, where there are tensions between Muslims and Christians, as there have been in Upper Egypt, the cause has been the desire of Muslim extremists to foment sectarian trouble as a means of dividing society and undermining the government. The reason is not that good Muslims are offended by having a Christian minority in their midst. And where, as has happened in most Arab countries, Islamic politicians have gained followings in the last ten years, the reason has not been that the people have suddenly become very devout, but that in the face of political and economic failure the Islamists have been seen as the only alternative to the discredited establishments.

Lastly in this chapter something should be said about the Arab economies, about where the people live and how they earn their livings. This is a large subject and can be dealt with here only in a very general fashion. The detailed functioning of the Arab economies will be explained in later chapters as part of the discussion of their weaknesses and the reforms now being imposed upon them by their governments and creditors.

The population of the Arab world totals 200 million – a rough estimated figure – and it is spread unevenly. Most Arabs live in North Africa. Morocco, Algeria and Tunisia have a combined population of some 60 million, Sudan has 25 million and Egypt, which is by far the most populous Arab country, has something between 56 and 60 million. The reason for Egypt's large population is the existence of the Nile which during millions of years has carried from Central Africa a colossal quantity of silt, forming a narrow band of cultivable land along the Nile valley and at the mouth of the river a large, flat delta. Both the valley and delta are immensely fertile. Seen from the air they stand out in stark, colourful contrast to the barren desert, which begins sharply where the irrigation stops. On the ground one sees the fertility in the large piles of melons, cabbages, carrots and other vegetables, all grown to prodigious sizes, that are stacked beside the roads. Something grows on every patch of land that has not been built on in the Nile valley. Virtually the entire population of the country lives in the valley and delta. Having a flat, densely populated, rich and fertile land as their home must be one of the reasons why the Egyptians have become a peaceful and sedentary people. The fact that the majority remain poor is a factor of the size of the population.

Most of the Arab population outside Egypt lives near the Mediterranean coast of North Africa and the Levant, on the central Moroccan plain and in the surprisingly fertile mountains of Yemen which receive some of the rains of the Indian Ocean. The only populated inland area is Iraq, through which flow the Tigris and Euphrates. These rivers together discharge almost as much water as the Nile brings to Egypt, but they have not produced a country that is nearly as fertile. The Euphrates water and much of the soil of southern Iraq is rather saline, and the Iraqi climate, which can be very cold in winter, does not allow the production of crops throughout the year, as does the climate of Egypt. Travelling through central and southern Iraq one is struck by how uncultivated most of the land appears.

A characteristic of populations in all parts of the Arab world other than Egypt and the southern marsh area of Iraq is that traditionally they have had to survive on the edge of deserts. This has given them a more outward looking and restless way of life than one would expect in a part of the world which until the last fifty years was very poor. Their culture has been influenced in part by the desert nomads. In the Sahara and the deserts of eastern Syria and the Arabian Peninsula there have always been bedouin populations, but the numbers have been small. Even in central Arabia before oil it is thought that the bedouin were outnumbered by the inhabitants of mud villages, earning a living from date palms and vegetable plots. A more important influence on Arab life, albeit one related to the bedouin, has been trade. Arab towns and cities developed as trading centres both because they were in areas which were not self-sufficient in manufactured or agricultural goods and because the Middle East lay between two populous and productive areas of the world, Europe to the west and the Indian subcontinent to the east. There used to be caravan routes between all the major cities and oases in the region. The longest ran from the Mediterranean to the head of the Persian Gulf and from the Mediterranean along the Red Sea coast to Yemen, which with Ethiopia was a source of spices and coffee. It must be partly because of the trading tradition that the Arabs

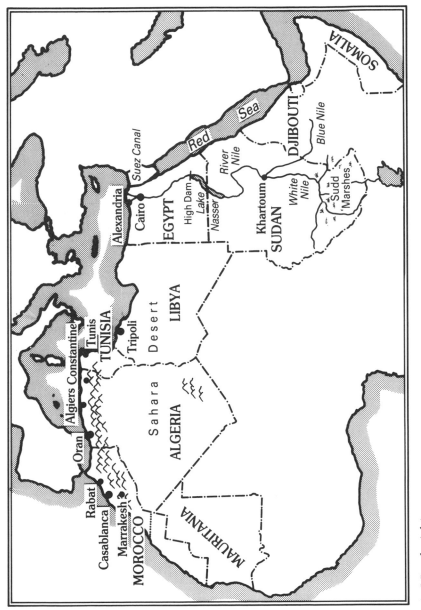

1. North Africa

in the twentieth century have taken to international travel with such ease and enthusiasm.

In all Arab countries the most popular type of work is in service businesses, particularly those concerned with trade, distribution and shop-keeping. Private businessmen who have made money have done so through real estate development, contracting, importing, transport, retailing and most recently tourism. In Egypt in the early 1990s tourism became roughly as big a source of foreign exchange as oil exports, American aid and the remittances of Egyptians working abroad. In every country some attempt has been made to develop industry, though nowhere, except in the petrochemical industries of Saudi Arabia, have there been striking successes. No Arab country has a major industrial sector, apart from petrochemicals and perhaps garment manufacture in Morocco and Tunisia, that is fast growing, internationally competitive and a major source of income for the population. Private investors, outside Saudi Arabia, have not liked to put their money into industry for a combination of political and temperamental reasons, which has meant that the major investors have been inefficient state-owned corporations. In the more left-wing republican countries the state corporations have had very much the character of state industrial organizations in the old eastern Europe.

Most of the Arab countries produce and export oil, and the Gulf states (except Bahrain), Saudi Arabia, Iraq, Libya and Algeria export it in large quantities. Most of the Arab reserves are concentrated in Iraq and the Gulf region, which together with Iran have more than half the world's commercially recoverable reserves. The bigger Gulf oil fields are of a size that have never been found elsewhere. The biggest of all, Ghawar in Saudi Arabia, discovered in 1948, has reserves now estimated at 80 billion barrels. (A barrel is 35 imperial gallons or 42 US gallons.) Burgan in Kuwait, also discovered in 1948, has 70 billion barrels, and Safaniyah, off the Saudi coast, has 30 billion barrels. There are eleven other fields in the Gulf, Iraq and Iran with reserves of ten billion barrels or more. To put these figures in perspective the biggest field ever found in the western hemisphere, Prudoe Bay in Alaska, had 10 billion barrels when it was discovered, though it is likely that the oil companies operating that field pitched their figure more conservatively than has recently been the practice of governments in the Middle East. The biggest fields discovered in the North Sea have been in the 2 to 3 billion barrel range. The important point − even allowing for the fact that the United States and other oil bearing regions have most of their reserves scattered in numerous small fields − is that the Middle East has reserves on a completely different scale from the rest of the world. Oil men say that 'there will never be another Middle East', and given that all the big fields of the region were discovered before 1970, and most of them before 1960, and that the industry now has more than a hundred years of global exploration experience behind it, they are probably right.

At the rates of production running in the early 1990s there was enough oil in the Gulf region for 130 years, which suggests that even with increases in production in the future there is no near danger of the oil fields being exhausted, as people imagine when they ask 'what will the Arabs do when the oil runs dry?' The problem for the Gulf producers is more the reverse. It concerns how much of their oil will be left in the ground when the world finally is forced by slowly declining output and rising prices to switch to other forms of energy. Logically, not every barrel of the world's oil will eventually be consumed, with the last oil well running dry and then the last refinery being closed and the last car being scrapped, and as, therefore, there will be some oil left underground in the end, that oil is bound to be in the Middle East. The interest of Middle Eastern producers since they have realized the implications of this and seen what big drops in production they experience when they overprice their oil, as they did in the early 1980s, has been to keep their production competitive to sustain demand for as long as possible. Since 1985 this has meant maintaining 'reasonable' prices of around $US18–21 a barrel. The countries with the biggest reserves and least immediate demand for revenue, Saudi Arabia, Kuwait and Abu Dhabi, have been the most moderate in their stance on prices.

Since 1985 there has been a steady annual increase in world demand for oil of about 1 million barrels a day, or nearly 2 per cent. This additional demand has come entirely from newly industrialised developing countries. The established industrialised nations by 1985 had adjusted to the oil shocks of 1973–4 and 1979–80 by using oil more efficiently and to some extent developing other sources of energy. They have managed to keep their consumption fairly static and are likely to continue to do so in future. The developing world, however, seems set to continue to demand an extra 1 million barrels a day every year for the next twenty years, and there seems to be nowhere this oil can come from except the Gulf. Demand for Gulf oil will probably be further increased by the slow decline of fields elsewhere in the world. The net effect is that the Gulf can expect an increase in demand, and revenues, of about 6 per cent a year. No doubt in times of crisis there will be sudden surges in the price, but as of 1993 the consensus in the oil industry is that the Gulf countries appreciate their long-term interests well enough to make sure that the surges will be short-lived.

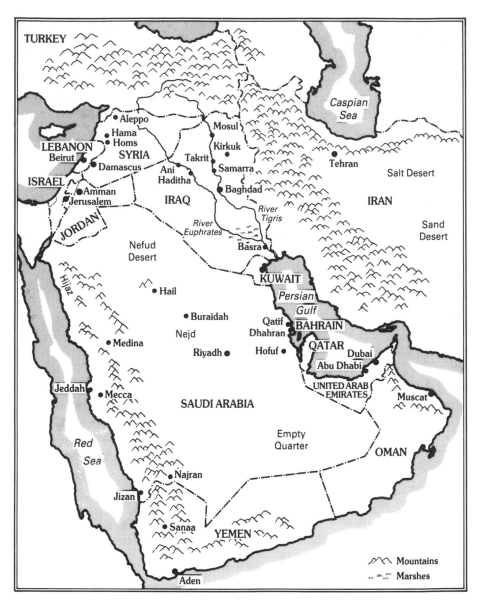

2. The Middle East

In assessing the effects of oil revenues on the Middle Eastern and North African countries one can divide the exporters into three categories: first there is a group of countries which have big populations but small volumes of oil production. These are Egypt, Syria, Tunisia and Yemen. For them oil is simply a very useful additional source of foreign exchange, comparable to tourism, phosphates or textiles. They are not considered as 'oil states' in the normal sense of the term.

Then there are Iran, Iraq and Algeria, which also have substantial populations but have much bigger oil revenues. These countries' economies are dominated by their large foreign exchange incomes and the effects, indirectly, have not been beneficial. In Algeria and Iran oil revenues encouraged the governments and populations to live beyond their means, caused the development of industrial white elephants and made uneconomic small existing industries that had been competitive before the economies in which they operated were swamped by oil wealth. In Iran economic mismanagement caused the 1979 Revolution and in Algeria it bankrupted the country and brought it to the brink of revolution. In Iraq the combination of oil and a large population, 19 million, gave Saddam Hussein the opportunity of developing an enormous military machine, which he used to invade Iran in 1980 and Kuwait in 1990, both with disastrous results.

The last group of oil producers is made up of those that are normally referred to as 'oil states'. They are the countries that have very large revenues relative to the size of their populations: Saudi Arabia, Kuwait, the United Arab Emirates, Qatar, Oman and Libya. The last of these countries, Libya, which has a population of less than 5 million, has been like Iraq in spending much of its money on misguided military and political adventures. Its people have benefited relatively little from its high income. Saudi Arabia and the Gulf states, which are similar to each other in having conservative monarchical systems of government, have developed broadly similar economies in which the thrust of the governments' policies has been to pump revenues into the pockets of their people. This has been done through the creation of extremely generous welfare states providing free education and health services, free medical trips abroad for those who need them, free telephone calls, enormously subsidized water, electricity and fuel, and moderately subsidized basic foodstuffs. Further money is pumped into the economies through land buying and cheap loans for industrial development and agriculture. The governments levy virtually no taxes on their people. The total population of these countries runs to no more than 15 million, of whom 5 million are expatriate workers and managers and 10 million citizens. It is the citizens who receive the lion's share of the benefits of government spending, not only on welfare but on all the other current and capital items in the budgets. Only they are allowed to own real estate, equity shares or import agencies. Foreign contracting and service companies have to operate in joint ventures with local businessmen as partners. It is the Saudi and Gulf Arabs who constitute the Arab rich.

MIDDLE EAST COUNTRIES: POPULATIONS AND OIL RESOURCES

	Population	Oil reserves in bn barrels	Approx. annual oil income ($bn)
Saudi Arabia	13m	260	43
Iran	56m	90	15
Iraq	19m	100	See note 2
Kuwait	2.2m	94	See note 2
United Arab Emirates	1.8m	98	14
Qatar	0.3m	4	2.2
Bahrain	0.3m	0.1	0.5
Oman	1.5m	4	4
Yemen	12	4	0.5
Syria	13	2	1.1
Turkey	57	0.5	nil
Jordan	3.6	nil	nil
Lebanon	3	nil	nil
Israel	5	nil	nil
Egypt	57	4.5	1.2
Sudan	25	see note	nil
Libya	4.8	23	10
Tunisia	8	2	0.5
Algeria	26	9	10
Morocco	26	nil	nil

Notes
1. The populations of Saudi Arabia and the Gulf states include expatriates.
2. Iraq's oil production has been closed since August 1990. Kuwait's production was closed from August 1990 to late 1991, and has since been slowly rebuilt. In 1989, the last year of full production before Iraq's invasion of Kuwait, Iraq had revenues of $12bn and Kuwait revenues of $8.7bn.
3. Bahrain's oil revenues include income from refining Saudi oil and a share of revenues it is given from a Saudi offshore field.
4. Oil has been found in Sudan, but the discoveries have not been properly appraised because exploration has been stopped by the civil war in the south of the country.

2

Deception and Division
1914–48

Diplomacy of First World War and Versailles conference –
creation of Syria, Lebanon, Jordan, Iraq, Saudi Arabia, Israel

The political failure of the modern Arab world has its origins in the time it was created at the end of the First World War. Nationalists, or at least some of the more secular nationalists, had been hoping for independence from Turkish rule and for unity, but what they got instead was division, colonial rule and the imposition of kings they did not want. They also had the beginnings of a Jewish state established on their soil. The whole post-war settlement made for instability.

The new Arab states of Syria, Lebanon, Jordan, Palestine and Iraq were awkward creations. They were not entirely artificial, and it is quite possible that a united Arab state would have been just as unhappy and unstable as the divided states have been. But neither was there such a neat cultural and historical logic to each of them that they could easily be accepted. What aroused the nationalists of the 1920s and led to conflict later on were not mere details of borders, but fundamental issues of whether the states should have been created at all and, if so, which Ottoman districts should have been included in each and which left out. The way the states were constructed sowed the resentments that were eventually to lead to the many Kurdish and Shia uprisings in Iraq and to the Lebanese civil war of the 1970s and 1980s.

The imposition of foreign rule and the immigration of foreign Jews into Palestine caused even greater anger than the division of territories. For patriotic Arabs it became a duty to expel the colonial powers, the kings, who were regarded as their surrogates, and the Zionists. This led to popular rebellions, *coups d'état* and attempted coups, and in due course to four full-scale Arab-Israeli wars.

The idea of unity, once it had been briefly aired but not achieved, itself became a source of tension. At the time of the First World War it was not particularly strong, but it grew in the 1930s and 1940s and became the main theme of nationalists in the 1950s and 1960s. Given that the Arab governments were not only different in character but also had their own vested interests in remaining in being – or only uniting with other states if they could be leader – most of them found themselves paying lip service to unity but resisting it in practice. The frustrations of unity unattained, like the wars with Israel, have poisoned relations between Arab governments ever since. They have contributed to the governments' lack of popular support, their ineffectiveness and the increasing brutality with which they have dealt with their own populations.

The roots of all these problems go back to the settlement imposed on the Middle East in 1918–22. This is the period to which Arabs trace back the political unhappiness of their world, and it is where I shall begin this chapter. I shall then go on in the latter part of this chapter and in the next two chapters to describe the broad development of Arab politics between the First World War and the present, in other words the background against which there is now a ferment for change.

The Arab world at the beginning of the First World War was already partly under European rule. The French governed Tunisia and Morocco as protectorates, and Algeria as a colony which officially was part of metropolitan France, though it was not administered in the same way as the French departments on the other side of the Mediterranean. Egypt had been run by the British, on behalf of the Sultan in Constantinople, since 1882. On the outbreak of war in 1914 it was taken as a protectorate. Oman and the Gulf states since the early years of the twentieth century had likewise been under British protection, and Aden had been a British colony since the middle of the previous century. The central part of the Arabian Peninsula was being fought over by the families of Saud, based in Riyadh, and Rashid, in Hail. This left the regions of Mesopotamia, greater Syria, including Palestine, and the Hijaz, the western edge of the Peninsula, which together constituted, and still constitute, much of the political and emotional heart of the Arab world, under the authority of the Ottoman Empire.

In Egypt and the Ottoman territories there had for half a century been nationalist movements. At first these were almost entirely pan-Islamic in character. They criticized Ottoman rule because it was weak. It was not properly representing the Islamic body politic, the Caliphate, the succession to the rule of the Prophet, which for the last five hundred years had been vested in the Turkish sultans. The imperial government was seen to be failing particularly in its inability to prevent the encroachment of greedy European powers on its territories, or on territories which it had once ruled directly but which for the last century or so had been more or less independent, under rulers who were supposed to be representing the Sultans. The nationalists did not want so much to overthrow the Ottoman rulers as to reinvigorate them.

From the 1880s a parallel anti-Turkish Arab nationalist sentiment began to emerge, and this was greatly strengthened after 1909 when the secular modernizing Committee of Union and Progress (the Young Turks) seized power in Constantinople and began its own efforts to reinvigorate the Empire, partly through stirring Turkish nationalism. The Young Turks were trying to create a political base for themselves quite different from that of the normally tolerant Ottoman sultans, whose legitimacy, in the secular sense, was based on their acceptance of the equality of their different subject races. Inevitably the Young Turks set off hostile nationalist reactions, particularly amongst Arabs. Arab secret societies were founded in Damascus, Baghdad and Beirut, with the purpose of obtaining administrative independence for the Arab provinces and the acceptance in these provinces and in the parliament in Constantinople of the Arabic language as equal to Turkish. There was an idea that the leadership of the Islamic community should be restored to the Arabs, possibly in the form of some joint Turkish-Arab monarchy. Only a few extremists, those who had been arrested or mistreated by the Turkish governors, wanted the overthrow of the Ottomans or complete independence for the Arabs. When war came in 1914 most Arabs loyally supported the Turks, and more Arabs fought in the Turkish army than joined the Arab revolt.

The Arabs at the time of the First World War, therefore, were not on the point of rebellion, nor longing to be liberated from the Turks. When the Turks were expelled from their territories Arabs regarded their liberators with only limited and short-lived goodwill. The British hoped, and believed, from the beginning of the war that the secret societies supported their intervention. In reality, if they had enjoyed the choice, the societies would have preferred to remain under Ottoman rule than to swap it for French or British. Even the Sherif Hussein of Mecca, who raised the standard of the Arab revolt in June 1916, acted with reluctance. He did not like the Turks, but had hoped to remain neutral, receiving money from both sides. What persuaded him to act were rather cautious and ambiguous promises of independence and territory, contained in the letters he received from Sir Henry McMahon, the British High Commissioner in Egypt, and, much more important, the discovery in the spring of 1916 that the Turks were planning to depose him.

The imperial powers were as indifferent to the Arabs as the Arabs were to them. They were anxious to enlist Arab allies against the Turks, but in a broader sense they did not care much what the Arabs felt. Nor was the fate of the Middle East in itself central to the powers' concerns. They saw their interests there mainly as part of much bigger strategic interests. Their objectives in the region, consequently, were not quite what Arab nationalists, who are naturally preoccupied with their own countries as the centre of their political world, have since come to believe. This is worth explaining because it puts a more precise perspective on the events of the period and what happened afterwards, and also because Arab misunderstanding of the events of 1914–22 has been the basis of numerous popular myths and conspiracy theories. According to the conventional Arab wisdom of the last forty years, Britain and France divided the territories of greater Syria and Mesopotamia into separate states to stop them becoming strong. It is said that they wanted to separate the centres of population from the regions that had oil, and, of course, it is central to the Arab version of events that the powers' overriding aim was to seize potential oil-bearing lands for themselves. These ideas are appealing to the Arabs because they make them seem important, but none of them is true. The imperial powers were certainly not acting in Arab interests in 1914–22, but their motives were different from what they are now supposed to have been.

There have been similar misunderstandings, and a little myth making, surrounding the central promises the allies made to the Arabs and each other during the war. The version of events one hears in the Middle East is that British and French policy at the time was a straightforward betrayal of the Arabs. The account begins with the Sherif Hussein being persuaded to revolt by promises of independence. It is less often mentioned that the Turkish governor of Syria, Djemal Pasha, had begun brutally crushing Arab dissent in 1915, and that Hussein feared some of those being tortured might reveal details of his treasonous correspondence with the British. In the following year he was almost forced into preemptive rebellion by the news that Djemal had assembled a German officered force to march through his territory, the Hijaz, to establish a telegraph station near the tip of the Peninsula.

By this time the promises made to Hussein had been superceded by the Sykes-Picot Agreement of February 1916, in which the British and French divided the Turks' Arab territories between themselves. Neither Hussein nor any other Arab learned of this until the Russians published the Agreement after the revolution of the autumn of 1917. A final act of double dealing was the Balfour Declaration in November 1917, when the British promised part of the Arab lands to the Jews.

The promises made to the Sherif Hussein, the Sykes-Picot Agreement and the Balfour Declaration are all, of course, historical facts, but what was promised and agreed took place against a more complicated and changing background than is generally understood. And the behaviour of all the parties concerned is also more ambiguous than it has been made out to be.*

A basic fact underlying Britain's, and France's, policy in the Middle East during the war was that neither country ever imagined that the region should or could be independent in the modern sense of the word. For some decades it had been taken for granted in Europe that the Ottoman Empire would collapse and that when this happened the European powers would have to take responsibility for much of its territory. No European statesman of the time thought for a moment that the Arabs would be able to govern themselves. When British officials spoke of 'independence', referring to the Sherif Hussein or Arab territories, their normal meaning was independence from the Turks with some form of British or French supervision or protection.

The Arabs were not seen as one people; that idea was new (and controversial) in the Middle East at the time and had not been heard of in Europe. Sometimes the European statesmen referred to the 'Arabic-speaking peoples' of the Ottoman Empire, but more often they talked of the Egyptians, Arabians, Syrians and Palestinians, and they were most at ease using the geographical names with which they were familiar from the Bible and the classics, which they had studied at school and university. They knew more about the region as it had been two thousand years before than as it was in their own time. Their tendency to think of it as being made up of many different peoples was strengthened by the Ottomans' habit of encouraging the development in the bigger towns of separate quarters for the different races and sects, Armenians, Greeks, Kurds, Jews and various others. This made the Middle East seem to outsiders a patchwork of races, some with

---

* By far the best source of information on this subject is a very readable book by David Fromkin called *A Peace to End All Peace – Creating the Modern Middle East 1914–1922*, Henry Holt, 1989

pleasantly Biblical names. It certainly appeared very different from the sort of society that is conjured up by the modern expression, 'the Arab world'.

It thus simply did not occur to European politicians after the First World War that the Middle East should be united. That would have seemed to them forced and unnatural. Nor did it occur to them that a united Arab country would be undesirable because it would be powerful. They did not imagine that the Arabs would be able to run their own affairs, let alone create a regional power.

British and French policies in the eight years from 1914 to 1922 were far from static: they evolved continuously with the changing circumstances of the war and the international balance of power. In 1915 the British concern was to gain a secure land route from the Mediterranean to the head of the Persian Gulf. The intention was that a railway should be built here for the movement of troops between Europe and India. An equally important concern was to keep Russia out of this area. For a hundred years it had been a cardinal principle of the British Government's policy to stop the Russians gaining ports on the Mediterranean or garrisons in Iran or Afghanistan, from which they might put armies on to the plains of India, and at the beginning of the war the Government had been forced into a major departure from this policy which made it all the more important that a new line be made secure a little further south. It had been agreed that when the Ottoman Empire was defeated the Russians would be given Constantinople and the territory of Anatolia, which is now the Asiatic part of Turkey. Therefore it became desirable for the British to have the French occupying an area to the north of them, to act as a buffer between them and the Russians. This area was defined as a broad strip of land running from Mount Lebanon eastwards, to include the Turkish province of Mosul in what is now northern Iraq. These ideas of strategic balance were much more important than the thought of oil. The British were already aware that 'the Mesopotamian provinces' might contain oil, and they had also mooted the possibility of incorporating them into the Indian empire and developing their agricultural potential. But when an important strategic interest ran against these ideas they were quite prepared to sacrifice the province of Mosul, which was where most of the oil was thought to be.

France's interests fitted quite well with those of the British. The French had had a long association with the Christians around Mount Lebanon, whom they had intervened to protect from the neighbouring Druze in the 1860s, during a particularly bloody war in the area. Since then the small province of Mount Lebanon had been ruled by a

Christian military governor serving directly under the office of the Grand Vizier, the Sultan's chief minister, who was obliged to act there only in consultation with the European powers. France's political involvement had been accompanied by growing commercial ties. French shipping and trading interests, particularly silk importers, developed business in Beirut and Damascus. Old memories were stirred of the Frankish kingdom that was established in Syria during the Crusades. From the moment the Ottoman Empire entered the war in November 1914 it seemed natural to the French Government that it should seek to acquire the Syrian provinces. The plan, as it evolved, was that France should rule a 'Greater Lebanon' and exert exclusive influence on the rest of Syria and Mosul. It was this division of the Middle East into two bands of territory, one French and one British, with their borders very loosely defined, that was incorporated in the Sykes-Picot Agreement of February 1916.

The ink was hardly dry on this Agreement before officials on both sides were thinking of ways in which it might be reinterpreted, and by late 1917 it had been largely forgotten. The British by now were interested in acquiring territory for its own sake. Given the enormous loss of life and impoverishment the war had caused, they wanted to have something to show for their struggle, and the obvious areas for the expansion of the Empire were East Africa and, more importantly, the Middle East. The idea was conceived of creating a vast arc of solidly British territory that would run from South Africa through the Rhodesias and East Africa (in part newly won from Germany) and then through Sudan, Egypt, Palestine, Mesopotamia, southern Persia and the Persian Gulf, the Indian Empire, Burma and Malaya, and finally to Australia and New Zealand. The arc's Middle East portion would secure the route to India, which remained a vital concern, and guard the Suez Canal.

At this time too the British concerns with Russian expansion were changing. When Russia withdrew from the war after the revolution it no longer had a claim to a share of the spoils of victory and, anyway, the new Communist government was making some play of renouncing all the imperial ambitions and attitudes of the old regime. This meant that the Soviet Union, as it became, was not to get Anatolia. That territory was to be divided between the victorious European powers and would itself be a buffer between the Soviet Union and the Middle East. In these circumstances Britain became interested in territory further north than the area it had awarded itself in the Sykes-Picot Agreement and it began to manoeuvre to acquire most of the areas formerly promised to the French, the exception being greater Lebanon.

As the war came to an end in the autumn of 1918 British Indian forces in Mesopotamia were ordered to occupy as large a portion as possible of the potential oil-bearing regions around Mosul. During the following two years of the treaty negotiations in Versailles the British Prime Minister, David Lloyd George, argued hard for the British being given Syria as well, on the grounds that as it was British and Dominion troops who had taken the area from the Turks it should be the British Empire that was given the mandate for it. The Prime Minister and the rest of the British Government were also beginning to worry about the influence of the Bolsheviks, who were credited with organizing the disturbances that occurred throughout the region at this time. As he and his colleagues believed in the domino theory – that if one country fell to Bolshevism, so would the next, and so on all the way to India – they were anxious to have as much territory as possible under British control between India and the new enemy.

Given that by the end of the war the British had an army of a million in different parts of the Middle East they would have been in a strong position to keep Syria had they really cared about it. But as Winston Churchill, the Secretary of State for War, continually reminded Lloyd George, the British forces were being rapidly demobilized and by the beginning of 1920 there were few British troops left in the region to enforce the settlement the Prime Minister wanted. Eventually he had to let the French seize Syria.

Just as the strategic aims of the British were not static, so their policies towards their Arab allies changed. Seen as a whole these were a mixture of deceit and loyalty, with the latter being prompted partly by guilty conscience. Policies were dictated pre-eminently, however, by self-interest.

In the early stages of the war the British administration in Cairo believed that the Sherif Hussein of Mecca was seeking to exercise only a spiritual authority in the region. British officers and civil servants were not well informed on the culture, or even the geography, of the Middle East. They did not understand that in Islam, in theory, secular and religious authority are not separate; some officials even persuaded themselves that the Arabs would welcome British administration of the secular aspects of government as an alternative to Ottoman rule. By the time of the Sykes-Picot Agreement in early 1916, however, they had been disabused of these ideas and when later the Sherif entered the war on Britain's side there were senior figures in Cairo and London who knew that they had already deceived him and who felt unhappy about it. The Sherif, on the other hand, had not been totally honest with the British. In order to extract bigger promises of territory he had exaggerated the scale of support he had in the secret societies in Damascus and the size of the tribal force he could muster. And his forces were not very effective. Great publicity was given to them and to one of their commanders, T.E. Lawrence, during the latter stages of the war and afterwards, but their only major success was the capture of Aqaba in July 1917. When in the early days of the revolt they attacked the Turkish garrison in Medina, which was isolated some way inside the Arabian Peninsula, they had come up against artillery fire and fled. Medina remained in Turkish hands until the end of the war. During the latter part of 1917 and 1918 Lawrence's forces were used purely to harass the Turks and disrupt their communications on the right flank of General Allenby's army advancing from Egypt. Allenby began his advance at Gaza in October 1917 and took Jerusalem by Christmas. Immediately after this his British troops were withdrawn to face the expected German offensive on the Western Front, and it was only in the late summer of 1918, when the offensive had been contained and was being pushed back, that his army was returned to him. Allenby resumed his attack in September 1918 and took Damascus within a fortnight.

After the war in the Middle East came to an end on 30 October, the British found themselves faced with the contradictions between their commitments to the Sherif Hussein, their understandings with the French, their promises to the Zionist movement and a dozen other pledges and statements of principle which had been made by them and the other allied powers during the conflict. These promises were presented by various minority peoples and other claimants to be honoured at the Versailles peace negotiations, and it goes without saying that they were not all compatible with each other. The allies, particularly the British, made a great fuss of reconciling, or pretending to reconcile, their commitments, and Lloyd George claimed that 'no race has done better out of the fidelity with which the allies redeemed their promises to the oppressed races than the Arabs'. But the reality was that the allies always knew that they would be letting down some of the Ottoman subject races and the ministers and senior civil servants concerned justified this by referring to the exigencies of war.

In the case of the Arabs the British by the end of 1918 were coming to know the Sherif Hussein as a difficult and eccentric ally, and in spite of his claim to be King of the whole Arab Middle East they were content to leave him ruling the Hijaz. They felt a stronger obligation towards the Sherif's most able son, Faisal, who had been the commander of the Arab armies in the revolt and who had gained the respect and friendship of Lawrence and other senior British officials. They felt they had to find Faisal a kingdom and it seemed at the same time that the prince might be the answer to some of their own problems in reconciling their different promises. Sir Mark Sykes, the co-author of the Sykes-Picot Agreement and one of the assistants of the Cabinet Secretary, believed it might be possible to tie up a deal for the whole of Syria (bar Lebanon) and Palestine, which would have Faisal as an 'independent' monarch under the loose supervision of the British and/or French. Faisal approved of this idea and he was not opposed to there being some Jewish settlement in Palestine. It was hoped that under him Arab agreement might be given to the development of the 'Jewish national home in Palestine' that had been promised in the Balfour Declaration. What brought these ideas to nought was that the intelligentsia and traders of Damascus, by far the most important city of the territories, did not want to be ruled by Prince Faisal; and the French had no intention of exercising merely a loose supervision of any area they claimed in the Middle East.

The British installed Prince Faisal in Damascus as ruler, or, nominally, as viceroy for his father, at the end of 1918. Most of the next year he spent, with Lawrence, at the Versailles conference, pursuing his and the Arabs' claim to independence. Damascus meanwhile was in a state of continuous unrest, being administered in his absence by feuding local politicians. These people were interested in Faisal only if he could spare them from French rule, and the French, as he found out at Versailles, were prepared to tolerate him only if he could curb the nationalists and usher in peacefully some form of French government. In the event, when he returned to Damascus early in 1920, Faisal found himself forced to speak on the nationalists' behalf and at one point referred to winning Arab independence from France 'by the sword'. Guerilla attacks followed on French positions on the coast, and finally on 26 July 1920 a French force marched from Beirut, occupied Damascus and sent Faisal into exile. It was at this point, one can say, that the modern state of Syria was formed, because whereas the nationalist clubs and Faisal had been talking about their claims to 'greater Syria', including Palestine, the area the French took and set about administering corresponded to the present state. When Damascus was taken, the French Prime Minister announced that Syria from then on would be held by France, 'the whole of it and forever'. His proclamation showed the difference between the French and British concepts of empire in the Middle East. While the British saw their territories as protectorates the French saw theirs as colonies. This was not altered by the fact that later, in 1922, the two powers were given the same type of mandate by the League of Nations.

The French occupation of Syria put an end to the possibility of there emerging a single united state at the heart of the Arab world. For such a state to have been created there would have had to be agreement on some form of joint supervision by the British and French, as well as British willingness to coerce the Zionists in Palestine and French willingness to ignore the Maronite Christians in Lebanon. Had all these conditions existed, which in retrospect one can see would have been extraordinary, they might have led to the creation of a state of Greater Syria. Whether it would have been feasible to expand this to include the former Turkish provinces of Mosul, Baghdad and Basra, which were later put together to form Iraq, is even more speculative. At the General Syrian Congress, in which the nationalists debated in Damascus during 1919 and early 1920, there was unanimity on the desirability of a greater Syria, but not on this including Iraq. Some of the delegates from Mesopotamia wanted their provinces to be included, but most favoured a separate government.

Already when the French occupied Damascus they had arranged to separate Lebanon from the rest of Syria. The district of Mount Lebanon was the one piece of territory which from 1916 onwards it was acknowledged by all parties – the French, the British and all realistic Arabs – would be French. The reason was not just that the French had had a long historical and commercial association with the area and felt themselves entitled to it, but also that the Maronite Christians themselves very much wanted to be brought under French government. The Maronites had always felt vulnerable. They were surrounded by Muslims and had a particularly long-standing enmity with the Druze, a Syrian mountain people which believes in a heretical form of Shiism holding that God has on many occasions come down to earth incarnate as man. The Maronites had survived by entrenching themselves on the slopes of Mount Lebanon, while the Druze occupied the southern extension of the massif, the Chouf, as well as Jebel Druze, south east of Damascus. The Maronites made it their custom to grasp whatever foreign, Christian protection they could get, whether from the Crusaders in the twelfth century or Napoleon III in the 1860s. Although during the early twentieth century they had become the biggest, best organized and most powerful community in the area, their desire for foreign alliances was unabated, and on this occasion it led them to embrace France of the Third Republic.

The Maronites maintained close contact with the French during the First World War and at the end pushed their willing allies to establish Le Grand Liban, the present Lebanon. The state was proclaimed on 1 August 1920. It was very much bigger than the Maronite homeland.

3. Syria, Lebanon, Israel, Jordan

To make it economically viable it was given the mainly Sunni Muslim ports of Tripoli, Beirut, Sidon and Tyre, as well as the Bekaa Valley in the east and the hilly Shia Muslim country to the south. The boundaries were drawn in such a way that the Maronites and other Christian sects just constituted a majority of the population – 51 per cent according to a French census in 1931. Only the Christians, of course, were happy with this arrangement. The Syrian nationalists saw it as removing a substantial area of land that was properly part of Syria, and they believed, quite rightly, that one of the reasons France had done this was to weaken their country and make it more easily governable. The Muslims in what became Lebanon were similarly disappointed. They were not consulted, and if they had been they would have favoured remaining part of Syria, which was predominantly Muslim and looked towards the rest of the Arab and Muslim world, and not towards Europe. In due course, however, the Sunni Muslims found they prospered in their new state with the Christians and French, and for half a century they accepted the situation.

A few months after the proclamation of the state of Lebanon another new country was formed in the Middle East. At the beginning of 1921 one of Prince Faisal's elder brothers, Abdullah, marched into the area east of the Dead Sea and the river Jordan at the head of a small Arabian tribal force, announcing that he was going to continue to Damascus to avenge his brother's expulsion. Abdullah must have known that he had no chance of defeating the French and it seems likely that his expedition was designed mainly to get a response from the British. If this was the case he succeeded. The British did not want to have the embarrassment of another member of the family they had promoted as ruler of parts of the Arab territories confronting the French and being humiliated. They feared that if Abdullah fought the French, the latter might retaliate by invading the Palestine mandate, which included areas on both sides of the river Jordan. So they decided to see if they could make some advantage from Abdullah's initiative. They heard the news of his advance in March 1921 at the time of the Cairo Conference. This had been called by Winston Churchill, then Colonial Secretary, for the senior officials in the area to discuss how they should govern the British mandates and, in particular, how they could reduce expenditure in doing so.

Churchill decided to intervene in person. He went to Jerusalem with T.E. Lawrence at the end of March and summoned Abdullah to meet him. Abdullah, of course, claimed that the whole of greater Syria properly belonged to his family and that at the very least he should be given Palestine and Iraq, but eventually he was bargained down to accepting, as a 'temporary' measure, a new emirate of Transjordan, together with a British subsidy. There were advantages in this arrangement for the British. Disorder had prevailed in the largely bedouin region of Transjordan since 1918 and the British no longer had the troops, or the money or inclination, to police the area. Giving it to Abdullah seemed a good way of restoring order, and, in future, restraining anti-French and anti-Zionist movements which it was feared would attempt to establish bases in the region. There was also some moral justice in this settlement. During Prince Faisal's brief reign in Damascus, Transjordan had been part of his territories, which made it seem right that it should now be given to another Hashemite. Gradually Abdullah came to accept his small desert territory, while those British officials who feared that he would be an ineffective ruler, or that he would provoke the ruler of Nejd to the south, or that supporting him would be too costly, came to accept him as the best solution for the government of Transjordan. The 'temporary' emirate gradually became permanent.

While the British were installing Abdullah in Transjordan they were arranging with more determination and guile to make his brother, Faisal, King of Iraq. This was part of the business of the Cairo Conference.

Baghdad had been taken by the British, at the second attempt, in March 1917. The campaign had been organized by the Government of India, as opposed to the authorities in Cairo, and it was British Indian officials, who were also responsible for Persia and the Persian Gulf, who ran the country after its capture. They had great hopes for it. They were impressed by its agricultural potential, which made them think of bringing in Indian settlers to farm it. They were also aware that there might be oil in the province of Mosul to the north of Mesopotamia, though this was not formally taken from the Turks and incorporated in the new country of Iraq until 1926. Most of all, though they did not often say it, they were impressed by the fact that the country's well-educated, urban, secular middle class, albeit partly Turkish, gave it the potential to become modern and developed on the lines of a European country. Gertrude Bell, the archaeologist, traveller and diplomat, who was one of the founders of the British administration, claimed that once the British had made it 'a centre of Arab civilisation and prosperity', there would not be 'an Arab of Syria or Palestine who would not want to be part of it'. What Miss Bell and other somewhat romantic British officials did not take sufficiently into account was the extraordinary violence and lack of homogeneity of the country. On the map the area appeared to be bound together by the Tigris and Euphrates, but in reality it was divided between peoples of the lower river basin, mostly Shias and ultimately descendants of the Sumerians and Babylonians, who had looked to the south, and the central peoples, mainly Sunni, whom an American missionary pointed out to Miss Bell were the descendants of the Assyrians, who had looked to the west and north. There were numerous ethnic and religious minorities, including Jews and Nestorian Christians, and when the province of Mosul was added the country was given a large population of Kurds. The British were surprised and shocked in June 1920 when a succession of murders, mostly of young officers, was suddenly followed by a major rebellion along the Euphrates. This was put down at a cost of 450 British and 10,000 Arab dead. The Government rather wildly blamed the influence of the Turks, the Bolsheviks, Prince Faisal, pan-Islamism and urban nationalists. It was decided that these elements had worked on the resentments of the simple Shia villagers and their leaders, who under the Ottoman regime had been left largely to themselves and now objected to the intrusion of an organized government and its tax collectors.

Order was not finally restored in Iraq until July 1921, when the Cairo Conference was about to assemble. Naturally the Conference was much concerned with what had happened in the country, and its members quickly endorsed the idea that the installation of Prince Faisal as King, under a British mandate, would be much more effective, and cheaper, than direct government. It would simultaneously discharge Britain's responsibilities to an old friend, albeit one whose loyalty had recently been called into question. It was therefore arranged that the Prince would send cables to the leading figures in Iraq saying that he had been urged by friends to come to the country and had decided to offer his services to the people. Faisal then travelled from London to Mecca to settle the matter with his father. Meanwhile the principal local political leader, Sayyid Talib, mounted a campaign to put forward 'an Iraqi ruler for Iraq' and it became clear to the British that he was gaining much more support than Prince Faisal was likely to find. So the Resident, Sir Percy Cox, invited Sayyid Talib to tea at the Residency in Baghdad, had him arrested on the grounds that he had been threatening to incite violence, and deported him to Ceylon. Prince Faisal arrived two months later, on 24 June. On 11 July the Council of Ministers voted to make him monarch, and in August its vote was endorsed by an overwhelming majority in a well-managed plebiscite.

The problems of the British in Iraq did not end when Faisal became King. No sooner had he been installed than he proposed a treaty to replace the mandate and when negotiations became long and devious the British began to think either of deposing him or evacuating the country. In late 1921 the attitude of the British towards the Middle East was very different from what it had been during the later stages of the First World War. People's thinking had been changed by the Russian Revolution and America's ideas of self-determination. British society was losing interest in both the idealistic case for empire, that it would extend the benefits of civilization to less fortunate peoples, and the practical case, that it would be of material benefit to Britain to expand the areas under its control. The Empire was beginning to be seen as a cost, by a country which needed all its revenues to rebuild itself. One reason why these ideas did not result in immediate British withdrawal from Iraq and other territories was that Winston Churchill and his staff were able to work out a low-cost policing policy, using small air forces and armoured cars. Another was that Lloyd George was against a policy of 'scuttle'. He referred to the belief that there was oil in Iraq and said that if the British left it might find in a year or so it had handed over to the French and Americans some of the richest oil fields in the world. He was quite right. Oil was found by a consortium, which included British, French and American interests, in 1927 at Kirkuk. It was the first oil discovery in an Arab country.

In 1932 Britain ended its mandate in Iraq, though it continued to bind the Hashemite regime to it by treaties. Immediately after independence the Iraqi army carried out a massacre of Nestorian Christians (Assyrians, in the modern sense of the word in Iraq) who had been closely associated with the mandate government. Two years later there was a second Shia revolt along the Euphrates, and as soon as the army had suppressed this it overthrew the government (but not the monarchy) in a coup. During the Second World War a new coup established a pro-German regime in Baghdad, which led immediately to a pogrom in the city's Jewish quarters. The coup was rapidly crushed by the British. The whole period of the 1930s and 1940s was punctuated by riots, the murder of British officials, tension between the different ethnic groups and a simmering demand for Kurdish independence. Yet through all this the country continued to hold the affections of a large number of British engineers, oil men, government advisers and other officials who together served it with more honesty and better effect than any other Iraqi executive, before or since. In due course Americans and Europeans who went there, diplomats as well as businessmen, came to share the goodwill and enthusiasm of the British. What impressed everybody was the apparent potential of the country. Iraq became the country in which the Western Arabist establishments believed. It was the state they most wanted to succeed and have as an ally.

The last Arab territory to be carved, in part, out of what had been the Ottoman Empire was Saudi Arabia. In this the British played only a minor role. The Kingdom was built almost entirely by the efforts of one man, Abdel-Aziz bin Abdel-Rahman al-Saud. The family of Abdel-Aziz had originally come to prominence in the Nejd, central Arabia, in the mid-eighteenth century, when its founder, Mohammad bin Saud, had allied himself with a revivalist preacher, Mohammed bin Abdel-Wahab. Inspired by this man, who wanted to purge Islam of the interest in saints and the impure superstitions that had crept into it during the previous centuries, Mohammad bin Saud embarked on a career of conquest which brought him much of the Arabian Peninsula. His descendants took Mecca and Medina and raided into Mesopotamia where they sacked the Shia shrines at Najaf and Kerbala. Eventually, in 1818, the Ottoman ruler of Egypt, the great Mohammad Ali, sent an army to curb the family. Its capital, Diriyyah, was taken and destroyed – the ruins can still be seen a few miles outside Riyadh – and Mohammad bin Saud's great grandson, Abdullah, was sent to Constantinople, where his head was cut off. For the next seventy years the fortunes of the Sauds alternatively rose and fell, until in 1887 their second capital, Riyadh, was taken by the Rashid family of Hail and they went into exile in Kuwait.

Fifteen years after this humiliation the family found a new young leader in Abdel-Aziz. In 1902 he rode across the desert with a small band of followers and retook Riyadh, storming the mud brick Masmak fort (which has been preserved) and slaying the Rashids' governor. In 1913 he took from the Turks the region of Hasa, now the Eastern Province, which lies beside the Gulf, and after the First World War he destroyed the Rashid family and took Hail, then conquered what are now the Saudi provinces of Asir, Najran and Jizan in the south west, and finally in 1925 and 1926 took the Hijaz. The Sherif went into voluntary exile, in Cyprus, soon after the war with Abdel-Aziz began, and when Jeddah was taken, in January 1926, he was followed by his son Ali, the brother of Faisal and Abdullah, whom he had left behind as governor. In 1922 Abdel-Aziz consolidated his domains of Nejd and Hijaz into the Kingdom of Saudi Arabia, which he named after his own family.

These are the bare facts of the creation of Saudi Arabia. Abdel-Aziz would no doubt have conquered all of the Arabian Peninsula, had he not been checked by the mountainous nature of the territory of Yemen, ruled by its Imam, and by the presence of the British in various protected territories to the south and east. These were the Aden protectorates, Oman, the Trucial States (now the United Arab Emirates), Qatar,

Bahrain and Kuwait. Ironically the British had first become involved in those territories that lay within the Gulf in the early nineteenth century when they had sent marines to the area to suppress the piracy that had been inspired partly by the fundamentalist movement of King Abdel-Aziz's ancestors. In later years they had signed several series of treaties with the local rulers, first banning piracy and then undertaking to protect the fledgling states in return for their rulers promising to have no dealings with foreign powers, notably Russia and Germany, without British permission. It was a treaty of 1899 with the ruler of Kuwait, whose family had achieved a *de facto* independence from the Turkish governor of Basra in the mid-eighteenth century, that prevented King Abdel-Aziz from adding that small state to his territories after the First World War. The borders of Saudi Arabia with Kuwait and Iraq were determined with a few strokes of a pencil by Sir Percy Cox, the British Resident in Baghdad, in November 1922. Sir Percy had taken a ship down the Gulf to the small village of Uqair, on the Arabian coast just south of Bahrain, to talk about frontiers to Abdel-Aziz, and when he found the ruler's claims on British protected territories to be unreasonably grandiose he had taken a red pencil from his coat and marked the borders without further ado. He was rather generous to Iraq, giving it much territory that had a distinctly Nejdi character, but a large piece of the land claimed by the Sabah family of Kuwait he gave to Abdel-Aziz.

Modern Arab nationalists, including the Iraqi President, Saddam Hussein, have often claimed that in defining the boundaries of Saudi Arabia and bringing into being the Gulf states, which before they signed treaties with the Government of India had been no more than fishing villages, each led by a chief and his son, the British conspired to separate the areas of large population, in Iraq, from the oil fields of the Gulf coast. This idea is simply wrong. The Gulf states all came under British protection long before there was an idea of there being oil under them. By the time the Uqair treaty was signed, it was suspected that there might be oil in Bahrain and Saudi Arabia, but these suspicions were much less definite than the belief that there was oil in Iraq, and they were irrelevant to the position of the lines that Sir Percy Cox drew so confidently. The Resident's concern at the time was mainly to control the raiding of Abdel-Aziz's bedouin, who in 1920 had nearly taken the town of Kuwait and who were regularly penetrating into Iraq. He would have liked, as part of a secondary agreement at Uqair, to have had Abdel-Aziz agree to give an oil concession only to a company approved by Britain, as Iraq and all the Gulf states had bound themselves to do, but on this he was rebuffed. Abdel-Aziz signed a concession first with a New Zealand speculator and then, in 1933, with Standard

Oil of California (now known as Chevron). Oil was not discovered in Saudi Arabia until 1938.

By far the most disruptive, but the most idealistically inspired, part of the post-war division of the Middle East was the blessing given by the British to the seeds of a Jewish state in Palestine. The idea went back nearly forty years.

From 1882 there had been a trickle of Jewish immigrants into Palestine, most of them coming from Russia and eastern Europe. The early arrivals were driven by a mixture of the need to escape persecution and fashionable ideas of bringing about the regeneration of Jewish culture by honest toil on the land. After the late 1890s, when the writer Theodor Herzl formulated the idea of Zionism – a return of the Jewish people to their ancient homeland and ultimately the foundation of a Jewish state – a new wave of more politically active settlers moved into Palestine. Neither Herzl nor the other leaders and thinkers in the Zionist movement talked openly of establishing a state because that would have alarmed the Turks, but the concept of a state and of that state having to be won by force was inherent in Jewish immigration from the time of Herzl onwards. The Palestinian Arabs sensed the threat. In some areas they saw to their surprise that the Jews settled on swamps and drained them, but in others it was found they bought land from absentee landlords and had the tenants evicted. The Arab farmers would then raid the settlements and carry off crops and livestock, but after a time they found it was more profitable to work on 'their' land for the new farmers, and so in the early period of settlement they took employment as labourers. Where the early-twentieth-century Jewish settlers were different from those who arrived in the 1880s and 1890s was in their attempts to be self-sufficient. If they could, they avoided either doing business with the Arabs or employing those they had evicted. By 1914 the Jewish population of Palestine had grown to 85,000.

The event that gave the Zionists the opportunity to take their first formal step towards statehood was the First World War. In 1916 and 1917 the ideas of Jewish immigration into a post-war Palestine and of the Jews having some sort of home under a British mandate were put by Jewish leaders to members of the British Cabinet, and to other important people in the establishment, and many of them responded favourably. Just as they had become familiar with the Near East as a whole through reading Roman history, they knew about Palestine through the Old Testament, and it seemed to them right and natural that the Jews should now be allowed to return to their home. As David Fromkin says in *A Peace to End All Peace*, 'Biblical prophecy was the first and most endearing of the many motives that led Britons to want to restore the Jews to Zion'. The idea also seemed modern and practical. During the war Zionism and Arab nationalism were not seen as incompatible. There were many who supported both and who felt it would be a fine thing for Britain to have a Jewish home under its protection. It was hoped that the Jews would bring agricultural knowledge and help improve the land, to the benefit of all its inhabitants.

Parallel to these idealistic but rather naïve ideas was the more cynical, but less important, reasoning that there would be a benefit in winning Jewish goodwill. At different times during the war members of the British Government, holding a conspiratorial view of the world that would do credit to the Arabs today, believed that the Jews controlled the Young Turk movement, the German Government and the Russian Revolution. These ideas, which embodied a long-established anti-semitism, did not in any sense contradict the pro-Zionist sentiments of the same people. The two ideas sat happily side by side. Both were exploited by Jewish leaders, particularly Chaim Weizmann, who mounted a patient campaign to get the British Government to translate its sympathies, fears and suspicions into a document which could be the legal basis for a state. He eventually succeeded on 2 November 1917 when the Foreign Secretary, Arthur Balfour, wrote the following letter to the most eminent of the British Zionists:

Dear Lord Rothshild,

I have much pleasure in conveying to you, on behalf of His Majesty's Government, the following declaration of sympathy with Jewish Zionist aspirations which has been submitted to, and approved by the Cabinet:

'His Majesty's Government views with favour the establishment in Palestine of a national home for the Jewish people, and will use its best endeavours to facilitate the achievement of this object, it being clearly understood that nothing shall be done which may prejudice the civil and religious rights of the existing non-Jewish communities in Palestine, or the rights and political status enjoyed by Jews in any other country.'

I shall be grateful if you would bring this declaration to the knowledge of the Zionist Federation.

Yours sincerely,
Arthur Balfour

This letter did not lead to any sudden surge in Jewish immigration – in fact the Jewish population of Palestine fell during the war. But it committed the British Government to supporting Zionism, which from the Jewish point of view was vital, because very soon after the war the Government was disabused of its ideas that Zionism and Arab nationalism might be compatible. The military officials who moved from Cairo to Jerusalem to administer Palestine in 1918 realized that the immigration of Jews, however skilled and well financed they might be, was not going to be accepted by the Palestinians. Violence broke out in Galilee in late 1919 and in Jerusalem in the spring of 1920. After the second episode a British military court passed exemplary sentences on the Jews who had distributed arms and organized self-defence groups, even though they had not been involved in the fighting. The officials in Jerusalem were open in their view that the London government's policy of allowing, and even promoting, Jewish immigration had been devised by people who had no knowledge of conditions on the ground. They said it was bound to lead to disaster. This contrast in sympathies between the colonial government and its master remained a feature of British policy in Palestine for the next twenty years.

In spite of the riots the Prime Minister, Lloyd George, and most of the rest of the cabinet remained resolute in backing Zionism and in 1920 they appointed to Jerusalem a civilian government headed by a former cabinet minister, Sir Herbert Samuel, to replace the military administration. But they were slowly coming to realize that Palestine was going to give them at least as much trouble as their other new Arab territories.

The disillusionment of the British grew in May 1921 when a serious riot occurred in Jaffa, a mainly Arab town next to the growing new Jewish town of Tel Aviv. On 1 May there was a clash between two Jewish labour unions, one Communist and the other social democrat, and the Arabs, instead of watching the alien phenomenon, as had been their custom in the past, suddenly attacked both sides and then went on a rampage of looting and murder in the Jewish quarters. By the time the army quelled the riots several days later nearly 200 Jews and 120 Arabs were dead or wounded. Similar violence occurred in Jerusalem in August 1929, provoked by young Jewish militants at a time when Arab and Jewish religious festivals happened to coincide. In these riots and the riots that followed in Hebron, Haifa and other places in Palestine the casualties numbered nearly 500. After both series of riots, and on several other occasions in the 1920s and 1930s, the British Government appointed commissions of enquiry. In each case the commissions reported that the violence was not premeditated but that it came out of a sense of Arab helplessness in the face of the steady Judaization of the country. By 1929 there were 156,000 Jews in Palestine, compared to some 800,000 Arabs, and they owned 14 per cent of the cultivable land. They continued to keep themselves separate from the Arabs, excluding them from their schools and hospitals and all other institutions.

In 1936 the Arabs rose in a general rebellion which continued for three years before it was suppressed with considerable brutality by the British army, with some Jewish help, in the spring of 1939. The British established yet another commission of enquiry, headed by the Colonial Secretary, Malcolm MacDonald. This reached much the same conclusion as its numerous predecessors, but unlike them it recommended quotas for Jewish immigration; by this time, stimulated by Nazi persecution, the Jewish population of Palestine had reached 400,000. It also recommended the regulation of land sales and the introduction of self-governing institutions which would lead to the creation of an independent Palestinian state in ten years. The British Government adopted the proposals and stated that it was not part of its policy that Palestine should become a Jewish state. The Palestinians, characteristically, split in their response to the plan. The Mufti of Jerusalem, Haj Amin Husseini, rejected it because he did not see why his people should make any concessions over the government and ownership of their own land. His rivals, members of the Nashashibi family, accepted it, partly to spite the Mufti. For their part, the Jews were horrified by Mac-Donald's White Paper. The fact that it proposed to limit Jewish immigration to 75,000 over the next five years and then stop it ran directly against Zionist aspirations to a state. The Jews promptly abandoned the policy of 'self-restraint' they had followed in the past, when they had often been extremely provocative but had stopped short of waging war on either the British or Arabs. There were demonstrations, attacks on Government offices and the beginning of an anti-British and anti-Arab terrorist campaign. The rebellion was brought sharply to a halt by the outbreak of war in September 1939, when the Jews found themselves obliged in their own self-interest to support the allied cause and join the British forces.

When the Second World War came to an end it remained British policy to limit immigration and move Palestine towards independence, but these ideas were now totally impracticable. The Zionist leaders meeting at the Biltmore Hotel in New York in May 1942 had for the first time announced their aims formally and publicly. They called for the gates of Palestine to be opened and for the country to be established as a Jewish commonwealth that would be integrated into the new structure of the democratic world. The Jews, in other words, were in open confrontation with the British – and by May 1945 there were large numbers of them who had experience of battle and were trained, armed and ready to fight for a state of their own. There were also some hundreds of thousands of Jews in Europe, the survivors of the Nazi holocaust, who wanted to go to Palestine. In 1945 and 1946 these people poured into the country increasing its Jewish population by the end of 1946 to some 600,000. Inside Palestine the Jewish Agency, which was the major organizer of Jewish immigration and land acquisition, formed its own military organization, the Haganah, which later became the Israeli army. It was supported by two terrorist groups, the Irgun and the Stern Gang. Together these forces waged war on the British and the Arabs. Their most spectacular act was the blowing up of the King David Hotel in Jerusalem, which acted as British headquarters, in July 1946. Most of the Zionist campaign was a mixture of smaller acts of guerilla war and terrorism – the sabotage of bridges, roads and railway lines, hit-and-run raids on barracks and air fields, and the murder of British servicemen, including two sergeants who were hanged from a tree and then booby trapped.

The British were in no state to resist these attacks. They were weary from six years of war, they were under great American pressure to allow the formation of a Jewish state and they were themselves divided in their sympathies between Jews and Arabs. Most of the troops in Palestine sympathized with the Arabs, but many in the British establishment were pro-Jewish and some were not above conniving with the Zionists in acts that would weaken their own forces and help the Haganah. In April 1947 the British Government asked the United Nations to consider the issue and in November that year the General Assembly, pushed by America, voted for a complicated partition plan which would have involved two states, one Arab and one Jewish, occupying several different parcels of land separated by winding and unpoliceable boundaries. The British finally terminated their mandate and left Palestine on 14 May 1948.

It was about a month before the withdrawal that the Jews swung their main attacks on to the Arab population. In April the Irgun and Stern Gang massacred the village of Deir Yassin. There followed many more smaller attacks on villages, in which houses were blown up and anyone who resisted killed. The thrust of the Jewish campaign was to force the Arabs to leave. This was not done only through violence. Secret radio stations and loudspeakers mounted on armoured cars broadcast reports of spreading epidemics. They spoke also of the treachery of Arab leaders and their collaboration with the Zionists. They claimed that those leaders who were assumed to be true to their people were urging them to flee. The campaign was extremely effective. By the date of the British withdrawal nearly 400,000 Arabs, about a third of the total Arab population of Palestine at that time, had left their homes and become refugees.

One minute after the British mandate ended at 6 p.m. Washington time on 14 May 1948, the state of Israel was established, and ten minutes later it was recognized by the United States. The following day five Arab countries, Egypt, Transjordan, Syria, Lebanon and Iraq sent forces to attack the new state, a total of 20,000 men with a few light tanks and aircraft. These armies were considerably outnumbered by the Israelis, whose fully mobilized regular forces alone totalled 30,000, and naturally the Israelis were far better trained and better equipped. As happened in later wars, the bluster of Arab leaders lead their own people to believe that they were going to achieve an easy victory and persuaded much of the rest of the world, which saw Israel as a tiny community of 600,000 pitted against 40 million, to rally round the new state. The President of Syria told an astounded Palestinian writer and community leader, Musa Alami, that his country had manufactured an atomic bomb, and the Secretary General of the Arab League stated that if the Arabs did not win the war against the Jews 'in an outright offensive' they could 'hang all their leaders and statesmen'. In the event the Israelis easily defeated four of the Arab armies. The only force that fought effectively was the Transjordanian army, and that was hampered by its Government's policy of scrupulously observing the UN Partition Plan; it defended Arab territory but would not move into the attack on Israeli land. By early 1949 the Transjordanians too had been defeated and Israel was able to sign armistice agreements one by one with its Arab neighbours. These confirmed Israel's boundaries on the basis of the military *status quo*, which gave Israel the territory it is internationally recognized as having today. This included a substantial amount of what the United Nations had intended should be the partitioned state of Palestine. One of the parts of Palestine that remained , the Gaza strip, was brought under Egyptian administration, and the other, the West Bank, was seized by King Abdullah in April 1950, to form the state of Jordan.

During the nine months of war that followed the declaration of the state of Israel, a further 400,000 Palestinian Arabs left their homes, and on several occasions during the next seven years the Israelis seized opportunities to evict more Palestinians from inconvenient villages, most of them near the West Bank frontier. The methods were the ones that had been used in 1948: the dynamiting of houses and the murder of the inhabitants. In other cases the Israelis simply seized Arab property. Throughout this period there was remarkably little international criticism of Israel, though the acts it was committing on its territories were much more brutal than anything it did in the occupied territories in the 1970s, 1980s or early 1990s.

For their part the Palestinians were remarkably supine. There was no uprising among those who had remained in Israel and until 1953 there were virtually no raids into Israel by those who had left. Occasionally farmers would slip across the frontier to visit relations or pick oranges from their orchards, but they did nothing of a military nature. Their defeat and humiliation had left them and the rest of the Arab world in a state of shock.

3

Hope and Disaster
1948–70

*The liberal age – revolution in Egypt – Suez and the influence
of Nasserism – 1967 war – rise of the fedayeen – war
in Jordan*

Had it not been for what happened in Palestine, the post-Second
World War years might have been the beginning of a period of happiness and prosperity for the Arabs. It was a time when they were starting
to gain their independence and earn some oil revenues.

The two French mandates, Syria and Lebanon, were given their independence in stages between the mid-1930s and 1946. The French
governments of the period did not part with them easily. They tried to
maintain for themselves a military presence and various other privileges,
which would have secured what the Free French leader, General de
Gaulle, referred to as 'France's dominant position in the Levant'. In
May 1945, to counter mounting nationalist agitation, the French landed
some of their much feared Senegalese troops in Beirut, and when riots
broke out in Syria they bombarded Damascus. It was only under pressure from the other great powers that they finally withdrew in April
1946.

Syria then turned its back on France. The whole history of French
rule from 1920 had been an unhappy one. The French had tried to
impose their culture on the country. An Italian diplomat who visited
it in 1935 told how he had seen a class of school children reciting the
words *'nos ancêtres les Gaulois etaient blonds'*. The French were seen,
with justification, as having seized the country by force and as having
been partly responsible for the division of greater Syria, which is what

the nationalists felt their country was in a natural cultural sense and should have been as a political unit.

The Lebanese, however, remained close to France after 1946. The Maronite Christians liked French culture and were as happy to speak French as Arabic. Privately, they also continued to look to France as a protector. The new government in Lebanon, unlike that in Syria, remained a democracy, albeit one organized on sectarian lines. In 1943 the main religious groups in the country had concluded an unwritten National Pact, which established a division of parliamentary seats and all the important offices of government between the different religious groups. The Maronites were given the Presidency, the Sunnis the office of Prime Minister and the Shias the office of Speaker in the National Assembly; all state bodies were to be staffed according to the ratio of six Christians to five Muslims. The Pact was based on the assumption that the Christians were a majority of the population, which even at this early date may not have been quite the case. It did not prevent the different sects having their own militias and it did not prevent considerable violence, vendettas and killings within each community, which gave Lebanese democracy a distinctively gangland flavour. But as a means of preventing the country from fragmenting and allowing the development of a rich and glittering trading, banking and tourist economy, the Pact worked well, for most of the time, for more than thirty years. The Lebanese bourgeoisie watched the military governments and *coups d'état* of much of the rest of the Arab world and congratulated itself on its political maturity, sense of balance and understanding of democracy.

Another state which gained its independence at this time was Jordan. Like its neighbours it went through the process in stages, being allowed control of part of its internal affairs in 1928 and then being given independence in 1946. Britain had just promoted the formation of the Arab League, which it hoped would foster a harmonious and pro-British independent Arab world, so it could hardly have kept Jordan as a protectorate. Nevertheless, independence under the Anglo-Jordanian treaty was highly circumscribed. The United States would not recognize the country, and it was only after the treaty was modified in 1948, allowing Britain just some base facilities and a training role with the army, that Jordan's independence was accepted internationally.

At the same time as Syria, Lebanon and Jordan were becoming independent, several other Arab countries to the east and south began to become rich, or, at least, they began to receive some revenues that were to lift them out of the poverty that had been their lot in the past. Saudi Arabia and Kuwait both began to export oil in 1946 and Qatar started exporting three years later. In Kuwait's case there was an extraordinary surge in oil revenues in the early 1950s when the Anglo-Iranian Oil Company (which later became British Petroleum) had its operations in Iran nationalized and turned mainly to Kuwait to make up the shortfall in supplies. Kuwait's revenues rose from $18 million in 1951 to $56 million in 1952, when it also began to benefit from the 50:50 profit split that had recently been negotiated between oil producers and concessionaires. In 1953, when Kuwait became the biggest oil producer in the Middle East and fourth biggest in the world, its income reached $168 million. Iraq, which had begun producing oil in 1934, saw its revenues multiply five times in this period.

Initially, of course, the revenues of the four oil producers were spent at home on basic development projects, and some reckless consumer spending. But some of the money began to trickle into the other Arab countries. The three Arabian Peninsula producers, and especially Kuwait, had become home to thousands of displaced Palestinians, who began to remit part of their wages and profits back to relations in Jordan and Lebanon. Lebanese and Egyptian contractors did highly profitable business in all the oil states, and the newly rich ruling families and the businessmen of these states started going to Cairo and Beirut for their holidays, and buying property there. By the standards of other parts of the world that were about to become independent, the Middle East was economically fortunate.

It was also relatively fortunate in its rulers. In most Arab countries, those that were or had been under the wing of the British, there were monarchies; Lebanon and Syria were republics. Both types of regime, it is true, were financially corrupt and incompetent. Even in the strongly nationalist republic of Syria in the late 1940s and 1950s the Sunni Muslim mercantile establishment of Damascus, which produced the country's presidents, civilian and military, devoted much of its energy to internal fighting over business deals. The virtue of all of the regimes, however, was that they were mild in their dealings with their own people. Society was reasonably free. People could travel easily, the foreign press was not censored and the domestic press was able to say pretty much what it wanted. Civil society – professional, academic and cultural – flourished. Foreigners were made welcome. Private businessmen felt reasonably confident in investing in their own countries and the governments' modest development projects, partly planned by foreigners, were well thought out and not motivated by a desire for political prestige. Looking back on this period and the decade or so that preceeded it, the Arab intelligentsia is now quite nostalgic. The fashionable attitude was summed up for me by an Egyptian professor:

'the years of the British and their lackeys, such as Nuri Said [the monarchist and Anglophile Prime Minister who dominated Iraqi politics in the 1940s and 1950s], were a liberal age. In our youth we condemned these people, but little did we know that those who would come and claim to be our liberators would be so frightful'.

This 'liberal age' was to come to an abrupt end, however. Palestine had acted as a fermenting agent for Arab nationalist ideas in the 1930s and 1940s. The intervention of the colonial powers in the region and its 'artificial' division into separate states had increased the discontent of the Arab middle classes. People began to think about left-wing philosophies of government and about ways in which the Arab states could be made stronger. Then, when five Arab armies tried to crush Israel in 1948, and four of them were defeated within three months, the established government order was humiliated. It was shown to be incapable of dealing with the challenges that faced the newly independent Arab nation. The general public, and particularly the young officers in the Arab armies, who had experienced the effects of government incompetence at first hand on the battlefield, asked themselves why their governments were so ineffective, and quickly came to the conclusion that it was because they were under the influence of the British, did not represent the people and were not properly 'democratic'. Had it not been for Palestine it is possible that the young nationalists would not have been so resentful of the continuing British presence in the region, nor of the fact that their homelands had been divided after the First World War. In the event, the military disasters of 1948 brought discredit on the entire political fabric.

The result was revolution. It began in Egypt, which in one sense was an unlikely place, because the country was not naturally or passionately pan-Arab. Arab nationalist philosophy had been debated in Egypt during the past half century and had been as often rejected as accepted. On the other hand Egypt had been through the same experience of colonial rule as its neighbours in the Levant. In some ways it had been more humiliated than they had been. From 1882 until 1914 it had been ruled by the British, acting, in theory, on behalf of the Sultan in Constantinople. When the First World War broke out it had been made a protectorate and in 1922 it had been given independence – unilaterally, because the British had not been able to find any Egyptian politician sufficiently servile to sign a treaty reserving to them authority in four important areas: the defence of the country, the security of the communications of the Empire (in effect the Suez Canal), the protection of foreign interests and minorities, and the government of the Sudan, which in theory was an Anglo-Egyptian condominion but in practice a British colony. After many attempts the British finally got a modified treaty signed in 1936, formally terminating the occupation and giving Egypt authority over its own minorities, but empowering the British to station troops in the canal zone and leaving the Sudan under their rule.

During the Second World War Egypt fulfilled its treaty obligations as a British base, but the population, and some members of the government, wavered between Allied and German sympathies. It was a dispute between the young King Farouk and the British ambassador, Sir Miles Lampson, in January 1942 over the appointment of a new government that led to the ambassador driving to the Abdine Palace with three tanks. He walked into the royal apartments, handed the King an act of abdication and told him that unless the British nominee, Nahas Pasha, was asked forthwith to form a government the King would either have to abdicate or be deposed. Farouk gave in. His submission made him even more anti-British than he had been before, it lost him the respect of his people and of his own army, and it embittered young officers and other educated but poor members of the middle classes – those who did not mix socially with the British. All of these sentiments were compounded six years later when the British withdrew from Palestine and the Egyptian army was humiliated there. The one honourable episode in the Egyptian campaign was the resistance of a brigade from October 1948 to February 1949 in the Falluja pocket, where it was surrounded by enemy forces and had no hope of relief. Among those trapped was Major Gamal Abdel-Nasser, and when he and other young, idealistic officers returned to Cairo they talked of the dishonest communiqués the Government had issued on the progress of the battle, the corruption in the medical and supply departments and the uselessness of their equipment, which had included rifles made in 1912. It was at this time that Nasser and other officers came to the conclusion not only that the British had to be removed but that the entire system of government had to be changed.

In the next three years events in Egypt slid slowly out of the Government's control. In 1951, in an attempt to regain some popular support, Nahas Pasha, who was once again Prime Minister, abrogated the 1936 treaty and proclaimed Farouk King of the Sudan. (The Egyptians at this time could not accept that the Sudan, which had unhappy memories of being ruthlessly exploited by them in the nineteenth century, wanted to be ruled by neither Britain nor Egypt, but to be independent.) The British bases on the canal were subjected to economic sanctions, essentially a refusal to supply them with food. Guerilla attacks were organized, with the Government's blessing, by the Muslim Brotherhood, an Islamic political group that had been established in Cairo in 1929. The

British retaliated. They destroyed a village from which guerillas had sabotaged their water supplies, they took prisoner a police post and finally, in January 1952, they fought a pitched battle with another police post at Ismailia, which had refused to surrender. By the time the defenders gave in, with their ammunition exhausted, forty-three of them were dead. The people of Cairo exploded with fury when they heard the news. On 26 January, Black Saturday, they burnt almost every bar, hotel, cinema, club and restaurant in the city centre that they associated with the British and their friends of the Turco-Egyptian pasha class. The riots showed Nasser and the Free Officers he had gathered round him that the country was more ripe for revolution than they had thought. They brought forward their plans for a coup and struck on 23 July 1952. Three days later King Farouk was allowed to sail away in the royal yacht to permanent exile.

The new regime did not have a revolutionary political programme, nor, indeed, any definite ideas on how Egypt would be governed. The officers hoped at first to appoint a professional politician to run the government and then step back to exercise a purely supervisory role. They believed that the enthusiasm of the newly liberated Egyptian people would suggest to the Government the necessary measures for the reinvigoration of the country. This was, of course, politically naïve. The officers found themselves sucked more and more into the business of active government and in due course Nasser himself became President, replacing the respected figurehead, General Neguib, who had been appointed to the post after the coup. Even then the officers had only two important revolutionary aims. One was land reform, the redistribution of the land of large estates to the people who farmed it, which was begun within two months of the revolution. The other was the eviction of the British. This objective was achieved relatively easily by negotiation in 1954. Nasser called off the attacks of the guerillas and the British Government, which had slowly come to see the futility of maintaining bases which themselves provoked attacks, felt it should try to establish a more cooperative relationship with the new republic. In October 1954 the two sides agreed that all British troops should be withdrawn by June 1956 and that thereafter the canal bases should be shared.

The agreement was a triumph for the young republican leaders. The British at the time were regarded in the Middle East as being immensely powerful, as well as manipulative, and it was known by everybody in the region what an important asset the Suez Canal was and how Egypt had been the base for all British interests in the area. The fact that the revolution had been able to force the British to retreat suggested a

strength and patriotism that had been lacking from previous governments. The Egyptians felt liberated by the agreement: it gave them a
new sense of dignity. The rest of the Arab world was inspired by it.
The leaders and people of other Arab countries, those already independent as well as those still under colonial rule, started to look to Nasser's
government as an example. And Nasser responded. Although he had
never been outside Egypt before the revolution – except on the army's
foray into Palestine in 1948 – since the war with Israel he had begun
to see Egypt's problems as just part of the problems of the Arab world
as a whole. Once he had evicted the British from his own country he
felt bound to help the other Arabs evict them from theirs. His radio
station, Voice of the Arabs, began to broadcast anti-imperialist propaganda, attacking in particular the British-supported regimes in Jordan
and Iraq. The director and chief announcer of the station, Ahmed Said,
had a very emotional style and he was often none too accurate in his
facts, but what he said captured people's imaginations throughout the
Arab world. He soon became famous. The bedouin in Saudi Arabia,
who had a habit of personalizing objects by calling them by their brand
names, started to refer to radios as 'Ahmed Saids'.

Nasser's philosophy and his non-aligned Afro-Asian policy, as well
as his attacks on the Arab monarchies, was bound to bring him into
conflict with the British and Americans, even though in the early years
of his government he enjoyed good relations with the United States and
after 1954 said he wanted to be on equally good terms with the British.
The major problem was that the two powers at this time were promoting the Baghdad Pact, which was intended to be one of three alliances
with NATO and SEATO which would surround the Soviet Union and
prevent the spread of Communism. The United States Secretary of State,
John Foster Dulles, had arranged a Turko-Pakistani accord in 1954
and in 1955 created the Pact by bringing in Iraq. He then hoped to
persuade Syria and Jordan to join. The Pact was clearly contrary not
only to Nasser's ideas of non-alignment but also to his hopes of ridding
the Arab world of a foreign military presence. It created an underlying
tension in America's and Britain's relations with Egypt which served
to aggravate the crisis that began in July 1955.

It was in this month that the Israelis raided the Gaza Strip which
had been under Egyptian government since 1949. Until this time Nasser
had tried quietly to ignore Israel, knowing that he would lose any battle
and being unwilling to spend what little foreign currency he had on
arms. Like other Arab governments he had tried to hold back the
Palestinians on his territory after the ex-Mufti of Jerusalem in 1953
had awoken some of his people from their state of shock by calling for

them to begin armed raids on their enemy. What few raids had taken place had been ineffective, and during the relatively moderate government of Moshe Sharett the Israelis had ignored them. Their policy changed as soon as the militant David Ben Gurion came back to power. Within one week of his return the Israelis readopted their policy of massive reprisal for any incursion. They attacked the Egyptian base in Gaza and killed thirty-nine soldiers. Humiliated, Nasser was forced into retaliating. He started to organize the Palestinian guerillas on his territory and from August that year used their raids as part of Egyptian policy. This change in approach meant that Egypt had to arm itself, and when the Western powers would not oblige him he turned to the Soviets. In September he announced that he was buying Soviet arms from Czechoslovakia. This, like his recognition of the Communist Chinese government early in 1956, was exactly the type of decision on the part of a non-aligned leader of the period that was most likely to alarm the Americans. On 19 July 1956, after being further annoyed by Cairo Radio's continuing attacks on their allies, the Americans and British announced that they were withdrawing the offer of a loan to finance the building of the Aswan High Dam, whose electricity was to fuel Egypt's industrialization. A week later Nasser responded by nationalizing the Suez Canal, which was owned by Britain and France. In a brilliant speech, broadcast live by Voice of the Arabs, he said that Egypt would build the dam with the canal's revenues and that 'the imperialists could choke on their rage'. The speech caused jubilation throughout the Arab world.

The British and French promptly withdrew their pilots, hoping that without them traffic in the canal would come to a halt. Nasser responded by appointing an exceptionally able young engineer to run the new Suez Canal Authority and getting the Egyptian pilots to work overtime. The canal continued to operate normally. The French and British then began to consider military action. The British Prime Minister, Sir Anthony Eden, was motivated in this extraordinary overreaction by his association of Nasser with the Fascist dictators with whom he had dealt as a junior minister and then Foreign Secretary before the Second World War. He saw everything that happened in the Middle East to hamper Britain's policies as engineered by Nasser. He had been particularly incensed by Cairo Radio's support for the Mau Mau rebellion in Kenya. He therefore found himself joining a Franco-Israeli conspiracy to invade Egypt, which the Israelis hoped would end the Palestinian raids and the French believed would curb the country that they saw as the principal backer of the rebellion in Algeria, which had begun in 1954. In accordance with the agreed plan the Israelis invaded Egypt on 29 October 1956 and the British and French moved into the canal zone on 5 November with the ostensible purpose of separating the two sides and guarding a strategic asset. The Egyptians promptly sank ships to block the canal. The Syrians blew up the two oil pipelines that ran across their territory from Iraq and Saudi Arabia to the Mediterranean. Throughout the Arab world there were riots, demonstrations and attacks on British and French property. The two powers were condemned internationally, not least by the Americans who refused to help Britain when the invasion caused an unexpectedly heavy run on sterling. After a few days the powers were forced to halt their action. All three invaders withdrew. For the British the withdrawal marked the moment when they realized that their country was no longer a major world power and that they would soon have to withdraw from the rest of what remained of their empire.

For Nasser the crisis was a colossal political victory. It made him the undisputed hero and leader of the Arabs. Already he was the major influence in Arab politics. He gave confidence to the nationalist movements in Morocco and Tunisia, both of which gained independence in 1956. His propaganda embarrassed the young King Hussein of Jordan into dismissing General Glubb, the British commander of his army, early that year. It certainly helped sustain the rebellion in Algeria, even if it was not the underlying cause, as the French would have liked to believe. After Suez, Egyptian influence forced King Hussein to cancel the treaty with Britain that his grandfather had signed in 1948. All British troops were withdrawn from Jordan by the summer of 1957. More remarkably the government in Syria, the country which Nasser described as 'the beating heart of Arabism', demanded immediate political union with Egypt. The Syrians were tired of being fought over by Egypt and Iraq, both of which wanted to move Syria decisively into its own non-aligned or pro-Western camp. The British and Americans had a notion of joining Syria and Iraq under Hashemite rule, and the Soviet Union, responding to the challenge, had been promoting the Syrian Communist Party. The Syrian regime was vulnerable to this type of politics not just because it ruled a relatively small but important country, but because it was chronically unstable. Ever since the country had been created in 1920 it had lacked proper legitimacy, in its own people's eyes and in the eyes of outsiders, because it was seen as not being quite whole. It did not cover all of the area of 'Syria' that the name had implied in Ottoman times. Its governments lacked confidence and had been changed more rapidly by *coups d'état* than those of any other country. Becoming part of Egypt, therefore, seemed to the leaders of the Syrian Government in 1957 a good way of sheltering under

Nasser's umbrella while, they hoped, being able to run their own terri-
tory. Nasser was sceptical, but having become the great proponent of
Arab unity he could hardly veto the idea. In February 1958 Syria and
Egypt proclaimed themselves the United Arab Republic.

There were further extraordinary developments later in the year.
In July in Iraq an ardent but mentally unstable nationalist, Brigadier
Abdel-Karim Kassem, overthrew the Hashemite monarchy in a bloody
coup, which saw the bodies of the King, the Crown Prince and the
Prime Minister dragged through the streets and mutilated by the crowd.
As a relatively populous and potentially rich country, Iraq had been
the bastion of Anglo-American influence in the Arab world and its 'fall'
was a shock to these powers. It seemed at the time that Lebanon too was
in danger of civil war or revolution, caused by a small-scale rebellion in
which the Muslim militias were trying to prevent the Christian President, Camille Chamoun, altering the constitution to give himself a
second term in office, which would have enabled him to ally his country
more firmly with the West. In accordance with the Eisenhower doctrine,
which pledged support for any Middle Eastern country threatened by
international Communism, and responding to the President's request,
the United States landed marines in Lebanon, while Britain flew troops
to Jordan to help protect the remaining Hashemite monarchy.

The year 1958 was the high point of the Arab nationalist tide and
of Nasserism. It seemed then that Nasser's ideas might sweep all before
them, that the old pro-Western monarchies would inevitably fall and
that the individual Arab countries might be able to unite – or reunite,
as the more fervent nationalists saw it. Domestically, as well as in
inter-Arab politics, it was a time of hope. The leaders of the new governments may have been violent and unpredictable, in the case of Kassem,
and opportunist, in the case of the Syrians, but they combined these
characteristics with some idealism. President Bourguiba of Tunisia,
King Mohammed V of Morocco and Nasser himself were men of an
altogether superior stamp, driven principally by idealism, albeit mixed
with a desire for power. All three had their own philosophies, Bourguiba's revolving around the development of Tunisia as a modern,
secular, European-orientated state, Mohammed V's being concerned
with the national integrity of Morocco, and Nasser's dwelling on the
independence, non-alignment and dignity of the Arab nation.

The people of the Arab world looked to their new leaders with hope;
in retrospect Arabs today say that hope was the distinguishing feature
of this period. They believed that they were being liberated, and, just
as Nasser had supposed in 1952–3, they thought that once they were
free and independent they would be better governed, become more

productive, and would enjoy more of the fruits of their own labour. They would be new men. There was great enthusiasm for projects such as the Aswan High Dam, which became the focus of the hopes of the Egyptian people. The belief was that the great national effort in the form of taxes and foreign exchange, together with Soviet credit, put into this project during the fifteen years it took to build would lift the country on to a new economic plane alongside the industrial powers.

The optimism of the late 1950s and early 1960s led the Arab people as a whole to tolerate some increasingly repressive regimes with little complaint. They were prepared to accept that some limitation of their human rights and freedoms was reasonable while their governments pursued broader goals. Above all they honestly believed that the new, independent, republican nation states would enable them to defeat Israel.

It was not long before the Arabs began to be disillusioned. The union between Egypt and Syria, the pride of the Arab world when it was made, was unhappy from the start. Part of the problem was that neither side knew or understood the other. At the time of the union Nasser had never been to Syria and he had only once met its leaders. He was already becoming impatient with other parties' and people's views, as successful leaders sometimes do, and with little thought he imposed on Syria Egypt's political system and its increasingly socialist economics. The Syrian political parties were dissolved and replaced by Egypt's National Union, and parts of the Syrian economy were nationalized. The business and political classes of Damascus, who were more factious, individualistic and politically minded than the Egyptians, came to resent Egyptian rule. They rejoiced in September 1961 when a group of army officers overthrew the regional government and took Syria out of the union.

A year later Nasser was sucked into another equally unhappy enterprise. A revolution occurred in Yemen, the most backward of the Arab states, and although the republicans took the capital, Sanaa, they failed to seize control of the whole country or destroy the royal family. The royalists, receiving help from Saudi Arabia and Britain, raised a counter rebellion in the country areas and the republicans called on Egypt for support. Nasser could not refuse, any more than he could have refused Syria's appeal for unity in 1957–8. He despatched increasing numbers of Egyptian troops to Yemen and was committed for five years to a civil war which only served to remind the world that the Arabs were still utterly divided in their political aims and that the Egyptian army was far from competent. The Egyptian officers knew nothing of Yemen or its people and the troops, most of whom had never seen a mountain or a hill before, were frightened by the terrain. They proved useless at guerilla warfare in the mountains and their bombing of villages, including some in the Saudi province of Najran, did nothing for Nasser's reputation as an Arab patriot. Egypt's enemies in the Arab world were able to represent the country as increasingly arrogant and overweening. These enemies by the mid-1960s included not only the remaining conservatives, principally Jordan, the Arabian Peninsula monarchies, Morocco and Libya, but also the new regimes in Syria and Iraq. Brigadier Kassem had been overthrown and killed in another bloody Iraqi coup in 1963, by which time his violence, eccentricities and purges of his opponents at home had long alienated Nasser. The two new Iraqi regimes that came to power in 1963 both proposed union with Egypt, but the first fell out with the Egyptian President during negotiations and the second was rebuffed.

At home too Nasser was becoming increasingly intolerant and suspicious. Anyone who was a critic, or who might be suspected of conspiring against him, came to live in fear of the midnight knock at the door and a long period of imprisonment.

In 1967 Nasser, and the entire Arab world, suffered a far worse disaster than the break-up of the United Arab Republic or the Yemeni war. Egypt was drawn into fighting a war with Israel, the fault lying ultimately with Syria and the Palestinians. The Palestinians had become much more active since the Suez crisis. In 1959 a Palestinian engineer, Yasser Arafat, had founded the organization Al-Fatah, which for several years had contented itself with publishing a crude magazine called *Our Palestine*. Then, in 1964, the leaders of the Arab governments, at a summit meeting, established the Palestine Liberation Organization which they intended should lead Palestinian resistance. But the aim was to keep it firmly under their control, particularly under the control of the Egyptian government, and not allow it to operate against Israel except under their supervision. Arafat meanwhile formed around himself a band of guerillas and got the backing of the radical Baathist government in Syria. His group's first 'operation', on New Year's Day 1965, was a total failure. It seems that word of his plans was leaked to the Lebanese authorities and a team of Al-Fatah 'commandoes' planning to carry out a raid into Israel was arrested by the Lebanese security forces before it set out. A little later the group suffered its first fatality at the hands of a Jordanian soldier. Nevertheless Arafat's group eventually managed to mount a campaign of periodic sabotage of Israeli installations, operating mostly across the Syrian and Jordanian borders. It issued ecstatic communiqués, and the Israelis dramatized the raids for their own propaganda purposes, but in fact in two and a half years of campaigning Al-Fatah only killed eleven of its enemy.

The main political effect of Arafat's attacks was to expose Syria, his backer, to Israeli retaliation – which the Syrians further provoked through relentless anti-Israeli propaganda. In November 1965 they asked Nasser to sign a defence agreement with them and Nasser found himself obliged to agree, feeling, once again, that he could not reject an offer of co-operation from a brother Arab government. The fact that Egypt did not enjoy good relations with the Baathist regime then in power in Damascus and worked even less happily with the extremist wing of the Baath that came to power in February 1966 made no difference to the basic logic of the situation. In the spring of 1967 tension on the Syrian and Jordanian borders mounted. It was fuelled partly by a calculated Israeli policy of over-retaliation for Palestinian raids and periodic Syrian bombardments, which themselves were sometimes provoked by Israeli intrusion into land in the demilitarized zone, which the Syrians said was owned by Arab farmers. In a particularly fierce exchange in April 1967 the Israelis shot down six Syrian aircraft, one of them over Damascus. In the next month it seemed that an Israeli attack on Syria was imminent and Nasser was obliged to act. He had often been taunted by other Arab governments about his hiding behind the United Nations force in Sinai which had taken up positions on the Egyptian side of the frontier (only) after the Suez crisis. It was said that if Egypt had the strongest armed forces in the Arab world, as it claimed, it should have asked for the UN force to be withdrawn so that it could put pressure on Israel by closing the Gulf of Aqaba to shipping going to the Israeli port of Eilat. On 18 May 1967 Nasser made this request. The United Nations Secretary General promptly complied and Nasser then had no alternative but to reoccupy Sharm el-Shaikh at the mouth of the Gulf and close the straits. In Israeli eyes this was a *causus belli*; indeed from their aggressive reactions to the Palestinian raids and from what some of their leaders have said and written since it seems that for two years the Israelis had been only too anxious to have a decisive battle with their Arab enemies.

While the Arab world worked itself into a state of jubilation, believing that it was about to win a mighty victory, and the Western public feared that Israel was about to be crushed, the Israelis put the final touches to a well-prepared plan, and struck. On the morning of 5 June 1967 they destroyed most of the Egyptian air force on the ground, by the evening of the 7th they had taken the West Bank of Palestine from Jordan, on the 9th they reached the Suez Canal and on that day and the next they took the Golan Heights from Syria.

Nasser felt that he was personally responsible for this disaster. He broadcast his resignation on 9 June, but at that moment of shock his people did not want to lose the familiar and inspiring figure they had grown to love during the previous fifteen years. Even while he was speaking they poured on to the streets, not only in Cairo but in other Arab capitals, and demanded that he stay at his post.

During the weeks and months that followed the Arabs had time to absorb the implications of the defeat. The hopes they had come to cherish had turned to dust. The ideas that independence and the creation of the republican nation state would give them power and prosperity were discredited. The people's disillusionment marked the beginning of the moral and political confusion, and the decline in the standards of government, that became such a marked feature of the Arab world during the next twenty years.

In the immediate aftermath of defeat, however, both people and governments remained defiant. In August the Arab leaders met in Khartoum and agreed that there would be no recognition of Israel and no negotiations with it. The richest of the oil producers, Saudi Arabia, Kuwait and Libya, agreed to pay subsidies to the front-line states. On the Suez Canal front there developed a war of attrition, of air raids and artillery bombardments.

It was the Palestinians, surprisingly, who took up the next stage of the fight. With the nation states humiliated in conventional warfare, they were no longer in a position to insist on controlling the Palestinian irregulars. Guerilla operations seemed the best prospect for hurting Israel. Soon after the ceasefire in June Yasser Arafat 'transferred' Al-Fatah's headquarters to the newly occupied West Bank, hoping, in accordance with the revolutionary fashion of the time, to organize a self-sustaining rebellion among the Palestinian population that had remained there. He failed. He discovered what has been a fundamental fact of Palestinian life since, that there is a big difference in attitude between the people living in camps in exile and those living under Israeli occupation. The first group had already lost their country and their homes and, feeling that they had nothing further to lose except their lives, were prepared to join the fedayeen (literally, those who sacrifice themselves) and risk dying, in the hope of regaining what they had lost. The West Bankers, in contrast, still had something to lose from Israeli reprisals and they were not prepared to risk a great sacrifice for an organization whose effectiveness they doubted. They preferred to hope that an Israeli withdrawal would eventually be arranged by diplomatic means. Arafat and his men quickly became demoralized and in January

1968 Arafat escaped from a sympathizer's house in Ramallah and crossed on to the east bank of the Jordan.

Then his fortunes turned. In February the guerillas, whose ranks had recently been swelled by the formation of the militant Popular Front for the Liberation of Palestine, managed to take over the direction of the PLO and demanded the resignation of Ahmed Shuqairy, the Chairman and Nasser's protégé. In due course he was replaced by Arafat. More extraordinarily, in March 1968 the guerillas won a military victory. It happened when the Israelis, responding to the explosion of a mine under a school bus, sent 15,000 men across the Jordan to attack the village of Karameh. The fedayeen stood firm. They took big casualties, losing perhaps 150, but they killed at least 30 Israelis, destroyed a number of tanks and forced the enemy to withdraw. It was not a very big action by the standards of what had gone before, but it was the first definite Arab military success against Israel and it generated enormous enthusiasm. Thousands, from all over the Arab world, flocked to join the guerillas. From some 200 before the 1967 war their numbers grew in three years to 30,000. Their operations changed. The mine laying and sabotage of 1965–7 were replaced by the bombing of supermarkets, bus stops and other civilian targets in Israeli cities, rocket attacks on border settlements and direct assaults on frontier posts.

None of these operations was as successful, or as justifiable in any moral sense, as the battle of Karameh, and quite quickly the Israelis managed to control them. They drove the fedayeen out of their own and the occupied territories and prevented further penetrations. The guerillas were forced to turn to sniping and shelling across the borders, and the more extremist elements, particularly the PFLP, turned to outright terrorism against international and civilian targets in an attempt to get publicity. One of the PFLP's early attacks was the machine gunning of an Israeli jet at Athens airport, which led to the Israelis mounting a retaliatory raid on Beirut in which they blew up thirteen aircraft of the Lebanese Middle East Airlines. The terrorist attacks increased in number and horror during the next four years. Aircraft were hijacked or blown up in mid-air, the Israeli team at the Munich Olympics was murdered, a group of hired Japanese machine-gunned passengers at Tel Aviv airport. It was not until mid-1973 that Yasser Arafat and the other Palestinian leaders decided that terrorism had served its purpose and, under pressure from Arab quarters, began to control the groups that were responsible.

It is an unpleasant thought, but in an international sense terrorism served the Palestinians in that it drew them to the attention of the Western world and made people realize for the first time that there was such a race as the Palestinians and that they had lost their country. In the Middle East, however, terrorism was less beneficial to them. It was partly responsible for leading the Palestinians into a war with the Jordanian Government, the first of two major disasters.

The causes of the war lay partly in the guerillas' arrogance, their inflated claims of success in their minor raids into Israel and the greed of a hooligan fringe who bullied and exploited the Lebanese and Jordanian villagers. From being heroes in 1968, by 1970 the guerillas had become thoroughly unpopular and were periodically fired on, particularly by the well-armed villagers of Lebanon. More important, they attracted Israeli retaliation, which normally came in the form of bombing raids on Palestinian camps and other Lebanese and Jordanian targets. They seemed likely to provoke even bigger Israeli incursions than the raid on Beirut airport. In Jordan they earned the enmity of the army, which was largely composed of bedouin and townsmen of the east bank, who did not feel a strong affinity with the people from the west of the river Jordan. It was not only that the guerillas seemed likely to embroil the Jordanians in a war with Israel, the regular soldiers and the King were angered by the guerillas' appearance of running a state within a state. They did not like the Palestinians claiming that Amman, the Hashemite capital, was about to become a liberated revolutionary city, an 'Arab Hanoi' as they called it, and a base for revolutionary war throughout the Arab world, which would lead to the eventual liberation of the homeland. When in September 1970 the PFLP hijacked three jets belonging to TWA, British Overseas Airways Corporation and Swissair, flew them to the desert of eastern Jordan and threatened to blow them up unless their comrades in prison in Israel and Britain were released, the patience of the King and the army snapped. It is said that the King was goaded into action by seeing a bra flying from the radio antenna of a tank. When he asked what it was doing there he was told by his troops that it meant they were being expected to behave like women. On 17 September the King turned his army on the guerillas and crushed them. Some armoured forces sent by Syria to help the Palestinians were driven back. At the end of ten days of fighting a truce was arranged by the intervention of Nasser – though nine months later the King renewed his attacks, crushed the last Palestinian bases in the north of his country, and drove the guerillas out of his realm for good. It was an Arab army, not the Israelis, which inflicted on the guerillas their worst defeat and deprived them of their best base for operations against their enemy.

Gamal Abdel-Nasser, in negotiating the ceasefire of 28 September 1970 at an Arab summit meeting in Cairo, seemed to be full of his old flair and authority, but in truth he was exhausted. On his way home from escorting the Ruler of Kuwait to the airport, he had a heart attack and a few hours later he died. The whole Arab world went into mourning. At his funeral on 1 October there were extraordinary scenes of grief. Nasser was still not blamed for the disaster of 1967. He was remembered for having freed the Arabs from the domination of the colonial powers and for giving them self-respect and hope.

4

Despair: 1970–93

The October war and Egyptian-Israeli peace settlement – Arab demoralization – rise of political Islam – Lebanese civil war – Iran-Iraq war – Gulf crisis

Nasser was succeeded by his Vice-President, Anwar Sadat. The succession was smooth but the tone of Sadat's presidency was different from what had gone before. Sadat was a less inspiring man than Nasser, more of a realist, more cynical, though still in some ways a dreamer, and not quite so austere in his personal finances. Just as Nasser had put his stamp on the 1950s and 1960s, Sadat put his on the 1970s.

From an early stage in his presidency Sadat realized that he had to move away from the Soviet Union, whose support for Egypt had been limited and not very effective, and he saw that he had to do something to break the stalemate with Israel on the Suez Canal and make some sort of peace. Part of the reason was that Egypt simply could not afford indefinitely to continue the war. The first of his objectives he began to achieve in his first two years in power by expelling a large number of Soviet advisers and removing the most pro-Soviet elements from his government. The second he planned with remarkable secrecy during 1972 and the first nine months of 1973, involving at a fairly late stage the new, more pragmatic government of Hafez Assad, which had seized power in Syria in November 1970. On 6 October 1973 the Egyptian army crossed the Canal and the Syrians advanced into the occupied Golan Heights. During the next three weeks they and the Israelis fought a far bigger and more costly war than had been seen in the Middle East before. On some days there were more tanks engaged on the two fronts than had been used in some of the big battles on the eastern front in the Second World War. Eventually the Israelis pushed the

Syrians back beyond the 1967 ceasefire line and managed to push a bridgehead across the canal but at the end of the fighting there were still large Egyptian forces in Sinai. In a strict military sense the Israelis had won, but they had been taken by surprise and were shocked by the efficiency with which Egyptian units had breached their defences. They had also been struck by the bravery of the Arab troops. The Arabs, the Israelis and the Western governments had all been impressed by the sheer scale of the fighting. Both the Americans and the Soviets had mounted airlifts of supplies to their clients. It was clear that if nothing was done to resolve the conflict, not only would there be a bigger war in the future, but the superpowers might one day confront each other in the Middle East.

The October, or Yom Kippur, War was also important for the use the Arabs made of the oil weapon. During the three years before the war the oil market had switched quickly from a condition of steady surplus to increasing tightness, caused by the growth in American demand. During the summer of 1973 the producers of the Organization of Petroleum Exporting Countries, only half of which were Arab, had come to realize that, regardless of the agreements they had made with the oil companies, consumers would pay for oil whatever was asked. It happened that on the day war broke out an OPEC team had begun negotiations in Vienna with some representatives of the oil companies, and when these broke down ten days later the OPEC delegates flew to Kuwait and there announced a price rise on 17 October of an extraordinary 70 per cent. Later on the same day, the Arab producers announced that they would be reducing oil production in stages until the Israelis withdrew from all the territories occupied in 1967 and the rights of the Palestinian people were restored. A few days later the oil weapon was sharpened by further production cuts which reflected a complete embargo on deliveries of Arab oil to the United States and the Netherlands. In the eyes of the consumers, not surprisingly, the issue of prices, which was not political, became confused with the oil weapon, not least because the shortage created by the production cuts drove open-market prices even higher and led to a further large price rise of 120 per cent when OPEC met again in December. Added to the shock of the war, the effect of the oil crisis was to make a settlement of the Middle East conflict the most pressing diplomatic challenge for America and the rest of the Western world.

Sadat, therefore, had succeeded very well in his strategy. Dr Henry Kissinger, the American Secretary of State, began an epic round of shuttle diplomacy and in January 1974 in Sinai and in May of the same year on the Golan Heights he negotiated disengagement agreements which separated Arab and Israeli forces. Sadat then wanted to build on these agreements to move towards peace with Israel. He and many other Egyptians felt that their country had sacrificed enough for the Palestinians in the previous thirty years. They were beginning to distance themselves from the pan-Arab nationalism of Nasser's period and think more of Egypt's own interests. (The dual nationalist sentiment, pan-Arab and nation state, which this change reflected is something unique to Egypt in the Arab world; it reflects the size of the country's population and a culture and history that is separate from that of the other Arab countries.) In the mid-1970s the Egyptians wanted to reform their economy and do more business with the Western world, which they saw as a potential source of investment. President Sadat found as he dealt more with the American leaders that he liked them – he developed special friendships with Henry Kissinger and President Jimmy Carter – and he had always believed that because America was the only country able to put real pressure on Israel it held 90 per cent of the cards for peace. His desire for a peace agreement and his links with the Americans developed together and nurtured each other. In August 1975 Kissinger was able to negotiate for him a further disengagement agreement which gave him back more territory in Sinai.

Two years later, finding himself frustrated by the endless debate about what the shape of further moves towards peace might be, he announced suddenly on 9 November 1977 in a speech to the Egyptian People's Assembly that he would be willing to go to Jerusalem to the Knesset itself, and negotiate with the Israelis. The suggestion amazed the world, but it was promptly taken up by the Israeli Prime Minister, Menachem Begin, and ten days later Sadat flew to Jerusalem. On the following day he made a passionate appeal for peace to the members of the Israeli parliament and the massed cameras of the world's television networks. Sadat's visit was followed by meetings with President Carter and further meetings with Begin, and finally, in September 1978, by a summit meeting at the US Presidential retreat at Camp David. Here an Egyptian-Israeli agreement was arranged which led to an Israeli withdrawal in stages from the rest of the Sinai peninsula, finishing in April 1982. Egypt recognized Israel and exchanged ambassadors with it, and the two sides agreed that they should encourage trade and tourism between them. A separate agreement outlined a procedure for the Israelis granting autonomy to the Palestinians in the West Bank and Gaza, and eventually entering negotiations to determine the final status of the territories. This agreement, to which of course no Palestinian was a party, remained the foundation of the American peace initiative in the Middle East.

The rest of the Arab world was utterly opposed to what it saw Egypt doing. The unity that had given the Arabs success in the 1973 war and immediately afterwards disintegrated from 1975 onwards. All of the Arabs had known for years that it was Israel's aim to conclude a separate peace with a major Arab power, preferably Egypt, so that the others would no longer be able to threaten it. President Sadat had been as aware of this as anyone, and yet he had pushed ahead with his second disengagement deal and his peace treaty. In his heart President Assad of Syria might have liked to join him, especially at the time of the 1975 agreement, but as leader of the country that was the keeper of the Arab conscience and the most resolute backer of the Palestinian cause he could do nothing. He knew that there was not nearly enough being offered by the Israelis to the Palestinians for it to be possible for him to follow Sadat; indeed, one of the reasons why the Israelis wanted to divide the Arabs was that if they succeeded they would not have to offer anything to the Palestinians. If Assad could not join the peace process neither could any of the remaining Arab countries, unless they wanted to be ostracized by their brethren and have their supplies of aid cut off by the oil producers. Also, it is fair to say, there was little incentive for most of the other states to conclude peace with Israel because, with the exception of Jordan, they were not in the front line and had not been significantly involved in fighting. So when the Camp David accords were finally signed in March 1979 the leaders of the rest of the Arab world condemned Egypt. They held a summit in Baghdad and imposed a political and economic boycott on the country, which involved their withdrawing ambassadors, suspending aid and moving the headquarters of the Arab League to Tunis.

Egypt's withdrawal from the conflict, which has not been seriously questioned in that country since, left the other Arabs to come to terms with the fact that for them the military option no longer existed. If that was so, it meant that all their effort, sacrifice and rhetoric during the previous thirty years had been in vain. Their cause had been taken from them. As nations and individuals they may not have greatly loved the Palestinians, but they had supported them because they were fellow Arabs and because the Palestinian cause had come to represent Arab nationhood, and once they had all suffered losses of men, territory, money, or pride on behalf of it, they had had their own reasons for continuing the fight. Now they had to start admitting to themselves that they had lost and that eventually they too would have to accept Israel and make peace with it. They felt bitter and embarrassed – embarrassed because the governments knew straight away the reality of the situation but could not admit it to each other or to their own people.

It was not only their political failure, and the further proof of their disunity, that hurt the Arabs in the late 1970s. They were equally disenchanted by what they saw as their growing materialism and corruption. This stemmed from the oil price explosion of 1973. At first, as the oil producers took stock of the situation and watched the inexorable rise in their revenues that occurred in 1974 and 1975, it seemed that a new age had dawned. This impression was enhanced by increases in the prices of other basic mineral and agricultural commodities. At last raw materials exported by the developing world were to be priced at their 'proper' level and there would be a huge transfer of wealth, in particular technology, from the rich industrialized countries to the poor. In part the transfer was to be supervised by conferences, such as the New International Economic Order and the Arab European Dialogue; in part it was to come about simply through the poor countries having the money to buy the goods and technology they needed. The Arabs, as the biggest group among the producers of the most important commodity, found themselves at the very centre of this process. They commanded the attention of the world. Politicians, scholars, businessmen, all wanted to develop connections in the Middle East.

While discussing the global implications of the transfer of wealth and power, the Arabs enjoyed spending their revenues. The richer oil exporters, Saudi Arabia and the Gulf states, were able to embark on the projects of their dreams, which in many cases involved the biggest infrastructure developments and the best quality public buildings being constructed anywhere in the world. The poorer Arab countries benefited from an increase in the value of their own small oil exports, together with aid and investment from the Gulf states, the remittances of their citizens working there, and the profits made by their traders, contractors, middlemen and wheeler-dealers, who flocked to help the newly rich Gulf Arabs manage their money. Numerous joint companies were launched by governments to exploit the rich countries' capital and the poor countries' labour, agricultural land and markets. Great faith was placed in co-operation.

Yet within a few years, it was clear that the poorer Arab economies were not being transformed. The joint companies were mostly failures and the other money that was flowing from the rich to the poor states was going more into consumption than investment. Instead of a new class of industrialist in Egypt, Jordan and Syria, there emerged a new class of conspicuous spender. There was a big increase in flashiness and corruption. When they saw this happening at the same time as the abandoning of the Palestinian cause, a connection became established in the minds of more idealistic Arabs between the loss of political ideals and the new money.

Their anguish was deepened yet further by the realization that their world was becoming far more violent. In the 1950s and early 1960s there had been a long and cruel war of independence in Algeria (1954–62) and some very bloody *coups d'état* in Iraq. But elsewhere, although there was considerable instability, with coups and attempted coups, not many people were killed. Syria's numerous *coups d'état* between 1949 and 1962 were almost entirely bloodless and in many cases the losers were not kept in prison for very long. From the time of the 1967 war this changed. The Palestinian attacks on Israel and the huge scale of the Israeli reprisals, and then the Palestinians' international terrorist campaign of 1969–73, were the most obvious signs of the change. Other shocking episodes were the Jordanian-Palestinian wars of 1970 and 1971. Then in 1973 the October war claimed 20,000 casualties in three weeks.

In the mid-1970s a new strand of violence appeared. All over the Middle East at this time there were born small, initially unobtrusive Islamic fundamentalist movements. These emerged as a direct consequence of past political failures. The people who joined them were reacting to the disaster of 1967, the failure of socialism, Arab nationalism and the established nation states, and the increasing corruption they saw around them. They were looking for a new ideal – something which was not an import, as socialism, nationalism and the whole concept of the nation state had been, but which came from their own culture. Inevitably they found the answer in Islam, which provides rules for all aspects of life, including government. Islam promises that a state which follows its laws will be rich, powerful and happy. People who follow God's law cannot but succeed. It also implies that the nation state will be superseded and that the Arab world – indeed the whole Islamic world – will be united, as part of it was in Ottoman times, because under good government guided by God there would do nothing to divide the Muslims.

The spread of these ideas was accompanied by a related but non-political trend towards social conservatism, noticed by few Westerners in the region but very visible to the Arabs. People began to return to Islam in a personal and moral sense. They prayed more, went more often to the mosques on Friday, became more traditional in the dress they wore and began to employ a correct classical style of language. None of these changes was objectionable, indeed in many ways they were desirable, except that they tended to distance Arab families from the foreigners living in their countries. Gradually, as Arab society became more conservative, the two groups had less contact with each other.

What was also undesirable was that some of the Islamic political movements, instead of just campaigning for political change, which admittedly would not have been easy in the restricting conditions of the Arab world, turned to violence. In the mid-1970s a newly revived part of the Muslim Brotherhood in Syria began to attack President Assad's regime through a campaign of bombings and assassinations, which eventually led to the government destroying a large part of the town of Hama and massacring its inhabitants (see Chapter 5). And in Iran in February 1979 there was an Islamic revolution. This was an event on an altogether different scale. It was the work of the entire population, inspired by clerical leaders, rather than of any single political party, and in the decade that followed it came to have a large influence on Islamic movements elsewhere. A combination of clerics, students and unemployed members of the new industrial working class swept away what appeared to be one of the strongest and most confident regimes in the Middle East. The ultimate causes of the revolution were the Shah's attempts to alter – Westernize – his country's culture and suppress the role of the clergy, and appalling economic mismanagement in which the post-1973 tide of oil revenues had first raised the expectations of the population and then led to huge unemployment when the government overspent and ran out of money.

Nine months after the Iranian revolution, in Saudi Arabia there was an alarming manifestation of Islamic zeal when a strange group of revolutionaries occupied the Grand Mosque in Mecca, believing that an 'army of the north' was going to come and help them usher in a new Islamic age. After mounting an embarrassingly long siege of two weeks and fighting their way through the cellars, the Saudi security forces eventually recaptured the mosque. Those of the rebels who were taken alive were executed. Two years after this, in October 1981, an Egyptian group of Islamic militants assassinated President Sadat, whom it considered had betrayed the Arab world by making peace with Israel.

The rising tides of secular and Islamic violence at their most callous came together in the course of the civil war that erupted in 1975 in Lebanon. This war was not only exceptionally cruel and bloody – it eventually left well over 100,000 dead – it happened in a society that had been admired for being 'civilized', in the sense that it allowed its different sects to live relatively peacefully side by side and encouraged those who could afford them to pursue the good things of life. Lebanon called itself a democracy and held regular elections, though its political system was really a carefully balanced contract between the sects, with democratic trappings. It had a free press, part of which would happily sell its loyalty to whatever foreign government paid it, and, in the American University of Beirut, it had the best university in the Middle East. It was a place where people from the other Arab countries could enjoy themselves without feeling inhibited by the more austere social customs and restrictive politics of their own countries. They could drink and gamble in Lebanon, meet politicians, or exiles, from other countries, gossip, engage in political speculation, or conspire.

Lebanon, and particularly the capital, Beirut, was the last remaining place in which flourished the pre-First World War culture of the Levant, which had once thrived in Smyrna (renamed Izmir by the Turkish republic), Constantinople, Salonica, Aleppo and Alexandria, but had been overcome by the aggressive twentieth-century nationalisms that emerged after the Ottoman Empire broke up. The culture had been created in the nineteenth century by traders, missionaries, diplomats and other travellers coming from Europe and introducing Western ideas to the local populations. The people retained their 'tribal' loyalties to their particular sects or national groups, but they overlaid them with a genteel, tolerant attitude to life and each other. In Beirut it was the Levantine spirit that enabled seventeen Christian, Muslim and Druze sects to live together, often forming business partnerships and sometimes intermarrying. It imbued only the upper and middle classes though, and it was essentially an urban phenomenon. There were large parts of the Lebanese population, notably the Shia community in the south, that had nothing to do with Beirut culture and felt despised by it. In most areas of the hinterland people lived and did business only with members of their own sects and remained suspicious of the others. From the point of view of the outside world, including the other Arab countries, the hinterland was not very important. What mattered in Lebanon was Beirut and its middle-class world. It was with this world that outsiders mostly came into contact and they were horrified to see it submerged in civil war in the late 1970s.

The origins of the war lay in demographic change. The National Pact, the distribution of government jobs on sectarian lines (but in the Christians' favour) and the Western orientation of the country worked well enough while the Christians made up roughly half the population. But by the early 1970s they were only a third, and the Shia Muslims had become the biggest single sect. There was an additional refugee community of Palestinians, predominantly Muslim, which served to make the Lebanese Muslim majority appear even bigger than it was. The Palestinians, of course, commanded much more support from the Muslims than they did from the Christians, and they reminded the two Lebanese communities of how their ambitions for their country diverged, one seeing it as an outpost of Europe in the Middle East and the other as part of the Arab world.

After 1970–1, when they were expelled from Jordan, the Palestinians adopted Lebanon as their base for operations against Israel. This made the country the target of Israel's retaliation raids. The Christian establishment feared, rightly as it turned out, that its country was being turned into a Palestinian-Israeli battleground. It tried to use the Lebanese army to control the guerillas and would have liked to have had it evict them, as the Jordanians had done, but the army was too weak and the country too disunited internally for this to be possible. Part of the intention of the Christians in trying to control the guerillas was to weaken the Muslims' claim for greater political power in the country, and the Muslims opposed military action partly because they had come to see the PLO forces as their biggest domestic militia. The Christian militias meanwhile wanted to take matters into their own hands. The war that followed was enormously complicated and the following account is only a simple summary of what happened. It is intended mainly to show how low Arab politics fell in the course of the conflict.

The first shots in the war were fired in April 1975 when some Christian militiamen machine-gunned a bus of Palestinians on the outskirts of Beirut. The fighting rapidly spread and grew in intensity, with two Christian militias, principally the Phalange, which was inspired by the Nazi and Fascist movements of the 1930s, on one side and the Sunni Muslim militias on the other. The PLO stayed aloof from the fighting in the early months but found itself drawn in during the autumn. The war was brought to an end, temporarily, in November 1976, when the Syrian army occupied Beirut. In sending in his forces President Assad's intention was not to reincorporate Lebanon into Syria, but to stop the Palestinians creating a radical state, which might drag him into another war with Israel, and prevent the further sectarian disintegration of the country, which he feared would start to affect Syria. In essence Assad wanted the old constitution upheld, even if he was not averse to having more influence in the country. For this reason, before his army moved, he had the Lebanese President invite him to intervene.

For a year after the Syrians arrived the main fighting switched to the south, where the Palestinians were engaged in their war against the Israelis. The principal victims were the Shia villagers who suffered from Israeli bombardment and Palestinian extortion. In March 1978 the Israelis mounted a major raid into southern Lebanon, killed some 2,000 Palestinians and Lebanese, and, when they withdrew, left behind a security zone controlled by Christian gunmen, who were drawn partly from the Christian villages in the south east.

The invasion was a disaster for Lebanon in every way. It forced the Syrians to arm the Palestinians and the Lebanese Muslims, both Sunni and Shia. It was after the 1978 Israeli incursion that the first Shia militia, Amal, came into being. The Israelis responded by giving more arms to the Christians, which had the effect of increasing the already growing division between the Christian militias and the Syrians, who were working to frustrate what appeared to be a Christian scheme to establish a state of their own. In effect the Israeli incursion caused the reversal of the Syrians' policy of disarmament and pacification.

The Syrians were further encouraged in their arming of the Palestinians by what they saw as President Sadat's abandonment of them when he embarked on his peace initiative to Israel. In the climate of Arab politics at the time arming the Palestinians was the necessary patriotic thing to do. And yet neither Syria nor any of the other Arab governments that sent arms or money wanted the Palestinians to be strong enough to take over Lebanon or cause another war with Israel. In truth they all regarded the Palestinian groups as thoroughly dangerous and would have liked to see them 'cut down to size'. They armed them out of a sense of short-term political obligation and what they saw as a need to protect themselves from each other. Ever since the late 1960s, when the proliferation of Palestinian groups took place and the PLO fell into the hands of the guerillas, different Arab governments had tried to give themselves some control of the movement by sponsoring their own guerilla groups. Syria established an organization called Al-Saiqa, Iraq founded the Arab Liberation Front and others backed other groups on an *ad hoc* basis. Now, in the late 1970s and early 1980s, they used the militias in Lebanon to fight wars among themselves by proxy. For example, the Egyptians, when they were attacked by Syria after the 1975 disengagement agreement, were able to hit back at their tormentors by giving backing, through the Saudis, to Lebanese and Palestinian groups that were opposed to President Assad's army and his groups. The Iraqi Baath Party, which was normally at daggers drawn with the Syrian Baath, did the same. The Syrians retaliated. The idea was that if parties found their proxies were losing and needing further support and money, or if the Syrians found their army was taking casualties, they would mellow their attacks on their brother Arab governments in the hope of concluding a truce.

These rivalries made for steadily increasing chaos. The extortion of the Palestinians in west (Muslim) Beirut and the south grew more greedy and violent. In these areas the PLO succeeded in establishing states within a state, with its own security police and its own cadres of corrupt, flashy, over-rewarded officers and officials. Its leaders never acknowledged that Lebanon was really somebody else's country: they regarded their own cause as so important that it was worth any sacrifice by any other Arab. Meanwhile the Syrian officers, in their parts of the country, became involved in protection rackets and the massive cultivation of cannabis in the Bekaa valley.

In 1982 matters took a decisive turn for the worse. Bashir Gemayel, the principal Christian leader at the time, had sent his militia on the offensive against the Syrians, ostensibly to protect a Greek Orthodox community in the town of Zahle, and in the tradition of the Christian Lebanese leaders had looked for some support from outsiders, in this case the Israelis. The Israelis had shot down some Syrian helicopters and the Syrians had then moved missile batteries into the Bekaa valley. This raised tension through the latter part of 1981 and early 1982 and finally in June that year it led to a new Israeli invasion of Lebanon. The Israelis destroyed part of the Syrian army in the Bekaa and seventy Syrian aircraft. They advanced up the coast to Beirut, meeting resistance only from the PLO and Amal, and after eight days entered east (Christian) Beirut. For the next two months they laid siege to west Beirut, killing some 4,000 civilians, until it was agreed, through the mediation of the Americans, that the PLO forces should leave the city and be dispersed to various Arab countries, Iraq, Yemen and Tunisia, all of which were well away from the Arab-Israeli front line. A multinational American, French and Italian force supervised the withdrawal and then itself left. At the same time Bashir Gemayel was elected President, after the Phalange had put some very heavy pressure on members of the Lebanese Parliament, but on 14 September he was assassinated by a car bomb. The Israelis then occupied west Beirut. During two days between 16 and 18 September the Christian militias, who moved in in the wake of their protectors, carried out a sadistic massacre in the Sabra and Chatilla Palestinian refugee camps, leaving between one and two thousand dead, and in many cases mutilated as well. This appalling act prompted the return of the multinational force.

The Israelis, who remained in east Beirut and the southern half of the country, had three objectives which they thought were clear and obtainable. They wanted to cleanse Lebanon of 'terrorists', in other words Palestinians, re-establish the Lebanese government, and sign a peace treaty with it. In the first of these aims it seems, in retrospect, they more or less succeeded. A large part of the PLO forces left by sea from Beirut in August 1982, firing their guns into the air and claiming, with their usual self-deception, that they had won a victory by bringing their cause to the world's attention. In the following year Yasser Arafat, the PLO Chairman, returned to the country and tried to re-enter its politics or civil war, but he was crushed by the Syrian army and Palestinian forces under Syrian control, and left from the port of Tripoli in December having destroyed a large part of the city. He sailed once again under the supervision of the multinational force, and once again he was bound for Tunis. There remained in northern and eastern Lebanon some 6,000 guerillas associated with the PLO, but they were kept under careful Syrian control. They and new recruits to their cause were involved in the Palestinian-Shia battles around the refugee camps in the mid-1980s, but they did not again represent a major force in the civil war and they were only able to launch occasional attacks on Israel. Their expulsion from Lebanon marked the Palestinians' second major military defeat and the removal of the PLO from the last base from which its guerillas could confront their principal enemy. They had been expelled from Jordan twelve years earlier and after the mid-1960s there had never been the slightest chance that the Syrians, for all their loyal rhetoric, would allow them to operate across the Golan frontier. It took a little while for the Palestinians to accept the fact, but 1983 marked the end of direct military confrontation between the PLO and Israel.

In the second and third objectives of their invasion the Israelis failed utterly. As had happened after the incursion of 1978, Lebanon was destabilized further by their action. In May 1983 the Israelis obliged the Lebanese government to sign a treaty, under which the former agreed to withdraw from the country if the Syrians would do the same, but the Syrians had not the slightest intention of leaving, so the agreement meant nothing. A year later the Lebanese government revoked it. The multinational force stayed on in the country until early 1984 but its mission was hopeless almost from the beginning. It too had the purpose of re-establishing a proper Lebanese government, but the current one, headed by Bashir Gemayel's elegantly coiffured brother, Amin, was little more than an instrument of the Phalange, and as it disintegrated in a new round of fighting with its enemies, principally the Druze and the Shias, the multinational force found itself in the unhappy position of supporting what was in most Lebanese eyes a single, losing militia group. The force was truck-bombed by Shia suicide drivers, who destroyed the American embassy and the American and French military headquarters. It retreated from its small territory of west Beirut in July 1984.

The Israelis pulled out of Lebanon in stages, finally leaving in the summer of 1985. From mid-1983 they were facing a vicious guerilla war and carrying out equally vicious retaliation in the southern areas they occupied. They suffered a steady stream of casualties, the worst single loss being in November 1983, when their headquarters in Tyre was bombed and demolished, killing seventy-five. They counted their invasion, in effect their fifth war with the Arabs, as a defeat.

What Israel left behind by 1985 was described by a British ambassador as 'a black hole of criminality, chaos and murder'. At the time of the invasion in 1982 thirty-three different militia groups had been counted in Lebanon, and although their number did not increase, or their behaviour become more brutal, they became more nihilistic in their aims. Much of the fighting, murder and kidnapping of the mid- and later 1980s was almost purposeless. It served only to promote the new militia leaders from *petit bourgeois* obscurity to positions of prominence, where they found themselves dealing with members of the big Lebanese families that dominated the country's politics and led its long-established militias. The only group that had a definite programme was Hizbollah, the Party of God, which with its associate, Islamic Jihad, hoped to make Lebanon the first Arab Islamic republic. Hizbollah was sponsored by the revolutionary government of Iran. It came to prominence as a direct result of the devastation caused by the Israeli invasion. The people it represented were the poorest refugees from the south who had never been part of the prosperous Levantine culture of Beirut and who now devoted themselves to destroying what remained of it.

The final stages of the war began in September 1988 when the Lebanese parliament failed to elect a new president and separate prime ministers took office in west and east Beirut. In effect the country was divided. Early the following year the Christian Prime Minister, General Michel Aoun, who had been commander-in-chief of the Lebanese army, declared that in his view the only future for his country lay in a Syrian withdrawal. He began to get large supplies of arms from the Syrians' enemies, the Iraqis, who had recently won their long war with Iran. His forces went to war first with the Muslim militias backed by the Syrians and then with the Syrian army itself. Much of what remained of Beirut, particularly the western part, was destroyed by shelling. Aoun attempted to gain support by internationalizing the crisis and involving the French, whom he saw as his main protectors, the Americans, Russians and other Arab states. The result was not one that pleased him. In September 1989 the Lebanese National Assembly met under Arab sponsorship in the Saudi mountain resort town of Taif and its members agreed to a revision of the famous National Pact of 1943 – the first there had been in fourteen years of civil war. They drew up a Charter of National Reconciliation which stated that in future seats in the cabinet and the Assembly would be divided equally between Christians and Muslims and that executive power should be transferred from the President to the cabinet. Aoun, predictably, denounced the Charter as illegal. The Assembly, however, met again in Lebanon and chose a new President, a Christian, and appointed the leader of the 1988 Muslim government, Selim El-Hoss, as Prime Minister, which was strictly in accord with both the National Pact and the new Charter. Aoun was dismissed from his position at the head of the army and increasingly isolated by the new government and the Syrians in his stronghold in east Beirut. In September 1990, after his backer, Iraq, had been subjected to an international embargo as a result of its invasion of Kuwait, his supply of arms was cut off. The government of what had become the Lebanese Second Republic, led by President Elias Hrawi, ordered the blockade of Aoun's headquarters and then invited the help of the Syrian army. At last the Syrians were free to act without inhibition. They had joined the international alliance against Iraq, and they knew that none of the major powers was going to criticize them, however violent they were. Aoun was duly crushed in three days and on 13 October 1990 went into exile in France.

After this seemingly decisive denouement Lebanon came under close Syrian supervision, giving it almost the status of a protectorate. Gradually the militias were disarmed, except in the extreme south where the Syrians dared not go for fear of confronting the Israelis. The hostages kidnapped by Hizbollah were released. Reconstruction began. Not all was peace, because the Shias in the south continued their war to get the Israelis out of the security zone they had seized in 1978, and occasionally some small, reformed Palestinian groups made raids across the zone into Israel – and the Israelis retaliated. The fighting, though, was on a pre-1975 scale. Slowly the Arab world decided that Lebanon was at 'peace'. The question people asked was whether the country would remain a Syrian client state, or whether, perhaps, some of the old, free, Levantine spirit might be rekindled and slowly bring about the liberalization of Syria.

The strongest emotion of the Arabs when they looked back on the fifteen years of the Lebanese civil war was shame. Many of the richer people and the intelligentsia felt a personal loss because they had known the country well and had enjoyed going there for business or holidays. Everyone who had followed the course of the war felt ashamed that sixteen brother states had watched disaster after disaster and never acted to stop it. They felt even more embarrassed by the knowledge that their governments had fought each other in Lebanon by proxy. They were exasperated by the Palestinian involvement in the destruction of Lebanon, which in the process destroyed their own military capability. They were horrified by the sheer numbers of people killed.

The civil war ate into Arab self-confidence. As they had known it before the war, Lebanon may have been imperfect, but it had been a success. Beirut had been the one place in the Arab world that had been free, prosperous, as glamorous and sophisticated as any city on the Mediterranean, and a meeting place for east and west. It had been a place which most Arabs could criticize but of which they all felt proud. When they saw it destroyed, mainly by fellow Arabs, they asked themselves what it was in their culture that could cause such a thing to happen.

For much of the time that the Lebanese war was being fought a very different type of war was taking place on the borders of Iraq and Iran. It did not command the same popular interest as Lebanon because it took place well away from the centre of the Arab world, did not destroy cities that many people knew and did not involve the Palestinians or the Israelis. It was important because of the scale of the military operations and because it led eventually to Iraq's disastrous invasion of Kuwait, which split the Arab world more thoroughly than it had ever been split before.

Both the Iranian war and the invasion of Kuwait were the work of Saddam Hussein, a tough Baath Party activist, conspirator and bully who had been the effective leader of Iraq since soon after he and his associates overthrew the government of Abdel-Rahman Aref in 1968. For the first eleven years of the new regime Saddam had been Vice-President, but in 1979 he had eased aside his superior, Ahmed Hassan Al-Bakr, taken the Presidency for himself and changing his cabinet by having most of its members killed. A year later, in September 1980, he sent his army to invade Iran. Part of his reason for doing so was that he felt himself under attack from the Islamic revolution of Ayatollah Khomeini which had come to power in February 1979. Khomeini had spent fourteen years in exile in the holy Iraqi city of Najaf but in 1978 had been expelled by Saddam at the request of the Shah. In the following two years a number of his friends and colleagues who had remained in Iraq had been murdered. Khomeini and all his associates knew that any Iraqi religious leader who tried to introduce religion into politics in that country would be removed from circulation and probably killed. He therefore bore Saddam no goodwill. He saw Iraq as an obvious target for the export of the Islamic revolution, not least because a majority of its population was Shia, and his government began broadcasting subversive propaganda in the hope of fermenting an uprising such as he had directed against the Shah. Iranian propagandists travelling in the region carried the message of their revolution to the Shia communities in the Gulf states, particularly Bahrain and Kuwait, and Saudi Arabia. They helped cause two serious outbreaks of rioting in the Saudi Shia oasis town of Qatif in November 1979 and February 1980. The Gulf rulers did little to reply to the Iranian attacks, which were often very personal and were particularly directed against the institution of monarchy, but Saddam Hussein not only beamed back his own propaganda to the Arab population of south western Iran, he had his army begin shelling Iranian border positions. The Iranians fired back.

The propaganda and the bombardments gave Saddam a pretext for hostilities, but he had two other unspoken reasons for his invasion. One was that he wanted to regain for Iraq complete sovereignty over the Shatt al-Arab waterway that is formed by the confluence of the Tigris and Euphrates and makes up the extreme southern part of the Iraq/Iran border. During the mandate the British had given the entire river to Iraq – rather against the international norm which puts river boundaries in the centre of the stream. In 1975, as a condition for the Shah withdrawing his support for the rebellion in Kurdistan, the Iraqis had had to surrender half of the river, but the concession had rankled and now the Iraqi leadership saw an opportunity to regain what it passionately believed was part of the homeland.

Saddam's other reason for attacking Iran was that he wanted to become leader of the Arab world, and thinking, as an uneducated man might, that a country in a state of revolutionary chaos would be an easy target, he told himself that he would win a quick and glorious victory. Had this occurred he would certainly have been able to dominate the Gulf states and Saudi Arabia, and establish himself as the major force in Arab politics. Egypt, the natural leader of the region, had recently withdrawn from the arena by signing the Camp David peace treaty. In Saddam's mind was the knowledge that under the monarchy and Nuri Said in the 1940s and 1950s, Baghdad had been the great rival of Cairo in the battle for influence, and now it must have seemed to him that the leadership was his to take.

Saddam may have had in mind some comparison between himself and the late Gamal Abdel-Nasser, though none was justified. Nasser was driven by a desire to liberate and unite the Arab world; he was a brilliant orator – it was said that he had 'a voice like honey' – and he inspired the love of the Arab peoples. Saddam, at best, impressed people. He was obviously patriotic in a crude way, in that he wanted to destroy Israel and pretended to rise above petty Arab squabbles, and he ran a state that seemed to outsiders to be efficient, even if cruel. But he was certainly no orator: his speeches were long, rambling, flowery in places, boring in others and generally inarticulate. He was known to preside over one of the most unpleasant regimes in the world and was believed, probably rightly, to have killed people with his own hands. Dr Ghazi Algosaibi, the Saudi ambassador in London, says in his book *The Gulf Crisis* that the keys to Saddam's character were a thirst for power for its own sake, a persecution complex and an instinct for adventurism.* The last trait meant that Saddam saw the taking of calculated initiatives fraught with danger as being the natural way of politics. His persecution complex led him to see these initiatives as being forced upon him. Soon after he had begun his war with Iran he was saying that he had undertaken it on behalf of the Gulf countries, which he expected to pay for it, and that its purpose was to protect the eastern gateway of the Arab nation.

From the beginning Saddam's invasion of Iran was a failure. His army penetrated no more than fifty miles in the first six months of the war and after a year's stalemate in early 1982 it was evicted in a rout, which nearly led to the Iranians taking Basra and cutting off Iraq from the Gulf. There followed six years of almost static warfare in which all the attacking was done by the Iranians and both sides suffered huge casualties. During much of this time the feeling among many journalists and diplomats in the region was that eventually the Iranians would win, because of their superior morale and much bigger population – 50 million at the time. During the whole of the period from 1982 to 1988 the Iraqis seemed to think only of how they could survive. They had the equipment to attack, but their troops lacked the motivation. As it turned out the Iraqi defense succeeded because the Iranians had the opposite problem: they simply lacked the tanks, artillery and aircraft to knock a hole in the Iraqi lines.

What won the war for the Iraqis was a sudden crack in the Iranian spirit in the spring of 1988. A point came when the Iranian leaders, the population and the troops realized that they could not win, and the morale of the troops at the front disintegrated. The first blow came when the American navy, which was protecting Kuwaiti oil tankers, fought a series of engagements in the Gulf, in which it sank nearly half of the Iranian navy without incurring any casualties itself. The loss of a few Iranian frigates and minelayers was not of enormous importance to their war effort, but it demonstrated to the population that it was

---

* Dr Ghazi Algosaibi, *The Gulf Crisis – An Attempt to Understand*, Kegan Paul, 1993

impotent against America, the 'Great Satan', and this the Iranians found embarrassing and depressing.

At the same time, in March and April, Iraq launched some 150 missiles at Tehran in the space of seven weeks. The Iranians in three years had managed to send only seventy-five missiles against Baghdad. Although Tehran is a vast, sprawling city of nearly 10 million, its inhabitants were terrified by the random and unpredictable nature of the missile strikes.

Lastly the Iraqis in May 1988 dropped poison gas on the Kurdish village of Halabja, in a part of Kurdistan that the Iranians had just taken, in their last successful attack of the war. The gas killed 5,000 civilians, mostly women and children, who literally choked to death. The Iranian press and television made great play of this atrocity, which was condemned all over the world, but what they reported only frightened their own people further. Iranian civilians, especially in towns near the frontier, began to wonder what Saddam might do to them, if he was prepared to gas his own people – albeit those who were in rebellion.

The Iraqi army had already achieved success at the beginning of the year when it had acted on satellite intelligence fed to it by the Americans and retaken the ill-defended town of Fao at the head of the Gulf. From the time of Halabja onwards it began to make similar attacks on poorly defended parts of the line, and it found that wherever it attacked the Iranians ran away. By the beginning of July it was pushing well into Iran. Later that month Ayatollah Khomeini, declaring that it was 'worse than drinking poison', accepted a ceasefire. A million people – two thirds Iranians, one third Iraqis – are thought to have been killed or maimed in the war.

For Saddam the victory, if that is what it was, did not taste as sweet as he would have liked. The Iranians did not concede control of the Shatt al-Arab waterway or other bits of territory; the two armies returned to the lines on which they had stood in 1980. The revolutionary government in Tehran stayed in power and the Arab governments, particularly those in the Gulf, seemed more nervous of Iraq than grateful for what it had done. The Iraqi economy was bankrupt. It had some $60 billion of debt to Western countries and the Soviet Union and $40 billion of debt to Arab countries, which it clearly had no intention of repaying. The Government saw little prospect of it earning sufficient oil revenues, after servicing Western and Soviet debt, for it to be able to restart spending on development and reabsorb into the economy some of the million men it had under arms. The problem was not that Iraq lacked big reserves of oil but that, for both financial and technical reasons, it could not repair and develop its fields quickly. Nor could it be sure of selling more oil even if it could produce it.

It is not known how soon Saddam decided that the annexation of Kuwait would be the answer to his difficulties, but viewed in retrospect his policies suggest that it might have been quite soon after the end of the war. Almost no attempt was made to demobilize his army, and the programme for the production of weapons of mass destruction, including missiles, which had been so important in winning the struggle with Iran, was stepped up. The Iraqi forces considerably expanded their complement of tanks and aircraft, buying from the Soviet Union. Air defence equipment was bought from France.

At the same time Saddam worked at tying the Arab countries to him, one by one. In the autumn of 1988 he invited King Fahd of Saudi Arabia to Baghdad and asked him to sign a non-aggression pact. The King was more than a little surprised, because he felt that his country had backed Iraq sufficiently loyally during its war with Iran. The Saudis had not wanted Saddam to instigate war and had even warned him against it, but when he appeared likely to lose they realized that an Iranian-installed revolutionary Shia regime in Baghdad would be disastrous for them. They and the Kuwaitis had therefore lent and given Iraq $38 billion. In spite of his surprise, King Fahd, who is a peaceful and friendly man, found it impossible to refuse the proffered treaty, and he signed as requested. Looking back on the episode, the Saudis say they assume Saddam's intention was to try to prevent them inviting foreign forces to the Kingdom when he invaded Kuwait.

In February 1989 Saddam took another initiative. He promoted the formation of a new regional body, the Arab Co-operation Council, to combine Iraq with Jordan, Yemen and Egypt, which, following its long period of isolation after the Camp David accords, had only recently been welcomed back into Arab councils. There seemed little economic logic to the ACC; it was speculated that it was intended to rehabilitate Egypt under the wing of Saddam and promote Iraq as a regional leader. In fact it was probably an attempt to neutralize the most powerful Arab state.

A little later the gratitude of Sudan was won by Saddam providing the government with arms to fight its civil war in the south. Further arms captured from Iran were given to Jordan. The countries of the Maghreb, Morocco, Algeria and Tunisia, received school books with 'Gift of the Iraqi Government' printed on them; students were invited to Iraq for four years to study free. To Western minds this sort of initiative might appear rather crude – it amounts to interference in the domestic affairs of the countries concerned – but to the citizens of developing countries who receive poor quality education from their own governments but are very earnest about learning, the gifts seemed both generous and patriotic. They were remarkably effective in winning support for Saddam from the ordinary people.

A final group, the Palestinians, already backed Iraq because of Saddam's aggressive rhetoric and his opposition to Syrian hegemony in Lebanon. Yasser Arafat had been given an aircraft and Iraqi crew by Saddam, and he and some of the other Palestinian leaders regarded Baghdad virtually as a second home. In 1990 Saddam earned further Palestinian goodwill by making it plain that sooner or later he was going to confront Israel. He seemed to be the only Arab leader who was still threatening the state in his speeches, and certainly he was the only one who gave any sign of being prepared to back harsh words with action. At one point he promised that if the Israelis hit him, as they had done when they bombed the Osirak nuclear reactor in 1981, he would 'burn half Israel'. Like most of Saddam's other ploys, his speeches were effective. Hardly a day passed in 1989 and early 1990 when a newspaper editorial in some part of the Arab world did not declare Saddam to be the most truly patriotic Arab leader.

In the months of June and July 1990 Saddam pursued a series of claims on Kuwait, which he told himself, and the world, were justified by his having sacrificed his own country to defend the Gulf from Iran. He demanded that Kuwait should cancel the debts of $12 billion that he owed it and that it should pay him $2.4 billion for oil allegedly stolen from a field that straddles the border of the two countries; he also demanded a lease on the islands of Warbah and Bubiyan at the head of the Gulf. When the Kuwaitis refused to give in to these demands and the threats that accompanied them, on 2 August he invaded their country. At first he said that he had been invited to intervene to help some Kuwaiti radicals who had seized power; a week later Kuwait was annexed as the nineteenth province of Iraq. The response of the Western powers and the United Nations was first to impose sanctions on Iraq and then to send troops to Saudi Arabia.

Saddam had greatly underestimated the international reaction, partly because he knew little about Western democracies. From what he understood of them he believed they would not risk the lives of thousands of their young men in resisting him, knowing that he would willingly sacrifice tens of thousands of his own men, as he told Claude Cheysson, a former French Foreign Minister, during the crisis. As it turned out, the West reacted vigorously and with surprisingly little hesitation. It was concerned mostly about oil. It was obviously not desirable for Saddam to be left in a position where he would have been able to dictate the pricing and production policies of countries that contained half the world's resources. There were other important considerations. It was unacceptable that one member of the United Nations should simply invade and annex another member, the first time this had happened since the UN was founded at the end of the Second World War. There was also a moral and political obligation for America and Britain, in particular, to help the defence of Saudi Arabia and the Gulf states, which in the previous forty years had become as good friends as any countries outside the industrialized world. For Britain the Gulf was its biggest market after Europe and North America. There were big flows of investments in both directions, large numbers of British and Americans worked in the Gulf and equally large numbers of Saudis and Gulf Arabs sent their children to school in Britain and the USA and spent their holidays there. On the basis of these commercial and cultural contacts a network of personal friendships had been established.

A final reason for Western intervention, and not the least strong, was the discovery that Saddam had been building a large arsenal of missiles and non-conventional weapons, poison gas, and nuclear and biological weapons. Given his predilection for using the weapons at his disposal, it was thought that this stockpile should be destroyed.

Saddam's assumptions about the Arab reaction to the invasion were more accurate than his assumptions about the West. In the fortnight after the invasion there was an attempt to find 'an Arab solution', which would have meant a virtual Kuwaiti surrender, and when it failed the Arab countries split into opposing camps guided by their most basic self-interest. Yemen, Jordan, with its big Palestinian population, the Palestine Liberation Organization and Sudan backed Iraq. Both the Yemenis' and the Palestinians' reaction was emotional as well as political. The Yemenis had long had an awkward relationship with Saudi Arabia, where almost half their labour force worked in menial jobs. They resented Saudi Arabia's involvement with their northern tribes, which since the revolution of 1962 had helped keep the central government weak. They may have been told by Saddam that if he won his confrontation they would be given back some of the territory that Abdel-Aziz bin Saud had taken from the Imam of Yemen after the First World War. The Palestinians were influenced by Saddam's aggressive stance towards Israel and by their jealousy of the Kuwaitis. Some 400,000 Palestinians lived in Kuwait and many had become rich there, but they were still bitter about the Kuwaitis' even greater wealth and their own exclusion from Kuwaiti citizenship.

The countries on which Saddam miscalculated badly, in fact fatally, were Saudi Arabia and Egypt. King Fahd was so appalled by the Iraqi leader's aggression and dishonesty that he invited the Americans to send forces to the Kingdom. In Egypt President Hosni Mubarak was furious about Saddam's lie at the end of July, when he had promised that he had no intention of attacking Kuwait. It seems that Saddam had supposed that his role through the Arab Co-operation Council in rehabilitating Egypt in the Arab world would count for more with Mubarak than Egypt's links with America and Saudi Arabia. He also failed to realize that heads of state, like other people, can feel moral indignation and, in spite of the odd expedient compromise, like to think that their policies are guided by moral principles. As Ghazi Algosaibi says in his book on the Gulf crisis, 'it is rare, if not impossible, to find a decision maker whose decisions do not take principles into account'. Saddam, being largely amoral, from the beginning of the crisis found himself, to his surprise, faced with the hostility of the biggest Arab state. Unlike the people in other Arab countries in North Africa, who were more pro-Iraqi than their governments, most of the Egyptian people were hostile to Iraq. In part this was because some of them, the middle classes, resented Iraq's pretensions to the leadership of the Arab world. During the previous twelve months Egyptians had also been alarmed to discover that large numbers of their compatriots working as labourers in Iraq had been murdered, it was thought by soldiers who had returned home to find that Egyptians had been given their jobs or seduced their wives. A great fuss was made when the bodies were returned to Egypt. As the Gulf crisis developed it turned out that Egypt's political and material advantage matched its moral stance. The crisis re-established it as the centre of Arab diplomacy and led to the Arab League headquarters being moved back to Cairo from Tunis. Egypt's Arab and Western creditors wrote off a large part of its debt.

In the five and a half months between the invasion and mid-January most Arabs, in all countries of the region, expected there would be some sort of compromise solution, possibly one which would leave Iraq controlling a slice of northern Kuwait. They were surprised when on 17 January 1991 the allied air forces began a bombing campaign. At the end of February this was followed by a four-day ground campaign and the total rout of the Iraqi army, or that part of it which was still in Kuwait. There were then two uprisings in Iraq, one in the south, where a broadly based revolt was taken over by Shia Islamic revolutionaries supported by Iraq, and the other in the north, where there was a rebellion by the Kurds. Saddam's army crushed both rebellions, doing huge damage in the south and, it is thought, killing more people than had been killed by both the allied air and land campaigns. To stop it doing the same in Kurdistan, and to look after the Kurdish refugees, the allied powers then established a safe area for the Kurds and announced that Iraqi aircraft were to be excluded from a much wider 'no fly zone'. In 1992 a similar zone was established in the south, to hamper Saddam in his continued pursuit of the Shia rebels. The United Nations sanctions on trade with Iraq and on flights into and out of the country remained in force and were supplemented with further resolutions which despatched UN teams to the country to destroy its stocks of missiles and non-conventional weapons. Saddam remained in power only thanks to the efficiency of the security organizations that protected him. Since the colonial period no Arab leader and no country had been so totally humiliated.

The Arab world as a whole was more upset by the Gulf crisis than by any other event since the disaster of 1967. For those who had backed Saddam, and who had seen him as a champion against the West and against Israel, there was embarrassment and shame. Many Palestinians, typically, had clung to hopes of a military victory even after the land campaign had begun, and once again they had seen their dreams turn to dust.

There was more widespread shock at the degree of disunity the crisis had caused. It was soon realized after the war that the divisions that had emerged in Arab ranks were permanent, or, at least, would last a very long time. Before January the Arabs' expectations had been that like many other regional crises the Iraqi occupation of Kuwait would eventually be resolved with a compromise, not perhaps a durable compromise, but at least one which would last for a few years and save the face of everyone involved. People had in their minds something like the end of one of the rounds of the Lebanese civil war or a minor inter-Arab war such as those that were fought between the two Yemens before they were joined in 1990. Then the various leaders had kissed, made up and turned in a matter of days from being bitter enemies to outward friends, swearing eternal brotherly love. During the Gulf crisis, Yasser Arafat, who had kissed more of his enemies than most, had said that the schism in the Arab world was no different from past schisms amd that it would end 'at the appropriate time'.

The fact that this crisis did not end in false and temporary reconciliation was the result of Saddam being too proud and fatalistic to retreat and the Western powers wanting a decisive outcome. The 'hand was played out' and when it reached its end the different parties had been pushed so far apart, and some had been so embarrassed, that they were bound to remain divided for many years. The Saudis and the Gulf Arabs, and especially the Kuwaitis, remained extremely bitter about the Iraqi betrayal and about the Palestinians' support for Iraq. They had discovered during the crisis that on practical matters of security their interests and the West's were the same, which made the Western democracies, in effect, more reliable friends than their brother Arabs. Elsewhere in North Africa and Jordan, the crisis showed again that charismatic leaders, hope of Arab unity, confrontation with other countries in and outside the Arab world, and dreams of victory – if they were all likely to end in failure – were of no use to the people in solving their countries' economic and social problems, of which they were becoming increasingly aware.

Throughout the Arab world in the aftermath of the crisis governments and peoples realized that for the time being each country would do better to look to its own interests and try to resolve its own problems, than to dream about being rescued by a pan-Arab political initiative or a great Arab leader. The practical result of the Gulf crisis was that Arab countries turned in on themselves.*

---

* The outline of the history of the Arab world during this century given in this and the two previous chapters has been intended as a basis for the analysis in the rest of this book of the changes now underway in the region. Five books to which I have referred and which give a far more detailed account of the events described are: Peter Mansfield, *The Arabs*, Penguin, 1978; Anthony Nutting, *Nasser*, Constable, 1972; David Hirst, *The Gun and the Olive Branch*, Faber, 1977; David Friedman, *From Beirut to Jerusalem*, Fontana, 1990; and Robert Fisk, *Pity the Nation*, André Deutsch, 1990.

5

The Corruption of the State

The early nationalist coups – introduction of socialism in Egypt – effect of 1967 – growing brutality of governments – Baathists in Syria and Iraq – the 'security state' – encouragement of corruption

For the ordinary Arab in the streets of Cairo, Amman or Casablanca the Arab-Israeli conflict, Lebanon and the Gulf crisis matter much more than equivalent issues matter to his European or American counterparts. In the Western industrialized nations any issues that are outside domestic politics are likely to be less important in the eyes of the electorates, even if their own armed forces are involved, than domestic economic and social issues. In the Arab world it is the reverse: in an emotional sense, and in assessing their leaders, Arabs are less concerned with their economies, or with improving or deteriorating social services, and more concerned with national pride and military success. If their countries go to war they are not going to worry over much about the morality of the conflict, and certainly not about the losses of the enemy (as part of the Western liberal classes did during the Gulf war), as long as they win. They want to have, and see the outward signs of, power and prestige. They want this for the Arab world as a whole, as well as for their own nation states. They also want not to have to watch their brother Arab states tearing themselves apart in civil conflicts. This is why the sequence of military defeats and civil wars described in the last three chapters has not only led to perpetual instability in the region but has also caused great pain to Arabs individually.

Even so, in a day-to-day sense, domestic politics, the types of government they have and the amount of freedom they are given are bound to have great influence on their lives. Likewise the success or failure of their governments' economic policies will help determine how rich or poor they are. As this and the following chapter will show, Arab government and economic management have fallen to as low an ebb as the politics of the region.

In Arab domestic government, as in regional politics, hopes have been raised and then dashed. The governments that ran the Arab world in the years after the Second World War are seen in retrospect to have been quite humane, even if they were not very effective; but at the time they were regarded as corrupt, unpatriotic and incompetent, and gradually they were overthrown by colonels and generals holding various types of nationalist ideas. The first post-war *coup d'état* where an army officer replaced a civilian government occurred in Syria in 1949. There were then further coups overturning monarchies or civilian republics in Egypt in 1952, Iraq and Sudan in 1958, Yemen in 1962 and Libya in 1969. During these years republican military regimes also came to power, after the French and British withdrawals, in Algeria in 1962 and southern Yemen in 1967. In every case the new regimes were greeted by their peoples with enthusiasm. It is said that after the first, bloodless, coup in Syria in 1949 the new President, Colonel Husni Zaim, put the deposed president and prime minister in an armoured car and had them driven around Damascus so that they could see the crowds dancing in the streets. The new regimes stood for Arab unity, the prosecution of the struggle with Israel, independence from foreign influence by old colonial powers and oil companies, and, in a non-specific way, for the development of their countries' economies. This was to be achieved by the revolutionaries wresting control from foreigners of their countries' principal assets and by their organizing a more equitable distribution of wealth within their own societies. In the early days the governments needed only to promise to bring about these changes for the people to believe that they were as good as done. The new leaders did not have well worked out programmes of reform and they had no idea of the practical problems they would encounter.

The classic early case of a revolution running into difficulties, and then becoming steadily more radical, intolerant and inefficient, was Egypt. It was here that were first tried out the policies which came to be known as 'Arab Socialism'. These proved to be a recipe for restricting freedom and bankrupting the economy. They were well intentioned at the beginning, but failed.

When he came to power in 1952, Colonel Nasser had only one clear economic objective, which was land reform. He and his colleagues saw that the richest half of 1 per cent of the landowners held a third of the cultivable land, while at the other end of the scale 72 per cent of the people who actually worked on the land owned plots of less than one feddan – a feddan being just over an acre. Within a few months the new government set a maximum holding for an individual of 200 feddans. Lands above this ceiling were confiscated and a slow and rather inefficient programme was instituted to distribute them to the fellahin (peasants) in lots of between two and five feddans. At the same time there was some moderate political reform. The monarchy, the titles of *pasha* and *bey* and the old political parties were abolished. This was as far as the revolution went. Nasser and his colleagues, a few of whom were from fairly comfortable backgrounds themselves, were pleased to have broken the political and economic power of the big landowners, who had been a barrier to reform for decades, but they were anxious to promote the traders, industrialists and bankers of the middle class. For nine years after the revolution these people prospered. Those who had owned land benefited from the compensation they received under the reform programme and many were able to buy into the foreign businesses that were forced after the Suez crisis to 'Egyptianize' themselves by offering some of their shares to the public. They also put much money into buildings, which have always been the favourite Arab investment. This was a disappointment to the government, which had hoped to see entrepreneurs providing more long-term employment for the country's fast-expanding population. The old established industrial and trading firms, including Ahmed Abboud's company, the Misr group, which was quoted, and the Delta and National steel companies, also quoted, were more effective in giving employment. The fault of the new companies in the government's view was mainly that they were not expanding as fast as it hoped.

What turned Nasser decisively against the capitalist middle classes was a development that had nothing to do with the economy. It was the failure of the union with Syria in 1961. The President believed that the people who had worked to have Syria break away from the union in such a humiliating fashion were the Syrian landowners and merchants, a numerous and influential class of fairly small businessmen who had been untouched by the many coups their country had endured before the union. He further imagined that these people would now try to influence their bigger counterparts in Egypt, to turn them against the Revolution and undermine all that had been achieved since 1952. And as he thought about this he told his colleagues that he remembered some of the big Egyptian industrialists in 1957 and 1958 had backed the union with Syria, which now suggested that they had been hoping that the Syrian bourgeoisie would curb the trend towards state control and socialism that was becoming apparent in Egypt even in those early days. These notions were unduly conspiratorial, but typical of Nasser. Distrust and suspicion of all the people with whom he dealt, including his closest colleagues, was the major flaw of his character, and he admitted as much. More than once he told the British ambassador and other friends that having been a conspirator for a large part of his life he could not get out of the habit of suspecting everybody.

During the later 1950s Nasser had already made some moves towards socialism. He was pushed in this direction by the fashion of the time and by the steadily growing bureaucracy of his government which, in the normal manner of bureaucracies, sought to bring more and more aspects of the country's life under its control. After the Suez crisis, at the same time as the 'Egyptianization' laws were passed, all the French and British companies in Egypt were nationalized, which gave the state control of most of the banking system. In 1960 the major Egyptian bank, Banque Misr, was nationalized, to extend the government's control. What happened after the failed union with Syria was the considerable expansion of these policies. In October 1961, only a month after the fatal *coup d'état* in Damascus, forty prominent Egyptian businessmen were arrested and their property and the property of more than a hundred other people was confiscated. A month later 400 more people had their businesses seized and a further list of banks, insurance companies and other quoted companies was nationalized. In December there was a similar wave of seizures, and in 1963 the government took even more comprehensive measures, which left it owning 80 per cent of the country's industry. The nationalized companies were grouped under new state agencies, run, initially, by army officers, which added another layer to the country's bureaucracy.

Hand in hand with the economic measures went various political changes. In 1960 the Egyptian press was nationalized. For several years it had been under government supervision, with each newspaper having a state appointee on its staff to make sure that its opinions were politically correct, but when Nasser found himself running into difficulties in Syria he decided that more direct control was needed. In 1962 the National Charter was published, declaring Egypt to be a socialist state and in the same year a new single political party, the Arab Socialist Union, was launched. The natural constituents of this body were the hundreds of thousands – later millions – of new state functionaries whose jobs were created by the revolution. These people formed a new republican middle class. Most of them came from humble *petit bourgeois* or working-class backgrounds, and unlike their smarter and richer predecessors, the bankers and industrialists, many of whom were of Turkish or Circassian stock, they were 'true' Egyptians. Nasser himself was typical of the breed; he was the son of a post office worker from the town of Assiut, in upper Egypt, who had moved to Alexandria and married there. The new class had a stake in the continuation of the revolution and its institutions. Its members have dominated Eygptian life since the late 1950s, and are making it difficult for the country to reform its economy and politics in the 1990s.

The 'Arab socialism' that evolved in Egypt under Nasser was not the product of any revolutionary philosophy. It came from a series of pragmatic, albeit often misguided, decisions made in response to particular circumstances. It was considerably more left wing than any brand of west European socialism, but less totalitarian than east European socialism or Communism, the principal difference between it and the latter being that it allowed more private ownership. In Egypt, even after the 1963 nationalizations, most of the smaller service industries and contractors remained private. People could still own their own houses, agricultural land remained with the fellahin and minor entrepreneurs continued to run the country's small business premises, the cafés, shops, garages, hotels, workshops and bakeries. The government had taken what were supposed to be the 'commanding heights' of the economy, which, under its patriotic management, were to become the motor of the modernization of society.

Even after their government became more socialist and authoritarian in the early 1960s, the Egyptian people continued to enjoy the independence and influence that Nasser's leadership gave them. They believed that they were building a new society which would eventually be prosperous and powerful. Their faith in this idea received a terrible shock when they were defeated in the Six Day War in June 1967. In all the Arab countries people lost the confidence they had gained in the previous fifteen years. They could no longer assume that independence, the republican nation state and socialism would bring them success. Their faith in the progress of their countries, in the very idea that their lives would improve under a new type of patriotic government, was shattered.

On turning to look for a reason for their defeat there were several practical explanations available to the Arabs. Israel was a stronger, more developed state and many of its citizens had lived a large part of their lives in Europe. Its leaders were more able and better educated than most Arab leaders. They were infinitely more cunning than the military rulers of Syria, who had done most to provoke the war. They ran an institutionalized society in which those at the top of government trusted their subordinates and responsibility was delegated, which made their army better organized and flexible. Israel also had the advantage of having as its backer the United States, a more loyal and powerful ally than the Soviet Union.

The Arabs were unable to accept these realities. They could not admit they were almost bound to be defeated by Israel, and that to become as strong as their enemy they should work slowly and practically at developing their countries. The trouble with this pragmatic logic was that it involved an admission of weakness. It was also politically unacceptable because it did not hold out the prospect of victory in less than a matter of decades. It was much easier for both people and governments to regard their defeat as the equivalent of a natural disaster and so absolve themselves from responsibility. It became customary for people to refer to it as *al nakba*, the catastrophe, and blame it on the West.

As to what might be done there were two main strands of thought. One held, utterly illogically, that as the West had brought about the catastrophe and been responsible for creating the state of Israel, it was only the West that would be able to solve the problem. The other, which existed as a supplement to this approach, rejected the long slow process of development, and looked for some magic political formula which would work faster.

The Arabs' search, predictably, led them to take up the unpleasant, extremist and facile political ideas that were fashionable in the 1960s. The effectiveness of these ideas were apparently born out by the success of the Cubans and Vietnamese in resisting American 'imperialism'. The period saw the strengthening of Baathism and other extreme forms of socialism in the Arab world, as well as the first rumblings of Islamic revival. Struggle, violence and revolution were glorified. Respectable intellectuals defended international terrorism. From the time they were able to chant slogans children in the Palestinian refugee camps and in the harder-line republics were taught revolutionary ideas. I remember visiting a camp in Syria early in 1972 and seeing children aged about twelve being put through an assault course and trained to handle automatic weapons. At the end of each stage of the drill they shouted in chorus '*assifa, thawra, nasr*', 'storm, revolution, victory'. I asked the Syrian and Palestinian officials who were with me whether they did not think that to indoctrinate children in this way might not be laying the foundations of trouble in the future, but they denied this, saying it was a necessary and 'inevitable' stage in their regaining their homeland. It need hardly be said that it was precisely these types of children who became the gunmen of Lebanon in the later 1970s and 1980s.

It was not only the school children, students, refugees in the camps, journalists and various members of the intelligentsia who espoused the violent ideas of the late 1960s. Army officers and governments adopted them as well. In their hands the simplistic revolutionary philosophies seemed to justify any sort of coercion and brutality directed against their own people, in the cause, they said, of creating the type of disciplined, strong, modern society that was made necessary by the state of war they were in.

The governments were made still more unpleasant by their insecurity. Before the June war they believed they had the confidence of their people, but afterwards they feared they were losing it, and this, combined with their knowing how easy it was for regimes to be overthrown by *coup d'état*, made them nervous. In Egypt critics of the regime were imprisoned, foreign newspapers were censored, or banned, and the President fell into the habit of taking decisions on his own, or with one or two colleagues, without consulting his cabinet. Yet Nasser's government never resorted to killing its opponents. The same could not be said for three other revolutionary regimes that came to power at this time, in Iraq in July 1968, Sudan in May 1969 and Libya in September 1969. All of these drew their short-lived legitimacy from the claim that they were replacing ineffective governments that had betrayed their people in the struggle against Israel. The Iraqi regime of Ahmed Hassan al-Bakr and Saddam Hussein, discussed below, rapidly became known as one of the most repressive in the world. The new Libyan leader, Colonel Muammar Gaddafi, crushed all internal opposition in the course of imposing on his country his own egalitarian, Islamic version of socialism. Those accused of attempting to overthrow his regime at home were executed and thousands accused of obstructing it were imprisoned. Enemies of the regime abroad were hunted down and killed. In Sudan, within two and a half years of coming to power, Jaafar Nimeri crushed an incipient Islamic uprising, killing thousands, and then defeated an attempted Communist coup. He executed the leading conspirators and imprisoned the rest. Thereafter, although his government suffered several domestic crises and undertook some sudden changes in policy, its human rights record was reasonably good. By the standards of other Arab republics Sudan was quite a relaxed country.*

Two countries from the 1960s onwards sank to an especially grim level of brutality in their dealings with their people. Syria and Iraq have not been typical of Arab countries in the last thirty years, because of the degree and consistency of their governments' ruthlessness. Almost all the Arab regimes have used torture; many of them have killed quite large numbers of their own people, executing political prisoners, suppressing demonstrations or putting down local uprisings. Some run more than one brutal internal security service. The governments of Syria and Iraq embrace all of these faults at once, and so they have come to be seen both inside and outside the Arab world as symbolizing all that is worst in the region's governments. For this reason their story is worth telling in some detail. The two countries' misfortunes have been a special cause of despair to the Arabs because Syria is the historical heart of the region, and Iraq, with its oil reserves and two big rivers, used to be regarded as the country with the most economic potential. Both countries have relatively large educated middle classes, which in the 1950s, before people started to emigrate, were larger still.

---

* The background to the new regimes in Libya and Sudan is as follows: the *coup d' état* in Libya overthrew the government of King Idris. Libya had been part of the Ottoman Empire until Italy invaded and conquered it in 1911. The Italians were expelled in 1943, and after a period of British government, in 1951 the country became independent under the rule of Idris al-Sanussi. The King was the leader of the Sanussi religious order, which had been formed in the mid-nineteenth century to return its people to the values of early Islam.

Sudan was invaded and partially conquered in the 1820s by the Egyptians, who exploited it for gold, ivory and slaves. In the 1870s the Khedive Ismail appointed British governors, Sir Samuel Baker and General Charles Gordon, to pacify the country and suppress slavery. On Gordon's retirement in 1879 the Khedive reappointed Egyptian governors whose cruelty and corruption led to the rebellion in 1882 of Mohammad Ahmed Abdullah, the Mahdi. Gordon was sent back to Khartoum to arrange the evacuation of the foreign population but he stayed with 'his people' and was killed when the city fell in January 1885. The Mahdi died five months later and the country suffered a succession of military disasters and plagues (of locusts, mice and disease) under his successor, the Khalifa. It was conquered by General Kitchener after the battle of Omdurman in 1898, and then ruled by the British, acting supposedly in partnership with the Egyptians, until it was given independence in 1956. During the 1930s, 1940s and early 1950s the Egyptians hoped that, when the British left, Sudan would be united with their country, but in 1955 Nasser reluctantly accepted that the Sudanese wanted to be independent. Colonel (later Field Marshal) Nimeri's government was Sudan's fourth since independence.

In Syria the regime that broke away from Egypt was overthrown in 1963 by a group of military and civilian members of the Baath Party led by General Amin Al-Hafiz. It was this government that turned Syria into a socialist state. In the two years after it came to power it nationalized the banks and many of the country's industries, and in 1965 it established a special military court to deal with 'all offences in word and deed' against the nationalization measures and the socialist revolution. From this time on Syria's economy has been virtually immobile. The only input of capital it has received has been from the government's spending on projects, which, until some oil revenues began to flow in the late 1980s, was not a very big stimulus. In 1966 the Hafiz regime was removed by an even more extreme Baathist clique. In due course this was partly responsible for leading Nasser into the 1967 war with Israel and in 1970 it launched the incompetent Syrian intervention in the Jordanian-Palestinian civil war. It was that small humiliation that led a pragmatic element in the government, under the Minister of Defence, Hafez Assad, to stage a bloodless coup in November 1970. Assad, a cruel, tough, ascetic man, has ruled Syria ever since.

In Iraq the monarchy was destroyed in 1958 by Brigadier Abdel-Karim Kassem, whose chaotic and violent rule lasted nearly five years. In 1963 there were two further coups. The first, which killed Kassem, was organized by the Baath and the second stemmed from a split in the Party in which moderate elements led by the President, Abdel-Salem Aref, were able to purge the extremists. It was the second government of 1963, which was in effect more Nasserite than Baathist, that carried out the nationalization of the Iraqi economy and established a single political party, known as the Iraqi Arab Socialist Union. Abdel-Salem Aref died in a helicopter accident in 1966 and his brother, Abdel-Rahman, who succeeded him, was overthrown in 1968 by a new Baathist coup. The coup itself was bloodless, but soon afterwards the new regime began murdering former ministers and other opponents and hanged a number of alleged spies from lampposts in Tahrir Square in the centre of Baghdad. An oil executive who worked in Iraq under the monarchy and the early republican regimes told me that that the 1968 coup marked a cruel new departure. 'It was after Ahmed Hassan Al-Bakr and Saddam Hussein came to power', he said, 'that we started to hear of people we knew — friends — being found dead in ditches.'

The simple reason for this regime's brutality — apart from the temperaments of its leaders — was that it did not want to be overthrown

itself. In the previous decade Iraq had suffered four successful coups
and several attempted ones. Saddam Hussein had undertaken the murder
of an official in Kassem's government and had once tried to assassinate the President himself. He and his fellow assassins had left him for
dead, omitting to put a bullet through Kassem's head, as they had been
told to do. In fact Kassem was only wounded. Some of Saddam's
co-conspirators were arrested and sent to prison, with death sentences hanging over them to encourage the good behaviour of their
friends. Saddam himself escaped to Cairo, only returning after the
coup of 1963. He then served briefly as head of security. Later that
year he was imprisoned by the Aref regime, but he and some friends
escaped and lived the underground lives of conspirators, until they
seized power again in 1968. Once Saddam and his colleagues were
back in control they saw that everyone who might possibly be a threat
to them was eliminated.

Although Hafez Assad of Syria had a less adventurous early career,
in power he has been as security conscious and almost as brutal as
Saddam.

The Baath Party to which Hafez Assad and Saddam belong is,
in theory, one body, even though its internal divisions and the con-
trasting characters and international rivalry of the two presidents
have made their regimes bitter enemies since the early 1970s. The
Party was founded in Damascus in the 1940s by two school
teachers, Michel Aflaq and Salah Bitar. Their writings are difficult
to follow, but the general thrust of their thinking has nevertheless
evoked a response from certain types of intellectual and would-be
revolutionary thoughout the Arab world for the past fifty years. It is
a mixture of Marxism, nineteenth-century German nationalism and
traditional Arab nationalism; and the governments it has produced,
as one might expect, have been part socialist and part Fascist. There
is much talk of rebirth − the word *baath* means 'resurrection' − and
the release of the 'hidden vitality' of the Arab people. The popular
slogans of the Party are 'Freedom, Unity, Socialism' and 'One Arab
Nation with an Eternal Mission'. Clearly, both Saddam Hussein
and Hafez Assad have failed to translate any part of these slogans
into reality, except in so far as their countries became more socialist
in the early stages of their rule. But in the 1970s and 1980s they did
succeed in the implied Baathist aim of making their countries strong.
Syria under Assad has become a force in the Arab world in its own
right, instead of being fought over by other powers as it used to
be, and Iraq in the 1980s was at least as influential in Arab politics

as any other country – until in 1990 Saddam made the mistake of invading Kuwait.

Both Saddam and Assad have narrow power bases that are at odds with their Party's, and their own, pan-Arab ideals. Assad and most of the generals who support his regime are members of the Alawite sect, which makes up about 10 per cent of the Syrian population. The sect has its home in the mountains inland from the ports of Latakia and Tartous. The sect is an extremist offshoot of the mainstream of Shiism, and its members believe that the Prophet Mohammad was a mere fore-runner of his cousin, Ali, and that the latter was the incarnation of God. Around this belief, which became established in the early days of Islam, it incorporated various Christian and pagan ideas, including a belief in the holiness of certain springs. Like Shia sects generally it is secretive. In practice Assad and his colleagues are not at all re-ligious – the present Syrian government is the most secular of all Arab regimes – but their Alawite background defines their loyalties. In the early years of this century the Alawites were a downtrodden class, peasants and labourers, the providers of maids to families in the Sunni cities of Damascus and Aleppo and a good source of soldiers and junior officers for the army. Professions other than the army were closed to them, and the French during the colonial period pushed them in that direction because they believed that they could be re-lied upon to stay loyal if the Sunni majority rose in rebellion (as it did in 1925). In later years the Alawites found themselves attracted by the slogans of the Baath because it seemed to them that socialism would give them equality with the rest of society. Gradually members of the sect rose in seniority in the army and the Party until by the early 1960s they were strong enough to dominate both. Since that time all Syria's governments have been based on military elements of the Baath Party, and within these groups the closest bonds have been between generals who are Alawite. The Alawites have known that if the regime falls the power of their sect will fall with it. Given the severity with which the Alawites/Baathists have suppressed Sunni Muslim rebellions in Hama in 1964 and 1982, the demise of Alawite power at the hands of other sects would be bound to be bloody.

In Iraq Saddam Hussein's power has been based on people from a handful of small Sunni Muslim towns in the north-west of the country: Samarra, Ani, Haditha and, above all, his own home, Takrit. One of the reasons why, in the months after the 1968 coup, the then Vice-President stopped calling himself Saddam Hussein Takriti was that he saw that if he and other members of the government continued to use the names of their towns as surnames it would only remind Iraqis of the tribe-like nature of their regime.* Within the circle of Takritis and their neighbours the people closest to Saddam are those who enjoy a blood relationship with him. In the late 1980s most of the government agencies that were involved with defence, military procurement and internal security were headed by relations of the President. All of these people, of course, were members of the Baath, but their links with each other through the Party were much less important than the mutual trust they gained from being related.

In both Syria and Iraq the regimes have systematically destroyed all opposition. Each of them runs a dozen or so overlapping internal security organizations which are used to watch the minorities, religious fundamentalists, the armed forces, civilian ministries, and each other – in case their own bosses might be harbouring disloyal thoughts. The effect of there being so many intelligence services, secret police forces and corps of bodyguards has been to produce a climate of perpetual fear, suspicion and political manœuvring, which in Iraq has led to the regular execution of officials as one after another has fallen under suspicion. Iraq has been the worse of the two countries both for the fear it has instilled in its own citizens and for the sheer numbers of people it has killed. From the time the regime came to power there has been a steady stream of political killings that has been quite separate from the well-publicized atrocities, such as the gassing of the Kurds in 1988 and the persecution of the Shias since the rebellion of 1991. As the Baathists established themselves in the late 1960s and early 1970s they concentrated on weeding out Communists and potentially disloyal elements in the army. In the 1980s the main victims of the regime were religious fundamentalists, incompetent army officers, officers who were too successful and therefore liable to pose a challenge to Saddam, and corrupt civil servants. The execution of corrupt officials, as well as discouraging embezzlement, was seen as having the benefit of enhancing the general climate of fear and therefore encouraging loyalty. Among the dead in the civil service were an under-secretary in the Ministry of Oil, a mayor of Baghdad, two ministers of health and twenty-two senior officials in that ministry.

---

* The name Saddam Hussein signifies only 'Saddam son of Hussein', which is why in the Arab world, and in this book, the Iraqi president is referred to simply as Saddam or Mr Saddam. At one point in the early 1970s in the Revolutionary Council building in Baghdad a name plate appeared on Saddam's chair reading 'Saddam Hussein Al-Majid' – Majid having been the name of his grandfather – which suggested that he had thought of adopting a new family name, but the idea did not last.

The case of the second minister of health provides a good example of the procedure used in disposing of a corrupt official. The minister, Sadeq Al-Wash, was instructed to go before the National Assembly (a parliament used to give the country a totally misleading appearance of democracy), confess that he and his twenty-two officials were not doing their jobs properly and ask that they be allowed to resign. He did this in May 1988 and then he and the officials disappeared. Two months later it became known that they had been executed. It was assumed, in this case and others, that the confessions to the Assembly were induced by the officials being told that if they made a clean breast of their embezzlement their lives might be spared. It is a testimony to the unruly and ill-disciplined nature of Iraqi society that anyone at this time was still tempted to be corrupt. Not only were the penalties severe, but high-level officials were well paid, which was not the case in all Arab countries, specifically because Saddam wanted to stop corruption.

The even broader question of why any competent and well-educated Iraqi who could obtain a passport would want to remain in a country ruled by Saddam is answered by the enormous importance of family ties in the Arab world. A quarter of Iraqis are married to their first cousins. Without his family around him, an Iraqi, or indeed any Arab, feels very alone. A desire to be near their families led many voluntary Iraqi exiles to be persuaded by the government in the 1980s to return home, only to be hanged when they got there.

In February 1992 an attempt was made to give some numbers for killings in Iraq. Max van Stoel, a former Dutch foreign minister, prepared a report for the United Nations Human Rights Commission which stated that he had the names of 17,000 people who were alleged to have disappeared, and it was assumed that this list would not have included many of those killed before the mid-1980s. The report stated that 'the violations of human rights which have occurred are so grave and are of such a massive nature that since the Second World War few parallels can be found', and it added, 'nor is it likely that these violations will come to an end as long as the security forces have the power to decide on the freedom or imprisonment, or even life or death, of any Iraqi citizen'.

In Syria many – perhaps most – of the deaths inflicted by the Assad regime on its subjects occurred in a single horrible episode in 1982. It stemmed from a terrorist campaign that had been waged aginst the regime by an Islamic fundamentalist group, the Muslim Brotherhood. This group drew its members from the less prosperous and more religious elements of the Sunni Muslim majority of the population, particularly those who lived in Hama, not only the most devout city of Syria but also one of the oldest and most beautiful cities in a beautiful country. The supporters of the Brotherhood were mainly young urban poor who brooded on their misfortunes and noticed the favour being shown to the members of the Alawite sect. They attributed their own poverty to the regime and to its modernizing and secular policies. Many of them came from families that lived in the old quarters of Hama and other towns and had businesses in the slowly declining craft industries. They were backed by members of the country's trade union movement, which had been suppressed since the early days of the Baathist government.

From the mid-1970s the Brotherhood and its supporters began a campaign of bombing and assassination, aimed at members of the Baath Party, the armed forces and the Russians, who were the main foreign backers of the regime. They achieved some notable successes. They killed more than sixty army cadets, mostly Alawites, in June 1979 and they regularly shot Baathist officials in broad daylight. The regime retaliated by murdering, or imprisoning and torturing those it thought might be responsible. After an attempt on Assad's life nearly succeeded in June 1980 it sent members of the Defence Brigades, a huge presidential bodyguard, to the prison at Palmyra where it held some 600 to 1,000 members of the Brotherhood, and killed them all. Finally in February 1982 the Defence Brigades, commanded by the President's brother, Rifaat, and two armoured brigades were dispatched to Hama to root out and destroy the movement in its den. Promptly the Brotherhood raised a rebellion in the city, declared war on the regime and called on the rest of Syria to join it. For a short time it resisted extremely effectively. All the Baath Party officials in the rebellious part of the city were murdered, many of them being shot or stabbed by many hands, which is exactly what happened to Iraqi Baath officials when the Shia regions and Kurdistan rose in revolt at the end of the Gulf war in 1991.

The success of the rebels lasted for only two days. The army called in reinforcements and gradually its tanks reduced the old quarters of the city to ruins. It surrounded buildings, or small neighbourhoods where there was resistance, and shelled them until every structure had collapsed or all shooting had stopped. At the end of two weeks, when all the rebel quarters had been subdued, it systematically dynamited what remained of the buildings. Most of the religious teachers and judges, and junior mosque employees who remained in other quarters of the city were shot. Houses in which it was thought insurgents might still be hiding were fumigated with cyanide gas. When the Government was sure all the rebels were dead, the Muslim Brotherhood in Cairo claims, it brought in religious students from other towns to sweep the streets, gather the bodies and catch the packs of dogs that were roaming the city. Eventually the quarters that had been destroyed were bulldozed and then steamrollered flat, with whatever corpses remained being buried under the rubble. Nobody has an accurate figure for the final death toll. In the year or so after the event the consensus in Damascus diplomatic circles was somewhere in the very wide range of 10,000 to 30,000.

The Syrian people were allowed to see the razed quarters of Hama quite soon after the fighting had stopped. The section of the main road that runs through the city from Damascus and Homs to Aleppo was reopened in April while debris was still being cleared and the rebel quarters levelled. The assumption is that the Government wanted its people to see what had happened and draw the appropriate lesson.*

For the ordinary citizens of Iraq, Syria and Libya, the main consequence of their living under such oppressive regimes is that politics is entirely removed from their lives. In the press and on the radio and television they are fed a purely official version of events. The newspapers are owned by the governments and run as extensions of the ministries of information or ruling parties. On most days the front page carries an article about a speech or meeting of the head of state. No photograph of another person ever appears higher on the page than the president's. Except to members of their family and their closest friends, people have to be careful what they say about their leaders, and they have to be particularly careful about any contact they have with foreigners, which might be noted by a neighbour in the pay of one of the security services. From the point of view of a foreigner, especially a journalist, this makes meeting Arab friends or contacts potentially dangerous, not for the visitor but for the nationals themselves. The difficulty they had in getting access to 'ordinary' Iraqis was one of the reasons why journalists in Baghdad during the Gulf crisis so often seemed to reflect the official version of events, to which they were directed by the Ministry of Information guides who were attached to them.

Contact with the outside world is restricted because satellite TV, fax machines and foreign newspapers (except occasionally in Syria) are totally banned. In Iraq even photocopiers are tightly controlled because

---

* The best detailed account of the Hama massacre in a book published in Europe and America is in Thomas Friedman, *From Beirut to Jerusalem*, 1990, pp. 76–87

the government believes they might be used to print anti-regime tracts. Anyone who goes to a photocopying shop or to a photocopier in a government building will be questioned about what he wants to copy. Journalists entering the country are liable to have their lap-top computers (and formerly typewriters) confiscated, or at the very least recorded in their passports, for fear that otherwise they might sell them. Passports for nationals are restricted to those who are of proven loyalty. In effect the only regular news that Iraqis, Syrians and Libyans receive from the rest of the world comes from other Arab countries' radios and, most importantly, the BBC Arabic Service.

The restrictions placed on citizens make them extremely cautious. Iraqis believe that all late-night taxi drivers in Baghdad are members of one or other of the security services, which makes them reluctant to take taxis after dark. Day-time taxi drivers avoid going near buildings known to belong to the security services, or even to the entrances of the big hotels if they see unsmiling, leather-jacketed security men standing around. Nervousness about security can even extend to diplomats. Once when I was being told a story about the President's son by the ambassador of one of the industrialized countries, I was surprised to see that my informant had no sooner begun his tale than he fell silent. He put his finger to his mouth, beckoned me to his desk, wrote out the essence of the story, which involved the young man's second murder (see below), on a piece of paper and then, when I told him I already knew about it, tore the paper into little pieces and put it in a basket of rubbish to be shredded. I was impressed that the ambassador of a Western country was worried about telling the story aloud in his own office in his own, admittedly rather small, embassy.

In the other Arab countries life is much freer. There is no climate of fear. People do not hesitate to meet foreigners or buy satellite dishes for their televisions, whether they are legal or not. They are free to own photocopiers and fax machines and to travel where they like. The Saudis and Gulf Arabs have an enormous amount of business contact with the industrialized world.

The ways in which these countries are not free lie principally in their treatment of parliaments and the media. No Arab country has a parliament with the authority to remove a government, and none has free television and radio networks. The press varies from being almost completely free in Egypt to being tightly controlled, or conformist by habit, in Saudi Arabia.

The particular sensitivities of governments vary. Saudi Arabia and the Gulf states are especially sensitive to what is said about them on television or written about them in books or newspapers, though the reasons for this are more cultural than political. There is a deeply engrained feeling in these countries that to say in public things that may embarrass people – not only individuals in government but all other members of society – is bad mannered and unproductive. It would be liable to damage people's reputations, which are regarded as being overwhelmingly important. Therefore almost anything that foreigners write about Saudi Arabia, the most sensitive of these countries, will not be allowed to circulate in the Kingdom. Articles on the country are deleted from foreign newspapers, and books, other than picture books sponsored by the government, are not imported. The bookstalls of Riyadh and Jeddah are full of volumes with such titles as *Insects of the Nejd* or *The Bird Life of Jubail and Yanbu*, while holding nothing on the politics or the economy of the Kingdom.

The domestic press, in Saudi Arabia and the Gulf states, operates a system of self-censorship. Journalists have learnt which topics they can mention and which they must pretend do not exist. They can report foreign affairs, as long as they are careful what they say about other Arab governments, and record the arrivals, departures and meetings of members of the ruling families. They are not allowed to write about internal political arguments, power struggles, the sacking of senior officials, corruption, scandal or anything else of major domestic importance.

In most of the republican Arab countries, and in Morocco and Jordan, the press is allowed greater freedom. It can attack the governments' domestic policies and individual ministers, and because it is not constrained by libel laws its attacks are sometimes personal and malicious. The subjects on which journalists have to be careful are anything to do with heads of state, the security services, and sensitive areas of policy, such as border disputes and their governments' attitudes towards making peace with Israel.

Paradoxically, those countries which have a rather more liberal attitude than the Gulf states towards the press have a worse record on human rights. In the Gulf and Saudi Arabia, there is much contact between the ruling families and the people. Saudis and Gulf Arabs can call on the princes and sheikhs and express their opinions on any matters that concern them. This provides an outlet for grievances and keeps the large ruling families well informed about the views of their people. It has helped produce fairly harmonious and loyal societies. There has been relatively little subversive activity, except when the influence of the Iranian revolution was at its height in the early 1980s, and the few political prisoners, mostly members of underground Shia organizations, have been convicted of possessing arms or conspiracy to murder. In the republics and Morocco there are many more political prisoners. In most cases, again, they are members of subversive groups, but many have been imprisoned after mass arrests and have not received proper trials.

In ways that are just as important as their attitudes to the press and human rights, the Arab governments in the 1970s and 1980s developed a character in common. The wars, internal violence, political fear and economic failure of the period produced regimes which may have been led by a president or a king and may have been more or less authoritarian, but which in terms of ideology and the tone of their political thinking were remarkably similar. They were not attractive creations. They had no moral purpose; they were not trying to change society or build a new world; they were neither traditional nor revolutionary.

During this time those governments that had once been revolutionary abandoned socialist rhetoric. The awkward jargon of socialist economics and political theory disappeared from their newspapers. They began to wish they could re-embrace capitalism. Some of the generals around President Assad and the mainly civilian friends and relations of Saddam not only became very rich and maintained lavish lifestyles, they were open in their pro-capitalist sentiments and their admiration of the United States. They were prevented from changing the system by their regimes' need to control every aspect of their countries' lives, as well as by some of the Syrian generals having financial interests in those industries that were controlled by the armed forces. In the other republics the barrier was the huge body of bureaucratic vested interest that inhabited every part of the government and the state corporations.

The leaders of the republics, having learnt how internal security measures could guard them against coups, were staying in power for so long that they began to be referred to as 'rulers', as if they were the heads of Gulf sheikhdoms or one of the Arab monarchies. In the early 1980s it is thought that President Assad, who was having treatment for diabetes and leukaemia, had it in mind to make his flamboyant and violent younger brother, Rifaat, his heir, and in 1992 and 1993 there was speculation that he was thinking of his son, Bassel, for the job. In the later 1980s in Iraq it seemed that Saddam's particularly violent elder son, Udei, was being groomed as a successor. (Udei came under a cloud in the autumn of 1988, when in a fit of temper he killed his father's bodyguard and foodtaster, who was the son of the presidential cook.) The notion of hereditary republicanism does not seem as strange to Arabs as it does to Westerners. The concept of loyalty to family is so strong in the Arab world that it can seem more important than the notion of a job going to the person best qualified for it. In Lebanon many parliamentary seats have been family property since independence. Even so, the thought of Syria or Iraq becoming hereditary republics is a long way from the ideals of those who introduced socialism to the two countries in the 1960s.

The true monarchies, by the 1980s, no longer felt ideologically threatened by the republics, as they had done in Nasser's day. There was no reason for them to feel threatened. It was obvious that there was little difference between them and the republics in the social and economic problems they faced and in the policies they were adopting to deal with them. Their political rhetoric was much the same as the republics'. In their relations with other Arab states King Fahd of Saudi Arabia, King Hussein of Jordan and King Hassan of Morocco would align themselves as readily with republican friends as they would with each other or the Gulf states.

It would be wrong to suggest that the fact that Arab governments had become so similar, and basically conservative, by the 1980s meant that nothing had been achieved during the early idealistic days of Nasser. Firstly, the region had been liberated from the presence and/or influence of the colonial powers. The people had been given the idea (now greatly weakened) that their economic and political lot could improve; some of the fatalism of centuries had been shaken off. The populations had become more socially mobile. Schools and technical colleges had been built. The need of modern governments for civil servants had brought into being a new educated – or partially educated – middle class, drawn from the *petit bourgeoisie* and the working class. An idea of what constituted social justice had become established, and although that justice had not been maintained in most states – indeed, in some it withered soon after it was born – the idea itself had lived on. The disappointment for the Arab world was that the idealism of the 1950s and 1960s and the social change of that period had failed, in all the ways already described, to bring about economic, military and political success.

In the disenchanted Arab world of the mid-1980s governments were purely pragmatic. In the eyes of their people they seemed unchanging and unchangeable. Their principal concern had become the maintenance of their own security against real and imagined enemies, at home and abroad. They became known to political writers in the region as 'security states'.

In all Arab countries in the 1980s people lost interest in politics, either because they seemed pointless or because they were not safe. Governments did not want to have people commenting on what they were doing in those difficult times. Policies were worked out and implemented by the ruling parties or families, with the officials who ran the ministries, and there was little point in outsiders expressing opinions, let alone trying to change the policies. With politics being, essentially, illegal, civil society could not prosper. Trade unions were either banned or absorbed into the machinery of the ruling parties. Trade, professional and academic associations were suspect in the eyes of governments which were seeking to control everything around them.

The people became docile. In the 1950s and 1960s when an important event occurred crowds used to pour spontaneously on to the streets. When Nasser made a major speech there would be a public response not just in Cairo but in capitals all over the Arab world. In the 1980s this stopped, much to the disgust of the Arab intelligentsia, particularly those of the older generation who had nationalist and republican sympathies. There was hardly any public reaction when Israel invaded Lebanon in 1982, or when the *intifadah*, the 'uprising', gathered force in the Israeli-occupied territories at the end of 1987 and in 1988.

The only outlet left for energy and initiative in the age of the security state was personal financial gain. Some of this was legitimate and laudable. Even in the socialist states some parts of the economy had always been left in the private sector, and in those fairly rare cases where businessmen were prepared to commit some capital and managed to establish profitable enterprises, a much-needed stimulus was given to the local economies. In Saudi Arabia and the Gulf states, which had big private sectors, large, honestly acquired business fortunes, belonging to nationals and to Arabs from other countries, were common. But alongside these legitimate fortunes, in every Arab country there were those acquired from corruption. In some cases this took the form of government officials accepting bribes. In others it involved members of the Gulf and Saudi ruling families exploiting their powerful positions to acquire land or win government contracts for companies they represented, normally at the expense of the middle-class merchants. The commissions charged for these services were often exorbitant. In all Arab countries there flourished a breed of middle-men and influence brokers, who without being official representatives managed to insinuate themselves into profitable deals of every sort. It was noticeable in the 1980s that there were operating in Europe nearly as many rich businessmen from the socialist countries and other poor Arab states, as there were from Saudi Arabia and the Gulf. Some of these, admittedly, were 'fronting' for members of Arabian ruling families, but more were handling fortunes of their own, many of them corrupt.

Corruption was not something to which most of the regimes –

republics or monarchies — very much objected. This was because it was seen as politically safe. It was not an activity that represented an immediate threat to security. It kept people in and around the government machines rich, and therefore happy. The people at the top of the governments could tell themselves that those who were getting rich from cheating the treasuries might in other types of societies have been going into politics or journalism, or some similar undesirable activity.

However, corruption did not go unnoticed by the people as a whole. It obviously made them poorer, in that it wasted scarce resources, and it made them envious and bitter. In Algeria it was people's realization that the regime was corrupt as well as incompetent, that caused the riots that led to the collapse of the Front de Libération Nationale government, the near creation of an Islamic republic, and a military intervention that produced a state of guerilla war between the security forces and Islamic militants. In other countries corruption has made the economic and political reforms, which some governments have been attempting since the late 1980s, even more difficult and dangerous than they would have been anyway.

6

Economic Stagnation

Socialist economic thinking – price controls and subsidies multiple exchange rates – short-term mentality of private sector – mismanagement of development spending – failure of inter-Arab investment

In the twenty years after the oil price explosion of 1973 the Arab oil producers received $2 trillion (million million) in revenues. Most of this colossal sum was paid to Saudi Arabia and the Gulf states, but large amounts also went to Iraq, Libya and Algeria, and well over $100 billion was transferred, or lent, to the poor Arab countries. Nowhere did the money create an economic miracle. Not one Arab state developed an economy to resemble South Korea, Taiwan, Singapore or any of the other vigorous, fast-growing countries of East Asia. Some Arab countries, notably Algeria, which had promised that it would make itself Africa's first Japan, were surprised and disappointed by this.

The reason for the failure is simply that vast injections of capital are not particularly useful in stimulating development. Some capital is needed for building ports, roads, telecommunications and other basic pieces of infrastructure, as well as schools and hospitals, but for the sustained growth of productive industry and services a country needs more than capital. It was not merely capital being poured in from outside that made the East Asian economies rich. Those countries prospered because they had political stability, large, industrious and disciplined work forces, the example of Japan, and reasonably prosperous but not too sophisticated markets close by. No similar conditions existed in the Arab world.

The Arab countries had only oil income, and this on its own tended to stimulate consumption rather than production. As a former colleague of mine on the Financial Times, Patrick Cockburn, once remarked dryly, 'the trouble with oil is that it doesn't do anything except teach people to enjoy spending the revenues'. This law applies to both rich and poor in the Arab world. The poor countries consumed the oil money they received, from their own small production and transfers from the Gulf, with just as much relish as the rich countries.

Oil money is what people outside the Middle East know about and associate with the Arab economies, yet the misuse of these revenues was not the chief cause of the economic failure of most Arab countries in the 1970s and 1980s. In the poor countries, which are the main subject of this chapter, the spending of what oil revenues come their way is a secondary matter. The management of their own people and resources is far more important. Unfortunately, in practically every Arab country outside the Arabian Peninsula oil states, the governments stifled their economies by imposing rigid state control during the age of socialist enthusiasm in the 1960s.

The underlying idea of governments in this period was that they should mobilize their countries' potential for the benefit of their populations as a whole, not just for the capitalist classes. In doing this the governments tended to think of potential just in terms of tangible material resources – agricultural land, mined raw materials, energy, physical manufacturing capacity and human labour – and not of intangibles, such as human initiative and motivation. They paid equally little attention to markets. The type of thinking that combines a manufacturing idea, a well-motivated labour force, demand in the domestic market and the prospect of profit was completely alien to them. Outside the United States it would have been against the thinking of the time.

The governments nationalized private companies and founded new enterprises of their own, creating state corporations that specialized in particular areas of production, such as building materials, steel products or beverages. The corporations were not necessarily monopolies – private firms that were nationalized were not always merged – but they were certainly not encouraged to compete with each other. They were told how much of their product they should manufacture, or aim to manufacture, at what price they should sell it, and whether it should go to the home market or be allocated to export under a barter or contra deal with another socialist Arab country or eastern European state. The products were seldom of a quality which would have appealed to Western markets or the Arabian Peninsula states. If by any chance they made a profit it was either to be reinvested to create further production for the benefit of the people or handed over to the government to be absorbed into the national budget. As much as possible the corporations were directed to producing import substitutes to make the countries self-sufficient. It did not matter whether they were able to make a product well or profitably; in the planned economies of the day officials would identify a need and command that it be filled, and in the eyes of everybody concerned that seemed to make good economic sense.

This socialist system was imposed first on Egypt and then on Tunisia, Algeria, Iraq, Syria, Sudan, Libya, and, in so far as it had any industrial production, Southern Yemen. In Morocco in 1973 the government established some big state enterprises in an attempt to supplement the work of the private sector, which lacked the capital to invest in large projects. No private business was nationalized, though foreign companies were obliged to sell shares in their businesses to Moroccans, the government's hope being that this would stimulate the investment of small parcels of private capital in the economy. The only poor country that escaped the creation of state corporations, except in a handful of capital intensive industries, was Jordan – and even here the government gradually introduced much of the other paraphernalia of socialism, in the form of an array of subsidies and controls on private businesses, particularly the banks.

From the beginning the Arab command economies were inefficient, though it took more than a decade for the true scale of their failure to become visible. Part of the problem lay in the policy of import substitution. The idea seemed patriotic, but it normally led to countries putting their resources of manpower and capital into industries in which they were not able to be competitive. They would have done better to have invested in businesses which might have seemed less important but which produced products for export, receiving in return cash rather than east European barter goods. An example of an import substitution initiative which failed was Egypt's decision to invest in spinning mills which would use the superb long staple cotton of the Nile valley to produce yarn. The theory was that this would give the country some of the potential added value from its own resources, because yarn would obviously command a higher price than raw cotton, but this was not what happened in practice. The yarn produced was not of sufficient quality to sell well on the international market, and because at the same time foreign spinners were being starved of high-quality cotton the price of good yarn being produced outside Egypt rose. This, in turn, gave an incentive to European and American cloth manufacturers to invest in technology which would enable them to produce good-quality fabrics with poor-quality yarn, from Egypt or elsewhere. Meanwhile growers in America were encouraged to improve the strains of cotton they produced. The result was that Egypt gained nothing from its investment in spinning mills and lost part of the market for its raw cotton.

This type of mistake was repeated many times. In the early 1990s the Sudanese government was trying to switch the production of some of its big plantations from cotton, to which the land and climate is well suited, to wheat. The reason was partly that Sudan's ginning, transport and marketing of its cotton crop had become so inefficient that it could not sell it profitably. But more important in a country that had made itself unpopular internationally and had developed something of a siege mentality was that growing wheat for hungry Sudanese looked more patriotic than growing cotton for rich, unfriendly foreigners.

The state corporations not only invested in the wrong businesses, they were burdened with too many employees. In Egypt the Nasser government in the early 1960s promised that it would give a job to every university graduate, and ten years later the promise was extended to the graduates of technical colleges and secondary schools. The purpose was not so much to encourage people to go into higher education, or to feed them, as to secure their support for the regime. The government was creating a new middle class, which was to be its constituency, and it wanted to make sure that the class stayed loyal. Millions of those graduates who took the government up on its offer during the following decades were pushed into the civil service, many more went into state corporations. When it was faced with rising working-class unemployment the government told the corporations to take on more labourers. When the corporations could not meet their wage bills, even though individual salaries and wage packets were miserably low, the state banks were told to lend to them. In effect the banks were given the job of financing the corporations' losses.

It goes without saying that the corporations were extremely unproductive. A European diplomat who was shown round a brick factory in the late 1980s calculated that it was producing only 25 units per man per day, not counting a fair number of broken or misshapen rejects.

The type of organizational system and mentality that lies behind such low levels of production is well illustrated by what happens if a person wants to buy a loaf of bread at the baker's shop that is attached to one of Cairo's big state-owned hotels. This shop in Europe would employ one or two people but in Cairo it manages eight. The procedure it has devised to keep these people busy is as follows. The customer goes up to the man behind the counter and says that he wants to buy a loaf. The assistant writes this on a small form and gives one copy to the customer and keeps another for himself. The customer then joins a queue and eventually gives his piece of paper to the cashier who puts a form in quadruplicate into a machine, types out the price, takes the customer's money, keeps the bottom copy of the form and hands to the customer the top three copies. The customer returns to the assistant behind the counter and gives him all the copies. The assistant compares these with the note he retained at the beginning, and then hands over the loaf of bread. Of the three pieces of paper that came from the till, one is kept by the assistant, another passed back to the cashier and the third given to the customer, in case he should want it for his records.

The Arab socialist economies have been further distorted by comprehensive sets of controls, applying both to state corporations and what remains of the private sectors. The banks, after they had been nationalized, were ordered to buy low-yielding treasury bills, which was a disguised way of the governments channelling private savings to themselves, and taxing them at the same time. The customers, of course, had no option of placing their money with banks abroad because the authorities operated strict exchange controls. Banks were also obliged to lend certain percentages of their money to industry, agriculture, construction and other sectors of the economy deemed desirable by governments, and they were told what rates of interest to charge to each sector.

Private importers, in those countries where they were allowed to operate at all, were restricted to buying unimportant non-strategic items. They were either given very little foreign exchange by the central banks, or were told that they had to earn their own foreign exchange by exporting, or buying it from other private exporters. These import and exchange controls led to the appearance of currency black markets.

The most common and comprehensive controls were imposed, and in many cases are maintained, on the prices of essential commodities. These include food, which may be controlled both at the point where the farmer sells to the wholesaler and at the retail level, simple manufactured goods and rents. In Egypt Nasser fixed rents for homes and apartments for the benefit of his new middle classes, and the rents remained fixed for two decades. Likewise farmers' land rents were fixed. Both sets of controls led to extraordinary distortions in the markets. In effect people within the private sector found themselves subsidizing each other, as normally happens when controls are imposed on them. In the towns, because tenancies in rent-controlled buildings could be inherited or transferred, any Egyptian who did not own his own home would try to make sure that if he and his family had to move they went into another rent-controlled apartment. This of course led to the appearance of a market in tenancies – rights to rent – which in effect became leases, but it did nothing for the supply of new accommodation. For many years in Cairo it was uneconomic for landlords to build new accommodation for letting.

Similar anomalies were found in the countryside. In the 1980s, when rents were still fixed at 1950s levels but controls on agricultural prices had been lifted, many farmers were able to make enough money to buy more land, and as they found that the more land they owned with sitting tenants the less they needed to work, in some villages full-time landlords began to outnumber cultivators. The best that could be said for this state of affairs was that it made easier the process of lifting rent controls, which began in the early 1990s, because it seemed that in many places the liberalization would benefit more people than it hurt.

One of the other bad effects of the battery of price controls in Egypt and elsewhere was that it drove some of the most productive and enterprising parts of the economies underground, to a world of second jobs and unofficial business, where prices were free. This, of course, lost governments potential tax revenues and led to their running bigger deficits than they would have done otherwise. The deficits were financed by printing money, which caused inflation.

The governments' spending was increased and the operation of the Arab economies further damaged by state subsidies. These began in some countries at the time of the Second World War, they became bigger and more formal in the 1950s and then grew enormously in the 1970s, when the governments felt themselves rich but were politically on the defensive. The items to which they were most often applied were gasoline and diesel, electricity, domestic bottled gas, bus fares, and a range of basic foodstuffs – bread, rice, semolina (for couscous in North Africa), cooking oil, sugar and milk.

The purpose of the subsidies, always, was to look after the poor, just as rent controls and guaranteed jobs cared for the middle classes. The fear was, and still is, that if the poor go hungry or find their meagre standard of living declining they will give their support to subversive Islamic fundamentalist movements. As one would expect, in the 1970s when governments still had the money to try to buy themselves out of difficulties, the worse the political threat seemed to be the more generous the subsidies became. At one stage in Egypt under Sadat even televisions and refrigerators were subsidized. As an official in the Prime Minister's office in Cairo later remarked, 'at that time any disturbance used to be handled by throwing money at it'.

By the early 1980s subsidies were absorbing nearly a quarter of the Egyptian government's spending. And this was separate from the losses of foreign exchange and extra debt that the country was incurring through disguising some of its subsidies in special exchange rates. These special rates became common in Middle Eastern countries during the 1980s. They came about through governments wanting to be able to hide the amount of money they were spending on purposes of which they were slightly ashamed, notably giving subsidies and servicing their foreign debts. They worked as follows: a government could import wheat, for example, pay for it in dollars, pretend that each of the dollars in its dwindling reserves was worth only five units of its local currency, when actually on the free market the dollar was worth ten units, and so be able to sell the wheat cheaply to its people while the transaction was seen to be costing the budget only half what it really cost. The government could then persuade itself that actually its accounts were better than an accountant would have found them because the five-units rate was really just as valid as the free-market rate – the difference being simply that one was set by the state and the other by bankers and other market operators. In this way a government that was really anxious to deceive itself could pretend that it was not making any loss at all.

Most of the poor Middle Eastern countries in the mid-1980s had two exchange rates – an official one and an illegal, or semi-legal, 'black' or 'free' market one. Three countries, Iran, Syria and Egypt, had a range of rates, each of which had been introduced as a weak response to a specific pressing economic problem during the previous ten years. In Egypt, where transactions at different rates were financed by drawing on different 'pools' of foreign exchange, such as oil revenues, state cotton sales and Suez Canal dues, the dollar exchange rates in operation in early 1987 were:

For trade with Eastern bloc countries – 40 piastres (0.4 Egyptian pounds)
For servicing the government's foreign debt and buying strategic raw materials, including wheat – 70 piastres
For banking transactions including payments for authorized private sector imports – £E1.35
For the payment of customs dues – £E1.75
For all unregulated purposes, including most transactions of the private sector, a 'black', 'grey' or 'free' floating rate of around £E2.35

In May 1987 the Egyptian government decided that in order to introduce a little realism into its country's accounts and if possible suck some of the foreign exchange in the free/black market into the banking system, the banks' rate should be devalued to around £E2.20 to the dollar, which was very close to the 'grey' market. The new rate, known as the 'banks' free market rate' was not entirely free, however. It was set daily by a committee of representatives from eight banks, who were never quite able to bring themselves to align the currency with the genuinely free market, with the result that the black/grey/free market never quite disappeared. When one of the bankers was asked by a Western colleague why they did not just let the rate float, his reply perfectly summed up the bureaucrat trained in the Nasser era. 'If we left it to the market,' he said, 'who would control it?'

The whole edifice of government intervention in the poor Arab countries – state corporations, controls and subsidies – created economies which consumed but did not produce, exactly the same weakness as beset the oil states. In both types of country the people were being given by their governments wealth they had not created, in the form of goods and services subsidized by the state or the private sector. The difference between the oil states and the poor countries was that the first group could finance its generosity with oil revenues while the second was living beyond its means.

The Arabian oil states' economies were also helped by their being capitalist, which meant that they had quite vigorous private sectors. The poor countries, being mostly socialist, had reduced their private sectors to a point where they were small, speculative minded and involved only with the least important parts of the economies. Even in the two poor monarchies, Jordan and Morocco, private businessmen had to abide by (or evade) a host of bureaucratic rules and regulations, and were hedged about with controls on how their banks should lend and what they could import without paying punitive tariffs.

In all the poor countries private business initiative was discouraged by the states controlling so much of the economic, political and social lives of their people. In countries where governments are not democratic and present themselves to their citizens as being the great providers, businessmen are put in a subordinate position. They are not able to criticize, argue with the authorities or suggest policies of their own. They find themselves looking to their governments for a lead, for instructions or for special incentives.

Businessmen have been further discouraged by the instability of the region. They have not been confident of the stability of their own governments or of the peace of the area as a whole. Anyone living near the borders of Israel (or Iraq under Saddam) cannot be sure that his investment will not be destroyed by war. As an economist in Amman in 1992 put it, 'here we're living under the threat of our neighbour, so who would invest for seven years from now?'

All of these influences have reinforced the short-term mentality of Arab businessmen. This derives originally from the role of the commercial classes as traders rather than investors. Arab businessmen are not drawn to industry. They prefer to be importers, where they are allowed to be, or retailers. Alternatively their instinct is to get as close as possible to a person in government and win a contract, for construction or the supply of goods, for themselves or somebody else. They also like playing brokering roles, where they are paid or given a commitment to purchase by their client, which is often their government, before they commit themselves to doing business with the person whose property they are selling. In these types of operations the attraction is that they do not have to commit capital. In some cases the businessman may simply not have much personal capital; there are many men in the Arab world who drive expensive cars (above all Mercedes), wear flashy suits and cover their wives with jewellery, but who actually have very little money saved. Arab society is a display society. People like to show what wealth they have. It is quite different from the old society of Europe where there is considerable wealth in property, art and shares, but not necessarily much display.

Even allowing for this there is still a temperamental resistance to committing capital, even when it is available. The idea that one finds in the industrial economies of an entrepreneur looking at a market, projecting its growth, assessing possible changes in taste or government policy, and then investing to make a product that people might want to buy over the next five to seven years is completely against the instincts of most Arab businessmen. There *are* those who have invested for the long term in light industry, but they are not many. Most private businessmen who have substantial capital assets are in contracting or real estate. The attraction of real estate is that it is an unsophisticated, tangible business which owners have felt is secure. It is assumed that there will always be demand for housing, especially in countries with fast-increasing populations. It has also always been believed that although governments might regulate rents, with varying degrees of seriousness, they would never seize the buildings of anybody except their political enemies. And since the 1960s seizures have been virtually unheard of.

All of the faults of the Arab economies have been made worse by the mismanagement of the governments' development spending. In spite of the advice the governments have received from international bodies, particularly the World Bank, much of their own and foreign lenders' money has been put into poorly executed projects of the wrong type.

The poor execution, which means uneconomically executed more often than badly built, comes from bad planning. Governments have often seized on ideas for projects after they have identified what appear to be valuable resources which ought to be exploited. They have had technical studies carried out and arranged financing, and on this perfunctory basis they decide to go ahead. It is only when the project is being built that it is realized that new roads need to be laid for access, that the electricity grid needs to be extended to the site, that there has to be a temporary housing project for the construction work force, and that at a later stage there ought to be more permanent housing for the people who will run the project. In the course of adding these extra facilities the cost of the project doubles, rendering it uneconomic. Sometimes the problem with the 'add-ons' is not so much that the planners have failed totally to see that the extra facilities are needed, but they have been making do with second-rate arrangements. A middle man near the ministry has been able to persuade the people in charge that they really do need a bigger, higher-quality facility, which, it happens, he can provide through a company he represents.

In deciding what types of project to build governments have been too much attracted by big infrastructure schemes. These have appealed because they are prestigious and tangible. They are politically safer than universities, or factories that lead to the creation of a bigger urban working class, they provide good opportunities for corruption and they may impress one's neighbours. Arab governments have competed with each other in their infrastructure projects, often taking their cue from Saudi Arabia, where the official attitude has been that nothing but the best and most modern will do for the people. The classic example of this type of project is Riyadh airport, built in the early 1980s, carpeted and attractively tiled throughout, kept spotlessly clean by Filipino sweepers and decorated inside with flower-beds, trees, fountains, and cascades of running water. It is certainly the most beautiful airport in the world. For Saudi Arabia, in the rich and confident days of the early 1980s when it was built, it was ideal, but it was not useful as an inspiration to other Arab governments. The provision of this type of facility, even in more modest forms, presents governments to their citizens as the generous providers. The temptation is always to buy the best and to buy it immediately, even if that involves having a foreign-built project, which has to be financed with aid money and eventually repaid in foreign currency. Quite often governments have ignored opportunities to build projects much more cheaply, using their own contractors and local materials. They have been put off by the lack of glamour and the longer time for execution. Their impatience has even led to quite poor countries having to import foreigners from the Far East to build and run parts of unnecessarily sophisticated projects, when a more modest version could have absorbed some of the local unemployed.

An incidental effect of large infrastructure projects, many made necessary by the growth of the motor car population and inadequate public transport, has been the physical ruin of many beautiful cities. Some of the cities of the Middle East are now choked with traffic and shrouded in a pall of exhaust fumes; Tehran is the classic example. In others – Cairo, Istanbul and Damascus in particular – big road and bridge projects have destroyed old buildings, orchards and gardens and made once-attractive parts of the cities nondescript or ugly. These towns are becoming less attractive to the eye, less enjoyable to visit and less pleasant and relaxing places to live in.

Another mistake, which has been common to most developing countries, is that there has been too little attention paid to agriculture. Some money has been invested in the reclamation of marginal lands on the fringes of cultivated areas, but at the same time fertile, well-farmed land has been taken over by expanding towns and villages and industrial projects. The prices of agricultural products have been controlled, which has discouraged production, while food has been subsidized, encouraging consumption. When land has been redistributed under land-reform programmes not enough help has been given to the new owners to make them more efficient. The result of these mistakes has been that the Arab world has a huge food deficit. Twenty years ago the region's trade in foodstuffs and other agricultural raw materials was in near equilibrium. At the beginning of the 1990s there was a deficit of more than $20 billion.

In education, another badly managed area, a great deal of money has been spent on buildings – which look good as gifts to the people – but the quality of teaching has been neglected. At high school and university levels the work of teachers has been inhibited by politics; there is a great deal of history, geography, economics, politics, law and similar subjects that cannot be discussed in many Arab countries. There have been big increases in the last ten years in the religious content of the curriculum, to appease Islamic extremists. In Saudi Arabia children now have some fifteen lessons a week on Islam, including special subjects such as the Koran as literature, the nature of God and the life of the Prophet. In spite of the religious emphasis and the inhibition of other arts teaching, Arab students seem to be more attracted to liberal

arts subjects than to sciences. Consequently, Arab schools do not produce the numbers of doctors and engineers that developing countries
need.

Perhaps the most disappointing aspect of the Arab countries' development since the early 1970s has been the failure of the idea of inter-Arab
investment. This blossomed around the time of the 1973–4 oil revenues
explosion, when it was thought that in addition to the Arabian Peninsula oil producers giving grants and soft loans to the Arab poor, they
might also invest in those countries on a purely commercial basis, for
the benefit of both parties. The idea was to combine Gulf capital with
Western technology and the poor Arab countries' labour, resources and
markets. It was believed that the discipline of the marketplace, which
would go with commercial investment, might itself be useful to the
recipient countries.

Two Kuwaiti financial institutions, the Kuwait Real Estate Investment Consortium and the Kuwait Foreign Trading Contracting and
Investment Company, were given briefs to concentrate their operations
in other Arab countries. Kuwaiti, Saudi, Abu Dhabian and Qatari companies, often pushed by their governments, joined the governments of
other Arab countries in establishing a series of specialist joint-Arab
companies, for livestock rearing, mining, hotels, oil projects and a host
of other purposes. There was much logic in these initiatives and it is
surprising how unsuccessful they proved.

In the fifteen years that followed 1973–4 some hundreds of individual projects, or individual project companies, were established on
paper, or even given some full- or part-time staff. But very few projects
were actually built. In most cases the main inter-Arab investment company completed its first project, which was often the project which had
stimulated the idea for the company and led to it being established in
the first place. In many cases this project had been given the momentum
of an endorsement by an inter-government protocol. Once it had completed this project the inter-Arab company languished. Sometimes this
was because of disputes between the shareholders or the failure of the
poor countries to pay up their (small) share of its capital. Sometimes
it was because the first project had not proved a success. Often there
was no political will for further projects. Most of the projects were
intended to foster the economic interdependence of Arab countries, but
secretly many governments did not want this. They did not want to
give their rivals possible means of exerting pressure on them.

It was not only the government sponsored joint-Arab companies that
ran into difficulties. The Kuwaiti companies, which less often had the
complications of multinational shareholdings in their projects, became

as disenchanted as the rest with investment in other Arab countries. To anyone who asked them they would give a well-argued stream of complaints. They found, in general, that the supposed complementarity of the rich and poor Arab economies was an illusion. Some of the poor lacked sufficiently skilled labour forces to run the factories they hoped to build; in other countries the domestic markets were not rich enough to buy the goods they were supposed to produce. The north Yemenis seemed to regard investment as merely another form of aid. Yemen and several other countries lacked much of the basic infrastructure that was needed to make commercial projects feasible. All Arab countries hampered investment with bureaucracy. After ten years of effort the Kuwaitis said that their only profitable investments had been various ventures in industry, agriculture and real estate in Jordan, and a successful chain of hotels in Tunisia. Since then some rich individuals from the Gulf and Saudi Arabia have invested profitably in hotels in Egypt and Morocco.

The saddest cases of inter-Arab projects failing to live up to expectations occurred in Sudan. This country was being promoted in the mid-1970s as the 'breadbasket of the Arab world', but it turned out to be afflicted by every one of the problems of the other recipient countries. It was a casebook of development obstacles. When the Kuwaitis built a big hotel in Khartoum, its profitability was ruined by a delay of over a year in it being connected to the electricity grid. Other projects were made impossible by Sudan's huge size; it is the biggest country in Africa. The terrible quality of its roads, its inadequate ports, and fuel shortages which brought transport to a halt, caused enormous delays in materials getting to construction sites. The rapid changing of ministers by President Nimeri did not help solve any of these problems. As different people got to the President's ear projects were altered, or abandoned and replaced with new ones. In the words of a Sudanese businessman, 'Corruption set in when the clique around him was able to control whatever came into Nimeri's mind. They could get him to build a less important road that was twice the length of the important one, because there would be a bigger commission in that contract.'

A good example of the difficulties of operating in Sudan is the story of the Sudan Textile Industry Limited. This company, which was based on the enormous expansion of a firm already in existence, was established in 1982 by a well-known Sudanese entrepreneur, Dr Khalil Osman, and a group of Kuwaitis. Together they invested more than $100 million in the second biggest textile mill in Africa – the biggest being in Egypt. It was not easy building the factory, but eventually they succeeded. The serious problems came when they started to run it. They found that they could not get enough electricity. They needed and had been promised 16 megawatts, but in the early part of the summer they were given only 2.5 megawatts. The problem was that the period of peak domestic demand in May and June, the hottest months in Sudan, coincides with the head of water behind the Rosires Dam, the grid's main supplier, being at its lowest, before the Blue Nile floods begin in July. This lack of power was sufficient to destroy the economics of the plant.

Further difficulties lay with the company getting access to foreign exchange for spare parts. The government distributed what little hard currency it had between its ministries, and the ministries gave each applicant only a percentage of its needs. Machines in the mills had to be cannibalized so that some at least could be kept running.

The company found that it could not rely on the local market for simple back-up services. It needed 150 buses to transport its labour, but it was unable to find a bus company to do the job, and could not hire on the local market, so it had to buy its own in Kuwait. It bought second-hand vehicles, which are extremely cheap in that country, but when it began to run them it had difficulty in obtaining fuel and, inevitably, spare parts. After two years of steady cannibalization it was left with only two buses in working order. At this point it gave up with its transport operation and sold the two working buses and the bits of the rest. Interestingly, its managers noticed that soon after the auction most of the buses were running again. They had been bought in twos and threes by small family firms which had immediately had local mechanics, in typical African fashion, put them together with new engines and other parts of vehicles of completely different makes. The moral of this is that in a very simple economy there are things that are practical for small businesses but completely impossible for anyone operating on a large, Western scale.

Eventually, in 1988, when there were exceptionally high floods on the Blue Nile, the plant was inundated. It was closed and not reopened when the waters subsided. The Kuwaiti company in Sudan that acted for the shareholders was declared bankrupt after its owners had refused to pay the mill's debts or pay redundancy money to the workers. The Sudanese government asked the shareholders to help, but by this time they had reached such a state of despair and exasperation that they did not reply.

7

The Collapse of Algeria

*French rule – independence – emergence of Algerian identity –
character of FLN – failure of industrialization programme –
Chadli Benjedid – stagnation and unemployment – corruption
– riots of 1988 – reform – the FIS – cancellation of elections –
terrorism and national demoralization*

Algeria was once the most admired country in the Arab world. There
were few who loved it or enjoyed going there – it was too hard and
unsmiling for that – but for what it had achieved it was respected.
People believed it was going to be a success.

Its reputation was built on its victorious war of independence and
the remarkable discipline with which it tackled its problems afterwards.
For eight years, from 1954 to 1962, it fought the French. In the process
it lost a million men and women, a tenth of its population. Its struggle
became an inspiration to other colonial territories and to the left-wing
revolutionary groups of the 1960s and 1970s that were fighting to
overthrow post-colonial regimes. The lesson taught by the Front de
Libération Nationale, which led the Algerians to victory, was 'do not
deviate from your maximum terms'. This was a valid principle at the
time for any revolutionary group which did not care about human
life on its own side and found itself facing an enemy at a moral and
diplomatic disadvantage.

Once the Algerians had won their freedom they had to create for
themselves a new culture. The French had made their territory not just
a colony but part of France. The government of Charles X invaded it
in 1830 as a means of distracting the people from its incompetence at
home, using as a pretext an episode which had occurred three years

earlier, when the Dey of Algiers lost his temper with the French consul during an argument over a trade deal. The Dey, whose authority encompassed only a fraction of the territory which the French were eventually to take, struck the consul in the face with a fly-whisk and called him a 'wicked, faithless, idol-worshipping rascal'. During the course of the eighteen years following their invasion the French slowly reduced the Algerian tribes. Many of the tribes united to fight under the leadership of a young chief named Abdel-Kader, but what the French were facing was not in any sense a single nation. It was more a space on the map between Morocco, which had a very strong political and cultural identity, partly because it had never been conquered by the Ottoman Turks, and the small territory of Tunisia, which like Algeria was nominally part of the Ottoman Empire, but in practice had been ruled by the Beys of the Husseinite dynasty since the early eighteenth century.

Large-scale French colonization began after 1870. Some of those who arrived were hard-working, skilled Alsatians, whose homes had been taken by the Germans in the Franco-Prussian war; many more were poor Spaniards, Italians and Maltese. In spite of the fact that by the time of the First World War only one in five of the *colon* population of Algeria was reckoned to be French by origin, the government and other colonial institutions of the country were totally French. The schools were run in French, and Algerian children, or those of them who received an education, were taught about French history and French culture. The French reproduced the towns they knew at home, with their churches, cafés and band stands. Algiers, built on a long curving hillside above a magnificent bay, came to look like Marseilles.

The vigour of the French culture, combined with their own lack of nationhood before the invasion and the ethnic division between Berbers and Arabs, left the nationalists of the early twentieth century trying to define who they were.* They were all Muslims – and referred to as 'Muslims', not 'Arabs' or 'Berbers' by the *colons* – but otherwise they had no shared symbols or history. One of them, Ferhat Abbas, who was later the first Prime Minister of the provisional government established

---

* All of the Algerians are descended ultimately from Berber stock. Those who now think of themselves as being 'Arabs' are those whose ancestors adopted the Arabic language and culture. The people who retain Berber as their first language are the Kabyles, whose home is the mountainous Kabylia region south-east of Algiers, and the Chaouias from the Aures massif, further east. Together the Kabyles and the Chaouias make up about 30 per cent of the population. The Kabyles, and some of the Chaouias think of themselves as being Berber first and Algerian second. Many of them have little respect for Arab Algerians and are not at all impressed by the rest of the Arab world.

during the revolution, declared in the 1930s, that he would not die for the Algerian nation because 'it does not exist'. Later, in 1958, when the Front de Libération Nationale established its provisional government in Cairo, at the heart of the Arab world at a time of intense pan-Arab fervour, Abbas made this announcement in French, because that was the only language he spoke competently.

When the French government finally gave Algeria its independence in 1962, and the attempts of French extremists in the Organisation Armée Sécrète to overthrow the French state failed in an orgy of point-less murder in Algiers, more than a million *colons*, eight out of ten of the foreign population, left the country in a matter of months. The OAS in its later days had taken to murdering Algerians and the *colons* were afraid of reprisals. Among those who went were virtually all the teachers and doctors, most of the upper and middle echelons of the administration and most of the technicians. The Algerians were left to make of their country what they wished, or what they could.

The matter of nationhood had been defined by the war – even though intellectuals at the time and for years afterwards continued to argue that Algeria had no proper identity. The FLN had effectively created a nation in the process of fighting the French and bringing most of the population eventually to support its struggle. Those who backed it by fighting, helping the fighters or just listening to its broadcasts came to feel a sense of unity, of all being on one side against a common enemy, and so by the end of the war the majority of the people felt themselves to be 'Algerians' rather than 'French colonial subjects'. Within the Algerian nation, though, there remained some division between Arabs and Berbers, and a very stark divide between the educated, French-speaking, secular élite, who had adopted French ways of thought and took their holidays in France, and the Arab and Berber peasants.

The war moulded the Algerians socially. The struggle emancipated Algerian women, and although this process was partly reversed after independence, when Algeria became socially austere, women remained more important in intellectual and political life than they were in most other Arab countries. The war also determined Algeria's government. It gave the country a revolutionary government of its own, not a government created by a departing colonial power. It was socialist, but not Communist. It believed in the redistribution of wealth and in the economic development of Algeria and the rest of the Third World. In its foreign policy the government was non-aligned; it was a strong supporter of African liberation movements. In the 1960s and 1970s, it was known to have links with various terrorist organizations, but it did not sponsor terrorism. It was regarded by its critics as well as its friends as being honest; in hijack negotiations and other sensitive political matters it was trusted as an intermediary. At the top of the government it had a small cadre of excellent, serious-minded and honest ministers and ambassadors, some of the most able in the Arab world, who helped inspire the Algerians themselves and gave a favourable impression of the country to outsiders. Together these features of the new government defined what the country stood for, and that reinforced its identity.

Of most immediate concern to the new Algerian government in 1962 was the reconstruction of all parts of the administration. The necessity of creating almost from scratch a new professional class contributed to the seriousness of the regime, and to the radical approach it took to its problems. A massive programme was put in hand to educate the population. By the early 1970s the government was spending more than 10 per cent of the country's gross national product on education, though because of the engrained nature of the French syllabus and the weak knowledge of Arabic among the small educated class, all teaching was done in French until 1972. In the countryside, where the French farms had simply been abandoned, workers' committees took over vacant land with the idea of developing a system of 'autogestion', self-management. Foreign trade and industry were taken by the state to be run on eastern European lines. The only goods imported were those needed for the country's development; all but essential foods and the most basic consumer goods were deemed frivolous. The population was expected to keep its belt tightened.

In the mid-1970s it seemed to the government and its people that their sacrifices were to be rewarded. The huge rise in oil prices multiplied the state's oil revenues by five or six times in the space of two years. The government instituted a free health service as a present to its people. The rest of its revenues it continued to pour into industrialization. It took over the running of its own oil production and built refineries, liquified gas plants, steel mills and a large number of engineering industries. By the end of the 1970s it had the biggest industrial base on the continent, after South Africa. It was at this time that the Minister of Industry, Belaid Abdessalem, made the famous prediction that Algeria was going to become 'Africa's first and the world's second Japan'.

In their dealings with the foreign companies involved in their industrialization the Algerians were as determined and inflexible as they were with themselves. When they negotiated gas and oil contracts they would argue over every last cent, believing in the suspicious fashion of Arab radicals that to concede something to a foreigner was to betray their own nation. In a case in the 1980s, when their gas projects were on stream, their reluctance to compromise was to bring one of their customers to the verge of bankruptcy. By this time the Algerians were applying a similar unyielding approach to negotiating foreign loans, insisting always on paying the very lowest interest rates. It never occurred to the men at the top of government that in a commercial transaction there was a value in having people's goodwill. They seemed incapable of understanding that a successful long-term business relationship involves a certain amount of giving, rather than the extraction of every last cent out of the party who may temporarily seem to be the weaker.

Their commercial dealings revealed a trait in the Algerian personality which the Algerians themselves admit is one of the causes of their later misfortune. This is that although they are disciplined and hard-working, the impression this gives that they are a practical people is misleading because they tend to take things to extremes. Hence in the 1960s they embraced a very extreme form of socialism and an exceptionally severe social and economic regime. In the 1980s they could tolerate this no longer and were forced to abandon their principles. Later reform of the political system moved too quickly and decisively to democracy. A more pragmatic people, it is said, would accept some imperfection and compromise in running its affairs and although it might not immediately impress itself and outsiders by such behaviour, in the long run it would probably be more successful.

It is because everybody was so impressed by Algeria in its first twenty years of independence that the disasters of the late 1980s and 1990s came as such a surprise. In the space of four years Algeria changed in the eyes of the world from being a rather unattractive success to a complete economic, social and political failure. In spite of appearances the economy was actually hopelessly uncompetitive. And in its social policies and the way it ran its country the government had never been as honest or competent as it had seemed. From the very beginning the Algerian republic had been flawed. Those people aware of the flaws had regarded them as small beside the government's iron determination and its apparent success, and they were rarely discussed.

What makes Algeria particularly interesting is that it displayed all the different faults of the Arab countries. Its government suffered from the hypocrisy, corruption and ruthlessness of the other Arab governments, and in running its economy it combined inflexible socialism with over-ambitious development schemes and, later, a short-sighted desire to win favour with its own people. It so happened that the effects of all its mistakes and shortcomings hit the country at the same time, and in a particularly acute fashion, and in a very short period brought it to ruin. It is this that makes Algeria a useful case to study.

The important fact of the early years of the Front's existence is that it did not defeat the French army. By the summer of 1959, after nearly five years of war, the Front de Libération Nationale had been defeated, and had the French pursued their attacks for a few more months its forces inside the country would have been totally eliminated. But for political reasons the offensive was stopped. Algeria came to be seen by the new President, General de Gaulle, and by much of the French intelligentsia as an international embarrassment and a drain on France's economy. Therefore the President put his efforts into seeking a political solution and although the *colons* and parts of the army resisted this, and tried to overthrow the government, all they achieved was the humiliation of France and a more violent and confused withdrawal. The FLN from late 1959 had only to keep itself in being, mainly in the form of a large army built up by Colonel Houari Boumedienne in Tunisia, and ensure that there were no other *interlocuteurs valables* with whom the French could negotiate. It was able to do this and it had the sense not to compromise in its negotiations, and so in 1962 it stepped into the shoes of the departed French. The legitimacy of the Front as a new government came from the tenacity and bravery of its fighters and from its having constituted the opposition to French rule in this period.

The FLN may have been legitimate but it was not a pleasant organization. It was suspicious, cruel and ruthless. From the beginning it had killed people in the most brutal and disgusting ways, and it had killed a great many Algerians, mostly small functionaries working for the colonial administration or potential leaders who might have emerged as rivals of the Front in negotiations with the French. At the end of the war it put to death thousands of *harkis*, irregular Muslim troops who had fought for the French. It also killed many of its own leaders, not because of ideological disputes but because in the middle of the war its members feared they were being betrayed by people in their own ranks. These 'cleansings', as they were known, were accompanied by mock trials and trumped-up evidence. The FLN that came to power in 1962 was riven by internal rivalries. The Algerian people feared and respected it, but they had no cause to love it.

To be accurate, from a few years after independence it was not the FLN itself, but the FLN's army that ran Algeria. During the period of President Boumedienne, from 1965 to 1978, which is when the institutions of the republic became established, power was in the hands of the President and the military men closest to him. The governors of the provinces, who were also senior officers, were allowed considerable independence in how they ran their territories, as long as they did not challenge Boumedienne. The FLN was made to appear to be the government, but it had little power. It was used as a platform for speeches and its members were given privileges, access to luxury consumer goods and opportunities for enriching themselves. It remained in a secondary position even after 1977, when the country was given its first parliament, for which only FLN members were eligible.

Both inside the country and outside it was accepted by the articulate technocrats who ran the economic ministries and foreign academics and journalists who knew Algeria that the regime was a dictatorship. But because of its fashionable socialist credentials and the mood of optimism that surrounded the oil states' development projects at that time, it was given a greater reputation for enlightened dictatorial rule than it deserved. In reality the government reflected its origins. In the early days of independence a few of its opponents were murdered; later critics were exiled or imprisoned. Occasional popular movements against the government's policies were efficiently suppressed.

Much of the government's reputation rested on its famous industrialization programme. This was over-ambitious from the start, and it reflected a misunderstanding of the nature of industrialization which is common in developing countries. The government saw the process as being mainly a matter of using its oil revenues to pay foreign contractors to build industrial plants. Once they were finished it would announce to its people and the world that it had become self-sufficient in whatever products the plants were built to make. The problem was that the new industries did not operate at a profit. In later years the government was to blame out-of-date designs, but the fact was that many of the factories were too big and sophisticated for the country. In spite of the state's heroic efforts to educate its people, the labour force was not adequately skilled for the jobs it had to do. Many of the workers who went into the factories had recently come into the towns from the countryside and had no experience of any work except farming. And as the numbers coming on to the labour market increased the government pushed more of these people into its factories, thus increasing their production problems and making it even more difficult for them to be profitable. Most of the industries were unable to compete with imports in the home market, let alone compete in export markets. The government, of course, hid these facts by not importing what it was producing locally and setting its own prices in the domestic market. By direct and indirect means it was subsidizing its industries. Without profits the industries were not able to use their own resources to expand. Any new facilities they wanted to build had to be paid for by oil revenues. In the 1970s and early 1980s, while the government had the oil revenue to finance whatever losses or capital needs it liked, these faults were not apparent.

While industry was being built on foundations of sand agriculture was neglected. Farming had been enormously disrupted by the flight of the *colons* in 1962 and the workers' committees which took over the farms were less efficient and less independent than it was hoped they would be. Agriculture, like other parts of the economy, was directed by bureaucrats promoted by favour – because they had been good fighters in the war or because they were related to a senior official – and not because they had any experience of farming. Few of those people near the top of any of the ministries or state corporations had worked their way up from the bottom. In agriculture the result was that the country, which has extensive fertile land near the Mediterranean coast and had fed itself under the French, began to be an importer of food.

Algeria's economic policies changed – and took a turn for the worse – when Houari Boumedienne died of a rare illness at the end of 1978 and was succeeded as President a few weeks later by Chadli Benjedid, the military governor of the western province of Oran. Chadli, as he was always known, was a very different character from his predecessor. He did not have the same austere dedication to making Algeria the industrial giant of the revolutionary Third World. He was a pragmatic man, slow moving and avuncular, used to the relatively liberal ways of Oran, which had been the most French region of the country in colonial days and had maintained a small, prosperous private sector since independence. He wanted to be liked. It would be accurate to say of Chadli that he had no strong principles at all.

As it happened Chadli's arrival coincided with the Iranian revolution which triggered the second big round of oil-price rises, in 1979 and 1980. Already in the later years of Boumedienne the government had become more liberal in its social spending policies, in the wages it paid and the goods it imported. The changes went hand in hand with its aim of expanding its population – 10 million at the time of independence – so that the country could be more powerful militarily and industrially. A policy of increasing a population calls not only for the total avoidance of birth control, but also for more food imports and, above all, more subsidized food so that families feel they can feed more mouths. Given that in Algeria's socialist economy the government set its own exchange rate and set prices in the domestic market, the subsidies were invisible, and, because of that, all the more liable to grow. Under the Chadli regime, as more foreign exchange became available, the government began spending without stint. It started importing what were by Algerian standards luxury consumer goods – bananas, foreign cheese,

washing machines, refrigerators – and through adjusting prices it gradually moved into subsidizing these and other items, such as cars and
even the raw materials, steel and cement, needed for its own industries.
At their maximum, when prices on the international markets were high,
the subsidies applied to basic foodstuffs amounted to more than half
their true price. At the same time exit visas for Algerians were abolished
and foreign currency was made available for people to travel abroad
on holidays. The government launched a *programme anti-pénurie*. As
Algerians say, in the early years of Chadli the state came to stand not
so much for 'social justice' as for 'social assistance'. They add, with a
typical French reference, that the government's policy was like that of
the cicada in the La Fontaine fable of the cicada and the ant, in which
the cicada spends all summer singing while the ant builds itself a store
of food. No attempt was made by the government to accumulate a
financial reserve against the day when its circumstances might become
less favourable.

To be fair to Chadli, it must be said that these policies represented
not just his own instincts but a consensus at the top of Algerian society.
There was a feeling by the time Boumedienne died that the government
should become less centralized and that there should be more emphasis
on rewarding the people, on letting them consume some of their own
oil wealth, rather than putting it all into industry.

To help finance its more relaxed and expansive policies Algeria began
borrowing on the international markets in 1984, and two years later,
when oil prices collapsed from about $30 a barrel (and more for the
attractive light Algerian crude) to $10–15, it enormously increased its
borrowings. There was real panic in the government. The authorities
rushed into short-term debt, because that was easier to arrange than
long-term, and like all the other members of OPEC they believed
devoutly that the price fall could only be a temporary phenomenon
and that demand for oil, and therefore its price, would rise again at
the end of the decade. Investment in industry stopped. For political
reasons it was not possible for the government to make new money
available by withdrawing its array of subsidies or lowering wages. Factories ran out of spare parts, production fell. Imports of consumer
goods continued to rise with the growing population. Those people who
were receiving good government salaries had the money to continue to
buy the goods they wanted, which drained the state's reserves of foreign
exchange where the goods were imports and stimulated inflation where
they were locally produced. Out of pride the government would not
devalue the dinar to cut off some of the demand. Borrowings had to
be increased.

Worst of all there was a huge growth in unemployment, to the point where about a quarter of the male work force was out of a job. Among young men in the seventeen to twenty-three age range unemployment ran at nearly 70 per cent. These people did not even have the money to while away their days sipping a cup of Turkish coffee in a shabby café with friends. They spent their waking hours leaning against the walls in the poor quarters of the towns, bored, bitter and fearing that they would never have a job. They became known as *'haa'iteen'*, or 'wall people'. It was unemployment that was to bring Algeria to disaster.

In retrospect the Algerian people were to calculate that the government under Chadli's guidance, from 1979 to January 1992, had received $100 billion of oil revenues, whereas before him its revenues from the time of independence had been just $30 billion. When they examined how the money had been spent the conclusion of economists and much of the rest of the intelligentsia was that most of it must have gone on a standard of living that the country could not afford, but among all sections of society there also became rooted the idea that $26 billion had been syphoned off by corruption and secreted in foreign bank accounts. It is characteristic of the Arab attitude towards statistics, which is both relaxed and political, that this figure matched Algeria's foreign debt, which by 1993 was also $26 billion, and its population, which was 26 million. The implication was that if the corrupt people could be brought to justice and their money extracted from them the debt could be repaid, or every man, woman and child in the country given $1,000.

Since the late 1980s the Algerians have been obsessed with corruption. They realize that it goes back to the early years of the republic. Soon after independence Mohammad Khider, one of the *'neuf historiques'*, the founders of the revolution, fled to Switzerland taking with him much of the FLN treasury, which had been accumulated, partly by extortion, during the war. When he was murdered in 1967 the money remained inaccessible in his personal account. In the mid-1960s a large sum raised by public subscription for a National Fund disappeared into the government's pockets without the public ever being told where it went or what benefit they had got from it. Boumedienne was forced to admit in 1969 that 'you cannot have somebody working in honey without him having a taste of that honey'. This remark is now condemned by his critics, especially sympathizers of the Islamic parties, as being despicably weak.

In the 1970s and the Chadli years the scale of the corruption grew. Particularly corrupt parts of the government, inevitably, were those that had big contracts to award. These were the ministries and state agencies that dealt with oil, industrialization, infrastructure building and foreign purchasing. The Ministry of Commerce, which did the foreign purchasing, awarded foreign companies surprisingly large contracts which gave them responsibility for buying whole ranges of items on behalf of the government. Naturally there was considerable competition for these contracts, and much of the competition took the form not of reduced prices and squeezed margins, but increased prices and bigger bribes. The companies most often mentioned by Algerians as having indulged in these types of practices were Swiss, French, American and Japanese.

It was possible for officials to make money even in parts of the bureaucracy that had relatively low turnovers. An Algerian university lecturer told me that he came across an extraordinary example of corruption when he was giving evening classes for adults who wanted to sit the university entrance examination. One of his students, whom he used to visit, lived in an extremely comfortable penthouse furnished with oriental art, including Persian carpets, silk hangings, carved hardwood furniture and ivory *objets*. The lecturer was impressed by what he described as 'this insolence of luxury' – an expression with a distinct political Islamic flavour – and he asked how the furnishings had been collected. 'Oh,' the student replied, 'I used to be cultural attaché at our embassy in Delhi'.

In all Middle Eastern countries there is some nepotism. The family in these countries is so important that for a powerful person to help a relation is regarded almost as a moral and proper gesture of loyalty. There is also a certain amount of straight bribery, and a great deal of sharing of the benefits of business deals between officials and contractors. If people refuse to give bribes no decisions may be taken at all. 'Patronage and corruption are the drive belts of action,' a British ambassador in Algiers concluded in 1989.

If the corruption stays on only a moderate scale and the countries remain reasonably prosperous, no great offence is caused. In Algeria, however, not only did the government run out of money but the scale of corruption seems to have been particularly high, mainly because the centralized direction of the economy and the lack of a free market gave officials unusually big opportunities for selling their decisions. One could see the evidence of corruption in the 1980s not just in the award of contracts, but in the allocation of government housing, which tended to go to people who had friends in the bureaucracy, and in the way the health service was operated. In theory everybody could have free health care as of right, but good-quality care, including specialist treatment in France, was just for the more important or better-off officials. People near the top of the government helped themselves to cures in Geneva and Vichy.

The effect of corruption in Algeria, in the words of the lecturer, was that it made government spending 'like the sprinkling of rose water'. Those nearest the source of the water received plenty, those below received a few drops and the rest of the population caught merely the smell. Those who only saw and smelt the wealth of the privileged few were understandably bitter. Gradually they came to despise their government.

The resentment of the Algerian people exploded in 1988. Between 4 and 12 October there were riots in Algiers, Oran and other towns, in which crowds of mostly young people attacked government offices, shops selling luxury goods and, particularly, any building that was associated with the FLN. The authorities, of course, responded harshly and, by their own admission, killed 280. French journalists reported that more than 700 died. As the violence subsided the police tortured some of those they had arrested to discover who might be the ring leaders, or what hidden hand might be behind the riots – it being unthinkable to an Arab government that riots might occur spontaneously.

The riots were not the first disturbances to occur in the 1980s. There had been protests by students about poor living standards and bad tuition. The police had occasionally clashed with Islamic fundamentalist groups. Invariably there had been heavy reprisals. After student riots in Constantine in 1986 nearly 200 people had been sent to prison, and the leaders of the Algerian League for Human Rights had been sent into internal exile in the Sahara. The 1988 riots, however, were much bigger and goaded the government into making reforms.

The man who responded to the riots was Chadli. He saw that the disquiet might perhaps be turned to his advantage. It had been noticed during the week of violence that the President himself had not been a target. The riots even seemed to help him, to the point where it began to be whispered that he 'must' be behind them. This theory was based on the knowledge that Chadli had recently been in some difficulties with the senior FLN cadres. Realizing that the economy had to be made more efficient, he had successfully pushed through a liberalization of agriculture two years before and had then begun to think of breaking up the big industrial corporations. It was here that he was meeting opposition from the theoreticians and trade unions of the FLN, who had even organized some strikes against the changes. At the same time Chadli was running for his third Presidential term – elections were due in December – and he had an obvious interest in seeing that, if possible, he should be the unique candidate. According to the logic of this particular conspiracy theory a serious outbreak of rioting might frighten people in the party away from any idea of change. Potential challengers and their backers would abandon their plans, and Chadli would be left to win his third term and then pursue whatever reforms he thought were necessary. There is no non-circumstantial evidence to suggest that this theory is true, but it gives an idea of the atmosphere of Algerian politics at the time.

As soon as the riots were over Chadli proposed reforms. These included promises that non-FLN candidates would be allowed to stand in elections and that the Prime Minister would be responsible to the National Assembly rather than the President, who would in future stand above politics. At the same time the President indicated that there would in future be further changes in the same liberalizing and decentralizing direction. A referendum was held on 3 November and, without cheating, the President got 92 per cent approval for his proposals on an 83 per cent turnout.

In the next few months Chadli made further changes. He announced a programme of financial and administrative measures, including higher taxes on the rich and a reduction in the length of military service, that appealed to the young. After being re-elected President but dropping his post as Secretary General of the FLN, he published a new constitution. This completed the separation of the state from the party. It dropped the old constitution's 'irrevocable commitment to socialism' and it permitted the creation of 'associations of a political nature'; the reformers did not yet dare use the words 'political party'. Once again the changes were endorsed by a referendum.

Then in April and May 1989 there were more demonstrations, strikes and riots by young people protesting over food price rises, the corruption of petty officials and what they saw as the slow pace of reform. So the pace was increased. In July political parties were made legal, with the proviso that they had to be licensed by the Ministry of the Interior and were not to represent exclusively religious or regional interests. In September Chadli dismissed Kasdi Merbah, the Prime Minister he had appointed after the riots, because he felt that his links with officials in the FLN remained too strong, and brought in a new figure, Mouloud Hamrouche, who had been running the Presidential office.

It was now that the floodgates of reform were fully opened. Hamrouche promised straight away that he would, in effect, introduce democracy. He said that he would change the government from a single-party system to a parliamentary system, through conducting a dialogue with other parties, trade unions and the public. He promised transparency in decision making. The Ministry of Information was abolished – an admirable decision – because in the Prime Minister's opinion it had no place in a democracy. It had become irrelevant several months earlier when a new press code had allowed anybody who wanted to, to produce a newspaper – an unusual freedom in the Arab world. A flood of new publications appeared on the market. Censorship had ceased. People began to say in public whatever they liked.

Most important of all the actions of Hamrouche in the autumn of 1989 was that he began generously to license political parties. Most of the new bodies were little more than groups of friends. As parties they were just figments of intellectuals' imaginations. But there was one body which was not of this type and which, had the law been properly applied, would have been refused a licence because it was an overtly religious organization. It was the Front Islamique de Salut – the Islamic Salvation Front.

Up to this point it can be said that the government, or the President, was in control of the pace of reform and the evolution of politics in Algeria. Once the FIS became legal, however, control rapidly slipped from its grasp.

In hindsight, the Algerian intelligentsia now wonders what Chadli and Hamrouche thought they were doing in 1989. Hamrouche, it is accepted, was an idealist, but Chadli was not really a radical reformer or democrat by background, and even after the riots it is suggested that he underwent no intellectual conversion in favour of reform. Now that it is the fashion to pour scorn on Chadli, it is believed, perhaps accurately, that the President did not fully realize that democracy would mean a change in the whole Algerian way of political life, that it might easily result in elections sweeping away his party, the system he knew and himself as President. Instead it is thought he saw it as just another expedient concession to the people, to bring peace, just as food subsidies had been meant to do in the early 1980s. It may also be that this gesture seemed to Chadli a good way of strengthening his own position as President. It pushed the FLN to one side and put him above the government and party politics as the sole arbiter of the nation's future, the man who could say to the people 'above these feuding parties I am your one guarantor of stability'. Chadli may have wished to promote himself as a bigger national leader, more in the mould of Nasser. Whatever his secret motives, the undeniable fact is that Chadli, and his Prime Minister, enormously underestimated the power of Islamic politics. They introduced democracy too fast and too completely.

The Front Islamique de Salut, the FIS, when it was given a licence, was not emerging from total obscurity. Its leaders and many of its members had been active in a social-cum-political Islamic milieu for most of the 1980s. They had established a presence in the schools, where they had almost been encouraged by the government in the post-socialist, post-Boumedienne years. At that time the view had been that Algeria needed to have put back into it some of its Arab and Islamic culture which had been so weakened by the French, and the Party functionaries at the Ministry of Education were happy to place people with Islamic leanings in the schools. Not only Algerians were given these posts: Arabs from the eastern countries, particularly Egypt, were imported to work in schools and teacher-training colleges, and many of these people, being poorly qualified, unsuccessful and generally disaffected used Islamic platitudes to make up for their ignorance. The Ministry officials, many promoted through family connections and some barely literate themselves, were too inexperienced in the business of education to be able to translate a general policy aim – the reintroduction of some traditional culture into schools – into an effective policy being implemented by the right teachers.

The leaders of the Islamic movement meanwhile developed contacts with each other through the network of mosques and charitable societies. The imams who led the people in their prayers were rather ill-educated government employees. The people who directed the political movement had more prestigious jobs. Abbassi Madani and Ali Belhadj, who became leader and deputy-leader of the FIS, were university lecturers – Madani, who had received some of his education in London, taught sociology. These men and many like them promoted informal discussion groups, which encouraged people to look to the Koran as a source of political ideas. Occasionally they organized demonstrations. When they were allowed to, they would preach in the mosques. It was after Ali Belhadj had been prevented from preaching by the authorities in 1988 that he went to the chambers of a prominent lawyer, who was also President of the League for Human Rights, to protest. The lawyer had hardly heard of him at the time but he told me later that he was impressed by 'his utter certainty, his lack of doubt'. Belhadj explained how three years earlier he had been sentenced to five years in prison for political agitation. After he had served two and a half years the governor summoned him and told him that he was being freed. Apparently he replied, 'I refuse everything from this power [the government, as opposed to God], even its pardon'. But in spite of his obstinacy he was evicted from the jail. A few months after this episode the Islamic politicians contrived to prolong and intensify the riots of October 1988.

From that time on the names of Madani and Belhadj became well known.

The people who formed the core of the early supporters of the FIS were the *petits bourgeois* – the shopkeepers, artisans and owners of small businesses. They were men who had to take some decisions for themselves, even if that merely meant how much stock they should buy for their shops. Unlike the mass of Algerians who worked for the state, they were themselves responsible for the amount of money they took home to their families at the end of each week. They had a little education, which made them aware of the money-making possibilities there might be in a more liberal economy. They felt they had been pushed aside by socialism and now they took pride in having an organization of their own which made them strong. The mentality of these people was similar to that of the people who had rallied to the Fascists and Nazis in Europe in the 1920s and 1930s.

After the tradesmen, flocking to the FIS came the unemployed working class. Seen in the street both they and the Front's *petits bourgeois* supporters looked similar, wearing the standard Arab fundamentalist garb, a short *thobe* (a white cotton shirt falling to above the ankles), a long beard, a closely clipped moustache and, if they had a headdress, just a folded triangular piece of cloth with no black ring (*agal*) to weigh it down. Their womenfolk covered themselves in black gowns and wore no make-up, though they did not necessarily hide their faces. These forms of dress were imported from the eastern Arab countries. The male styles were supposed to reflect the example of the Prophet Mohammad, being a combination of how he dressed himself and advice he is said to have given on how a man should avoid being affected in his appearance by sporting a luxuriant moustache or allowing his robe to drag on the ground.

The '*intégristes*', as they are always known in north Africa, from the word '*intégrité*' meaning integrity or completeness, became more aggressive as they grew in power. They smashed the windows of bars, threatened journalists who criticized them and interrogated university lecturers about the content of their history and literature courses. They were particularly violent towards women who were behaving in ways which they considered 'liberated'. Girls on the beaches were harrassed. Some had acid thrown at their legs. When a woman in Annaba led a campaign against the FIS's demand that Islamic law be imposed the *intégristes* burnt down her home. Parties and weddings at which both men and women were guests were attacked and disrupted. The *intégristes* were neurotic about the role of 'liberated' women. They believed, rightly, that the education and liberation of women would lead to the disappearance of the society that nurtured their own supporters. They were embittered by seeing that women in factories had taken men's jobs. In a famous speech in 1989 Abbasi Madani told his audience that a woman should come out of her house only three times, 'when she is born, when she is married and when she goes to the cemetery'.

Quite quickly society responded to the *intégriste* pressure. The Ministry of Religious Affairs and the imams in the mosques began to accede to the demands of FIS members that they should be allowed to preach, and then they began to broadcast their sermons through the loudspeakers attached to the minarets, which had previously been used only for the calls to prayer. In hotel rooms there appeared on the bedside tables transparent stickers, indicating *qibla*, the direction of Mecca, for those devout travellers who wished to pray but did not have the time or energy to go to the mosques. A few middle-class Algerian women began to wear the Islamic shawl, the chador. Among them was Chadli's wife, who adopted a rather chic version of the garment. She seemed to be suggesting to the *intégristes* that she and her husband were on their side.

Most of the Algerian middle classes, the secular Francophone government officials, the Oran businessmen and the professionals, were horrified by the innovations. The same went for the Berber population. Islamic fundamentalism, being in part a substitute for Arab nationalism, appealed almost exclusively to the Arab element in the Algerian population.

Among the Arab poor the popularity of the FIS increased. The Front had only a few definite policies. One was that women were to be stopped from working and compensated by being given salaries as housewives. This idea was supposed to stop unemployment, though it was never explained where the money for the new salaries would come from. For the small businessman there was a promise of lower taxes and fewer regulations. Beyond this the FIS, like similar groups elsewhere in the Muslim world, confined its promises to generalities. Its favourite phrase in addressing any issue was that it would institute 'an Islamic solution'. With Islamic government, it said, there would be social justice, an end to corruption, and prosperity. Being God's perfect rule for mankind on earth it could not fail to produce success and happiness. Much of the Algerian male electorate believed these promises because they were desperate and partly, maybe, because having been brought up in a secular state they knew very little of Islam compared with, say, the Saudis or Gulf Arabs and were more prone to being impressed by apparently holy men. Working-class women, who became equally enthusiastic supporters of the Front, backed it out of a superstitious fear that if they made any other choice they would be consigning themselves to hell.

In June 1990, in the first free vote allowed in Algeria since independence, the FIS won a majority of the seats in local government elections. The result had been expected and the policies the Front immediately put into effect were predictable. It shut kindergartens to oblige women to stay at home to look after their children. Cinemas were made into mosques or FIS meeting places. Men and women were separated from each other in buses and given different counters in post offices. In the streets the FIS put up posters with verses from the Koran. Notices for hospitals were replaced with a verse which read 'If you are ill God alone can cure you'. The purpose was not to stop people going to hospital but to remind them that man's ability to cure was given to him by God. It was part of a rather self-conscious process of replacing Western symbols by Arab and Islamic ones.

The public was not particularly impressed by these achievements. The FIS brought no material improvement in people's conditions and quite a lot of inconvenience. There were signs of opposition, with a few protest strikes by municipal workers. Yet in a broad sense the Front benefited enormously by controlling local government. When it organized a rally in a stadium it would use the buses it had under its control to bring in thousands of its supporters from elsewhere. As the first free national parliamentary elections approached in June 1991 it ensured that people who were thought to be against it did not get polling cards or had their names kept off the electoral registers. The new secular parties, which by this time numbered some dozens, could not begin to compete with the FIS. They were not only disunited, they had no organization, no reputation and, except for one party associated with the Berbers, the Front des Forces Socialistes, no presence in local government.

In the weeks leading up to the polls the FIS claimed that the way the constituency boundaries had been drawn was biased against it. Its supporters clashed in the streets with the police and the confrontations became so serious, killing more than fifty people, that on 4 June Chadli felt forced to announce the indefinite postponement of the elections and declare martial law. Hamrouche was sacked and a new Prime Minister, Sid Ahmed Ghozali, a former Foreign Minister and one of the country's most able technocrats, was appointed.

As soon as he came into office Ghozali announced that his priority would be to organize new elections. Dates were set for two rounds in December and January, the second being for a run-off between the two leading candidates in seats in which there was no outright majority for a single person in the first round. This time the FIS was less overtly violent, partly because a large number of its members had been arrested after the confrontations in June. But on the day of the elections on 26 December in many towns it still had groups of youths standing outside the polling stations to intimidate secular-looking voters. The FIS duly won 188 seats, which left it needing only 28 more in the second round, due on 16 January 1992, to give it an outright majority in parliament.

The rest of the story is well known. For all the more modern minded Algerians, including the expatriates living in France, the prospect of FIS victory was appalling. For two weeks the government floundered. At one stage it is thought Chadli believed he might stay as a secular President 'cohabiting' with an *intégriste* government, but in the end he lacked the nerve to try. Other senior members of the government had lost faith in him. On 11 January 1992 he resigned and went into private life. The army, led by the Minister of Defence, General Khaled Nezzar, took control of the country, the second round of elections was cancelled, and a High Council of State was established to take over the role of the Presidency. Four days after the coup one of the surviving '*neufs historiques*', Mohammad Boudiaf, a man who was untainted by the abuses of power of the FLN, returned from 28 years of exile to lead the Council of State. The most powerful man in the Council, Nezzar, stayed in the background.

In the weeks that followed the coup most of the FIS leaders, including Madani and Belhadj, were arrested. In March the Front was declared illegal and in April nearly half of the town councils it had won in 1990 were dissolved. Gradually the FIS members, who seemed at first to have been disorientated by the cancellation of the elections, organized a campaign of bombings and assassinations, the targets normally being members of the security forces or people in or associated with the government. The campaign, slowly growing in intensity, continued through 1992 and 1993. The authorities responded by arresting thousands of FIS members. Hundreds more were killed in fighting.

At the end of June 1992 Mohammad Boudiaf was assassinated. The killer, who was arrested soon afterwards, was a member of the security forces who turned out to have *intégriste* sympathies, but, needless to say, most Algerians could not accept that the killing had been the work of one man and began looking for a plot. They had no difficulty in finding plausible theories. Boudiaf had been brought to power because the men of the FLN establishment thought that in his old age – he was 72 – he would be easily manipulated, but he had disappointed them. He had shown himself to be utterly honest and as much a revolutionary as when he had been exiled in 1963, after he had quarrelled with the first post-independence President, Ahmed Ben Bella. He had tried to address the concerns of young people, particularly their resentment of corruption. He had made enemies. Senior FLN members could see that he might be going to embarrass them personally, and elements of the FIS thought he might undermine their own popularity.

There was even a murky area of society in which the FLN and FIS came together in fearing him. The people involved were the *trabendo* class – the smugglers, whose name in Algeria is taken from the Spanish word *contrabendo*. The trabendos ran a flourishing business exporting subsidized basic foodstuffs from Algeria to Morocco and Tunisia, and hoarding and exporting other, locally produced, foodstuffs in order to create shortages and drive up prices inside the country. At the same time they were importing all the basic consumer goods and spare parts which were not available on the local market and which would normally have attracted high rates of duty. All of these transactions, of course, involved the sale or purchase of black-market foreign currency and the bribery of customs officials. The people who did the carrying – the youths in tracksuits any traveller would see on flights from Tunis or Casablanca, holding carrier bags bulging with china and pots and pans – were the *trabendo* labourers. The people behind them, who provided the money and fixed the customs, were the *trabendo* entrepreneurs, and among their number were just as many greedy FIS supporters as there were FLN functionaries. The popular theory, therefore, was that it might well have been some combination of the two interests that had killed Boudiaf. At his funeral Boudiaf was mourned by young people of all political views, and the more religious in the procession shouted Islamic political slogans, not, on this occasion, in support of a revolution, but in homage to the dead man.

After the assassination the High Council of State chose Ali Kafi, the little-known former director of the veterans' association, to be its chairman and appointed a new prime minister, Belaid Abdessalem. It was Abdessalem, in the role of Minister of Industry in the late 1960s and 1970s, who had launched the country's disastrous industrialization drive.

The new prime minister was faced with appalling problems. His country's population, which had been 9 million at the time of independence, had reached 26 million and was continuing to grow by 2.5 per cent a year. Unemployment was running at close to 25 per cent. The shortage of housing was so severe that in some of the poorer parts of the towns there were dozens of people living in single apartments. Factories were running at half capacity because they did not have access to foreign exchange to buy spare parts and raw materials. And the government had a debt of $26 billion and the most onerous debt service ratio of any country in the world. It was receiving $11–12 billion of oil and gas revenues a year and being obliged to make annual payments of interest and principal of some $8.5 billion. Because the country could not hope to live off just $3 billion of foreign exchange a year it was having to finance its repayments of principal with new short-term borrowings, and so its debt burden remained constant.

On top of its economic problems the government faced the continuing terrorist campaign of the FIS, which, it was rumoured, was being copied by elements of the FLN establishment. There were, no doubt, several terrorist factions associated with each body, but during 1993 two principal organizations were identified. One was the Groupe Islamist Armé, which was believed to join some obscure and unpleasant *intégriste* factions with the state's military intelligence organization. This group chose to kill distinguished non-political state servants and other members of the intelligentsia, such as professors and well-known journalists, and then in December 1993, after declaring that all foreigners should leave the country by the beginning of the month, moved on to murdering Europeans. It was assumed that the reasoning behind its killings was that if it could create a general atmosphere of fear and chaos, the Algerian middle classes, and perhaps some of the poor, would turn back to the FLN. They would see it as representing the stability they remembered from the 1960s and 1970s. The other terrorist organization, known as the Mouvement Islamist Armé, was associated with the FIS and reflected the attitudes of its more militant 'Afghani' elements – the people who had gone to Afghanistan in the 1980s to join the *mujahiddin* and fight the Russians. They had since returned, well-trained and aggressive, and were now intent on ridding their own country of un-Islamic elements. Like the Groupe, the Mouvement operated what amounted to death squads. In the period between the assassination of Boudiaf and the end of 1993 the two organizations together killed several hundreds. Their most distinguished victim was Kasdi Merbah, the first reforming prime minister, who was murdered in August 1993.

The response of the authorities to the wave of killings was initially to try to crush the terrorists. The mainstream of the military and the FLN, and the Western-educated middle classes, saw their country's problem chiefly as a matter of winning a war against subversion. They put much more emphasis on destroying the terrorists than on the reforms that were needed to undermine their support. This was true under both the Belaid Abdessalem government, which seemed always to be hankering after the old socialist certainties of the 1970s, and the more enlightened and practical government of Redha Malek, a former ambassador to Washington and member of the High Council of State, which succeeded it on 21 August 1993. By the end of 1993, however, it was clear that the policy of straight repression had failed and, encouraged by the French, the government began to pursue a two-pronged approach. On one hand it was keeping up its pressure on the FIS, arresting members it could identify and periodically killing terrorists in shoot-outs. The French authorities were helping by arresting the Front's representatives in France and trying to break up its fund-raising network. Under this relentless pressure, it was believed that the FIS was disbanding itself, though if this was true it was not leading to a drop in the number of terrorist incidents. At the same time the government was trying to find some moderate, or 'responsible', FIS or ex-FIS elements, with whom it might establish a dialogue on the country's future. Its intention was to move slowly towards reintroducing elections, for a parliament with limited powers, and it believed that if these were to bring an end to the violence and the parliament was to be an effective legislative body, part of the Islamic movement would have to be persuaded to co-operate. Success in its aim seemed likely to depend on whether it made sufficient progress in its anti-terrorist campaign, thus persuading the opposition to co-operate.

The Algerian people were profoundly depressed by the events of 1992 and 1993, not just because of the grim economic and political prospects, but because they felt the shame of failure. In the 1960s and 1970s they had developed an image of themselves as radical Third World revolutionaries, austere, disciplined and dedicated to making their country an industrial power. By the early 1990s this image had proved to be an illusion and their hopes had been shattered. The country's future was uncertain. People did not know whether in a few months they would still be living in a nominally socialist, secular state or in an Islamic republic. As they had done under the French, the Algerians in 1992 and 1993 were asking themselves what sort of a nation they were. Once more they were worrying about their identity.

8

The Search for a Reason

*The Arabs' disenchantment – divisions in society and between
states – the disruptive idea of unity – the longing for strength –
ill effects of bad government and people's tolerance of it –
ignorance and conspiracy theories*

The first seven chapters of this book tell an unhappy story of war
and defeat, bad government, corruption and economic failure. The
Arabs, needless to say, have been painfully aware of this history. They
have been particularly hurt and frustrated because their failure seems
to them so unjust and unexpected. In the back of every Arab's mind is
a memory of his people's past greatness, together with the knowledge
that Islam, which is God's last and most detailed revelation of His laws
to mankind, promises believers success. Muslim societies, armed with
God's rules for happiness, just government and prosperity, should be
the strongest in the world and the Arabs, being the people to whom
God first revealed his final law, should be the first among these societies.
They might not aspire to ruling the world, but the Arabs believe they
should at least be a major power. As evidence to support this idea they
have not only God's promise: when they look at their nation they see
they also have money and a large population. These alone ought to
have given them developed economies and military strength.

In their view of the world the Arabs are different from the peoples
of other developing countries. Obviously one can find some variation
in outlook between the peoples of Africa, South America and South-
East Asia, but the more prosperous classes of these regions have seemed
in the last decade or so to have shared a set of attitudes which are
secular, tolerant, materialistic and internationalist, and these have

tended in a loose fashion to link them to the industrialized countries. These 'modern' attitudes can certainly be found in the Arab world, but the Arabs *en masse* cannot embrace them and forget the older and deeper-rooted ideas of their culture. They cannot escape the knowledge that God has told them that they are special and superior. So in reacting to problems in recent years their instinct has been not to embrace foreign ideas but more vigorously to reject them and look back into their own history for an answer which is specifically Arab and Islamic.

This instinct is not new. In the eighteenth and nineteenth centuries it led the Arabs of the Ottoman empire to resist contact with Europeans, with the result that the communities which came to handle most of the region's foreign trade and so learned most from the foreigners were non-Arabs, or Arab Christians. In the later nineteenth century a similar reaction against foreign influence, materialism and corruption in Egypt produced the revolt of Arabi Pasha against the government of the Khedive Tewfiq and the Europeans who controlled his treasury.* In the last twenty years the atavistic instinct has helped the rise of Islamic fundamentalism. As has happened on previous occasions, while the present atavistic phase lasts relations between the Arabs and the outside world will no doubt deteriorate and the Arabs will become more bitter and resentful. Then there will be a gradual return to copying modern, foreign ideas, which is what happened during most of this century, up to about 1970.

If one takes the Arabs' failure, their unhappiness and their backward-looking reaction as given facts, it is reasonable to ask if there are any generalizations that can be made about why in the present century they were unsuccessful in the first place. There is obviously no key that unlocks a single complete explanation. Nor is it sensible to try to find a collection of causes wrapped up with the Arabs' psychology.

---

* In 1879 the British and French governments arranged for the Sultan in Constantinople to depose the man who was nominally his viceroy, the Khedive Ismail, who had become massively in debt to European banks. No debt relief was given to Ismail's successor, the Khedive Tewfiq, and the Egyptian people came increasingly to resent the European interference in its government's affairs. It had felt humiliated by its weakness in the face of the European powers since Napoleon's invasion at the end of the eighteenth century. In September 1881 a revolt of army officers under Arabi Pasha, backed by popular uprisings, forced the Khedive to install a nationalist government. European demands that this government resign led in May 1882 to serious riots in Alexandria, in which Europeans were killed and wounded. British forces intervened. Alexandria was bombarded and a force under Sir Garnet Wolseley defeated Arabi at Tel-el-Kebir in September. Arabi was exiled to Ceylon. From then until 1914 the British ruled Egypt, acting through the Khedive and representing, in theory, the Sultan.

Commenting on the psychology of peoples is interesting and relevant only on a general, fairly superficial level, and where it is mixed with other types of comments. Some of the comments I have to make on the Arabs' personality and culture I have made in Chapter 1 and others are woven into this and other chapters, but I do not propose to address the subject directly. An alternative approach is simply to tell the story of how events unfolded, as has been done in Chapters 2 to 4. Here I am going to comment on a few broad, and destructive, themes that seem to recur in any discussion of the Arab world.

If one asks the Arabs why they have had such an unhappy time in the last seventy years they will most often reply 'because we have been divided'. Nobody would argue with this answer, inside the Arab world or outside it.

The Arabs are divided at every level. In almost all their countries one can find serious rivalries within small towns and villages, as well as much bigger divisions between towns, tribes, regions and different ethnic and religious communities. The Palestinians' cause has been dogged by such divisions from the beginning. During the rebellion against the British in 1935–9 the instinct of much of the population was to put loyalty to family, village and district before loyalty to what they hoped would become their own independent country. The urban political leadership split between the Husseini family, which was militant, and its rival, the Nashashibi family, which was more prepared to co-operate with the authorities. This division was often reflected in the villages, where if one influential person supported the uprising his enemy would help the British. Rebel courts were used to settle old family scores. Volunteer fighters refused to join rebel bands that came from outside their own areas, or sometimes they were rejected if they tried to do so. Similar divisions have continued into modern times. The Israeli internal security service, Shin Bet, exploiting the little rivalries, has never had difficulty in recruiting Palestinian informers. The West Bank and Gaza leadership of the PLO, on the other hand, wasted a great deal of time after peace talks involving them got under way in October 1991 in organizing a different delegation for each round of the talks. The spokesmen and leaders of the teams remained the same from the beginning, but the delegates had to be changed so that each section of the population of the occupied territories – totalling under 2 million – was able to feel properly represented.

Most of the visible internal rivalries in the Arab countries are on a broader scale (though in Iraq when the south rose in rebellion at the end of the Gulf War and the strict hand of Saddam was temporarily lifted there were many family vendetta killings mixed with the assault on the army and the Baath Party). In Yemen, which admittedly is an especially lawless place, there are frequent tribal wars. In Algeria it has often been said since the military intervention of January 1992 that had the planned elections been allowed to take place and the FIS had won, there would have been civil war, because the Berber element in the population would not have accepted being governed by the Front.

The obvious disadvantage of these divisions, and many others like them, is that they make the Arab countries prone to manipulation by outsiders who can back a disaffected community in rebellion against the central government, as the Shah of Iran did with the Kurds in Iraq. They also weaken the countries in a more subtle way, in that they give every member of the population an ambivalent relationship with the state. This is best understood if one compares Arab attitudes with those in the West.

In the Western world the political process is accompanied by much bitter debate and appearance of disunity, but most members of the populations are fundamentally loyal to their governments and their countries, some of which have existed in their present shapes for several hundred years. However big and impersonal Western states may be, individuals have a sense, especially in times of war and in elections, of playing their own small roles as elements in the giant machine. In the Arab world, it would be wrong to say that this mentality does not exist at all. It was noticeable during the Iran-Iraq war that each side tried to encourage minorities in the other's army to desert – the Iranians appealed to Iraqi Shias and the Iraqis directed propaganda at the Arabs from the Iranian province of Khuzestan – but the minorities remained strikingly loyal to their nation states. Nevertheless, this type of loyalty is certainly weaker in the Arab world than it is in the West, because the countries, and indeed the very concept of the nation state, are new. Loyalty to the state exists side by side with several competing loyalties. These might come to the fore when people find themselves having to decide whether or not to help a relation get a job in the bureaucracy or, more seriously, shelter somebody who has been involved in subversive activity. In these cases they would have to take into account their obligations to their extended family, their village or town, their tribe, if they are part of one, their ethnic or religious group (Kurd, Alawite, Druze, Shia et cetera) and fellow members of the Islamic Umma, the community of the faithful. One consequence of this is that people's commitment to the state can never be more than partial. To give an extreme case as an example, a soldier of, say, Syria or Iraq might be personally brave and often fight well for his country, but, under pressure, it is always possible that he will decide that the continuation of his country and its government is less important to him than his village, tribe or ethnic or religious community and that he would rather desert, return home and help the smaller unit survive under whatever regime might be imposed by the victorious enemy. Thus the whole idea of the state is weaker, and therefore possibly less durable in the Arab countries than it is in the industrialized world.

The internal weakness of some of the Arab states in the last seventy years has been compounded by the fact that their rulers have been seen as representing just one faction of their peoples. In Lebanon after the French left the government was thought, rightly, by the population to represent first and foremost the Maronite Christians. In Iraq from 1922 to 1958 and in Jordan until about the mid-1960s the governments were believed to represent the Hashemite family, which had come from the Hijaz and been imposed on the people by the British. In the last twenty years the governments of Iraq and Syria have clearly represented in one case the factional interests of the Sunni Muslims of the region around Takrit and in the other the Alawites — albeit not exclusively.

The divisions inside the Arab states are mirrored in divisions between them. A few of these are based on important ideological differences which have led one country to interfere in the internal affairs of another. In the early 1990s Sudan offended Egypt, Saudi Arabia and the United Arab Emirates by backing militant Islamic groups in those countries, either through arming them, in Egypt's case, or sending them subversive propaganda in the form of tape-recorded sermons. More often the cause of division has been a mixture of a few matters of substance and a great deal of petty rivalry. Syria and Iraq have suffered from this type of quarrel, virtually without a break, since the Iraqi revolution of 1958. Almost the only substantial problem has been their argument over the division of the Euphrates waters; the rest of their antagonism has been based on clashes of personality and competition for influence in the Arab world. Equally pointless have been numerous frontier disputes dividing countries that ought to be friends. These have occurred particularly in the Gulf, where in the last few years there have been little crises over territory involving Saudi Arabia and Qatar, Qatar and Bahrain and the UAE and Oman. In only one of these instances has there been the remotest possibility of an undiscovered oil field lying under the disputed land; the major reason for dispute in every case has been old, deep-rooted family and tribal jealousy, often complicated by rivalries within the ruling families on each side. All of the countries involved have been members of the Gulf Co-operation Council, which was formed by the Arabian Peninsula oil producers in 1981 to co-ordinate their foreign and security policies.

Tension has also arisen from some Arab governments and peoples not wholly accepting the independence of other Arab states. Since the modern Arab world was constructed after the First World War, there has been a feeling in nationalist circles that greater Syria should not have been divided, and although this idea is not often translated into the specific statement that Syria, Lebanon and Jordan should not exist as independent states, it is sometimes implied that they do not have a right to completely independent action. It has been used in this way by the Palestinians. Having abandoned their country in the face of the Israeli assault in 1948, they have since relied on other Arab countries to help them get it back, and whenever any other Arab or foreigner has questioned whether they have had the right to inflict successive wars on their neighbours, their reply has been, in effect: 'Ah, but we were only divided by the work of the imperialists, we are really one country and it is the duty of our compatriots to help us.' This argument is generally extended to the Arabs of the other former Ottoman provinces, Iraq and parts of the Arabian Peninsula, and it can easily be widened to embrace North Africa.

More specific cases of states' existence being challenged concern the Gulf oil producers. The obvious example is Kuwait, which is claimed by Iraq, partly on the grounds that in the eighteenth century the land which makes up the state was part of the Ottoman province of Basra – before the Al-Sabah and other families established a settlement there and negotiated for themselves a form of autonomy, which much later was recognized by the British. The other, unstated, basis of Iraq's claim is that it would like to have Kuwait's large and easily operated oil fields. In this respect Iraq is only expressing a belief common, at an unofficial level, in the poor Arab countries that the Gulf states and Saudi Arabia are ridiculously rich for the small size of their populations and ought not to exist as independent states at all. Alternatively it is said they should share with their neighbours substantial parts of their revenues, not just the 2–5 per cent of gross national product they gave in the 1970s and 1980s. The poor Arabs' jealousy and appetite for more money is sharpened by what they see as the vulgar and hypocritical behaviour of the rich when they visit Egypt and Morocco on holiday. And the rich Arabs clearly feel a reciprocal sense of guilt. One sees this in their tolerance of corruption on the part of the 'poor' Arabs (and other 'poor' Muslims) who work for them, and in the way they pay foreign Arab journalists, particularly in London, to write nice things about them.* Their behaviour suggests they feel there is some justice in their being exploited by the people around them.

To give their claims intellectual substance the poor Arabs have advanced the theory that the presence of oil in the Arabian Peninsula is merely a geological coincidence, which does not give the people of that land any more right to the oil than the other Arabs have. They have further persuaded themselves that the struggle for 'control' of Arab oil, which before the mid-1970s was produced by foreign companies, was waged in Cairo, Baghdad, Damascus and Beirut, which were the intellectual centres of the Arab world. This notion is simply not true, though that did not prevent the Syrian editor of a dubious London-based magazine saying to me bluntly in 1988 'Kuwait's oil is my oil and my country's oil'.

A second justification for the claims of the poor is that the borders of the oil states, like those in the Levant, were drawn by the British with the intention of keeping the Arabs weak. This idea was expressed in typically flowery language by Saddam Hussein on 7 August 1990, five days after he had taken Kuwait. He began by greeting his troops and saying that new suns and moons would shine, stars glitter and light expel darkness. Then he explained that the darkness to which he was referring was the result of 'Baghdad's eye being put out and its mind ruined by the rule of the foreigner', and eventually he stated that 'the malicious Westerners intentionally multiplied the number of countries with the result that the Arab nation could not achieve the integration needed to realize its full capability. When fragmenting the Arab homeland they intentionally distanced the majority of the population and areas of cultural depth from riches and their source'.

The ideas put forward by Saddam have no historical validity, as one sees if one examines how Iraq, Saudi Arabia and the Gulf states were created, but to much of the Arab population they have great emotional appeal. Not the least part of their attraction is that they put the blame for Arab disunity squarely on the foreigner.

---

* In London in the late 1980s and early 1990s there were seven papers being published daily in Arabic, and some fifty Arabic magazines. The city had taken Beirut's role as the publishing centre of the Arab world. Several of the magazines existed mainly to make money out of blackmail. They would attack a person or government and wait to be paid to reverse their opinion, which they would do in the most obvious and shameless fashion, partly in order to show their next victim how the game was played. Alternatively they would hire themselves to flatter a person or attack his enemies.

It is not difficult to see from the experience of the Arabian Peninsula oil states that ideas of Arab unification are as likely to widen divisions between countries as narrow them. Unity on the terms envisaged by those who cast envious eyes at the Gulf means either the absorption of small states by bigger ones, or the sharing of national budgets. In these cases a call for unity can be as divisive an act as the reopening of a frontier dispute. An incidental consequence of this is that in discussing the Arab world, it is not always easy to decide which topics should come under the broad heading of 'division' and which under 'unity'.

The cause of unity is dear to the Arabs. Their traditional way of reacting to outside threats or disputes between themselves has been to declare that they should unite; the strongest calls have often come in the aftermath of small inter-Arab military confrontations. Sometimes the leaders making the calls have meant just that they should unite to co-ordinate their policies, sometimes they have been talking of the actual unification of their states.

Both of these concepts of unity blossomed in the 1950s, when the feeling of nationalist politicians, journalists and members of the intelligentsia in general was that it would be only through unity that the Arabs would regain Palestine and expel the imperial powers which hampered their development. The Palestinians had not yet found their voice after the shock of being expelled from their home and at this time contributed little to the nationalist ferment. The great exponent of unity was Gamal Abdel-Nasser, though the Egyptian President was more interested in uniting the Arab world in the informal sense, of having all the other governments loyally following his policies, than in joining together countries. As it happened, in the late 1950s Nasser achieved success, if that is the right word, on both these fronts. For a few years he dominated the politics of the Arab world and between 1958 and 1961 he was pulled into a union with Syria. Neither of these forms of unity was very happy. The union with Syria was more a take-over of that state by Egypt than a merger on equal terms, and it failed because it trampled on the interests of Syrian politicians and businessmen. And Nasser's leadership of the Arab world lasted for only a few years, from 1956 to about 1960, because however impressed by him they may have been the other Arab leaders had interests that did not necessarily coincide with his and eventually resented being bullied into following his policies. They were particularly sensitive to his appealing over their heads, via the radio station Voice of the Arabs, to their own peoples. There was then, and there remains, a strong element of political blackmail in Arab nationalism.

Since Nasser's day, in spite of the efforts of the Palestinians, attempts to unite the policies of the Arab countries have been feebler or shorter lived, and only the Libyan leader, Colonel Gaddafi, has been a passionate advocate of joining countries together. On several occasions Gaddafi has demanded the union of Libya with its neighbours, and once, in 1969, he managed to construct a loose confederation with Egypt, Sudan and Syria, though this never amounted to anything of substance. Gaddafi's other overtures were rejected, either before negotiations could begin or within days or weeks of the other states' leaders being persuaded to sign ill-considered declarations of union. None of the prospective partners, Malta, Egypt, for a second time, and Tunisia, twice, wanted to join an unpredictable leader with an eccentric ideology. In most cases these later proposals of unity were made by Gaddafi on impulse, though in 1973 his courtship of President Sadat took some months and had to be backed by a civilian army sent to demolish an Egyptian frontier post. When there were acceptances, by Egypt in September 1973 and Tunisia in January 1974, the latter after only two days of negotiations, the main thought of the other leaders was that they might get some of Libya's oil revenues. The eventual rejection of all Gaddafi's initiatives, like the end of attempts to unify policy by other states at other times, led to periods of recrimination and military incidents on the borders.

To all the Arab nationalists who backed the idea in the 1950s, 1960s and early 1970s, and have hankered after it since, part of the appeal of unity has been simply emotional. Given that the Arabs share a language and a history, in certain moods every one of them feels that they should be a single people, that his own state is artificial and that he should be united with his kith and kin. More important, though, is another more calculated belief. This is that if the Arabs unite they will be strong. They remember how successful they were in 1973 when for a brief moment two states joined forces to attack Israel and most of the rest backed them with oil production cuts. They feel that if they were able to sustain this sort of unity they would be able to defeat their enemy and show their independence of the West and their contempt for its culture. Unity, they imagine, would make them successful and give them pride in themselves. Though they may not acknowledge it, the desire for unity in this context is no more than a desire to find a formula for becoming great and powerful.

The longing to be strong is one of the great motivating forces in the Arab world; to appreciate this is a key to understanding what happens in the region. But the fact that a people wants something and appears to have the means of achieving it, by unity, does not mean that either the aim or the method are practicable.

In the Arabs' case there are two reasons why attempts at unity, applying to either policies or states, fail. One is that they damage established interests. The Arab countries may be only partly evolved as nation states in terms of their capturing the loyalties of their own peoples and being accepted by their neighbours, but they have still evolved far enough for there to be strong vested interests in favour of their remaining in being. Governments and political parties do not want to dissolve themselves, or share their revenues or have to pursue dangerous common policies, particularly the sorts of traditional Palestinian-inspired policy which used to involve conservative states being asked to risk their friendships with Western countries and expose themselves to attacks by Israel.

The other matter that makes unity difficult is that for all the periodic enthusiasm the people feel for ideas of brotherhood, there is no overwhelming cultural logic in unification. There are many similarities in character between the Arab peoples. They are mostly Muslim, their families play hugely important roles in their lives, they relate better to personalities than institutions, and they dislike confrontation, which may mean compromising rather than pursuing a dispute to the point of war, or not wanting to give a direct 'no' to a business proposition. They are also very sensitive to losing face. But at the same time it is striking how the citizens of each country think of themselves as different from and superior to their neighbours. Although to an outsider the Arabs may seem quite similar in a general sense, each country has a national personality which tends to separate it from its neighbours. It is remarkable how little even well-educated and well-travelled Arabs know about what is happening in the countries next to them. And it is striking what a lively disdain they have for them – how ready they are to say how primitive their human rights are, how they are going to have the most terrible trouble once the current ruler (who may have been in power for twenty years or so) goes, and, the most cunning insult of all, how they lack a middle class, which is a way of saying that the neighbour is less developed than the speaker's own state. Comments of this sort may stem more from differences in perception than from real differences, and this might make an outsider smile, but differences in perception are of great political importance. They indicate that the people of most Arab countries would feel unhappy at the thought of having their government run, in part, by people from other countries, or having to adopt the others' laws or administrative practices. This is before they even consider what unification might do to their private political or business interests.*

The Arabs' craving for success has not led them only into ill-conceived attempts at union. It has been one of the influences that have caused them, with even more unhappy results, to tolerate bad government. To a surprising degree since the early 1960s the Arabs have endured authoritarian and incompetent regimes with little protest in the form of uprisings (the Muslim Brotherhood's rebellion at Hama is the obvious exception) or even conspicuous agitation or criticism. It is only since the mid-1980s, as the rest of this book explains, that there has been a swell of political ferment across the Arab world.

From the time the liberal post-Second World War political society was swept away, the Arab regimes have been justifying the inroads they have made into the freedom of their peoples by saying that in order to confront Israel their societies have to be united behind them,

---

* In May 1990 two Arab states, the Yemen Arab Republic, northern Yemen, and the Popular Democratic Republic of Yemen, southern Yemen, joined in a union which at first seemed likely to be a success, but the circumstances were untypical of Arab politics, which is why the union is not discussed above. Although the countries had not before been under one government,their people had a common culture and considered themselves to be one nation.

The matter of vested interests did not initially obstruct the union because after the collapse of East Germany in late 1989 and early 1990 the southern government faced bankruptcy and possible revolution. The negotiation of a merger with the north, in which they would be given posts in the combined government, seemed to the southern leaders a rather attractive option.

After the union the frontier was abolished, but the south's army and security force remained separate from the north's. Some new social and economic tensions emerged. It was realized that the southerners, having lived for 150 years under British and then Communist rule, were very much more sophisticated and secular than the rather isolated and xenophobic people of the north. The southerners were disenchanted by the slow pace of economic liberalization and they claimed they were discriminated against in the civil service: northerners were being paid bigger salaries than they were.

In late 1993 and early 1994 the tension between the north and south became serious enough to threaten the union. In February 1994 the southern leadership moved tanks and artillery to the old border and to the area of its major oil field at Shabwa. What precipitated the crisis was its justified belief that Ali Abdullah Saleh, the President, was trying to squeeze it out of government and, in effect, run the whole country himself.

If the united Yemen was to break up the reason would be that, in the end, the vested interests of one of the parties had been trampled on. One would be able to say that the union had been too hasty, the rulers of the dominant party too greedy and ambitious, and the government machines in general too unsophisticated to have been able to tackle the difficult task of uniting two states. In other words the flaws that made unity impossible elsewhere were present in Yemen as well.

and therefore normal freedoms of speech and political opposition have to be temporarily suspended. The people have accepted these arguments, partly because the regimes' security services have seen that they have not had the option; but also because in the eyes of many the proposition the governments have been putting to them has not seemed unreasonable. Most Arabs would be prepared to tolerate bad government for a long time if that meant defeating the national enemy. The strength of this feeling came to the surface at the time of the Iraqi invasion of Kuwait when the populations of all the poor Arab countries, bar Egypt, rallied immediately to Saddam Hussein. Everybody knew that Saddam ran one of the most unpleasant regimes in the world, but this seemed unimportant beside the prospect of his using the wealth he would get from Kuwait to confront Israel. He had been saying that this was his intention for a year before the invasion; his famous threat to 'burn half Israel' had been published in all the Arab countries. Soon after the invasion he was made to look still more patriotic when the Western powers joined to expel him from Kuwait and he responded by linking the possibility of his withdrawal to Israel's withdrawal from the occupied territories. In these circumstances even people who should have known better found themselves caught up in the enthusiasm for Saddam. The Association of Tunisian Lawyers thought of chartering an aircraft to fly to Baghdad to make Saddam an honorary member, but it was frustrated by the air embargo that had been imposed on Iraq and by the mildly discouraging attitude of its own government. At the same time half of the members of the League of Human Rights in Tunis declared their support for the Iraqi leader by saying that 'the rights of peoples [in other words the Arabs in general and the Palestinians] come before the rights of individuals'.

The great disappointment for the Arabs, it need hardly be said, is that neither Saddam nor any other leader has been able to defeat Israel, and the people have been left – to different degrees in different countries – with the unhappiness and weakness that comes from being deprived of their freedom and none of the promised benefit. The ill effects of bad government are well known. It has caused many of the most able and most principled people to leave their countries and go to live in the free societies of Europe and America. This has not only impoverished intellectual and political life, which, admittedly, under the nastiest governments would have been rendered sterile anyway, it has deprived those countries where some private sector economic activity has been allowed to continue of the people who might have shown enterprise. It has also deprived them of those people's capital. The concentration of decision making at the top of governments and the fear of what might happen to people who make mistakes has discouraged the taking of responsibility, which has made Arab administration, and Arab armies, slow and rigid. The suppression of a free press and the threat of imprisonment that hangs over people who might be overheard, or betrayed, when criticizing their governments has stifled the debate that in freer societies exposes corruption and leads to the changing of failed policies.

Worst of all, bad government has led to wars, which in this context means not so much the war with Israel, the idea of which commands popular support, but some of the other large and small regional conflicts that have erupted during the last forty years. The list of these wars is a long and gloomy one and it includes two small wars between the previously divided Yemens and Egypt's expedition to north Yemen in the 1960s; the subversion in the southern Omani province of Dhofar which was backed by the south Yemen government in the late 1960s and early 1970s; the two long civil wars in southern Sudan; Libya's wars with almost all of its neighbours and particularly its long expedition into Chad; Syria's intervention in the Jordanian-Palestinian war of 1970 and its later intervention in Lebanon; Iraq's war against the Kurds and, on a much bigger scale, its wars against Iran in 1980–8 and the US-led coalition in 1991.

In some cases it is possible to sympathize with the governments that have gone to war: for example, Syria sent its army into Lebanon because it feared that the factional bloodshed there might spread into its own country. But more often the wars have been caused by the greed, personal ambition or petty quarrels of leaders, or their inability to negotiate and give ground without feeling they are losing face in the eyes of their people. All of these faults are characteristic of absolutist regimes, and particularly absolutist republican regimes. It is rare for democracies to become involved in wars on these grounds, and quite rare for monarchies to be involved. Certainly the monarchies in the Arab world have begun fewer wars than the republics. The weakness of the republics is that, having poor claims to legitimacy in many cases, they have come to represent themselves to their people as being perfect, or at least stronger and better than their predecessors. When the Iraqi regime, for example, pursues its claim to the whole of the Shatt al-Arab waterway, it cannot compromise and give away half, which would be in line with normal international practice and is what a democracy would do. To make such a gesture would be to show that it was incapable of giving its people the faultless leadership it promises. So it goes to war. The human life it expends hardly enters its thoughts. In the eyes of governments in all the more populous Middle Eastern countries, and in many other developing countries, human life is not something of great value. One reason, raised in the other contexts earlier, is that in the Middle East national pride matters more to people than it does in the West. Another is that the families of the people who are dying have no free press or parliaments to speak to their governments on those occasions when they decide that the cause being fought for is not worth the loss of their loved ones. Significantly, human life is valued more in the countries that have small populations, Saudi Arabia and the Gulf states, because here there is considerable contact between rulers and ruled.

The reasons why the Arabs have been prepared to tolerate such callous, incompetent and weakening government for so long – apart from their concern with the conflict with Israel – are rooted in the unsophisticated nature of their society, its fragmentation, the lack of emphasis on the rights of individuals and fears that more liberal governments might not be effective.

Much of the Arab population is little affected by the morality of its government – except when its children are killed in wars. People who cannot read and do not have enough money to travel abroad will not be concerned if their government censors newspapers or does not give them passports as of right. Other misdeeds, such as the execution of ministers, may affect the people a little in an indirect sense but are too far removed from anything with which they have had any contact to be of much interest. For most individuals in Arab countries the important aim in life is to ensure their own and their families' survival, helped by the government subsidies they receive, and if possible attain a modest degree of prosperity. If a member of a family that has climbed a few rungs up the professional ladder can get a post in the government, or finds himself working as a contractor for it, he will exploit this position for everything he can get. He will be far more concerned with benefiting himself and his family than he would be about honesty or his obligation to the government, which he may not recognize at all. The government is something which exists to benefit him, and he will not be interested in questions of whether it is decent or competent. Issues of human rights such as a free press, freedom of speech, governments consulting parliaments chosen by free elections and freedom from arbitrary arrest and imprisonment, only matter to the educated middle classes. These people, although they are growing in number, make up a much smaller proportion of the population than they do in the West, and are less important.

None of this means that the populations in Arab countries are not thoroughly cynical about their governments. They see that even in the most socialist countries the people at the top are rich. They have a vague feeling that the system is unfair and biased against them, and they believe that they are being exploited – though in the 1960s and 1970s governments were able to deflect this resentment on to foreigners, particularly America, the former imperial powers and the oil companies. It is partly because they are cynical about them that the people are so happy to exploit their governments if they are given the chance. What is important for the argument here, though, is that being cynical and caring about human rights issues are two different things. Ordinary people would like to have better, fairer governments, but they do not necessarily equate this with having elections or allowing a free press or freedom of speech, mainly for the benefit of the middle classes. They do not believe that a freer political society run by a broader section of the intelligentsia would necessarily be any less corrupt or of any greater benefit to them. They also have a suspicion in the back of their minds that democracy might lead to chaos.

Fundamental to this view of the relationship of government and the people is that the rights of the individual are not of overwhelming importance, in the eyes of either party. In the Arab world, and in other developing countries, the community – the family, village, ethnic or religious groups, or, occasionally, the nation state – carries more weight than the individual, and it is regarded as the individual's duty to be aware of the community and not bring embarrassment or dishonour on it. If a person does something rebellious, even if his act is dictated by conscience, and the authorities imprison and torture him for it, the opinion of society will be that he has mainly himself to blame. The lack of sympathy may stem either from the idea that the bigger social or political unit has been embarrassed, if society is opposed to the ideas of the person being held, or it may come simply from the view that the individual's conscience and his (questionable) right of protest are not of great value.

This attitude towards conformity and the rights of the individual was illustrated by a hypothetical example I was given once by two Arab journalists. They suggested that if a drunken man was arrested by the police in Britain or France, just for sitting on a pavement, civil liberties groups would object on the grounds that he had not been doing any harm to anyone. But in the Arab world – even in those countries (the majority) where alcohol is legal – there would be no objection because the drunk would be considered to have been behaving in an undignified and shameful way that did not conform to the norms of society. Individualism or eccentricity are qualities that are not much understood or valued in Arab society. This might seem surprising, given that the Arabs are not particularly good at working in teams in large corporations or relating to institutions rather than individuals. The key to the paradox is that to be individualistic in the sense of preferring to run a shop than to work for a corporation is to conform to the Arab tradition, but to be individualistic in the sense of being drunk in public or making a political protest is not.

It has often been said, within the Arab world and outside it, that this whole body of social values has been formed by Islam. The idea that Islam puts the public good before the individual is put forward by journalists and lawyers, and by officials of the two Islamic regimes in the Middle East, Iran and Sudan, who might be presumed to be speaking with authority. The idea was summed up in the remark that an Iranian minister made to me in an interview: 'our human rights are different from yours'. It is given substance by the response of the Sudanese government to the United Nations Committee on Human Rights, which in 1991 accused it of not having met its obligations under the International Covenant on Civil and Political Rights. To most of the charges levelled at it the government replied simply that the provisions of the Covenant did not conform to Islam. Further authority for these types of arguments comes from an often-quoted statement of the Prophet Mohammad, who is supposed to have said: 'Do not abuse those who bear rule. If they act uprightly they shall have their reward, and your duty is to show gratitude. If they do evil they shall bear the burden, and your duty is to endure patiently. They are a chastisement which God inflicts on those whom he will'.*

Islam is a religion that puts more stress on the community and less on the individual than Christianity does, but it is wrong to cite it as the main cause of the Arab governments' poor human rights records or the community orientation of Arab society. The tradition of people being urged by their teachers not to rebel against bad rulers, on the grounds that the strife rebellion would cause would be worse than the oppression it was meant to remove, is as much part of Christian belief as it is of Islam. Clerics spoke on this theme in Europe during the Middle Ages and the sixteenth century. Philip Melanchthon, a follower of Martin Luther and one of the thinkers of the early Reformation in Germany, wrote in 1521: 'The magistrates' administration of the sword

---

* The compilation of the actions and sayings of the Prophet is known as the Hadith. In the two centuries after the Prophet's death there was circulating in the Muslim world an increasing number of sayings, many of which are obviously false, and it became necessary for scholars to produce a definitive compilation. This was done in the ninth century. In spite of the scholars' claims that they had included only the best authenticated statements, there remains an element of doubt attached to some of the sayings.

is consonant with piety . . . If princes command anything contrary to God, this is to be obeyed . . . the magistrate is to be suffered for charity's sake in all cases where change is impossible without public commotion or sedition'. This statement, one of many similar in its period, is not dissimilar to the Prophet's.

The fact that officials of Islamic republics state that their societies' human rights are different from the West's is, likewise, not proof that this is so. Many (though not all) of the leaders and senior officials in Iran and Sudan are far from Godly men – they have joined the Islamic movement to gain power – and they use Islam as a means of defending their own brutal governments. To attribute whatever they do, good or bad, to Islam has become part of their self-justifying rhetoric.

The conventional wisdom of much of the liberal intelligentsia in the Middle East on Islam putting public good before the individual does not go unchallenged. The dissenting view was summed up by a left-wing Egyptian human rights lawyer who told me that, in his opinion, 'to say that Islam has a different concept of human rights is just an attempt to use it to stop the popular drive towards more freedom'. Those who support this view would argue that the Koran addresses each individual and makes him accountable for his own acts. It does not put over him a religious establishment with spiritual authority (except in Shia societies). Each individual has a direct relationship with God, which makes the ruler bound to treat his subjects justly and the individual bound to try to change whatever he sees in society that is wrong. The idea that the individual has a duty to endure bad rule without protest is a medieval accretion. It was added to Islam by jurists whose views reflected the values of a merchant society and their own need to compromise with their rulers.

If these lines of argument are right – and they are put forward by many people, both secular and devout – the conclusion must be that Middle Eastern attitudes to the individual, freedom, human rights and bad government in general have been determined less by Islam than by the fragmented, tribal or community-based nature of the region's society.

It is because the Arabs (and Iranians) are very aware of the fragmentation of their society, as well as having their attitudes conditioned by it, that many will say quite openly that authoritarian government may not be bad for them. This is a final, very conscious, reason why they tolerate it. They are aware not only of the major episodes of (partly) sectarian violence – the Lebanese civil war and the rebellion of the Muslim Brotherhood against Assad's government in Syria. They see all the minor family murders and feuds, the gang wars in the Nile delta, the settling of scores that occurs whenever law and order collapses as it did in Iraq in March 1991. In effect they look into the bubbling cauldron of Middle Eastern society and see the advantage of living under governments that are able to keep the lid on. It would be wrong to say, as it sometimes has been, that confronted with an episode such as the massacre at Hama, any Arab people who had been through the bombings and assassinations that the Syrians had endured during the previous few years would endorse the destruction of an entire quarter of a town. Most Arabs understand the reasons for such an action, but even simple people if asked for an opinion, say that a massacre on that scale was too brutal. It is acknowledged that in controlling turbulent elements governments have to be severe, but it is thought that the degree of severity should be proportionate to the crime.

One of the consequences of bad government, a controlled media and the introspective nature of Middle Eastern society, with its concentration on community loyalties, is that the Arabs (and the Iranians) are surprisingly ignorant of the world outside. This is something that strikes any Westerner who spends time in the region. Even in the Gulf states and Saudi Arabia, whose citizens have much contact with foreigners and travel to Europe and America frequently, one finds that people may be well informed on currency movements and the latest chat on the prospects of the Western economies but know surprisingly little about how Western societies and governments operate. Even those who live in the West or visit it frequently on holiday do not have much understanding of it because, in most cases, when they are there they mix with other Arabs, principally their own relations, and take no interest in the culture, history or institutions of the countries they are in. They enjoy the West for the social freedom (including the chance to read free, scurrilous newspapers) and the shopping.

It goes without saying that in the more isolated and authoritarian countries the less well educated people, who have never had the money to travel, have even less knowledge of the Western world. It is these types of people, who include minor functionaries in the civil service, whom Westerners find are suspicious of them when, for example, they say they want to travel to the provinces or visit a historical site because they are interested in learning about the country in which they are staying. Having no interest in any other country themselves, the officials are only too ready to believe that anyone who is interested in theirs must have a dubious motive, probably as a spy.

Ignorance leads the Arabs to a distorted view of how the Western countries regard them. This, obviously, puts them at a disadvantage in their dealings with the West. It is still widely believed in the Arab world and Iran that the former imperial powers and America want to manipulate these countries and curb their independence, if not actually recolonize them. A remarkable example of this belief was displayed by the Iraqi ambassador in London two years before the invasion of Kuwait. We were having lunch with an Arab theologian at the Athenaeum and after warming up with some rather suspicious remarks during the meal, over coffee in the reading room the ambassador launched into a tirade which began with the assertion that Britain, and in particular Mrs Thatcher, had never forgiven his country for the nationalization of the Iraq Petroleum Company (owned partly by BP and Shell) in 1972. He then claimed that the Foreign Office wanted to undermine Iraq because it was the only force that was able to put some resolution into the weak Saudi and Gulf rulers, whom the British and Americans were exploiting to force down the price of oil so that they could rob the Arabs of their only resource. One of the methods being used to discredit Iraq was the spreading of false rumours, such as the recent allegations that poisonous gas had been dropped on the Kurds (which it had). In the long run, the ambassador concluded, Britain would very much like to install a new puppet government (like the monarchy) in Baghdad, get back IPC's concession and control Iraq as it had in the days of the mandate. Most likely the ambassador would have acknowledged to himself that half of what he was saying was just the Baghdad party line, but the other half he probably believed. And he must have thought his ideas were at least intelligent enough to be worth telling to a Western journalist.

There would have been no point in my explaining to the ambassador that the idea of regaining an empire is of not the slightest interest to the British, or the French; that for much of the modern liberal intelligentsia memories of empire are an embarrassment; that since the 1960s there has been a complete change in the attitudes of electorates, establishments and governments in Britain and the other Western countries; that in the new 'caring' society human rights are genuinely important to the media and the public; and that the main interest of most Western governments in their foreign policies is the promotion of trade. Most Arabs, like the ambassador, know nothing of the social changes underlying these new attitudes, and they are not very interested in learning about them. Talking on these themes a young and intelligent banker in the Gulf revealed to me that he was completely ignorant of the fact that the Suez expedition had marked a watershed in Britain's view of itself in the world, knew nothing about what the '60s meant, and believed that British society was pretty much the same in the early 1990s as it had been at the end of the Second World War.

Both the ambassador's and the banker's views represent straightforward ignorance. But they are related to the Arab belief that the destinies of peoples and nations are not formed by complex economic and social pressures but directed by conspiracies. This idea is almost universal in the Middle East. Some of the conspiracy theories that have been put to me recently are: that the Bank of England and other Western central banks engineered the collapse of the Bank of Credit and Commerce International because they could not face the prospect of their own banks having to compete with a major successful bank from the Muslim world; that the United States and France had manipulated the military intervention in Algeria in January 1992, the proof being that there had been 'not one word of protest from those countries since'; that President Bush must have organized the break-up of the USSR, because America had been the main country to benefit; and that in early 1990 Mrs Thatcher had taken a provocatively tough line after the Iraqis had arrested the journalist Farzad Bazoft, so that Saddam would be forced into hanging him, the long-term purpose of this being to provoke a confrontation which would allow Thatcher and Bush to mount an expedition to destroy the one Arab country that was becoming an international power. The person who voiced this last, quite common, theory added that a further consideration for Mrs Thatcher was that she represented a constituency that had a large number of Jewish voters.

In most cases Arab conspiracy theories involve those who hold them blaming foreigners for what has gone wrong. Thereby they avoid the shame of having to admit that the event was their own societies' fault. The same thinking leads people to deny or alter actual historical facts, to make them coincide with what they would like to believe. After the end of the Gulf War a view put forward frequently in Yemen was that the reason the allied armies had left Iraq so promptly was that they had been driven out by Iraqi forces. Similarly, since 1988 Iraqis, Palestinians and many other Arab nationalists have maintained that Saddam Hussein never used poison gas on the Kurds, ignoring the testimony of the Kurds themselves, the accounts of the journalists who went to the region soon afterwards and the photographs of the dead bodies. This tendency to self-deception is remarked on even by the Arabs themselves. An Egyptian ex-minister told me that 'people here think with their emotions more than they think with their minds'.

It will be argued that the Arabs' belief in plots and related fantasies is not politically important, that it is no more than a cultural quirk. This view might be supported by the fact that in their heart of hearts the Arabs know that part of what they are claiming when they put forward a conspiracy theory is coming from their own imaginations. Also 'the plot' is a more popular explanation for events among the older generation than it is among the young. This is because when people who are now in their fifties and sixties were young their countries really were ruled or influenced by Britain or France, and the people who were teaching them about politics knew the time when they had been ruled by the Ottomans. As a radical Iranian newspaper said in 1992, 'it is the people of the old school who tell you that the Revolution was a British plot and reply when you question this that "the proof is, there's no trace".'

The problem with dismissing the liking for conspiracy theories as an unimportant cultural quirk is that the trait is obviously linked to the theorists' general ignorance of the outside world, and this is clearly a disadvantage for any society. The belief in plots, combined with ignorance, leads the Arabs to exaggerate the power of the West and misjudge its motives, making them believe that it is hostile and manipulative when it is more likely to be morally censorious, occasionally concerned with upholding states' sovereignty and/or protecting its oil interests, generally interested in promoting its exports, and often indifferent to Arab issues – or concerned but unable to see how it can influence events. At the same time the plot theorists make themselves underestimate the power of their own countries and fail to blame their own governments for events for which they are culpable. Applying this to one of the theories listed earlier: if the Jordanian who produced the idea that the Algerian coup had been engineered by France and America could have brought himself to acknowledge that the Algerian army and the FLN were perfectly capable of carrying out a coup themselves, he would have been forced to take a view on whether their intervention had been right or wrong, and then he would have had to address the whole issue of how democracy should be introduced into the Arab world in a way which would avoid either military intervention or the electorate falling into the hands of Islamic fundamentalists.

In the same way one can argue that the Arabs' belief that they are only pawns in other peoples' political games for many years prevented them playing a more active diplomatic role in resolving the conflict with Israel and winning some sort of a state for the Palestinians. Their instinct between 1967 and 1993 was most often to turn to the West and say, in effect, 'we can do nothing, you have put us in this position, now you have to help us, the solution is in your hands'. In a sense this position was reasonable, given that the Arabs had failed to defeat Israel in battle and that Israel's willingness to make concessions depended partly on America's willingness to put pressure on it. Yet the Arabs themselves did little diplomatically to make Western governments and public opinion want to help them. They hardly ever put forward peace plans of their own to try to draw Israel and the West into talks and except in 1973, when they used the oil weapon, no leader (except Sadat) gave the West any political or economic incentive to arrange a peace between them and the Israelis. It is true that part of the reason for this was that Arab diplomacy was not very sophisticated; most Arab embassies (other than Egypt's) in Western capitals are in Western terms no more than expanded consular sections. But the more important reason is that the Arabs did not appreciate their own diplomatic and economic potential, except in crude confrontational terms, and overestimated the power of Western governments to put pressure on a country such as Israel without their electorates being fully behind the policy.

None of this analysis is intended to be patronizing. It is put forward because the Arabs' liking for conspiracy theories and their ignorance of the West are damaging to them and stem, in part, from bad government.

Obviously among members of the older generation there are people whose views are based on old suspicion and are not likely to be changed, but among the young belief in conspiracies is partly a product of the incomplete, boring and occasionally distorted information they are fed by their own countries' media. The television and radio is of a low standard everywhere in the Arab world. There are very few news comment programmes and those that are broadcast are uncontroversial. It is practically unheard of for Westerners or other foreigners to be interviewed. In four countries, Lebanon, Egypt, Algeria and Yemen, the press is virtually free, but elsewhere it is owned or controlled by governments. In most countries it is difficult for people to criticize their own governments, write about embarrassing issues such as the collapse of BCCI, or debate matters that are supposed to be the preserve of senior members of the governments, particularly the conduct of foreign policy.

In these conditions it is not surprising that the Arab public is ill informed. The lack of open discussion of the governments' successes and failures and other events of public interest that are regarded as being in some way 'sensitive' encourages the development of misunderstanding and myth. And when there has been a failure of government policy the lack of a public debate makes it all the more likely to be repeated.

2

Reform

9

The Demand for Legitimate Government

*Expectations of change – impact of satellite TV – definitions of
legitimacy – Moroccan and Saudi monarchies – balancing old
and new – legitimacy of Egyptian government – characteristics
of illegitimate government – destruction of institutions –
possibility of creating political legitimacy*

In the last ten years there has been a growing feeling in the Arab world
that there must be change. The realization by the people of the failures
of their governments has led to an intellectual ferment, within the region
and outside it. It has affected the Arabs in Europe, most of them workers
and students, but some of them businessmen, political exiles and
members of the rich leisured classes who spend much of their time in
their houses abroad. The debate spreads easily from one Arab people
to another. It is stimulated by the fact that the Arabs listen to each
other's radio stations and the BBC Arabic service. They mix with each
other when they travel, and when in London or Paris they read the
unofficial press, some of which is worth reading. The debate in itself
is a force for change. A public perception of failure and expectation of
change puts pressure on governments.

The pressure has been increased in recent years by the collapse of
the Communist regimes in eastern Europe and the former Soviet Union,
and by the introduction of democracy in the more sophisticated countries in these areas. Only one of the Arab countries, southern Yemen,
was ever Communist, but many once espoused strongly socialist ideas
and even after their idealism evaporated they continued to run their

economies on eastern European lines and allow their people no more freedom than had the eastern European regimes. The knowledge that governments which seemed as secure as the Communist ones can suddenly be swept away has led to the thought, particularly among the young, that the same might happen in the Arab world. The parallel in people's minds is strengthened by the fact that more than half of the Arab leaders, if not old men, have ruled as heads of state, or as the effective powers in their governments, for twenty years or more. When the political stage has been occupied for so long by so many familiar faces people are bound to think of change. They imagine that many of the leaders will die or be replaced in a short space of time, that a new generation will take over and a new era begin.

The expectation of change has been increased by a force which has taken all of the Arab governments by surprise – satellite television. Until five years ago there were only two Arab countries, Algeria and Tunisia, in which people were able to tune their televisions to receive the broadcasts of a European country, France, in a language which most of them understood. Being able to look at the success and prosperity of Europe made the Algerians all the more aware of their own failure and helped create the discontent that exploded in October 1988. Since then, French TV, like other European TV, has become more explicit in the sex it shows, particularly late in the evenings. This has had a morally corrupting influence which, through the reaction of conservatives, has increased support for the Front Islamique de Salut. Now, since the explosion of the availability of satellite channels, both the moral corruption and the images of freedom and wealth are available to all Arab countries. People are becoming better educated. They are learning more about scientific subjects, particularly the environment. They are able to watch political change not only in eastern Europe but in developing countries; they are learning what the rest of the world considers normal human rights. It is true that all of this information was available to the Arabs before, on their radios, but the visual images on the television have had a much stronger impact.

None of the Arab governments has welcomed satellite television, but except in Iraq, Syria and Libya, where people are genuinely frightened of the regimes and control their behaviour so as not to draw attention to themselves, there is not much that they have been able to do about it. They admit that a quiet revolution has crept up on them before they have been able to think how they might regulate satellite dishes, which ideally in their view would mean banning them. The confusion is well illustrated by the situation in Saudi Arabia. Here there is an actual ban on satellite dishes, and even if this were not the case, most of the population would assume that any innovation of this sort was of questionable legality unless it had been specifically sanctioned by the *ulema*, the judges and senior religious scholars. However, it is not the Saudi government's practice to try to regulate what goes on in people's homes, and so the authorities have done nothing about the dishes. The only action on the matter has come from a few religious fanatics who have tried shooting at them with .22 rifles. This may appeal to their militant mentality, but except in the case of the odd lucky shot that takes out the electronic apparatus, small bullet holes do not do much harm to dishes. The dishes are sold openly in all the Saudi towns, and because the population is quite rich, spends a huge amount of time watching television and is very craze-minded they have spread fast.

Realizing several years ago that satellite TV was the wave of the future and that nothing could be done about it, at the end of the 1980s King Fahd decided to embrace the revolution. He encouraged the establishment in London by Saudi businessmen and members of his entourage of the Kingdom's own satellite station, the Middle East Broadcasting Centre, to transmit programmes to the whole Arab world. This channel is now in operation, claims it has 30 million viewers and has become particularly popular in North Africa. Its output is characteristically Saudi: innocuous light entertainment, mixed with a few news items avoiding any obvious political bias. Nothing has been done meanwhile to remove the ban on dishes in the Kingdom. That would be against the style of Saudi government, which prefers change to take place slowly. It likes its population to be allowed to accept gradually the fact that an innovation is legal. Making announcements on such matters is felt likely to antagonize conservatives, particularly the religious extremists who have become so aggressive since 1990. The whole MEBC enterprise is also typical of Saudi government in that it has involved the creation of an organization that operates in parallel to the Ministry of Information, which runs the Saudi domestic television service. The King apparently, like the rest of the population, finds Saudi TV extremely boring, and knowing that changing the way Saudi bureaucracy runs this type of operation is almost impossible – civil servants in the softer Arab governments are as good at frustrating their masters as they are in Western democracies – has set up an entirely new organization. MEBC is not the only quasi-state institution that exists in Saudi government. The King and other senior members of the Saud family have their own foreign affairs staffs and two quite good-quality, fairly objective newspapers, *As-Sharq Al-Awsat* (*The Middle East*) and the *Arab News*. *As-Sharq Al-Awsat*, which appears on green newsprint, is produced in London and printed daily in seven or eight cities around the world.*

None of the other Arab governments has responded to the challenge of satellite television in such an ambitious and complicated way as Saudi Arabia. Most have found themselves powerless to do anything. In several countries the low technology parts of the dishes are being produced by local entrepreneurs, and in countries such as Morocco that have active private sectors businessmen have started to direct advertising at their domestic markets through the foreign satellite channels. So far in the poorer countries most of the people who have satellite television are middle class, but the dishes are being heavily advertized and prices are falling fast. Although, traditionally, it has not been the working classes in any part of the world who have brought about political change, the spread of satellite television lower down the social scale can only add strength to the demand for change that has been growing among the bourgeois intelligentsia.

Given that the crisis of Arab government is general rather than acute and that the internal politics and economic problems of the Arab countries are not all the same, the feeling that there must be change is not manifesting itself in any series of precise demands. It has taken the form, rather, of a consensus that the Arab world needs governments that treat their people better, principally by giving them more freedom, are more answerable to them, less corrupt, do not pursue petty quarrels with their neighbours and have more self-confidence. This last idea means that governments should not have to pretend to be perfect and should be able to tell their peoples when they have to make sacrifices, prepare themselves to receive fewer subsidies or accept compromise on a border dispute.

If a government is to say these things it should be legitimate, which means that it should have a moral authority which is accepted by its people. The same applies if it is to introduce orderly political reform. Even if it has legitimacy a government will find it difficult to begin

---

* The way in which the Saudi government has handled the coming of satellite TV recalls a comment of the late *Sunday Times* journalist, David Holden, in *Farewell to Arabia* (Faber, 1966) page 134. Here he spoke of Prince (later King) Faisal having 'the characteristic knack of the radical conservative of leading his people backwards into the future'. The controversial issues in Saudi Arabia then were the introduction of television, education for girls and the Kingdom's first secular 'commercial law'. The particular device used to make television palatable for the *ulema* was to have most of the first year or so of broadcasts taken up with readings from the Koran. Faisal's policy of reassuring conservatives while quietly promoting change has been the hallmark of Saudi government since.

these changes, but if it is not regarded as legitimate the process will be much harder, and more dangerous. People will be less willing to accept economic suffering from an illegitimate government than from a government they respect. And ethnic and religious interest groups will not restrain themselves from resorting to violence, or be restrained by society, or by the police with the backing of society, if an illegitimate or discredited government opens the door to political change, as happened in Algeria in 1989.

The idea of what constitutes a legitimate government in the Arab world, therefore, is a part of the debate on economic and political change. It will constitute a background to the discussion of change in the remainder of this book. In this chapter I shall discuss what it is that has made Arab governments legitimate or illegitimate in the past few decades, and what the people feel should give legitimacy to the new, reformed governments they would like to see emerge in the future.

The whole question of legitimacy is complicated by its being indefinite and subjective. There are no exact criteria, any more than there are definite rules on who should govern a state and how it should be governed. Similarly there is no universal agreement on exactly which of the modern regimes in the Arab world are legitimate. Much depends on the political bias of the person considering the issue; the views of the conservative tribal constituents of the Saudi royal family are not going to coincide with the opinions of Islamic militants or Palestinian radicals. The matter is further complicated by the impermanent nature of legitimacy. A regime can both win legitimacy and lose it.

In spite of these difficulties of analysis, in the debate of the last five years or so there has emerged a consensus of a sort on the subject. Across a broad band of moderate opinion, formed by Arabs from all countries with no special axes to grind, the view is that the list of legitimate governments might comprise Saudi Arabia, the Gulf states, Jordan, Egypt, and Morocco. One could add Iran to the list, if it were expanded to embrace the whole Muslim Middle East, on the grounds that the Islamic republican government came to power by a popular uprising and is accepted by a majority of its people, albeit with a large amount of open grumbling and political argument. The openness of debate in the country is one of the strengths of the regime.

Of the governments that have been left off the list some are borderline, in the sense that they are relatively new and as yet unproven in their ability to tackle their countries' problems and win the acceptance of their peoples. The governments of united Yemen, Tunisia and Lebanon would fall into this category. Others, the governments of Iraq,

Syria, Sudan, Libya and Algeria, are clearly not legitimate, having proved themselves incompetent and/or unacceptably brutal.

There is a similar consensus on the main qualities that are needed to make a government legitimate. The most important is that it should be competent and reasonably humane in its dealings with its people. Another is that it should have its people's support, and, a quality which it cannot itself create, it should have a long association with its country. The first two of these qualities do not need any elaboration, but the way in which the third bestows legitimacy is more complicated and interesting and is worth discussing in some detail. It is the quality which biases the membership of the list of legitimate governments in favour of monarchies.

Most of the surviving Arab royal and ruling families – 'ruling' being the expression applied to the families which run the Gulf states – have been governing their countries for two hundred years or more. During this time they have had close contact with their peoples, which in turn has led to their reflecting, and helping create, the traditions and customs of their countries. The best examples of how this has built the legitimacy of the families are provided by the Alaoui dynasty of Morocco and the Sauds of Saudi Arabia.

The legitimacy of the Alaoui family, in its historical aspect, is based partly on a connection with the Prophet. The family claims descent from Mohammad's cousin and son-in-law, Ali, hence its name. Nobody can prove this claim, nor those of many other families in the Muslim world which claim to be related to the Prophet, but nobody in Morocco is going to question it and so it is accepted as a fact, in a formal and symbolic rather than scientific way. Equally, or even more useful for the family is that it comes from the country it rules – unlike the Hashemites in Jordan and formerly Iraq, the Egyptian monarchy, whose members were the descendants of an ambitious Albanian officer, and the beys of Tunis, whose dynasty was established by a Turkish general of Cretan descent. The Alaouis emerged in the middle of the seventeenth century from Tafilalt, a remote oasis beyond the Atlas mountains, close to where the river Ziz disappears into the Sahara.* They took over the country at a time when it was in a state of anarchy and have ruled it ever since. Sometimes their rule has been extremely cruel, and certainly

---

* Tafilalt is traditionally a Berber area. During the last 350 years the Alaoui family has married into all parts of the Moroccan population and it is not regarded as belonging to any particular region or community. The distinction between the several Berber tribes and the Arabs in Morocco is much less important than it is in Algeria.

during the nineteenth century it was reactionary and stultifying; but at least it was unquestionably Moroccan. The kingdom was never part of the Ottoman Empire, and when it came under the authority of France, from 1912 to 1956, it was as a protectorate rather than a colony. The French ruled through the Sultan. The country had the good luck to have as its first Resident General, Marshal Lyautey, a man who respected Arab tradition and worked to restore the prestige of the royal family, which had fallen into decline in the early years of the century.

The family, and Morocco, were also fortunate between 1927 and 1961 in having a Sultan of exceptional stature in Mohammad V, who managed to win both the respect of the French and the affection of his people. At the beginning of the Second World War he asked his people to support the allied cause. Later, when his country was liberated from Vichy rule he sent troops to serve with the allied forces in Tunisia and Italy. At the same time he managed, skilfully, to put himself at the head of the nationalist movement, which was demanding independence from the French. The movement drew its main support from the towns, which are not the places, traditionally, where Arab monarchies have been strongest.

Gradually Mohammad's relations with the protecting power deteriorated. In 1953 the French, who were in dispute with him over his refusal to sign decrees on their behalf, allied themselves with some reactionary tribes opposed to the nationalists and sent him into exile. His replacement, a distant relative, carried no authority. Two attempts were made to assassinate the new ruler, outbreaks of violence occurred throughout the country and most of the population continued to look for leadership to Mohammad. Moroccans claimed at this time to be able to see his face in the moon. Eventually, in November 1955, Mohammad returned to his country and in March 1956 it was declared independent. Sadly the King, as he was known after independence, died during a minor sinus operation in 1961, when he was only fifty-two. He is buried in Rabat. His son has seen that at his tomb, day and night throughout the year, sits a scholar reading the Koran.

The present Moroccan monarch, Hassan II, is a thoroughly competent king in his own right. He is a clever politician and he has been lucky. In the early 1970s he survived two coup attempts, one of them involving an assault on his birthday party. His people believe he has *baraka*, divinely inspired good fortune. Yet the King's authority is undeniably increased by the religious aura which surrounds his family and by the achievements of his father. His family's descent from Ali has enabled him to give himself the title of Commander of the Faithful. His people venerate and respect him, though to say he is 'loved' in the way his father was would be wrong. The dual nature of his authority has made it possible for him to pre-empt much of the appeal of the *intégristes*, which is something the republican regimes of Tunisia and Algeria could never do. He has been helped in this by the retention of a well-educated religious leadership, which feels itself to be part of the establishment. In the Arab republics in the last forty years the religious leaders have either been aware that they have been occupying a very minor position in the state or have been in quiet (or recently noisy) opposition to the governments.

The King is strengthened further by his family having been part of Morocco's history for so long. This has led to the monarch being associated with many of the ordinary practices and habits of the country. These are practices which have been part of Moroccan custom for centuries and which inevitably have been adopted or endorsed by the monarch at some stage, with the result that in the minds of the population his authority had been enhanced, while the continuation of the practice has been made to seem in a small way dependent on the continuation and stability of the monarchy.

An interesting and unusual example of this concerns the tradition of religious toleration. For five centuries in Morocco there has been a substantial community of Jews. They arrived from Spain in the years after 1492, when the Castilian monarchy reconquered Granada, and although many left after the creation of Israel there are still some 40,000 in the country. There are also some 30,000 Roman Catholics, made up entirely of foreigners. Both groups are not merely tolerated, they are regarded as being an important part of Morocco's society. The Catholic church holds a substantial amount of property tax free in the country. The Moroccan Muslims revere Jewish as well as Muslim *marabouts* (saints), whose whitewashed, domed tombs form an attractive feature of the Moroccan countryside. They also think of Abraham, the other principal Jewish prophets and Christ as their own prophets. In theory this idea is accepted by all Muslims, it being part of Islamic doctrine that Mohammad was the last and most authoritative of a line of prophets who revealed God to mankind, but in other Muslim societies, and particularly Saudi Arabia, the earlier prophets are accorded very low importance.*

The monarchy has been associated with these tolerant traditions in

---

* A further minor example of Morocco's tolerant attitudes, which might be noticed by any visitor to the country, is the locally produced red wine called Rabbi Jacob. This is not something one would expect to find elsewhere in the Arab world.

various unselfconscious ways. During the Vichy regime from 1940 to 1942 Mohammad V refused to allow the French authorities to make Jews carry a yellow Star of David. King Hassan during his reign has had several Jewish associates; his present economic counsellor is a Jew. In the early 1980s when the Pope came to Morocco, the only Arab country he has visited, the King greeted him and was photographed with him.

In these acts the Moroccan monarchs were not being daringly independent, but nor were they being completely conformist. They were showing themselves to their people as leaders who were prepared to do things which they thought were right, or which merely suited them personally, and who were willing to lead the nation in protecting one of its traditions which at times could be difficult or controversial. In this way they were binding themselves to that tradition, and it was the monarchy a well as the nation that benefited.

The royal family of Saudi Arabia is in a similar position to the Alaouis in that it rules a country that has a strong, distinctive culture of its own, albeit not one that includes religious tolerance among its qualities. Central Saudi Arabia, the Nejd, which is culturally and politically the dominant part of the Kingdom, was never part of the Ottoman Empire, and no part of the Kingdom was ever ruled by a European colonial power. This lack of foreign influence has enabled Saudi government and society to evolve their own institutions. As in Morocco, the royal family has helped mould the traditions of society and draws strength from working within them.

The Sauds derive their legitimacy, ultimately, from an alliance made in the mid-eighteenth century between Mohammad bin Saud, the ruler of Diriyyah, a village close to the site of the modern city of Riyadh, and Mohammad bin Abdel-Wahab, a revivalist teacher (sheikh) who wanted to strip Islam of all wrong and superstitious practices, such as the worship of saints and the veneration of tombs, that had crept into it since the early days of the Caliphate. Inspired by the sheikh, Mohammad bin Saud and later his descendants embarked on a campaign of conquest and proselytization which in the course of seventy years gave them most of the Arabian Peninsula and saw them raiding into Iraq, where they zealously destroyed Shia shrines. The family was then crushed and Diriyyah destroyed in 1818 by Ibrahim Pasha, the son of the Governor of Egypt, acting on behalf of the Sultan in Constantinople. The family's fortunes revived and then fell again in the later nineteenth century, and finally rose for a third time in the first thirty years of this century when Abdel-Aziz bin Abdel-Rahman Al-Saud created the present Saudi kingdom. Through all the changes in their fortunes the

Sauds remained dedicated to spreading the very pure, austere, unitarian form of Islam that was preached by Mohammad bin Abdel-Wahab, and although the family and the style of Islam it espouses have now become conservative rather than revolutionary forces, the creation of a model state embodying these teachings remains the purpose of Saudi rule to this day. The Sauds have kept their alliance with the descendants of the teacher, who are known as the Al-as-Sheikh (the family of the teacher) and occupy senior judicial, ministerial and academic positions in the country. The two families are much inter-married.

To a striking and surprising extent the Sauds have succeeded in creating the type of state they intended. They have done this mainly by treating Shariah law as their constitution, their criminal code and the basis of their civil code. Given that the family has also been anxious to build a modern economy and has been expected to deliver a high standard of living to its people, it has often had to make compromises and think of ways of circumventing the law without appearing to do so. This has given rise to many inconsistencies and complications. For example, the authorities know that the Kingdom needs a modern banking system. They also know that Islamic banking, which involves profit sharing rather than the payment of interest, has not been a great success in the countries where it has been tried and has tended to exclude those countries' banks from the mainstream of international finance. They have therefore given a licence to only one Islamic bank, a former money exchanger. But being responsible for running a state dedicated to implementing Shariah law, the Government cannot openly support the payment of interest, which is condemned in the law as usury. Nor can it force the courts to order defaulting customers to repay loans with interest because to do so would be to change God's law, which would be blasphemous and against everything the state stands for. So over the years a series of compromises has been allowed to evolve. The banks refer to the sums they pay and receive as 'commission' or 'charges', to preserve the appearance of legality. When a dispute arises between a bank and one of its customers it is referred to the Banking Disputes Committee, a body established during the recession of the mid-1980s, which gives a purely secular judgement on the case, based on whatever undertakings the customer has given to the bank in the loan agreement. If a customer wants, he can still, in theory, appeal to the Shariah court, which will most likely deduct interest paid from his debt; but to lodge his appeal he needs the permission of the King, and in practice this is never given. Meanwhile the banks will have added his name to their list of customers who try to use Islam as a pretext for defaulting on their debts, and they will avoid doing business with him in future. The end result is that the law remains Islamic, while the practice of the banks and their better customers is secular.

There are worse inconsistencies than those that apply to the banking regulations. There is a great deal of corruption, greed, hypocrisy and immorality, not a little of it connected with members of the royal family and their followers, which certainly does not accord with the Shariah. This behaviour has long attracted the criticism (and in some cases the commercial envy) of members of the Western educated middle class, who are rich and hardly revolutionary. More recently it has been attacked by the new breed of Islamic militants. The mass of the Saudi population, though, remains reasonably content with its government. One reason is that the faults of the system are not easily visible to Saudis – or to foreign expatriates or the millions of pilgrims who come to Mecca and Medina. The moderately well-off, God-fearing majority of Saudis does not have its sensibilities offended by the sight of unveiled women, short skirts, bars and discotheques, as did the poor in Iran under the Shah. What behaviour is not in accordance with the Koran takes place behind the walls of private houses, outside the country or in people's financial dealings.

The basic workings of the system suit the people. The execution of criminals who commit murder, rape, other violent crimes and drug offences may horrify Western journalists who occasionally visit the Kingdom, but it pleases the great majority of the Saudis because they believe it helps create a more secure and peaceful state. Executions are quite common, but the other punishment which upsets Westerners, the amputation of the hands of thieves who have stolen on several occasions, is rare. One can monitor the frequency of the sentences by reading the Saudi papers on Saturdays, when there are matter-of-fact announcements of the executions and amputations carried out the day before. There is, of course, no other reporting of the punishments, in the form of interviews with relations of the victims or the criminal. This type of journalism would not be allowed and would anyway be considered distasteful and pointless by the public.

The same types of conformist attitude, uniting the government and the people but upsetting Westerners, apply to other aspects of society. Women in Saudi Arabia are not supposed to work, except as directors of their own businesses, or as teachers, doctors or nurses. They are not allowed to drive cars, or travel, except in the company of a male relative. These restrictions cause some discontent among the more sophisticated classes, and they run against international ideas of women's rights, but they are intended to help hold families together and the majority of the people think they are sensible. In a similar way there is support for the prohibition of Christian worship. Most Saudis think that other people's religions are mistaken and believe that their own country, blessed by the presence of the two holy cities, must be kept purely Islamic.

Most important of all the institutions of Saudi rule is the access that the people have to members of the royal family. This is also a feature of the Gulf states' governments and it is made possible in all these countries by the small size of the populations and the large size of the ruling families. Many Saudis have a personal connection with a prince, to whom they feel they can take their complaints, or with whom some of them – the better educated – can occasionally have a discussion about the state of the country's affairs. What people say when they talk to the junior princes filters up to the top of the family and keeps its leaders in touch with popular opinion.

Some of the senior princes and all the provincial and town governors are available to their people every day, or several times a week, in their *majles* (council chambers) where they receive petitions. Most of these concern small disputes, complaints about the bureaucracy and requests for financial help, for dowries, medical trips to London, the replacement of crashed vehicles and similar domestic needs. Some of these matters could be dealt with by government departments, but many of the ordinary Saudis of the older generation, especially the people of the Nejd, still prefer to take their requests to a prince and his secretariat, even if that puts them in the position of supplicants, rather than fill in forms and demand their rights from a civil servant, who might be a foreigner. Again, the big *majles* are useful in keeping the royal family informed. More importantly they give the people a sense of having contact with their rulers.

The Saudi government is very soft with its own people, in a way which runs counter to the severe, unsmiling image it has abroad. The Saudis are not taxed and benefit from a lavish welfare state and subsidies. The government often seems anxious to push money into their hands. It is extremely generous in the compensation it pays to anyone whose land it buys for a construction project. There have been occasions, after roads in the mountains of the south-west have been washed away by floods and their sites occupied by bedouin, when the government has paid the occupants to move from what they have claimed have been their 'grazing grounds'.

Saudi homes are regarded as inviolable. No Saudi household (nor most foreign households) would ever be searched for alcohol. Neither the Saudi government, nor any Gulf state government, can order the confiscation of a person's money, business, house or other property – which most of the republican Arab governments can do. The Saudi and

Gulf authorities are restrained in these matters by the Shariah law. It is likewise very difficult for a creditor to seize a person's property through the courts.

The consensus among the Saudi people is that their government may be far from perfect but is better than any likely alternative, republican or revolutionary Islamic. One often hears it said in the Kingdom that 'if there were elections tomorrow the Saud family would win by a huge margin'. This, at least, has been the case for most of the last thirty years, but recently the royal family has been openly challenged. It has long been obvious that the traditional forms of Saudi rule are not relevant to the growing numbers of educated middle-class Saudis, and since the beginning of the 1990s they have been under noisier and much more aggressive attack by Islamic extremists. These attacks and the government's reaction to them will be discussed in a later chapter. The purpose of the description of Saudi rule here has been to explain the workings of a government that has been effective in the past and is still accepted by a majority of its subjects today. Most Saudis feel that the royal family delivers its implied promise of a reasonably Islamic and thoroughly Arabian state, and in doing this it makes itself legitimate.

The secret of the successful government of the Moroccan and Saudi monarchies is that they manage to represent both the old and the new in their countries' cultures. This is important because their constituents, the people, live in two worlds. Some of their ideas, and their material aspirations, belong to a Western secular world and others to a traditional Islamic one. One sees this division very starkly in Tunisia, where until the early 1980s the population prospered under and seemed to support the very secular government of Habib Bourguiba but then turned quite suddenly in the 1980s to support the *intégristes*. Obviously there was a considerable economic deterioration in this period, and by no means the whole of the population altered its views, but the fact that there was such a radical change shows that many of the people can never have been quite happy in Bourguiba's society. They must have felt that part of their culture had been lost.

To modernize successfully an Arab government has to work with continual reference to tradition. It has either to justify its innovations with religious arguments or maintain an imperfect mixture of old and modern principles in its laws. This is what Morocco has done with its laws on alcohol. These state that alcohol is to be sold (and produced) only for the consumption of non-Muslims, which pleases conservatives. However, for the benefit of those who want to drink, the law is not enforced, except in two ways: it is applied strictly on religious feast days and during Ramadan, and anyone caught drunk in a public place is arrested. In this way both traditionalists and modernists are satisfied while the public's attitude towards alcohol is allowed to evolve gradually in whatever direction fashion takes it.

Moroccan law has a similar complicated approach to marriage and divorce. It acknowledges that a Muslim is allowed to take up to four wives, but it states that a man's first wife can ask for divorce on the grounds of her husband taking a second wife. It also states that before a man marries for a second, third or fourth time he must obtain a certificate saying whether he is single, married or divorced, so that the new wife can be sure of what household she is entering. This rule is not relevant to the modern middle classes in the towns, but it is useful in the countryside where a girl's marriage may be arranged for her by her parents. In practice the taking of more than one wife is now uncommon in even the most traditional Muslim societies, but to ban the practice outright, as Bourguiba did in Tunisia, causes offence because it puts a government of men in the position of confronting and contradicting the law of God.

A point of difference between the Arab countries and the West in these and similar areas of social and economic legislation, which include education, job security, bank interest and the control of television, is that whereas Western governments are generally passing laws to regulate more or less accepted principles or practices, Arab governments are actively trying to modernize their societies. They are trying to give their people the higher standard of living and the political and economic strength – the 'modernization' - for which they are clamouring, often without understanding exactly what the process will involve. On some matters this involves them introducing laws which run against the sensibilities of a majority of their people, or offend a large vocal minority. The secret for both the stability of society and their own legitimacy has been for the governments to achieve an equilibrium between the old and the new and the religious and the secular in their policies.

There is one Arab government, the Egyptian administration of Hosni Mubarak, that is legitimate but completely different from the governments of Morocco and Saudi Arabia in both its origins and its methods. It provides an atypical case of a legitimate, modern republican Arab government.

The legitimacy of the Egyptian government comes first from its being the constitutional descendant of the republic established by Gamal Abdel-Nasser, who was unquestionably legitimate in that he made his country truly independent, was loved and respected by his people and, in his early years in office, was successful. The two presidents who have followed him, Anwar Sadat and Hosni Mubarak, were both Vice-Presidents before they were elevated to the highest office on the deaths of their predecessors, and although they have been very different personalities from Nasser, and have altered his constitution, the fact that they head the republic he founded has given them some of the mantle of his legitimacy. They have been seen as representing the established, legal Egyptian government.

The present Egyptian government is also made legitimate by its being just adequately competent, by the rather charitable standards one has to apply in the Middle East. Neither the Sadat nor the Mubarak regimes have been uncorrupt, and Egyptians have been very cynical about both of them. But Mubarak's government allows its people considerable freedom – the country has an almost completely free press – and it is reasonably humane, except in its treatment of people associated with Islamic terrorist groups. The greater freedom Egyptians enjoy under their present government makes up for its lacking the inspiring quality of Nasser's regime.

The people have further benefited in a gradual and unspectacular way in the last two decades from their government's careful diplomacy and its having made the right long-term strategic decisions. It has made a lasting peace with Israel, which has given it back the Sinai peninsula and has given its people a higher standard of living than they would have had otherwise. After an eight year period in the Arab political wilderness, brought about by what was seen as a treacherous treaty, in 1987 the government managed to reinsert itself into Arab councils and was readmitted to the Arab League. Three years later it backed the winning side in the Gulf crisis, which enabled it to bring the League's headquarters back to Cairo, re-establish itself as the hub of Arab diplomacy and have a major part of its international debt forgiven. The government has proved itself adept at handling negotiations with the International Monetary Fund and the World Bank, giving the absolute minimum it needs to obtain the concessions it wants, and then often managing to delay the implementation of its promises. These achievements, though they appear quite impressive, are not enough to make the Egyptian government popular, and nor do they prove competent management, but taken with its ancestry they are enough to make the government legitimate.

President Mubarak both reflects and to some extent creates the character of his government. He is a sensible, decent man, more able than he is given credit for being, but uninspiring and accident prone in front of television cameras in a way which has made him the butt of jokes across the Arab world. There are many Mubarak stories which illustrate his knack of saying the wrong thing. One of them concerns a visit to a new factory, where he decided, in the proper presidential manner, to ask one of the workers about his job. The man demurred. The President insisted and told him not to be shy. There were some embarrassed mutterings between the man and members of the President's entourage, and eventually the man turned to Mubarak and said, 'Well sir, I'm your bodyguard'. These sorts of mistakes make people laugh, but they do not make the President disliked or feared in the way that the heads of some of the Arab republics are.

Both Mubarak and his government benefit from two characteristics of Egypt which make that country, in some ways, easy to govern and help its governments to be accepted. One is that because Egypt has been a nation for 5000 years – with Morocco it is one of only two Arab states that can claim to be nations in their own right – nobody inside or outside the country is going to challenge the basic legitimacy of the state. It does not have the anxiety on this score that Iraq and Kuwait have today or that Syria had in its early years of independence. The other is that the country is not seriously divided on community lines internally; the attacks of Islamic extremists on the Copts in upper Egypt in the late 1980s and early 1990s reflected the militants' desire to destabilize the country rather than a long-standing rift in society. It is not possible for the extremists or anyone else to claim that an Egyptian government represents just one section of the population in the way they might about the regimes in Iraq and Syria. In these respects Egypt is more united, self-confident and mature than the other Arab countries. Any Egyptian government has the advantage of knowing that it is ruling a single nation rather than a collection of villages, tribes or communities which are only partly committed to the state and therefore only partly loyal. This helps marry together the idea of the nation in Egypt and the idea of its government, and it bestows on the government some of the permanence of the nation.

The qualities that make a government illegitimate are, in the most obvious sense, the opposite of those that make it legitimate – namely, that it is incompetent, brutal, lacks popular support and is new, often having come to power by *coup d'état*. All of these characteristics of Arab governments have been discussed in earlier chapters. There are, however, three peculiar aspects of illegitimate governments that need to be described in more detail. These are that they have unfashionable philosophies, that they were once legitimate but have lost that quality and that they have helped to undermine their own legitimacy by destroying the institutions of the states they rule.

The first of these issues is related to the international loss of faith in socialism as a useful principle for government. The socialist years in the Arab world, and in other parts of the developing world, were from the late 1950s to the early 1970s. In that period the demand of the newly independent peoples was for modernization, the redistribution of wealth, the recreation of national pride and freedom from the influence of the former colonial powers. The new Arab republics seemed to represent these ideas, and their authoritarian side was less pronounced than it became later. They appeared to be more legitimate representatives of the people than the monarchies. But now that the intellectual climate has become more conservative and religious, and the loudest demand for change comes from the right, the socialist, or nominally socialist, republics cannot plausibly offer the types of changes or the style of rule the new radicals are demanding. They have been put on the defensive. The new political mood much better suits the monarchies, because they are in theory, more conservative and therefore apparently closer to the ideals of the militant Islamists, and they have links with the religious establishments which enable them better to control the new forces.

The second characteristic of illegitimate Arab governments – that most of them once had legitimacy but lost it – stems partly from the change in political fashion but also from the governments' incompetence. The ruling parties of Tunisia and Algeria, for example, once carried great prestige. They won independence for their countries and then in the 1960s and 1970s managed to give their people prosperity, or the hope of prosperity, and liberal social reform. In Iraq and Syria the governments of the period were dedicated to the struggle against Israel. The difficulty for all these governments was that the maintenance of their legitimacy depended on their continuing to be successful, or fulfilling their promises. When they failed in this, as they all did to different degrees, they were not able to fall back on a tradition of popular acceptance such as the Moroccan and Saudi governments enjoy. They were new governments and had none of the reserves of legitimacy which underpin old dynasties.

The last of the features of political illegitimacy, the destruction of institutions, has upset and destabilized Arab societies. 'Institution' in this context means not just bodies of people such as independent councils or associations, but, in the broader sense of the word, the customs and procedures to which people have become used. Chief among the institutions swept away, in those states that were once monarchies, was everything that was associated with the kings: the patronage, the ceremonies, the protection of traditions, minorities and tribal rights, in short all the institutionalized contacts that joined the monarchs to the people. The republican governments abolished political parties, other than the parties they created for themselves. They seized private companies, banks and the press. Religious bodies were pushed to the peripheries of the government establishment and either watched carefully or treated with contempt. Chambers of commerce, trade unions, local and tribal councils and similar minor institutions of civil society were made illegal or brought under the authority of the state. It was not just the more dogmatic regimes of Syria, Iraq, Libya and Algeria that did these things, the example they followed was set by Nasser's government in Egypt. The difference between the Egyptian government and most of the other republican regimes was that Nasser's flair and the moderation of Sadat and Mubarak compensated for some of the revolution's mistakes.

The republics were bound to act in the way they did because their leaders started with the idea that they represented a new era of social justice. They believed they embodied the force of history. They were doing what the people wanted, carrying out their wishes before the people acted for themselves, or even fully realized what their interests were. This put them above institutions, customs and tradition. They felt they did not need such things.

The new governments' destructive enthusiasm was increased by the political instability, the *coups d'état* and attempted coups, that the Arab world experienced during the early republican years. The regimes developed a fear of leaving intact any independent centre of power, influence or even debate, because they came to think that such institutions embodied the threat of subversion. Every aspect of society had to be brought under their control, which in due course meant that all surviving clubs, professional or academic associations and newspapers had to be licensed. Some of this passion for control came to affect the Arab monarchies during the security-conscious years of the 1980s, but it was always a worse habit in the republics and did more damage there.*

One of the results of their insecurity was that the republican regimes

---

* Many Arabs have been conditioned by their experience at home to suppose that the licensing of newspapers is the normal practice in Western democracies. When embassies and individuals from the Gulf states and Saudi Arabia have complained to the British authorities about attacks on them in the blackmailing Arabic gutter press in London they have often asked why H.M. Government has not withdrawn the papers' permission to publish.

became cut off from the views of their peoples. They worried about the details of their own ideologies and concentrated on their plans for changing society. As part of this they established channels of communication from themselves to the people, to tell them of the great things they were doing on their behalf, but having destroyed or seized all bodies through which the people might express their own views they prevented themselves from hearing a reply. Anything they did chance to hear disagreeing with their policies they persuaded themselves came from small groups of subversives. Of all the governments the one that lectured its people most and listened least was the FLN in Algeria.

The worst effect of the republics' policies was that they left for the people only one permissible focus for their political loyalty. Many of the old, familiar institutions that were abolished or ignored had been a focus for village, tribal, religious and professional loyalties, and they had represented their members, or the people who looked to them, in dealings with the old governments. They performed a role similar to that of trade unions, employers' federations and local councils in the West. When it was declared, in effect, that only a single party or its agencies could represent the people, the link between large parts of the populations and central governments was broken. All those who had a more direct stake in the institutions that were abolished, the people who had been their officers, those who had benefited from royal patronage, the owners of newspapers and companies that had been nationalized, were even more strongly alienated.

Under the form of rule that developed in most of the republican Arab countries anybody who was a committed member of the governing party could feel that he had a role in his country, but most of the people were left with a feeling of being separated from their governments.

The debate in the Arab world now is about how the region can be given better, legitimate governments in future. This implies not only finding ways in which illegitimate governments can be changed or reformed, but encouraging governments that are already accepted as legitimate to evolve so that they keep their people's support. What the politicians, academics and journalists who discuss these issues have in mind when they talk about the second part of the question is the development of the governments of Saudi Arabia and the Gulf states, which have tended to rest immobile while their societies have been changing around them.

There is no obvious pattern for the region to follow in bringing about the changes that are needed. There has not been any country (except Egypt to some extent) that has peacefully evolved away from authoritarian rule, and nor have there been any discredited regimes that have been turned into something better after quick, relatively bloodless revolutions. There is no reformed state which people can look to as an example or which academics can refer to as 'the such-and-such model'. Similarly, most of the people – the exception being the Muslim fundamentalists – who have been saying that there must be change do not have a definite idea of the type of government they want to create. The ideas of the moderate, thoughtful middle classes are still evolving.

The debate is complicated on the fringes by the fact that not everybody in the region accepts the boundaries of the present states. Nor does everybody accept the idea of 'national government' in the secular and precise geographical sense in which it is understood elsewhere in the world. The most dedicated of the Islamic militants would like to recreate the single state, guided by Shariah law, in which the Muslim community was briefly united in the early years of the Caliphate. Even among people of less fervent beliefs and less radical aims there is an uneasiness with the national divisions and with the secular nature of the governments that have ruled since the early 1920s. Many people, though they cannot say exactly what it is that they want, would be happier with states that were a bit more Islamic and a bit broader in geographical area than those that exist at present. It is this instinct that has led in recent years to a revival of interest in the Ottoman Empire, which embodied a Sultan who was acknowledged as the legal successor of the Prophet. The Empire did not impose artificial divisions on the land of the Muslims and for most of its history was reasonably humane and tolerant in its treatment of both believers and minorities. Nobody is talking of attempting to recreate anything to resemble the Empire, but there are people who would like to see some of its character incorporated in whatever new form of governments might evolve in future.

These ideas, though, are somewhat academic. The general view of most of the non-fundamentalist intelligentsia is that political change in the region will have to involve borders staying as they are and the international concept of the nation state being accepted. To attempt fundamental change in either of these areas would be to invite chaos. In considering what sorts of change should be introduced within these limits, people are looking to a mixture of Western and Islamic ideas and watching the results of the various fairly successful and unsuccessful attempts at political reform there have been in Arab countries so far. They are not looking at most of the accepted legitimate Arab governments because much of what makes the governments of Saudi Arabia, the Gulf states and Morocco legitimate simply cannot be reproduced elsewhere and is not relevant to political reform. The consensus, anyway, is that all of these states are themselves in need of reform.

There is, however, one legitimate regime, the Hashemite government in Jordan, to which people can look for ideas. The reason is precisely that its legitimacy does not depend at all on the royal family having ancient roots in its land, or on Jordan being a proper nation. It has achieved legitimacy in a purely pragmatic way by providing good government.

When the government of this state was created in 1922 it was definitely not legitimate. The Emir Abdullah did not belong to the area, and nobody, before he arrived there with his small army, had ever thought of Transjordan being turned into a state of its own. It was the British who protected the new Kingdom, drew its boundaries and advised the Emir's government. In 1952, after Abdullah had been assassinated by a Palestinian angered by his annexation of the West Bank, the young King Hussein found himself ruling a country which was on the borders of Israel and had Palestinians as a majority of its population. It is hard to think of a less auspicious background for a reign, yet the King survived by a mixture of flair, bravery, good luck, a judicious distancing of himself from the British, and pragmatic, reasonably humane government which took account of the fact that most of his subjects were Palestinian. Many Palestinians were given ministerial portfolios. They dominated the civil service. Even during the difficult period of the late 1960s and 1970, when the guerilla groups were at their most powerful, there was a moderate middle-class Palestinian constituency which supported the King.

Since the 1970s Hussein has been increasingly popular with his people. He was strengthened by his decision in 1988 to relinquish his formal claim to the West Bank. In 1989 he began some democratic reform and during the Gulf crisis he played the role of a constitutional monarch in speaking to reflect the views of his people, even though these were much more pro-Iraqi than his private views. The result of the King's good judgement is that Jordan is now a more united country than it has ever been before. In the last ten or twenty years the division between its different communities – the Palestinians, the East Bank townspeople and the bedouin – have become less important. There has not been a similar change in most other parts of the Arab world. In talking of the make-up of its society people now refer more to 'Jordanians', whereas a few years ago in any analysis they drew a distinction between 'Jordanians' and 'Palestinians', and added that the latter made up a majority of the population. Among much of the population King Hussein is now genuinely loved. In September 1992, when he returned from surgery for cancer in the United States, hundreds of thousands poured on to the streets to greet him. When his car, which was being driven by his brother, Crown Prince Hassan, was forced to stop, the King got out and sat on its bonnet, without a security guard in sight. No other Middle Eastern leader would have dared do such a thing.

What the case of Jordan shows those who want change in Arab government is that there is no need for the introduction of particular systems, taken from Islam or from foreign countries' governments or foreign political philosophies. Building legitimate governments can be a matter of competent rule in which governments try to respond to their people. In some ways this is not as difficult in the Arab world as it is in the West, because the Arab populations are very patient, accept that change can only come slowly and, because they know that there is an undercurrent of disorder and violence in their societies, do not expect all the same freedoms that Westerners demand. Arab governments that are moderately competent in managing their economies and provide stability, even if that is achieved by quite severe methods, will enjoy a large amount of popular support. The improvement of Arab government, therefore, does not require revolutionary change, except in Iraq, Syria and Libya, where the regimes are probably incapable of changing peacefully.

As to what type of change there should be, the general feeling among most of the middle classes is that it should be something of a democratic sort. People may not have in their minds a blueprint for a new system, and they may still be looking into the past to see if aspects of older successful Middle Eastern governments can be adapted to modern use, but they know that socialism and dictatorship have failed, they think that most of the monarchies need to change with society around them, and they do not want – or most of them do not want – the introduction of Islamic regimes. This leaves democracy as the only option.

There is a belief that democracy is becoming the internationally accepted system and that the Arabs have to embrace it. This does not mean that any country should try suddenly to introduce full-scale Western democracy. It means only that governments that want to respond to their people are expected slowly to introduce reforms of a democratic sort. These would involve creating or reviving representative institutions and giving the people greater freedom. It is hoped that one of the benefits of this will be the recreation of independent institutions, which will help build happier, more stable societies.

10

The IMF's Medicine

Societies living beyond their means – debt crises – reschedulings – reforms demanded by the IMF and World Bank – sensitivities of governments – success of reform in Jordan

There is a second force pushing the Arab countries towards change, which is related to the debate on legitimacy and the improvement of government. It is the realization by a large part of the populations of the poor countries that their economies have been incompetently managed during the last thirty years and have now reached a crisis. It is accepted that there has to be reform – and economic reform, because it is painful for the population as a whole and involves a redistribution of economic power to the private sector, produces its own pressure for political change.

The state-controlled Arab economies have been inefficient from the time socialist ideas were imposed on them, starting in Tunisia and Egypt in the late 1950s. For many years the inefficiencies were hidden. In the Arab world, as elsewhere, socialism worked at the beginning because it consumed wealth accumulated in the past – by using productive facilities and capital created by others – and the fact that governments were not able to invest enough to sustain the higher standard of living they had awarded their people was not immediately apparent. In the 1970s and early 1980s this was further disguised by the governments receiving what amounted to unearned income, directly and indirectly, from oil. Most of the poor Arab countries produced some oil of their own and profited directly from the high prices of that era. They also benefited from the large flows of aid – cheap loans and outright grants – and smaller amounts of investment from the rich oil states, together with the remittances of their citizens who had gone to work in those states. In all during the 1970s and 1980s the poor states received well over $100 billion from their neighbours. Some of these countries' capitals, particularly Amman, received so much remittance money that their richer quarters began to develop the glossy look of the Gulf states, with smart new villas, expensive cars and shops selling luxury goods.

Reality began to dawn in the mid-1980s, when oil prices collapsed and the flow of aid and remittances was much reduced. At this point governments and people were forced to accept that the achievement of the levels of income and benefit the people had been promised was just not possible. The strains could be seen in every part of the system. In Egypt the quality of state education had fallen so low that it was hardly worth having. Families that had any ambitions for their children were having to pay for extra lessons outside school hours, and teachers were grateful for the few extra pounds this was earning them. The Government found itself without the money to fulfil its promise of giving every graduate a job; it could not even pay the nominal salaries it had been paying in the past, which required its employees to take second and third jobs in the afternoons and evenings. It was forced to tell students that the jobs would not be available until three years after graduation, by which time it clearly hoped most of them would have found work in the private sector or gone abroad. A great many young men were not finding any work at all, or were finding only one part-time job instead of two. One of their complaints was that they could not see themselves saving enough money to get married until they were forty. These sorts of miserable experience, combined with governments in Egypt and elsewhere beginning to tell their people that they cannot continue to provide subsidies, free education, cheap housing and other benefits, are what have made a bigger part of the population than just the middle classes realize that some sort of economic change is unavoidable.

Action to implement the change, as often happens in these circumstances, has been forced on each government quite suddenly when its problems have become acute, which in each case has meant when it has had to seek outside help in rescheduling or refinancing its debts. These are themselves a product of the governments' living beyond their means. Most were incurred in the early and mid-1980s when the governments believed that the flow of money from the outside would continue indefinitely and that it would therefore be safe for them to borrow to accelerate their development, expand their armies and sustain those parts of their welfare programmes which were already seeming to be heavy burdens. Then, when Gulf aid and remittances fell from

1983–4 and the price of oil dropped in February 1986, the governments increased their borrowings in the hope that their difficulties would be temporary. By the end of the decade their total debts had risen to some $200 billion, a figure which included sums owed to Arab lenders and the large Iraqi and Syrian military debts due to the Soviet Union.

A feature of official Arab debt was that most of it was owed to government agencies, whereas the famous and bigger Latin American debts of the period were owed mainly to banks. In many cases the interest being charged on the debt, especially when it came from Arab sources, was well below commercial rates. What was worrying was that the debt represented an average of two thirds of the borrowers' gross domestic products, their annual output of goods and services, and that in Egypt, Sudan, Jordan, Morocco and Iraq the debts ran to well over 100 per cent of GDP.

As the 1980s progressed, one by one the Arab borrowers found themselves unable to service their debts. The first country to face the problem was Morocco, which had a slightly different economic history from the others. It was not an oil producer and few of its nationals worked in the Gulf, so high oil prices worked to its disadvantage. The only benefit it received from them was in the grants it was given, mainly by Saudi Arabia. Its debt had been incurred in the late 1970s and early 1980s when it was embarking on a major programme of investment in infrastructure and facilities for the production of phosphates, of which it has the biggest reserves in the world. For a few years a buoyant market seemed to justify its investment, but then suddenly it was hit by a fall in fertilizer prices, the second big round of oil price rises in 1979/80 and several years of drought. In 1983 it was forced to ask its creditors to agree that $14bn of its debts should be rescheduled.

Morocco's problems were followed in 1985 and 1986 by Algeria, which had been a market borrower, and Tunisia. Neither of these countries rescheduled their debts (and have not rescheduled since) because they did not want to be excluded from the commercial markets in the future, but both began programmes of refinancing, which has meant, in effect, replacing old debts with new. In 1987 Egypt, which had long been in default on some of its debt owed to the United States, negotiated a rescheduling, and Jordan did the same in March 1989, after going into default the previous autumn. Syria in the mid-1980s simply defaulted on much of its debt and refused to negotiate, while Iraq, after it ended its war with Iran in August 1988, told its creditors that if any of them insisted on even partial repayment it would avoid buying from them or using their contractors. Although Iraq had huge debts of some $60bn, owed half to Arab countries and half to the West and the Soviet Union, none of its suppliers demanded repayment. They all hoped that its oil reserves would make it a good risk.

The negotiations that have surrounded the reschedulings and refinancings, in those states that have been through the process, have followed a more or less standard pattern. In cases where countries have rescheduled the initial arrangements have been concluded with the International Monetary Fund, which discusses with the governments how they are going to improve their economic management to avoid having to default on their debts in the future, this being an essential prerequisite of any deal. The IMF is representing in these negotiations the government lenders of the industrialized world, which are grouped in what is known as the Paris Club, so called because the liaison between the Fund and the governments and some of the negotiations on the reschedulings are managed in Paris by a secretariat attached to the French Ministry of Finance. This body, which includes some officials from the other industrialized countries' treasuries, may meet in the Ministry, or in the IMF and World Bank offices or in the Organization for Economic Co-operation and Development (OECD) building; much depends on the sensitivities of the country with which it is dealing. Some countries do not mind being open about the fact that they are talking to the IMF, others consider it shameful and will try to disguise the fact. Whatever the label put on the negotiations, the procedure afterwards is the same: the lending governments sign separate but similar deals with the borrower.

The debts covered are normally made up of development assistance and overdue export credits; military debt is often dealt with separately on a bilateral basis. The rescheduling itself generally involves the lenders taking the interest and principal due to be paid in the year of default and converting it into a new loan. Typical terms include a five year grace period at the beginning and then repayments spread over ten years. Assuming that the borrower remains in financial difficulties for some time it will probably conclude a succession of annual reschedulings, covering each year's interest and principal as it comes due, but it is hoped that by the time repayments begin on its first rescheduling its economy will have improved sufficiently for it to be able to pay on time.

Once a deal has been done with the Paris Club it may be followed by the Gulf lenders and will probably lead to a further deal with the London Club of Western commercial banks. This body — misnamed because since the Latin American debt crisis of 1982 it has run most of its operations in New York – is less institutionalized than the Paris Club. It has no secretariat, the banks involved are different in every negotiation, and its work is handled by lawyers (the main reason why there are many more pages in a London Club deal than in a Paris one). In most cases the Club's reschedulings involve the banks issuing a new loan comprising all the outstanding principal and interest of the old one, stretching the loan over a longer term and giving the borrower a grace period before repayments start. It is with these types of arrangements that the difference between a rescheduling and a refinancing begins to be academic. A London Club rescheduling is, in effect, a refinancing and the type of refinancing that Algeria agreed with the Italian government and banks in 1992, when it reorganized several billion dollars of debt, is not unlike a combination of a Paris Club and a London Club rescheduling. Algeria and Tunisia are both proud of never having had to reschedule and stress the fact in their discussions with foreigners, but outside the two countries' governments it is questionable whether anybody is very concerned by the distinctions they draw.

In a very few cases reschedulings have been accompanied by the actual forgiving of debts, always for political reasons. This happened in two Arab transactions at the time of the Gulf crisis. Morocco in early 1991 was excused $2.6bn of debt by Saudi Arabia, as a result of King Hassan having dispatched a force to serve with the allied armies in the liberation of Kuwait. The King had told those of his people who had demonstrated in favour of Saddam Hussein that the dispatch of his army overseas was his own prerogative and he intended to exercise it. Likewise President Mubarak, who sent a much bigger force to Saudi Arabia, was excused $7bn of US military debt in December 1990 and $6bn owed to the countries of the Gulf Co-operation Council. A few months later, in May 1991, the Paris Club creditors agreed a complicated deal under which they undertook to write off half of the $20bn of debt owed to them, in three tranches of 15 per cent straight away, 15 per cent eighteen months later and 20 per cent three years later, provided that when the second two write-offs became due Egypt could satisfy them that it had stuck to the IMF's reform programme.

Nobody was surprised by the writing off of so much of Egypt's debt. It had been obvious to all the lenders for some time that Egypt had no hope of ever servicing the $50 billion odd of debt it had accumulated and that its strategy was to make itself politically indispensable to its friends, remind them what a disaster it would be if its economy were to collapse and the Islamic fundamentalists come to power, and wait for a stroke of luck, which Saddam provided. In these circumstances the whole industrialized world decided, as the Egyptians had calculated, that the country should be made a special case.*

In most cases the essence of the rescheduling deals is that the principal of the loans should not be written off – but nor should it be repaid, or at least it should not be repaid until it has become unimportant as a burden to the country concerned. The idea instead is that countries should be given time to expand their economies so that their total debt becomes smaller as a proportion of GDP and the annual debt service burden (of interest and part of principal) is reduced as a percentage of foreign currency earnings. This is a practical strategy which often works well. In Morocco, when the government first rescheduled in 1983, debt service was demanding nearly two-thirds of the country's export earnings, which did not allow it sufficient foreign exchange to buy all the materials it needed to keep its economy functioning, but after nine years, regular reschedulings, and some periods of vigorous economic growth, its debt-service requirement was down to some 33 per cent, which was well within its means. The government announced in 1992 that it would not be needing to reschedule again.

Where there is always a problem in putting these arrangements in place is, predictably, in getting governments to agree to the reforms that the IMF demands. These involve them abandoning the habits of living beyond their means and making promises to their people which they cannot fulfil. They are required, in effect, to adopt good housekeeping policies.

The governments have to reduce their budget deficits by eliminating or radically cutting the visible and disguised subsidies they give their economies. The idea of these measures, which apply to the losses of state corporations as well as the subsidies on food and energy given to the people, is to make corporations and people consume only the equivalent of what they produce. What budget deficits remain after the attack on subsidies are to be financed by borrowings from commercial sources rather than by printing money, which is inflationary. Bank

---

* To put these figures for debt relief into perspective, Egypt's main sources of foreign exchange in 1991 were as follows: oil revenues $2.2bn (a figure pushed up by the Gulf crisis from the normal $1.5bn); Suez Canal dues $1.5bn (increasing by about $100m a year); US grant aid and concessionary financing for civil and military purposes $2.3bn; aid of varying degrees of softness from Europe, the Gulf, the IMF and the World Bank $3bn; remittances from Egyptians abroad $3bn; tourism $1–2bn. Income from tourism, which was difficult to estimate, was thought to be close to $3bn in 1992 but fell to perhaps half this level in 1993.

interest rates are to be decontrolled, which always means that they will rise, and banks are directed to lend certain percentages of their balance sheets to specific economic sectors. The purpose of this is that people should be encouraged to save rather than spend and banks and borrowers should be forced to think harder about the likely profitability of projects that are financed with bank lending. Currencies have to be allowed to depreciate to a point where they reach their international market value, with the obvious effect of promoting exports and discouraging imports. Multiple exchange rates, which are a means of governments giving their people subsidies without their showing in the budgets, are eliminated as part of this process. The eventual aim is that when currencies have depreciated sufficiently and the governments and banks have been able to build adequate reserves of foreign exchange, the currencies should be made freely convertible at home and abroad.

Parallel to these budgetary and related financial reforms, the IMF's sister institution, the World Bank, supervises structural changes. These involve mainly the privatization of state manufacturing and service corporations. The feeling at the Fund and the Bank – and, in theory, among some of the debtor governments – is that the state in Arab countries has become involved in many parts of the economies which ought to be run by the private sectors. In two cases, Morocco, and Jordan to a lesser degree, the governments did this because they felt that their private sectors lacked the capital to develop big enterprises and wanted themselves to stimulate their economies. Elsewhere government involvement came about through the nationalization of existing companies, prompted by socialist ideology. Once they had taken over the bigger private companies the republican governments made them increase the numbers of their employees in a futile attempt to prevent unemployment. In the process they took away from them any chance of their making a profit or generating capital for expansion.

The new policy is to release these companies from state control. They are first to be deprived of government subsidies but allowed to charge whatever prices they like, and then sold back to the private sector. It is hoped that with new management, more capital and the stimulus of competition they will produce more, cheaper and better goods and invest in new plant. It is only in this way, it is thought, that the poor Arab economies will be able to achieve faster economic growth in the long term.

Part of the thinking behind the policy concerns a reappraisal of the value of human resources. The view of free-market economists is that governments in the past have failed to think of their people, their energies and intellects, as a source of wealth, and that if countries such as

Egypt, which have large populations and scarce physical resources, are to be successful it can only be through their people developing and selling new skills. This idea was summed up by an Egyptian banker, a particularly enthusiastic advocate of the new philosophy, to whom I spoke in Cairo in 1992. 'The miracle of the market,' he said, 'is that it gives every person a chance to contribute what he can to an economy. The market will expand people's outlook, it will tap their ingenuity, it will make them think of producing things that nobody has thought of producing in Egypt before.'

Another part of the new thinking concerns the best use of capital. It is suggested that the governments need all the money they can get for infrastructural development, education, health and other services that are still reckoned the state's preserve, and they should liberate the money they have tied up in making cement, sugar and steel. They also need from these industries tax revenues, which they will only receive if they can be run at a profit. The private sector, meanwhile, has large amounts of capital that are not being invested productively in the Arab economies and are not yielding tax revenues. In every poor Arab country it is said that citizens have vast sums abroad – around $25bn is the standard figure mentioned in Egypt, Syria and Algeria. This money is partly flight capital, partly the capital of old *émigré* families, and partly the savings of the new expatriate middle classes who have been working in the Gulf and Europe. There is also much middle-class capital in the domestic economies, particularly in property, and there are further large sums being held as cash by small traders. The small trader class, in particular, does not pay tax. In the view of the reformers there is an obvious logic in this capital being mobilized for economic growth, and taxed. Privatization and the parallel reform of the financial markets is seen as the best way of doing this.

Taken as a whole the IMF and World Bank ideas represent a radical departure from the way Arab governments have run their affairs in the past. They are not only painful to implement and politically embarrassing, they involve them relinquishing control of parts of the societies they govern.

A few governments have not been prepared to contemplate these ideas. This has been the case in Libya, where the government has sufficient oil revenues not to have to reform, and Iraq, where normal economic life has been suspended since the Gulf crisis. Even if their economic circumstances were not exceptional, these governments would not reform for ideological reasons. They operate too much as dictatorships and have the habit of control too deeply engrained in their systems. Syria is in nearly the same position. Since the late 1980s its economy has been helped by an increase in oil production, which has made its debts seem less serious and allowed the government to increase its spending. At the same time it has made itself aware of the World Bank's thinking and has implemented some of the easiest of its policies. It has allowed private businessmen to import more and invest in types of industries and services that were previously closed to them. This has produced a minor boom and given a superficial appearance of change. But there has been no serious reform, and it is difficult to imagine this happening while Assad remains in power.

Some slightly less inflexible Arab governments have been prepared to introduce IMF and World Bank reforms but have not wanted it known that they are talking to the two institutions. Their attitude has been like that of the government in Iran, where an official in the Central Bank told me in 1991 that no advice was being sought from the Fund and that 'if any is offered it will be ignored'. He added that the Islamic Republic had broken contact with the Fund ten years before because it was clearly an instrument of the United States Government. In fact at the time there was an IMF team in Tehran, officially for 'consultation and the preparation of a report on the Iranian economy', and after its visit the government had many other contacts with the Fund and went on to impose an exceptionally disciplined reform programme on its country.

Events in Sudan in 1991 and 1992 followed a roughly similar pattern. The government here stood as the biggest defaulter to the IMF and was being threatened with suspension of its membership of both the Fund and the Bank. It did not like taking orders from either body, and especially not from the IMF, which of the two is more strongly associated with the rich industrialized countries. However, it was desperate for aid, its relations with every other possible lender had been severed and the World Bank, which still maintained an office in Khartoum, was its last hope. In the summer of 1991, after the Government had loudly backed the losing side in the Gulf war and its fortunes seemed to have sunk as low as they could go, it was told by the Bank that if it did not put in place a reform programme that held out the possibility of it being able to service its debts, the Bank's office would have to close. It was made plain to it that because it had made so many promises to reform in the past and never done anything to put them into effect it no longer enjoyed goodwill or credibility. The Finance Minister was genuinely upset when he absorbed this news. The prospect loomed of Sudan becoming the first developing country to be totally cut off from financial help. He therefore persuaded his colleagues in the cabinet that this time the reforms had to be genuine, and so during the later months

of 1991 and early 1992 the government put into effect a reform programme that was more austere than the Fund or Bank would ever
have dared impose on a debtor country. Among its measures were the
abolition of virtually every price control and subsidy and a devaluation
of 70 per cent. As it planned and implemented its reforms the government talked to teams of advisers sent from the IMF, but the World
Bank's representative sat in on the meetings, and the government obviously preferred to have it appear that it was the Bank rather than the
Fund with which it was dealing. It was assumed that if the government's
relations with the industrialized lenders improved and it got to the stage
of again rescheduling its debts, it would be the Bank rather than the
Fund that would call a meeting of the Paris Club.

Sensitivity about being seen to be accepting IMF and World Bank
programmes extends to countries that have been quite willing
reformers. Tunisia and Algeria introduced reforms of their own accord,
partly as a means of protecting their pride and avoiding having to
reschedule. If they did not ask the IMF for special financial help, they
reasoned, the Fund would have no pretext for telling them that they
should change the management of their economies. Having saved their
amour propre both countries have consulted in detail with the IMF
and instituted classic IMF sets of reforms. In Algeria the process was
interrupted by the threat of the Front Islamique de Salut winning the
national elections and by the military intervention of January 1992.

Paradoxically it is the countries that are forced to reform but are
fairly happy to be seen talking to the Fund that argue hardest. Normally
as the time of an unavoidable default nears, or passes, an IMF team
comes to the debtor government and gives it an analysis of its economic
prospects. It then explains which features of the country's economy
need to be corrected. The government always agrees with both the
analysis and the recommendation, but then there is an argument over
when the reforms should start and how fast they should move forward.
The government wants to begin the programme after eighteen months,
when it has arranged some financial help, hoping, of course, that it
might avoid having to reform altogether. The Fund tells it that it must
put a reform programme in place, and then it will have its debts rescheduled. The argument continues until the government realizes that it has
no option but to do roughly what the Fund tells it.

Once they start putting the reforms into effect governments often
find that the early – budgetary and financial – stages are easier and
quicker acting than they expected. There have been some surprisingly
fast turn-rounds in reforming countries' budgetary positions, balance
of payments and domestic growth rates.

A classic success story has been Jordan. In October 1988, when this country defaulted, its financial state was as bad as that of any country in the Middle East. It had debts of $8bn, which represented 167 per cent of its GDP and made it the most indebted country per capita in the world. Economists calculated that its consumption was equivalent to rather more than its domestic product, which meant that it would have been running up debts even if it had been investing nothing in its own economy. When the Jordanian middle classes discovered, quite suddenly, that the government had no money to service its debts they were shocked and began immediately to blame the greed and corruption of some of the people around the King. Then as the government started raising taxes they were forced to admit to themselves that they were not part of the affluent Western world, as they had almost come to believe, but were still citizens of a developing country that had little industry and few natural resources. They found the experience demoralizing.

The government, though, rose to the challenge and had a reform programme in place by March 1989. It floated the dinar, completely deregulated interest rates and increased taxation. The number of deductible items individuals were allowed for income tax purposes was reduced, stamp duties were raised and a consumption tax, which was in effect a factory gate tax on consumer goods made in Jordan, was introduced. This type of tax in Arab countries is much more efficient than income tax, which is mostly evaded by anybody who is not a government employee. A further tax was imposed on people who were employing foreign servants, most often Filipino maids and nannies, and a special airport tax of some $40 was levied on Jordanians leaving the country. It was in particular the tax on servants that the newly comfortable Jordanian middle classes said at the time was going to be intolerable.

Within a few months the medicine seemed to take effect. The government was set to cut its budget deficit by 40 per cent, and thanks to the devaluation small factories that made such products as electrical fittings, sheet metal goods and medical supplies for the regional market were reopening. Then the whole programme was thrown off course by the Gulf crisis. The UN sanctions much reduced Jordan's trade with Iraq, which had been taking 20 per cent of its exports, and brought its trade with Saudi Arabia and the Gulf to a halt. The Jordanian people had incurred the wrath of the Gulf states by enthusiastically supporting Saddam Hussein, and their government had criticized Saudi Arabia for inviting the Western powers into a quarrel which it said should be resolved by the Arabs themselves. As the crisis deepened the country

received 300,000 Palestinians who had been living in Kuwait. These
people owned a large and useful amount of capital, later estimated to
be $1.5bn, but their most noticeable impact when they arrived was
to put a strain on the Kingdom's social services and increase its
unemployment.

When the crisis was over in the spring of 1991 the Iraqi and Gulf
markets remained closed but the government returned to its reform
programme. By the beginning of the following year in consultation with
the IMF it had drawn up a seven-year schedule of reforms which aimed
to allow the economy to grow, clearly necessary given the increase in
the population, but slowly to bring down government debt as a proportion of GDP to 137 per cent. It also aimed to balance the country's
current account by the end of 1998, the end of the programme, and
have the budget deficit down to 5 per cent of GDP. As a first step
towards these objectives the government increased the rate and scope
of the consumption tax, cut subsidies on food to a point where just
five items, bread, rice, sugar, animal feed and milk, remained receiving
any subsidy at all, and switched the subsidy it paid on several types of
fuel to a tax. The new tax was applied to heavy fuel oil, used by
factories, super gasoline, for luxury cars, and diesel fuel, much of which
was bought by lorries in transit between Europe and Saudi Arabia. The
revenue from these sources more than offset the small remaining subsidy
on ordinary gasoline and kerosene, used by the poorer Jordanians. An
interesting reflection of the way relations between debtor governments
and the IMF are conducted was that Jordan's 1992 rescheduling package was signed in early March a few days after the fuel taxes were
introduced. The Fund had wanted to see the tax levied before it recommended the rescheduling to the Paris Club.

Once again the economy responded well to its treatment. Further
small factories reopened or their production increased. They were
helped not only by the devaluation, which by the end of the crisis had
reached 50 per cent, but by the fall in wages that had taken place since
the mid-1980s' boom. They found new markets in Morocco, Tunisia,
Yemen, Sudan, eastern Europe and even the United States. As the Palestinian returnees, who were regarded as 'Kuwaitiized' and vulgar, settled
into their new home, they began building big expensive stone houses,
which caused a construction boom. They also established new
businesses, most conspicuously at first in retailing. Their capital produced a boom on the stock market, which rose by 30 per cent in 1992.
During that year the government saw its budget deficit as a proportion
of GDP fall to 7 per cent, which it had not expected to happen until
1997, and the country's economic growth rate reached an extraordinary

11 per cent. It was expected to run at 5 per cent a year for the next five years. If it did this it was thought that the country would be able to create the 50,000 new jobs it needed every year, and reduce its unemployment rate from the alarming level of 19 per cent.

Obviously the turn-round in Jordan's economy in 1992 was helped greatly by this influx of 300,000 rich new citizens. It is also true that Jordan is a small country – even with the returnees its population is only 3.6 million – and its people are well educated. This is one of the features that make its economy relatively easy to manage.

Equally important the country has not had to go through the structural reform part of the IMF and World Bank programme. Its economy has always run on market lines. It has an active stock market, it has not prohibited imports to protect local industries, and its banks, although previously tightly regulated, have never been regarded as arms of the state to be used for financing the losses of industrial monopolies. It has very few state-owned corporations. The national airline, the utilities, the large phosphates and potash companies, and its shares in the cement industry and some of Amman's major hotels would be a nearly complete list of the holdings the government has in businesses that might be sold to the private sector. Some of these companies are quite profitable, which is why the government has no plans so far to privatize them.

This lack of necessity for stuctural change has been the key to Jordan's rapid success. It has been noticeable that in all countries that have begun reform the financial management parts of the programme have gone well; even Algeria before the winter of 1991/2 was making good progress in these areas. What makes this stage of reform fairly easy is that much of it can be done, more or less, with a stroke of a pen. A government can devalue a currency, raise a tax or lower a subsidy by an administrative act in the finance minister's office, and as long as the people have been prepared for the decision and the financial shock is spread over several instalments, so that there are no riots, the act is immediately effective. It may be painful for the people and embarrassing for the government, but that is all.

Structural reform, on the other hand, involves the reorganization of whole economies through the agency of unenthusiastic and unskilled bureaucracies. It changes the fabric of societies and reduces the governments' control of their people. In every way it is more difficult than financial reform.

11

Structural Reform

IMF reforms in Egypt – slow implementation of structural reform – lack of understanding of market economy – obstruction of privatization in Tunisia – reform of banking systems – chances of reform succeeding – population growth – water shortages

Once the IMF and the World Bank have succeeded in imposing financial discipline on an Arab debtor they set about rooting socialism out of its economy. This process has been underway, guided by creditors or local governments, in many parts of the world since the mid-1980s. In the eastern European countries and the former Soviet Union it was begun by revolution which has given it momentum. In the Arab countries the situation is different. There have been no recent revolutions. The impetus for change is coming from the arm-twisting of the World Bank and the Western creditor governments and the sheer logical necessity of reform, which the Arab governments have tended to accept only reluctantly. This is making the process a slow one.

The main features of the second stage of the reform programme are privatization, the lifting of price controls and the opening of domestic markets to foreign goods. The trade liberalization, which is intended to encourage efficiency in the domestic manufacturers that are going to be privatized, involves the complete abandonment of lists of prohibited imports and import licensing systems, and the lowering of tariff barriers. On many categories of goods these have been as high as 100 or 200 per cent.

A complementary programme in the financial sector begins with the reorganization, and often recapitalization, of the banks, so that they are allowed, or forced, to operate on commercial principles. It involves the reopening of capital markets and the introduction of modern legislation to regulate financial transactions in a market economy.

The two strands of structural redevelopment are supposed to begin once governments have put in place the basic IMF financial reforms, but everywhere the programme is lagging far behind schedule. Egypt, where state supervision of the economy has been the most deeply entrenched and the most inefficient, is a good example. The country began its reforms with a standard IMF financial package. Its first efforts to implement the programme, in 1987, were unsuccessful because it could not bring itself to cut its budget deficit by anywhere near the amount the Fund demanded. But then during the Gulf crisis it was offered the prospect of a large amount of debt relief, and when it tried to reform again after the crisis it was more successful. In the space of about a year it put into effect a series of reforms which by its own standards were radical. It abolished its multiple exchange rates, which had the desirable effect of putting all its subsidies into its budget, where their true size became visible. The Egyptian pound was floated and far from sinking remained stable in the markets. It was helped by the decontrol of interest rates and the government's issue of tax-free treasury bills. Money poured into the country from Egyptians abroad and the government's reserves rose steadily, to the impressive figure of $14.5bn in March 1993. The government was even able to buy foreign grain for cash. At the same time it reduced its budget deficit, partly by slowly raising the prices of electricity and gasoline and, very tentatively, attacking the subsidy on bread. Some of the price rises were brought about by the technique, well practised by Middle East governments, of introducing an allegedly improved or bigger product at a significantly higher price and then gradually phasing out the smaller original product. When this formula was applied to bread it was noticed that the new five-piastre loaf was not really five times bigger or better than the slowly disappearing one-piastre loaf.

By the middle of 1992 the IMF was quite impressed by Egypt's performance and from the point of view of its own normal areas of responsibility would have been happy to approve the cancellation of the 15 per cent of outstanding Paris Club debt which was scheduled for November that year. The World Bank, however, was much less satisfied with the government's progress in the areas it was supposed to supervise. One of its officials remarked at the time that in his opinion the government had no more than a fifty-fifty chance of qualifying for the next tranche of relief, though he added, 'it might just wriggle through'. In the event the debt relief was granted, in mid-1993, but only after several rounds of talks on the acceleration of reforms and much nagging of the Egyptians by the principal Paris Club governments.

The process of structural reform, which was causing the Bank so much irritation, had begun in May 1991, when the government had put in place a legal framework for privatization in the form of a law which outlined how it was going to prepare state companies for sale. It cut off the companies from subsidies and freed them to manage themselves. They were allowed to make their own decisions on what types of goods and what quantities they should produce, how many people they should employ, and, in almost every case, what prices they should charge. The law also provided for the establishment of twenty-seven holding companies which would manage groups of state corporations as portfolios and would be responsible for making each company in their charge efficient and saleable. The idea behind this was that it would be better to put in charge of privatization people who had the sale of companies as their purpose, and who could expect to be rewarded for success, than to leave the process to the Ministry of Industry, which would be bound to feel that in privatizing companies it was doing away with its empire and many of its officials' jobs. Further legislation began the lowering of tariffs, cutting the maximum rate from 100 per cent to 80 per cent, and the cancellation in stages of the lists of prohibited imports.

Together the new laws and the establishment of the holding companies, both of which were designed largely by the World Bank, marked a promising beginning, but then very little happened. A few hotels were sold to private investors, and these were untypical of most state assets in that they were profitable and came under the authority of the energetic and reform-minded Minister of Tourism. In the spring of 1993 there were signs of new movement. The government started to gather bids for a further mixed batch of twenty companies and other state assets, among them some more hotels, a few Nile cruisers and a handful of industrial concerns, including the Suez Cement Company and the El Nasr Bottling Company. According to the plans it published, these were only the first of eighty-five concerns that were supposed to be privatized by 1997, but even as the bids began to be considered the programme was falling behind schedule. Officials were not prepared to name any further companies which might be included in the next batch to be sold, because, it was said, the government wanted to see how the marketing of the first twenty fared. The feeling among Western bankers and economists in Cairo was that this was a delaying tactic.

The most simple and charitable explanation of the slow pace of the Egyptians is that privatization is a difficult and dangerous business. What is to be sold, eventually, is the major part of the Egyptian economy, made up of all the bigger industrial, contracting and service enterprises. Together these are responsible for some 50 to 70 per cent of the country's

GDP – the figure depends on one's estimate of the size of the private sector black economy. They employ the greater part of the Egyptian labour force that is not involved in agriculture, and they are said to be overstaffed by anything from a third to 600 per cent. The exact amount cannot accurately be assessed. It varies from one enterprise to another and, anyway, the concept of overstaffing is itself to some extent a subjective one. One owner, or accountant, might employ more people at a lower wage than another might do. Even so, however the problem is measured there will clearly be huge redundancies as companies are privatized, and it will be some time before the work force will be given new jobs by the faster growing economy which restructuring is supposed to produce. There is a danger that unemployment will throw people into the hands of the militant Islamic groups, or lead to riots. This makes it sensible for the government to proceed slowly and see just how many people are made redundant by the early privatizations, and how they react.

An equally serious problem for the government is that it does not have the means to go faster on privatization. The officials in the ministries, the holding companies and the state corporations themselves are totally unqualified to organize the sale of companies, and they cannot put the business into the hands of Egyptian merchant banks because there are no such institutions. There are virtually no Egyptians working in the country who know about mergers and acquisitions, financial restructuring or company valuations. The authorities can draw on foreign merchant banks and on parts of the World Bank group, but the people they send will probably not know about Egyptian conditions, and may not speak Arabic. Thus they will have to have Egyptians working alongside them to explain how their ideas might be adapted to suit local conditions, and there are few Egyptians with experience of working with modern banks. No doubt eventually the authorities will develop useful relationships with Western banks, but the process will take time.

These are all fundamental difficulties, because in Egypt there is much more than the normal amount of preparatory work that needs to be done to make state corporations marketable. The companies have to be given better management structures, which in most cases will involve a weeding out of excessive numbers of executive directors. They need to have their labour forces much reduced before privatization. They also need to be given something resembling normal balance sheets. At present many of the companies are unsaleable because they have no assets, other than land and worn-out plant, and no prospect of making profits. Any Western company, rather than buy an Egyptian factory for even a nominal price, would invest from scratch. Finding Egyptian buyers, therefore, will involve the holding companies trying slowly to reduce the corporations'

losses and then selling them for very small sums to owners who have
experience of Egyptian industrial conditions and are able to make
profits out of businesses which Westerners would find impossible to
manage. It may be in the end that some of the companies will prove
impossible to sell and will have to be allowed quietly to fade away.

Those firms that can be sold need not just financial and management
restructuring, but whole new departments of people trained, or in Egypt
semi-trained, to manage research, quality control, accounting and
marketing. These are some of the most basic functions of any company
competing in a free market, but they hardly exist in Egyptian state
corporations. It is here that the work of privatization encounters one
of the most serious of all its problems, which is that the people who
are running the state corporations, in some cases the same as those
running the holding companies, have no idea about how a market
economy operates. They have spent all their working lives in a command economy, in which they have known no uncertainty. Those who
have been managing manufacturing companies have been told to produce certain amounts of particular products at fixed prices, and distribution companies have then delivered the products to the public. If the
goods have been too cheap or produced in insufficient quantity the
public has been allowed to queue; if they have not sold because they
have been too expensive or of inferior quality a ban has been put on
competing imports. The system has been run by engineers and tailored
to the way of thinking of the most simple production line manager. The
sole focus of the corporation directors' interest has been the numbers of
units their factories have been able to produce. The performance of the
managers has been judged according to how close they have been able
to get to their targets. Given the system of fixed prices and import
controls nobody has ever had to worry about quality or profits.

In future in a market economy, managers will be confronted with
hundreds of new, difficult decisions. The managers of, for example, a
shoe company will find that their shareholders will be judging them
not by the quantities they are producing but by how well their shoes
are selling. And if the shoes are not selling well they will have to find
out whether this is because the public prefers European imports and,
if this is the case, what it would like to see changed in the Egyptian
company's own shoes. It may be the quality, design, price or packaging.
It may be that the shoes are perfectly saleable but are being marketed
in the wrong way. Once they know what the problem is the managers
will have to pinpoint what part of the production process they should
change, and how they can control costs in doing this, and then get their
plans implemented by staff who may only half understand the reasons

for the changes. It is because these processes were so unfamiliar to Egyptian managers that there were surprisingly few changes in the prices of industrial goods in the later months of 1991 after the regime of price controls was lifted.

Not surprisingly, in view of the multitude of difficulties, the Egyptian government establishment is not enthusiastic about privatization. Mr Mubarak and most of his cabinet colleagues accept it as an unpleasant necessity which has to be put into operation, but at all levels below them there is quiet resistance to the idea.

The Egyptian civil servants have several reasons for opposing privatization. They do not understand market economies, though they hate to admit this. They also do not trust the private sector. This is because since the nationalizations of the early 1960s there have been hardly any private companies in Egypt that have seemed capable of running operations on the scale of those of the state corporations. Under a nominally socialist government there has been no development of the equivalent of the bigger family companies of the Arabian oil states, such as Juffali, Olayan, Alireza and Kanoo, which now have professional Arab/Western managements and a long-term approach to business which increasingly resembles that of Western corporations. Most private businessmen in Egypt operate on a small scale, and many think short term and are speculatively minded, looking for the quick deal which will yield them an immediate profit. The same goes for stock-exchange investors. The suspicion of the civil servants, therefore, is that whether the state corporations are floated on the stock market or sold to individuals or groups of investors, the new owners will not have any interest in keeping them in being in the long term.*

The officials' nervousness is increased by the odour of corruption

---

* The same lack of faith in private businessmen is preventing the governments in Egypt and in other poor Arab countries from allowing the private sector to invest in the development of natural gas, which according to current thinking should be used to fuel domestic power stations and industrial plants, leaving the countries' more easily exported oil production to earn foreign currency revenues. Natural gas requires large amounts of capital to develop and gives a much lower return than oil, and it ought therefore to be something which governments should happily privatize. Investors would be a combination of the domestic private sector and foreign oil companies. In practice governments have been reluctant to pursue this policy because they think of gas as a 'strategic' national asset and cannot face seeing it in private or foreign ownership. A similar worry surfaced in Morocco in 1991 and 1992 when development agencies suggested that a $50m pipeline running to a refinery near Casablanca might be built by the private sector. It was pointed out that private businessmen would hardly 'steal the pipe or put wine in it', but the government would not consider the idea.

which in Egypt and elsewhere surrounds dealings between the bureaucracy and the private sector. Their fear is that if they give approval for transactions that are of obvious benefit to private persons they may be accused of having accepted bribes (as many of them have in these circumstances) and this reinforces their engrained reluctance to take decisions. Quite petty matters of this sort have been known to pass up the bureaucracy to the desk of the President.

More fundamentally officials in both the state corporations and the ministries that supervise them are worried about privatization as a threat to their way of life as bureaucrats, as they have known it in the last thirty years. Some stand to lose their jobs. Many of the others will find themselves working for private employers in a competitive environment, rather than for the government. They may no longer be able to look to their employers for the job security and all the benefits, the housing, cars, pensions, foreign travel, expenses and opportunities for petty corruption through being paid to sign documents, which go with their positions at present. It is these advantages, coupled with the fact that there is no unemployment pay in Egypt, that make young men so anxious to get jobs in the bureaucracy and cause them to put such pressure on friends and relatives already working there to create posts for them.

The system of 'you scratch my back I'll scratch yours', which is highly developed in Egypt, will operate much less well after privatization. People will find the system around them changing slowly to one which demands that they work effectively for their salaries, probably bigger ones than they are getting at present, and then pay for the things they want to buy.

The people at the top of the Egyptian government are very aware of the bureaucracy's anxieties and take them seriously. The officials in the ministries and the state corporations are of the middle classes which were created by Nasser and which have been the principal constituents of the regime since the mid-1950s. If these people were to feel their security and status threatened in an immediate and acute sense, they might turn against the government. This would not only make it impossible for the structural reform programme to continue, it would remove the public support which is necessary for any government and would destroy the administration's self-confidence. This is a much more serious threat than the unhappiness of the poor who suffer the increases in the price of bread. The poor if they riot or join fundamentalist groups can probably be dealt with by the army or the police, but the loss of the confidence of the middle classes, which was a factor in the near collapse of the FLN government in Algeria after 1988, undermines a government from within and leaves it vulnerable to pressure from the bottom of society. It is because they know that they must keep the support of the middle classes that President Mubarak and the ministers and advisers around him are not pressing the bureaucracy too hard to implement the reform programme. They are letting it slowly become used to the idea.

The very fact that the Egyptian government has moved so cautiously on privatization makes it difficult for anyone to predict how its officials will behave when they actually begin pre-sale corporate reorganizations or negotiations with potential buyers. To see what might happen then one has to turn to Tunisia, where the programme is more advanced.

Tunisia, though a small country with a population a bit over 8 million and a much higher standard of living than Egypt's, is like Egypt in having been for thirty years under a socialist government. In some periods it has been more strongly socialist than Egypt. In the late 1950s and 1960s Habib Bourguiba was certainly a more pragmatic leader than Nasser, and the society he led was pushed into developing along liberal social lines, but in the 1970s, when the Egyptians under Sadat had lost interest in socialism as an idea and were looking for a way of escaping from it, the Tunisians stayed committed to their moderate version of the ideology. Then and for most of the 1980s the country remained much more socialist than it appeared to foreign visitors, either tourists or businessmen. Most of its industry was owned by the state. Since 1986, when it was forced by its burden of debt to begin reform, and 1987, when Zine El-Abidine Ben Ali replaced Habib Bourguiba, who was becoming senile, Tunisia has been moving away from socialism, albeit somewhat hesitantly, and has been implementing standard types of economic reforms. It has been very successful with the early parts of the IMF programme, and its government firmly supports the principle of privatization. In interviews Tunisian ministers are enthusiastic about the idea; they point out that in their eighth national development plan they are looking to the private sector for more than half the total investment.

Yet in Tunisia, as in Egypt, privatization has moved slowly. In 1986, as a condition of the first Structural Adjustment Loan it received from the World Bank, the government drew up a list of three hundred companies that would be privatized, but in the seven years that followed only some forty of these were sold. They included a tourism company, the national wood importer and various manufacturing concerns, including several producing textiles. One of the companies, a firm originally called Le Confort, which made refrigerators, provided a perfect example of what should be the benefits of privatization. As a state enterprise it suffered from very poor industrial relations – Tunisia is a highly trade-unionized country – and made regular large losses, which made it a burden on the government and caused it to be one of the first companies to be disposed of. Within a few months of its being transferred to the private sector, under the new name of Société Tunisienne Electromenager, it had been turned round to make a profit, without any of the labour force having been made redundant. The secret of its success was simply that its new owners understood basic financial disciplines and marketing. The officials in the government began to mutter that they had sold it too cheaply.

The reason, predictably, for the slow progress of sales has been that the officials in the ministries that own the companies have been obstructing them. They stress, at the beginning of every negotiation with a buyer, the government's desire not to increase unemployment. The government has been worried about this since early 1984, when a large and ineptly managed cut in the subsidy on bread and semolina led to riots, and its fears have been made worse by events in Algeria in recent years. Buyers of state companies, therefore, are being asked either to avoid lay-offs or to ensure that workers are given good severance pay. The emphasis put on this, combined with the officials' selection of the most unprofitable companies for early privatization, has succeeded in scaring away a number of potential buyers. Officials have emphasised the weak features of companies and concealed their good points, making the paperwork as complex as possible (including changing the requirements in mid-negotiation), and making as big a difficulty as possible out of the quite common complications in companies' property rights. In many cases although the government may own a company that is for sale, a municipality owns the land on which its factory has been built, and the municipality staff are often only too happy to help ministry officials frustrate a sale by refusing to part with their land, demanding higher rents or creating any one of a number of possible obstacles concerning leases or planning permissions.

The people in the ministries and municipalities are, of course, assisted in their obstruction by the staffs of the companies themselves. The managers resist the internal reorganization of their firms, which in most cases is undertaken on an *ad hoc* basis as part of the process of each company being offered for sale. No attempt is being made to prepare companies in advance of the time of sale, as the holding companies should, in theory, be doing in Egypt. Faced with having to reduce the numbers of their directors or establish new departments, the reaction of most company boards is to demand a subsidized state loan, or a grant, to help with the process. When told that they have to improve the quality of their products, the boards normally agree that this is desirable but then request another subsidized loan for new equipment. This is what they have been given whenever they have had to make changes in the past, and it is what seems natural to them.

It rarely occurs to the companies' directors that there are other sources of funds, which they might tap through selling assets, trying to cut costs and increase profits, or even going to the recently deregulated banks to negotiate a commercial loan. Doing any of these things would mean their entering the new world of the free market, which they do not understand and find frightening.

Fortunately for the governments and bureaucracies, not to mention their foreign advisers, reforming financial institutions and capital markets is easier than privatization. It does not create unemployment, nor trouble civil servants, though it does involve a huge break with the past.

In all the socialist Arab countries since the 1960s the commercial banks have been run as extensions of the finance ministries. The most hardline states have seen no need for even the appearance of competition and each has consolidated its entire banking system into a single institution, on the old eastern European and Soviet model. The more moderate governments, notably Tunisia, have kept many different banks but, until recently, instructed them on exactly what interest rates they should charge and what proportion of their lending should go to each sector of the economy. They also made the banks give low-interest loans to the government. In between the two types of regime were the Algerian and Egyptian systems, in which small numbers of state banks were ordered to lend to state corporations without applying any commercial criteria at all. They were not so much regulated as used as a method of printing money and taxing the private sector by transferring parts of its savings to the state.

In Egypt until 1991 the big four public-sector banks, Banque Misr, Banque du Caire, Bank of Alexandria and National Bank of Egypt, were given the job of financing the losses of the nationalized industries. The more workers the industries were forced to take on and the bigger their losses became, the bigger were the loans they were given. In effect, as an official of one of the governments lending to Egypt put it, 'the red ink on the companies' balance sheets was the banks' collateral'. It went without saying that few of the loans were ever serviced. It was in this way that the Egyptian public-sector corporations received most of their state subsidies.

Stock exchanges in the socialist countries and the more heavily regulated market economies, principally Morocco, have been small and inactive. Few companies have been listed and there have not been enough transactions each day for brokers to be able to quote prices that reflect stocks' proper market value. The owners of companies hardly think of the stock markets as a source of capital; if they need to raise equity they go to their extended families or networks of friends.

In none of the poor Arab countries has there been any of the legal framework that underpins private companies and capital markets in the industrialized world. In Morocco the law that governed these matters in 1992 was drawn ultimately from the French legislation of 1867, which had been adapted for the Kingdom's purposes in 1959. It laid down the most minimal capital requirements for limited liability companies – just 300 dirhams, about $30. It made no stipulation on the competence of auditors, their responsibilities, the standards they should apply or their fees. The result was that public companies in Morocco, other than those that wanted to have proper sets of accounts, were virtually unaudited, even though some hid the fact by producing quite glossy annual reports. A bank with total assets equivalent to $1.5bn, which might have spent $100,000 on its audit in the United States or Europe, would spend just $1,000 in Morocco, for work of a quality that matched the fee.

There were virtually no requirements for information to be given in public companies' reports. A company could give a figure for a profit or loss, but it was not required to state what accounting principles (if any) had been used, or how it had valued securities, stock or real estate, or give any other explanations. Private companies were not required to make available any information at all about themselves. In the industrialized countries anyone can go to the appropriate authority and find out who owns a company and what is its financial position. In 1992 it was still not possible for a person to do this in Morocco.

Pushed by their creditors, the governments of Morocco and the other Arab countries have accepted that their banking systems and capital markets have to be totally overhauled. An Egyptian banker has described his country as needing 'a rejuvenated stock exchange, a modern deregulated banking system, the usual body of legislation that goes with free markets, a re-educated judiciary with an understanding of commerce, organized regulating bodies, and an accepted code of free-market business ethics'. It will clearly take much more than a decade for these changes to be instituted and become established, but by 1992–3 most countries' governments were already working on new legislation and in some cases they were putting it into effect.

The Moroccans, for instance, were establishing a new body to supervise the Casablanca stock exchange, on which only sixty-nine shares

were quoted.* The parliament was debating a law on auditing requirements, which had as one of its provisions the establishment of a regulat-
ory body for the profession. The Casablanca business school, prompted
by the government, in 1990 had begun the training of accountants. It
was assumed here and in other Arab countries – not least Algeria,
where in 1992 there were only fifty accountants – that there would be
an enormous expansion of the auditing and legal professions.

Moroccan tax laws, applying to both individuals and companies,
were changed at the beginning of the 1990s to make them clearer and
to spell out the obligations and rights of both the tax payers and the
tax collecting agencies. Tax rates, which for companies ran up to 44 per
cent, were expected to be lowered. This had recently been done with great
success in Tunisia. In 1991 the top rate of Tunisian personal income tax
had been cut from 68 to 35 per cent while corporation tax had been cut
from 45 to 35 per cent. The coverage of taxes had been increased, but
collection had been enforced and the laws made simpler, to the point
where a banker could describe the 'whole structure' as being 'brilliantly
clear'. The predictable result was that the government had been able to
collect more tax, which had helped reduce its budget deficit.

Reform of the banking system in Tunisia has involved fairly thorough
deregulation. This allows the banks to lend where they please, though
out of force of habit the directors of most of them still look to the
Central Bank to be told what to do. In Egypt in 1991 the government
gave the four big banks a major infusion of capital at the same time
as it cut off the public sector corporations' subsidies. Then in June
1992 it passed a new banking law, Law 37, which obliged the banks
to classify their assets according to internationally accepted (Basle Committee) standards as good, doubtful, non-performing or bad. The same
law transferred control of the banks from the economics ministry to
the Central Bank, and in a later refinement in early 1993, permitted
the small foreign bank branches that had for some years been doing
international business in Egypt to deal in the local currency. This last

---

* Privatization in Morocco in the early 1990s was not moving much faster than in
Egypt or Tunisia. The government had outlined a privatization plan in 1989 and
published a list of seventy-five companies and thirty-seven hotels which it intended to
sell. All of these it had established itself as part of an excursion into state capitalism
in the 1960s and 1970s. Given that the country had no lingering socialist tradition,
privatization should have been easier than elsewhere, but by 1993 only a handful of
assets had been sold. Admittedly the flotations of some companies were very successful,
being oversubscribed several times. Many of their shares had gone to Moroccans living
abroad. The pro-private sector climate had encouraged a big increase of foreign investment in the country since 1988.

clause was expected to have a slow but radical effect in stimulating the introduction of new products and creating competition for the state banks.

At the same time as Law 37 was passed, a capital markets law, largely drafted by the World Bank, gave equity shares almost the same tax-free status that had encouraged such a big flow of capital into bank deposits and treasury bills in the previous two years. It cut capital gains tax and stamp duty on share transactions from a possible total of 25 per cent to 2 per cent. It also removed an old ceiling of 7 per cent on bond coupons, which had prevented companies competing with banks and the treasury in raising loan capital. The view of bankers and investors in Cairo was that there was, typically, too much emphasis in the law on ways of controlling a market that had hardly come into existence, but in comparison to what had gone before it was described by one as 'a huge leap forward'.

There remains the question of whether the whole series of reforms introduced to the Arab debtors by the IMF and the World Bank will work. The question is best divided into two parts, one dealing with the debt crisis and the other with overall economic reform and the Arabs' chances of developing prosperous, fast-growing economies.

The consensus in mid-1993 among bankers and lending governments was that the debt crisis was over. After some remarkably successful budgetry reforms, Tunisia and Morocco were servicing their debts, Jordan was still rescheduling, though on a predictable annual basis, and Egypt was servicing its commercial debt and having part of its government debt forgiven in accordance with an agreed programme. The creditors' opinion was that Tunisia and Jordan, if they had had the political will, could have tightened their belts further and achieved still greater success. Looking at the region as a whole an official of one of the lending governments commented that 'whereas in 1990 one could only see problems, now one can see a plausible return to normality'.

Nobody in 1993 was yet going so far as to predict a Latin American style recovery, which in the previous few years had seen countries which were once much more indebted than the Arabs emerge as the possible economic 'tigers' of the 1990s. In South and Central America growth rates were among the highest in the developing world, multinational companies were investing and stock exchanges were booming. It was difficult to imagine this happening in the Arab world because most of the countries there had been more socialist than the Latin American states.

The one Arab country that remained immersed in a seemingly intractable debt crisis was Algeria, which in terms of the ratio of its annual debt service ($8.5bn) to its foreign exchange income ($11–12bn) was the most seriously indebted country in the world. In the early 1990s it was surviving by borrowing enough short term to service each year's debt. Most of what it owed was high-interest commercial debt, much of it in yen. Its oil and gas income was in dollars, which were depreciating against the Japanese currency. The country was making no progress in reducing its total debt, and because of the short-term nature of its borrowings annual repayment demands were going to stay at the same level for the indefinite future. Algeria clearly needed to agree with its creditors a major rescheduling and reform package, and, in spite of its traditional sensitivity to the idea, this is what Redha Malek's government at the end of 1993 was preparing to do. Teams from the IMF had visited the country and terms had been agreed.

The second part of the question on reform – whether it will produce successful economies in the long term – is less easy to analyse. Much depends on whether the governments really want to pursue the reforms, and the evidence on this is unclear. In most countries governments have tended to introduce just enough reform at each stage of the process to satisfy their creditors. Then they have hesitated. The Tunisians in particular have been accused of resting on their laurels. The problem is not just a matter of obstruction by the bureaucracy, it comes right from the top of the governments. It is certainly true that the heads of state and the people around them appreciate both the theoretical benefits and the immediate practical necessity of reform. It must also be true that they see that getting out of debt and stimulating the growth of their economies will increase their political power, in the region and internationally. This would be particularly welcome to Mr Mubarak who leads a country which would be by far the most powerful in the region if it did not have to ask for charity from others. Yet none of these arguments means that reform appeals to the people at the top of the governments in an instinctive or emotional sense.

Explaining their caution, the cabinet members point to the political dangers of unemployment. They sometimes admit that reforms could be pushed ahead faster, but they say this would mean imposing them on the people rather than allowing a popular consensus to build in favour of them. Then, they say, if something were 'to go wrong politically' their governments would have to reintroduce much of the old systems, particularly the subsidies, and the reforms would have to begin again. One of the Tunisian ministers summed up his argument by quoting the famous remark of Talleyrand to his secretary, '*Allez lentement, je suis pressé*'.

This argument for slow reform is perfectly valid but it reflects only part of the governments' thinking. Their underlying concern is with losing control. The economies with which they have lived for the last thirty years may have been inefficient but they have at least been understood. If they press ahead with reforms, and each successive stage turns out to be a success and their economies grow fast and steadily they will create completely different types of societies, more like the successful economies of the Far East, or even southern Europe. The governments will find themselves dealing with large private corporations, local and foreign, which will wield considerable economic power. There will be still greater popular pressure for radical political change, and if this happens the ministers, the governing parties, in fact the entire government establishments, will most likely be swept away. In effect, without even admitting it to themselves, the people at the top of the governments are afraid of their countries becoming too successful. None of them thinks that in reality they are very likely to evolve in this way; they are more immediately worried about the possibility of reform failing and their facing an uprising of fundamentalist forces. The long-term effects of successful reform nevertheless make them cautious.

The likelihood, therefore, is that the structural parts of the IMF and World Bank reforms will continue to be implemented slowly. Probably the creditors will have to continue to push the Arab governments to privatize. The programmes may only be accelerated if they prove very popular with private investors and the governments find themselves earning attractive amounts of money from them. It may be that in Egypt structural reform will follow what is known as the Chinese model. This would involve the government keeping many of its state corporations in being but starving them of subsidies and letting them become gradually less important as an element in the economy, while a new private sector is allowed to grow up around them – though it is difficult to imagine the Egyptian private sector growing as fast as the Chinese.

If the Arab governments do pursue reform along roughly World Bank lines they will face the challenges of whether they can produce growth rates that are higher than the rates of increase of their populations, and whether they can control their economies' consumption of water, which is in short supply throughout the region.

In the last twenty years there has been an enormous growth in the population of the Arab world. Nearly 60 per cent of the region's people are under twenty-one, and 40 per cent are under fourteen. The average family has five children. In the Arabian Peninsula oil states, which admittedly are starting with small indigenous populations, the people are reproducing themselves nearly as fast as human populations are able to. The growth rate among Saudi and Gulf nationals, as opposed to immigrants, is above 4 per cent. In Jordan, another country with a small population, the rate is 3.5 per cent.

In Egypt, which in 1993 had about 58 million people, numbers are growing by a million every nine months. The country needs to create half a million new jobs a year, and if it is to maintain the present level of enrolment in schools, which is only 70 per cent of children of school age, it needs to open four new schools every day.

These figures are alarming, but they make the position look more dire than it really is. In some of the Arab countries with the biggest populations the rate of increase has been falling quite sharply for five or six years. In Egypt the number of babies being born has fallen from 1.92m in 1988 to 1.65m in 1992. This has helped reduce the annual growth in the country's population from well over 3 per cent in the 1970s and early 1980s to 2.3 per cent in 1991 and 1992. Morocco has experienced a similar decline and Tunisia, where the Bourguiba government was active in promoting birth control before the other Arab countries, had got its growth rate by 1992 down to only 1.9 per cent. These statistics, which are based on the careful monitoring of representative sections of the people, are reckoned to be more accurate than the figures for total population.

The reasons for the slower rate of increase in this region are connected with the changing economic and social role of women. More girls are going to school, they are staying there longer and they are marrying five or six years later. Men too are marrying later, though in their case the main reason is that they are taking longer to find jobs and gain the financial independence they need to marry. In Tunisia, Algeria (in spite of the protests of the *intégristes*) and Morocco more women are going out to work, and therefore wanting fewer babies. In Morocco women make up a third of the working population. They take jobs as clerks, secretaries and, above all, workers in textile plants, making garments to be exported to Europe. One of their motives is to give themselves some financial independence in case they are divorced. They also want to acquire new consumer durable goods, and increasingly they and their families are saving to buy their own homes. The possibility of people having their own homes full of their new possessions is itself an incentive for them to have fewer children; big families need bigger, less affordable apartments. It is significant that in Morocco families which are regarded as being middle class have an average of fewer than two children, while the poorest families in the country still have five or six.

Most of the social forces that are affecting the people in the Maghreb countries apply to some degree in Egypt. In this country recently there has also been the effect of a major birth-control campaign. The National Population Council, set up in 1985, has been telling women through billboard advertisements and a television campaign that fewer children, ideally two, mean a better life. It has enlisted the support of the Grand Mufti, the country's senior religious judge, to give his opinion that birth control does not run against the teachings of the Koran. The purpose of this has been to counter the propaganda of the fundamentalist groups. There have been calls by people promoting the birth-control programme, including members of the People's Assembly, for the government to back up its free distribution of contraceptive pills and intra-uterine devices, mostly coming from the American aid programme, by sending a female instructor to every village. In a debate in the Assembly in April 1992 it was claimed that this would not only help the government's campaign win the confidence of the wives of the peasant farmers, it would stop them using the pills to fatten their chickens.

The projections for population increase put forward by different authorities at the time of the debate ranged from one which assumed that the 2.3 per cent growth rate of that year would continue, giving Egypt a population of more than 100 million by 2020, to one which suggested that if the government implemented the idea of sending advisers into the villages the population by that date might be no more than 70 million. The Chairman of the Egyptian Demographic Centre, speaking at a symposium at the American University of Cairo, gave a prediction between the two extremes, which had the country's population stabilizing at the end of the 2020s at between 90 and 95 million.

Clearly if the moderate or optimistic projections turn out to be correct the economic reform programme now being implemented should be a success, because it will need to produce only a very moderate GDP growth rate to bring about a quite significant improvement in people's standard of living. If the programme can generate economic growth of more than the current rate of population growth, which ought to be possible, it should be successful for a few years. The problems will come in the early years of the next century. Then, whatever the country's rate of GDP growth, if it has a population that is expanding from 70 to 90 million, it will be facing shortages of agricultural land and water.*

---

* During the last thirty years much agricultural land in Egypt has been built on. It should, in theory, be possible for the government to stop further building, but such a policy would be hard to implement because Egyptians do not like the alternative of living in the desert. Home for them is the delta and the Nile valley, however crowded these places may be. The desert is hardly regarded as part of Egypt and the three new towns built there have not been popular. In the early 1990s there were 7.5 million

In the Maghreb countries the projections are for the rate of population increase to continue to fall quite steeply. In Tunisia it is expected that the population will be static before 2025. The speed of the fall in the growth rate here and in Morocco is quite worrying because it suggests that at some point early in the next century there may be a shortage of young people coming on to the labour market, causing the rate of economic growth to slow and the growing numbers of elderly people, who will be living longer, to find their standard of living falling.

Already there have been signs of labour shortages in Tunisia, even though between 15 and 20 per cent of the work force of that country is estimated to be unemployed. There have been cases of hotels, textile factories and construction sites finding it difficult to get labour. In some agricultural regions there have been too few people to harvest the crops; in the spring of 1992 army units had to be used to help with the olive harvest near the town of Sfax. Such action had never been taken before. The reason for the shortages was not so much an absolute lack of people, as a tendency for young people to be more selective about what employment they took. There were many youths who would not deign to work in hotels and who found labour on the land too hard and boring. They preferred to sit in cafés with their friends or chat up European girls on the beaches, while living off the wages of their sisters working in the textile factories. The lifestyles of these people, who were included in the unemployment statistics, were a sign of rising wages and living standards, brought about partly by successful economic reform.

The problems of water supply are more worrying than those of population because there is little sign as yet of how they are going to be resolved. In several traditionally fertile and populated parts of the Middle East and North Africa there are already actual shortages of water. In Amman domestic water is rationed. Families are able to fill the tanks they have on top of their homes twice a week, when water comes on-stream for thirty-six hours at a time. Similar rationing has been imposed in Damascus. In parts of the valley of the river Jordan farmers have been ordered not to plant more than a quarter of their acreage and the Jordanian government has been giving them ten dinars ($14) per uncultivated dunum (1,000 square metres). Licences are not given in Jordan for new industries that consume significant amounts of water as part of their processes.

---

acres cultivated in Egypt. It was estimated that if building on agricultural land was controlled and more water was made available from recycling, this, together with the construction of the Jonglei Canal (see p.227) and the exploitation of underground water reserves, would allow the cultivated area to be increased to 10 million acres.

In other parts of the Middle East shortages are expected within a decade, and where two or more states share a river basin the arguments of the governments are becoming steadily more acrimonious. In the Euphrates basin a water war by proxy has already begun. The Syrians, annoyed by the way the Turks have reduced the river's flow to fill the reservoir behind the vast new Ataturk dam, have provided arms and training for the guerrillas of the PKK, the Kurdish Workers' Party, which is in rebellion in eastern Turkey. The implied threat is that if, after the reservoir is full, the Turks continue to extract large amounts of water to feed the irrigation schemes of the new South-Eastern Anatolia Project, support for the PKK will be increased.

There is scope for many more conflicts in the Euphrates and Tigris basin, which has never been as well regulated as the Nile system. The Iranians' extraction of water from rivers flowing into the Tigris has been a traditional cause of friction between Iran and Iraq. Syria and Iraq have been arguing over the Euphrates waters since the Syrians built a large dam at Tabqa in the 1970s. In all of the disputes in this basin the ultimate losers are the Iraqis, who as the traditional users are the people first entitled to the water. In what short-lived and bad-tempered negotiations have taken place in the last two decades the upstream users' position has been that the Iraqis should make themselves more efficient in using water.

In theory, in all parts of the region it should be possible for governments to resolve their water problems without conflict, and without their countries suffering any shortage. The mathematics supporting this are straightforward. It is reckoned that the Arab countries, Iran and Turkey receive some 600 billion cubic metres of water a year from rainfall and one river, the Nile, which flows into the region from outside. Of this figure it is thought that it should be feasible for the populations to make use of 400 billion cubic metres, for agriculture, domestic purposes and industry. It is estimated that for domestic purposes – cooking and washing – the population uses about 200 litres per person per day, and even if one projects the population figures forward to the end of this century, this rate of consumption will mean that domestic use will then be accounting for only 25 billion cubic metres a year. There is therefore, on paper, no direct threat to the region's water resources from the growth of population.

The main challenge for governments is to make sure that this domestic water is made available to the people. In most of the region this involves building dams and reservoirs to catch and store the rain water which at present evaporates or flows into the sea. For Egypt, for both domestic and agricultural purposes, there is also the intriguing possibility of its increasing the quantity of water it receives from the Nile system by sponsoring the construction of the Jonglei Canal. This is a project, discussed for decades, for channelling the flow of the White Nile in southern Sudan into a canal, instead of letting it move slowly through the Sudd marshes, where huge amounts of water evaporate. Under the Nile Waters Agreement of 1959 Egypt (or in practice its aid donors) would be obliged to pay for the canal and would receive half of the extra flow of water – a share of 9 billion cubic metres. This would be added to the 55 billion cubic metres to which it is entitled under the Agreement at present. The problem with implementing the project is partly political; it would require better relations than have existed between the Egyptian and Sudanese governments since the Islamic republican regime came to power in Khartoum in 1989. There are also environmental and economic difficulties. Draining a large area of central Africa would totally change the ecology of the region and destroy the way of life of the cattle-raising tribes who live there.

A second way for the Middle Eastern governments to safeguard domestic water supplies is to see that water use in agriculture becomes more efficient. The Egyptian authorities reckon that they might be able to give themselves another 3 or 4 billion cubic metres by recycling more of the drainage water that comes out of irrigation systems. There is scope here and in other countries for more domestic sewerage water being recycled. Both of these types of economy will cost money but are not particularly difficult to implement.

Other methods of saving water are more complicated because they involve changing the habits of farmers. In some areas they would mean teaching farmers about drip systems of irrigation. They might also mean getting farmers to switch from growing ordinary foodstuffs to high value types of crops, such as melons, flowers and long staple cotton, which can be exported and, per unit of water that has to be used to grow them, earn much higher returns. These sorts of change are very difficult. Farmers tend to object out of engrained conservatism, unless they are given careful and sympathetic advice. And the governments themselves may resist because these measures would involve a step away from self-sufficiency in food, which is a sensitive political issue. The idea that the best incentive for getting farmers to change their habits might be a financial one, involving governments introducing some sort of charge for water, is even more dangerous. In Islamic societies the idea of people being able to take freely what water is available to them is deeply rooted in the culture. Any thought of governments charging their farmers for water is politically explosive and would play into the hands of the Islamic militants.

12

Political Islam

Pressures for political reform – Islam and government – Islamic and secular nationalist movements in early twentieth century – increase in conservative sentiment after 1967 – revolution in Iran – 'official Islam' – Islamic militants, violent and non-violent – reform societies and charities – Islamist politicians – sources of funds

In April 1989, a month after Jordan had agreed with the IMF its first package of economic reforms, the government announced cuts in some of the subsidies on basic foods. The cuts were quite big, ranging from 15 to 50 per cent, and they led immediately to riots. The trouble began in some of the towns in the south, particularly Maan, which had populations of bedouin and East Bank Jordanians who traditionally had been regarded as the people most loyal to the government. This was a most worrying development. King Hussein, who was on an official visit to the United States when he heard the news, cancelled his remaining engagements and returned home. He appointed a new government under Sherif Zaid bin Shaker, one of his relations, who had been commander-in-chief of the armed forces, but refused to make any concessions on the price increases. Instead he announced that later in the year the country would hold a general election, its first for twenty-two years.

These events in Jordan, which spanned no more than a week, represent the connections between cuts in subsidies and riots and between riots and steps towards democracy, which have become quite well established in the Arab world. Several of the Egyptian government's early attempts at cutting subsidies in the late 1970s and early 1980s led to riots, as did the Tunisian government's measures of January 1984. In both these countries the governments learnt that cuts have to be introduced very carefully. They also began to see that if there was going to be painful economic reform their people would have to be given at least some say in the running of their countries so that they could to a small extent choose how they would suffer. In Egypt these ideas remained on a somewhat intellectual level in government circles, and in Tunisia they were hardly mentioned at all until President Zine El-Abidine Ben Ali eased aside Habib Bourguiba in 1987, but in Jordan in 1989 they were discussed quite explicitly. One of the royal advisers remarked to me in that year, 'the problem is that with economic deregulation one gets losers as well as winners – and to compensate the losers you have got to give them some political freedom, because then they'll feel that eventually their turn will come'.

This logic sounds rather crude but it is no more than the reverse of the analysis of politics that was often made in the late 1970s and early 1980s. Then, at a time when the region seemed to be becoming more unstable under the influence of the Lebanese civil war and the Iranian revolution, there was a noticeable increase in censorship and a tightening of security, seen particularly in the arrests of Islamic dissidents. Yet because oil prices were high and the non-oil producing countries were receiving large sums of aid from the Gulf, governments were able to compensate their people by subsidizing their household spending. It used to be said that the governments were buying their people's freedom and the people, although they were aware of what was happening, seemed reasonably content with the bargain. Now the process is having to be reversed.

Further, gentler and longer-term pressure for political change is coming from the programmes of privatization and financial and legal reform. Governments are realizing that if the private sectors are to put large sums of capital into difficult, relatively high-risk investments, particularly industrial projects, they will want to see frameworks of commercial law that are properly established, understood and not liable to change at the whim of a minister who is answerable to nobody except his president. The same will go for the governments' economic policies. Investors will want these openly discussed. They will want to feel free to criticize the policies, sue government agencies, lobby and propose policy initiatives, just as companies do in the West. These points are being echoed by expatriates and by foreign companies, from both the industrialized world and the Arabian Peninsula, who will be investing in the poorer Arab countries. Their confidence is important because it is assumed that in future much less of the flow of capital to these countries will be coming as aid and more will be in the form of commercial investment.

These economic pressures are not the only influences pushing the governments towards reform. There is also the popular recognition of the regimes' past failures, the influence of foreign television and the growing demands of the intelligentsia for legitimate government. The impact of all these pressures together has been to push governments into relaxing censorship, legalizing opposition political parties, holding elections and then ceding some authority to parliaments that have traditionally been used just as a means of rubber-stamping decisions that have already been taken by the cabinets. There have been changes in this direction in Jordan, Egypt, Tunisia, Algeria, Morocco and, in rather different circumstances, in Yemen. The problem in most cases has been that the people who have moved most vigorously to seize the new political opportunities have been the militant Islamist groups which are not interested in continuing either the economic or the political reforms.

The prominence of the Islamists, or fundamentalists, in the early stages of political relaxation in any country comes from their being the best organized. In the 1970s and early 1980s, when opposition parties were banned and public political discussion was not allowed, the Islamists were able to meet, talk and form what amounted to political networks through their charitable societies. They were able to make political points through sympathizers preaching at the mosques on Fridays. It was very difficult for the governments to control either the societies or the preachers. If a preacher chose his words well the authorities could hardly criticize him for saying that the government was imperfect, as is everything except God himself, and that it should be run more on lines laid down by God in the Koran. In effect the societies became the only practicable and permitted form of opposition of the day. This gave them a political head-start on all secular opposition groups when Arab governments began to relax control in the later 1980s. The Islamist movements had the enormous additional advantage of standing for an idea which the people understood. Everyone knew what Shariah law was and roughly what an Islamic state was supposed to be, but nobody knew much about the leaders and policies of the multitude of new secular parties. Inevitably since the period of political change began it has been the Islamic parties that have dominated Arab politics.

There is nothing illogical about Islam being in politics. The religion is built on the message which God gave to the Prophet Mohammad in the early seventh century. This message, the Koran, is God's final revelation of His law to mankind. It says that God revealed himself through prophets (the Old Testament prophets and Christ) to the Jews and Christians, both of whom have built imperfect religions, and that now he is giving a very explicit message to Mohammad in order that he can preach a complete and perfect religion. Part of what God says concerns His own personality, the mysteries of creation and what a Muslim should believe, which basically is that there is one God and that Mohammad is His Messenger; but most concerns how men should live their lives. He gives instructions for all aspects of life and leaves (in theory) no room for doubt or misunderstanding. One of the most important matters God addresses, particularly in His later revelations when the Prophet has established the first Islamic state in Medina, is how a Muslim community should be governed.

In the years after the Prophet's death the rulers of the Muslim communities and Islamic scholars began the process of using the Koran to build a body of law, which became known as the Shariah, meaning 'the Path' by which a Muslim might reach heaven. In addition to the Koran they drew on people's recollections of the Prophet's actions and judgements, known as *hadiths*, together with elements of pre-Islamic customs and practices that had evolved in the government of the early Muslim rulers. For more than a hundred years many versions of the Shariah existed, but in the late eighth and ninth centuries there emerged in the Sunni community four major and quite similar schools of law, which have remained in being ever since. The law which these schools assembled was a complete code for the administration of society, dealing with prayer, ritual, commerce, government and all other civil and criminal matters. It became the foundation of the Muslim state. During the period of the Arab and early Turkish dynasties a small amount of interpretation of the law was allowed, but in early Ottoman times scholars decided that this 'door' should be closed, and it has remained closed since.

The Shariah is thus a rather inflexible body of law. There is little scope for any individual, however learned, to interpret it and none whatever for him to revise or update it. Nobody who believes in God can doubt that God is perfect, and therefore there cannot be any mistake in what he has said in the Koran. It follows in the mind of the modern fuundamentalist, that if God has laid down laws for government, society must try to put them into effect. The result will be the perfect state. In this matter the Shariah says that a ruler should be chosen by those in the community who are best qualified to represent the people, being those who are wisest, most experienced and of highest moral character. The ruler, it says, should be honest, just, modest, brave, merciful and, through these qualities, a good leader who understands his people and is able to command their respect. He must consult his people, or their representatives, listen to what they say and take decisions based on what he has heard. This is most important. In effect he must run his community as the Prophet ran the community in Medina between 622 and his death in 632.

For nearly thirteen centuries all the governments that followed the Prophet in the Muslim world claimed to rule by the Shariah, though in practice most fell a long way short of the ideal. It followed that opponents of these governments would use the Shariah as the basis of their criticism, claiming that the sultans, khedives, shahs or beys were abusing their positions by not ruling as the law said they should. The whole debate over good and bad rule was conducted in terms of the Shariah and even after the 1870s, when some secular and some purely nationalistic ideas were introduced into the politics of the Muslim world, most of the movements that were demanding reform couched their arguments in partly Islamic terms. Islam was so much part of people's lives, of their concept of government and of their concept of nationality, that it was bound to be tied into all their ideas on nationalism and political change. These sorts of attitudes continued well into the twentieth century, after the collapse of the Ottoman Empire and the creation of separate Arab states.

It was not until the late 1930s and 1940s that some specifically secular and purely Arab nationalist, as opposed to pan-Islamic nationalist, lines of thinking emerged. The most durable of the new parties that reflected these ideas has been the Baath. This type of secular party did not replace more religiously orientated organizations or leaders, it simply existed alongside them. New religious groups and parties continued to appear. Some lasted, others disappeared after their leaders died. The most important organization founded during this period was the Muslim Brotherhood, which was established in Cairo in 1929 by Hassan El-Banna, a sheikh at El-Azhar, the ancient Islamic university.* The Brotherhood was intended at first to be a religious revival move-

---

* The term 'sheikh' comes from the Arabic word for age and implies a person who is old and wise – a teacher. It is applied to religious scholars and judges and sometimes to wise old men who are the heads of villages or tribes. In the Gulf states it has become the title given to all members of the ruling families, though forty years ago it was applied only to the most senior members of these families. In Saudi Arabia the title has become almost meaningless. It is given to ministers, senior officials and to businessmen of all ages and degrees of wealth and importance. It has been particularly foreigners, both Asian immigrants and Western businessmen anxious to win contracts, who have been responsible for the spread of the title.

ment, but it rapidly took on a political character and by the 1940s was organizing demonstrations and terrorist attacks on the British forces. A shorter-lived but important group was that which formed round an elderly religious teacher, Sheikh Izzeddin Qassam, in Palestine in the early 1930s. It was the preaching and then the impetuous and suicidal rebellion of the sheikh in 1935 that sparked the Palestinian revolt of 1936–9.

In effect in the 1930s and 1940s the religious and secular nationalist groups worked alongside each other in trying to liberate their countries from the imperial powers. Often they co-operated. Both wanted to create an independent, successful and powerful nation. One of the differences between them was that for the religious nationalists the nation meant, in principle, the whole Islamic world, while for the secular nationalists it meant the Arab world. Another of the differences was that the religious parties saw the key to success as being the proper application of the Shariah, while the secular parties envisaged a new Arab society being created through the copying or adaptation of modern European ideas.

When the Arab states began to gain their independence after the Second World War the people who led them – monarchs and republicans – were supporters of the secular nationalist ideas and they opted for forms of government based on Western systems, initially some very imperfect versions of democracy and later, in several cases, socialism. The nationalists of an Islamic persuasion found themselves pushed into opposition. They saw the secular parties in government liberalizing the laws on alcohol and the rights of women, talking of 'modernizing' in an obviously Western sense and seizing private property through the introduction of land reform. In Egypt the Muslim Brotherhood helped create the chaotic conditions that enabled Nasser to stage his coup, but as soon as the new regime was in power it became clear that the young officers and the Brothers had different objectives. In 1954, after a Muslim zealot tried to assassinate him, Nasser had the Brotherhood banned and its leaders and five hundred of its other members thrown into prison.

It was at this point that the religious and secular nationalist movements turned against each other. In the later 1950s and 1960s, when Nasser's influence was at its strongest and the Egyptian government was waging a propaganda war against the Arab monarchies and other 'reactionaries', it was natural for King Hussein and King Faisal to turn to members of the Brotherhood and their sympathizers for support against the radical tide. King Faisal wanted to establish himself in the minds of his own people and other Arabs and Muslims as the exponent of an idea of modern Islamic government, which could be a counter to Nasser's socialist ideas. He established the Islamic Conference Organization, which he hoped would lead to the formation of an anti-socialist bloc of Muslim governments. He began financing Islamic organizations all over the Muslim world, and those members of Islamic political bodies who had had to flee their own countries, particularly the Egyptian brethren, he allowed to come to Saudi Arabia. Members of the Muslim Brotherhood took jobs in Saudi schools and in the Ministry of Education. They rapidly worked their way up the teaching and administrative ladder and soon came to dominate the Saudi educational system.

A decade later in Egypt Anwar Sadat made use of the Brotherhood when in the early years of his presidency he turned against the left wing of his government, represented by Ali Sabri, one of the vice-presidents, and began his move away from socialism. Wanting to increase the constituency backing these changes and neutralize the people still loyal to Nasser's ideas he courted the religious right. He let several hundred members of religious parties out of prison and had the state broadcasting authority increase the amount of religious programming on television. In one or two cases he arranged for subsidies to be given to religious groups. Some religious figures were elected to the committees of professional associations and similar bodies that the government controlled.

Throughout the Arab world at this time there was a general rise in conservative sentiment. The defeat of 1967 and the increasingly authoritarian character of government showed people that the new, independent, republican nation states in which they had put their faith since the Second World War were not as strong, competent or benign as they had hoped. Socialism and the habit of copying the West had been shown to be failures. People realized that the pace of change of the previous twenty years had been too fast, and they reacted by going back to Islam and the traditions of their own society. Many of the changes in people's behaviour were in matters which they hardly noticed at the time. They paid more attention to their prayers, which Muslims are supposed to say five times a day. In the Gulf those who had adopted Western dress in the 1960s found themselves gradually going back to wearing the long white robes known in Kuwait and Bahrain as *dishdashas*. Their speech became more formal. They began using traditional expressions, such as *'ya tawil al-'umr'*, 'oh long of life', when addressing people they respected. In the case of a misunderstanding, they turned to the old word *'sem'*, an abbreviation for 'in the name of God again', rather than *'ismahli'*, which was a literal translation of the English expression 'excuse me'. In all parts of the Arab world extended families began to spend more time together. Middle-class children who had been treating their parents in a slightly casual fashion, partly as a result of watching American films, became more formal and respectful.

The reaction against the West had another, more aggressive aspect. People began to criticize it for being Godless, fecklessly tolerant, crime-and drug-ridden (criticisms that were made long before Western societies themselves became preoccupied with these issues) and neglectful of old people and the family. Arabs from the Gulf and Saudi Arabia continued to go to Europe and America in the summer for shopping, the cool weather and in some cases some hypocritical indulgence in its vices. But most of the older generation who had been going for some years found they were less impressed by the West than they had been in the 1960s.

There was a particular religious reaction against the spread of Western culture. This stemmed from the fact that the great majority of Arabs and other Muslims, even members of the intelligentsia, had not lost their faith during the last fifty years. They still believed in God. Many of them therefore found increasingly that they disliked and resented the Western attitude that religion was a thing of the past or, alternatively, that all religions were permissible and interesting as long as they were seen only as colourful cultural phenomena and nobody seriously suggested that one of them might be right. A Sudanese writer, Abdelwahab El-Affendi, recently summed up objections to this attitude when he wrote that it left everybody 'free to worship the god of his choice', but entitled no one 'to ask which is the True God'.* He then suggested that Muslims were distancing themselves from Western culture not just because of political and economic envy, or because of frustration at their own failures, but because they had *faith*. And he added defiantly: 'At a time when most non-Western cultures – and, for that matter, most traditional aspects of Western culture, including its religious component – are bowing down – or out – in front of the dominant secular religion of the age, Islam is the only non-secular culture on the offensive today'.

Conservative and anti-Western sentiments of every sort in the Middle East were greatly strengthened by the Iranian revolution of 1979. To poor and disaffected Muslims everywhere the revolution proved that militant Islam was powerful. It showed them that people inspired by

---

* Abdelwahab El-Affendi, 'Studying My Movement: Social Change without Cynicism' from the *International Journal of Middle Eastern Studies*, 1991

faith could by their own action in the streets overthrow a long-
established Westernized regime supported by a fearsome secret police
and a large army. The Ayatollah Khomeini and the other leaders of the
revolution backed this lesson with powerful rhetoric. All were excellent
speakers. Like Muslim clerics everywhere they had been taught how to
speak in public and had had many years of practice. Once installed in
power they called on the poor in all parts of the Muslim world to
follow the Iranians' example. Their theme was that 'injustice', as they
called economic inequality, would disappear if monarchies and other
governments they considered illegitimate were overthrown or made to
rule properly, in accordance with the Shariah. They were fond of quoting a verse in the Koran in which God announces: 'We shall favour
those who were dispossessed [the *mostazafin*]. We shall make them
leaders and endow them with the earth'. This and similar verses became
an inspiration to Islamic revolutionary movements in the 1980s.

The new leaders' political ideas also attracted support at a more
intellectual level, among the thoughtful, religious members of the
Muslim middle classes. Most of these people would have agreed with
many of the criticisms made of Khomeini in the West: that he was
unworldly, in many ways naïve and fanatical in his pursuit of objectives
he considered morally necessary. Yet because they were interested in
the philosophical aspects of what the Imam, the Leader, as Khomeini
was known in Iran, was saying they found in his thinking some admirable characteristics. The core of his belief was that Muslims should not
be passive and fatalistic when confronted by injustice, as they had so
often been in the past, but should fight to overcome it. Chief among
the evils Khomeini had fought to remove during the previous fifty years
had been the Pahlavi dynasty of Mohammad Reza Shah and his father,
Reza Shah. This, in his view, had been steadily weakening Iran by
corrupting its culture and attacking its clergy, who had traditionally
had a role as protectors of society against tyrannical government and
foreign influences. He hated particularly the way the Pahlavis had introduced 'reforms' proposed by the Americans, including the emancipation
of women and land reform (which damaged the financial interests of
the clergy), and had given special legal privileges to American forces in
Iran. He despised the spread of America's popular culture. He referred
to the United States not only as 'the Great Satan' – one of his most
famous phrases – but as 'the World Devourer'.

Khomeini began to develop his ideas on the integrity of Iran and the
duties of Muslims when as a young man in the 1920s and 1930s he
lectured in the religious colleges in Qom, the holy city south of Tehran.
He taught jurisprudence and philosophy and was regarded as a particu-

larly fine lecturer on ethics. According to Ayatollah Mohammad-Javad Bahonar, a former student and later colleague, 'the two issues he emphasized were the necessity for Islam and Iran to be independent of colonialism and the need to get the clerics out of an academic straightjacket. He said the clergy had a responsibility for humanity not only in Iran but wherever people were hungry and oppressed'.* It was in this context that he reminded people that according to the Hadith the Prophet had said that he who saw wrong was obliged to try to put it right.

In the 1960s, when he was an exile in Iraq, Khomeini developed these ideas into the doctrine of the Velayat-e-Faqih, the Regency of the Jurist. This laid down that Muslims should not think of the perfect state as being an ideal to be achieved in some distant future, but as a form of government which they could create in the present generation. The idea of regency referred to the role of a leader, or a group of Muslim jurists, in the absence of the semi-mythical twelfth Shia imam, Mahdi, who had disappeared in the ninth century and was supposed to return one day to save the world. In effect Khomeini's doctrine was stating that Muslims should not wait for this event but be guided by a government which would act on the missing imam's behalf. When the clerics came to power in Iran they built the Velayat-e-Faqih into the new constitution, not without some argument among themselves, which gave the idea considerable publicity and increased its authority. Although the roots of the doctrine were Shia, in that they referred to a Shia imam, its conclusions were addressed to all Muslims and they struck a chord in the minds of religious intellectuals, as well as malcontents and revolutionaries, in all parts of the Islamic world. There were even a few of the broader-minded thinkers in Saudi Arabia, in the Hijaz rather than the Nejd, who thought Khomeini's ideas were interesting.

It was not just the spread of its political ideas that gave the new republic influence outside Iran. It worked by material means to export its revolution. It gave money to whatever Islamic groups – charitable societies, political parties and revolutionary organizations – sought its aid. It broadcast propaganda to the populations of Iraq, the Gulf states and Saudi Arabia and did what it could to foment uprisings or terrorist activity by the Shia elements in those countries. Most vigorously it worked to create a second Islamic republic in Lebanon.

Several of the early leaders of the Iranian republic, including Mohammad Beheshti, who led the Islamic Republican Party, and Mustapha

---

* See Shaul Bakhash, *The Reign of the Ayatollahs*, I.B. Tauris, 1985, p. 21

Chamran, who became Minister of Defence, had gone regularly to the Shia area of southern Lebanon before the revolution. They visited and taught at the Jebel Amel College which had been established in Tyre by an Iranian cleric named Mousa Sadr. They used to pray with the people who were later to become the leaders of the anti-Israeli Shia resistance in the region. A year after the revolution in Tehran the first Iranian Revolutionary Guards appeared in southern Lebanon, and in 1982 two Lebanese clerics who had been educated in Qom founded Hizbollah, the Party of God, in the town of Baalbek in the Bekaa valley. This party became steadily more powerful in the 1980s. It gradually superseded Amal as the principal Shia guerrilla group, winning the loyalty of both the Shias in the south and those refugees who had fled to the shanty towns around Beirut. Under the name of Islamic Jihad it organized the kidnapping of most of the Western hostages who were taken in the 1980s. Although the group appeared to be wholly Lebanese, it received its weapons and training from the Revolutionary Guards and it later emerged that it took its orders from the Iranian embassy in Damascus.

Given that the Shias lived mainly in the south and a small part of the centre of Lebanon, it was never likely that they would succeed in making the whole country an Islamic republic. They might have aspired to partition it and form an Islamic republic in the south, but even in this they would have been constrained by the fact that the ultimate power in the country was the Syrian army and the Syrians had always been opposed to the fragmentation of their neighbour. What the Iranians and the people they supported succeeded in doing was making Lebanon a centre for the dissemination of Islamic revolutionary ideas. In the 1980s it was to Lebanon that members of Islamic groups in other Arab countries came for training, arms and money.

The Iranians and the Islamist organizations in Arab countries in the 1980s and 1990s have been fighting not just against secular Arab governments but against the official religious establishments backed by these governments. They see themselves as representing true devout Islam, whereas most of the people running the mosques they claim represent something which they call 'official', 'state' or, worst of all, 'American' Islam. This involves going through the motions of devotion but has nothing to do with creating the sort of society God has ordained for mankind in the Koran.

In all the Arab countries the majority of the mosques and the clergy are controlled by governments. Originally, in medieval and Ottoman times, mosques, like churches in Europe, were built by rich Muslims who wished to do good and commend their souls to God. They paid for a muezzin to climb the minaret to call the people to prayer five times a day, and an imam to lead the prayers and preach a sermon, to the founder's taste, on Fridays. In their wills they would leave a sum of money, a *waqf* or religious endowment, to continue to support the mosques after their deaths. This system began to change in the early nineteenth century. When Mohammad Ali, an army officer of Albanian extraction, established himself as governor of Egypt, nominally on behalf of the Sultan in Constantinople but in practice as an independent ruler, he was helped to power by the *ulema*, the senior imams, judges and teachers. Then, seeing that these people were powerful and might one day support a rival to himself or his successors, and being influenced in his thinking on government by modern European ideas, in particular the centralizing policies of Napoleon, he decided to bring the mosques under his control. His government took over ownership of the more important mosques and their endowments and began to pay salaries to their staffs. His example was followed by his successors and by the twentieth-century colonial governments. These, like Mohammad Ali, quite rightly saw an independent *ulema* as a potential focus of opposition and in order to control it they put it under the authority of the rulers they installed or supported. It has remained more or less happily in this position ever since. The tradition in Sunni Islam has always been for the *ulema* to support the ruling power, and to try to influence it if it has not been governing in accordance with the Shariah. It has reasoned that to move into opposition would be likely to cause more chaos and misery than it would remedy.*

Today in the Arab world most mosques are owned and run by ministries of *awqaf* (the plural of *waqf*). These bodies have taken over all

---

* In this the Sunni *ulema* has been different from the Iranian religious establishment. In Iran, even though Shiism owes its dominance to Ismail Shah having imposed it on the country in the early sixteenth century, the clergy has always been a power in its own right, independent of the ruling dynasties. It has its own hierarchy of *rohani* (or mulla in popular speech), *hojatolislam* and *ayatollah*. It has been associated with the poor and, particularly, the bazaar class, from which many of its members come. Often it has stood in opposition to governments which it has seen as a threat to its supporters. Its financial independence has been assured by the same means that originally gave independence to the Sunni clergy – religious endowments.

The clergy's power has been enhanced by Shia Islam giving its leaders a spiritual authority which derives from their being the heirs of its early saints. The tradition of opposition, likewise, comes partly from the movement's history. In its early years Shiism was associated with the conquered peoples of the Arab empire. Its leaders were martyred and its rebellions suppressed.

old *awqaf* and receive new endowments, which in Saudi Arabia are still frequent and sometimes very big. The endowments may be not just for the general use of the ministries, but for specific charitable purposes, such as orphanages.

The ministries employ the staffs of the mosques, an imam and maybe a muezzin, possibly supplemented by a cleaner or two. In the smaller mosques the muezzins and cleaners are often volunteers. Both the professional muezzins and their unpaid helpers nowadays stand downstairs and broadcast the calls to prayer through microphones connected to loudspeakers at the top of the minarets. As well as being available at prayer times to lead the community in its devotions and give any necessary religious counselling to its members, the imams are expected to preach a sermon on Fridays. In a few of the most important mosques in the big towns sermons may be given by teachers from the religious departments at the universities or by judges from the Shariah courts, which in most Arab countries now have their activities confined to family law matters. In Saudi Arabia it has become the norm for outside preachers to be invited to give sermons in all the more important mosques. In that country there is a particularly large body of religious scholars, made up of both academics and the legal profession, which through the Shariah courts administers all criminal law and a large part of commercial law.

The question of sermons is a sensitive one. In theory in Islam a sermon can be about anything that is of concern to the community. This may mean simple matters of personal morality or social issues, such as the role of women, the influence of television and the right way for a person to conduct his banking affairs. A favourite theme in Saudi Arabia and the Gulf countries in recent years has been the dangers of letting 'foreigners' – in other words Filipino or Indian servants – into the household. It is, of course, the foreigners who are blamed for introducing immorality into homes, but it is also intended that the congregation should appreciate that there have to be two parties in any sexual act, that Arab householders or their wives are at least half to blame for the 'immorality' that occurs, and that they should control their lusts.

More controversially, sermons can be about corruption, the use of improper influence in business, personal greed in high places, the behaviour of neighbouring Arab governments, or economic policy, including the submission of governments to the dictates of the IMF and the World Bank. It is these topics which are sensitive to governments and which usually the ministries of *awqaf* and the interior try to control. They have their representatives mingling in the congregations on

Fridays to write reports on the sermons, and if they do not like what they read on Saturdays they will tell the preachers to avoid particular topics and may even order them to stop preaching. This is not always easy to do. If a preacher is popular, phrases his attacks cleverly and defends himself with spirit and well-chosen quotations from the Koran when he is questioned about what he has said, it may be impossible for the authorities to sack him. The Saudis have had difficulty particularly since 1991. In Algeria in the late 1980s the government totally lost control of its mosques – though the reason for this was not so much that it tried to control its preachers and failed, as that through carelessness, neglect and a long-established disdain for religious matters it allowed sympathizers of the Front Islamique de Salut to take over the system. In most Arab countries the governments make sure that their controls are effective. They have been particularly watchful since the Algerian débâcle.

In the eyes of the new breed of Islamic militants, the establishment *ulema*, or those of their number who do not rebel, are pathetically submissive. They are also commonly accused of being ignorant. When they discuss banking, for example, they clearly know the classical treatises on the subject but understand very little of modern practice. They talk in sermons about heredity and discuss genes and chromosomes and similar complex biological subjects without having more than the faintest familiarity with them. This lack of scientific knowledge is more serious than it might seem because, in theory, Islamic scholars should be versed in all matters relevant to the society of the day, as many of them were in the early centuries of Islam. The *ulema*'s ignorance is noticed particularly in the Arabian Peninsula, where on Fridays most of the Western-educated middle classes go to the mosques. One often hears middle-class Saudis, even people of a conservative bent, describing the official *ulema* as 'useless', or as a Jeddah businessman once put it to me, 'educated neither in Islam nor in science – which all good Muslims should understand'. The reference to their lack of education in Islam applied to their fear of tackling difficult social and political issues.

The people who condemn the official *ulema* so strongly are not part of a single movement, of the type that Communism was supposed to be. Some are just outspoken individuals. Others belong to different societies, political parties and extremist groups, which have a variety of ideas and objectives.

At the most militant and violent end of the spectrum are terrorist groups such as those that killed President Sadat in 1981 and have since been waging a bombing campaign in Egypt. The most prominent of the Egyptian organizations in the early 1990s were the Gamaa al-Islamiyya and a body called Islamic Jihad (Islamic Holy War), a name that had previously been associated with Hizbollah in Lebanon. Like similar groups all over the world, these and other bodies in Arab countries were rather hazily defined, being liable under pressure from the security forces to disappear, merge, reform and change their names. They had no detailed political programmes. Their objective was simply to destabilize whichever country they were attacking in the hope that this would lead to revolution, followed by the emergence of a more Godly order.

A second strand of violence has come from more substantial bodies which have tried to take control of countries, either by adopting violent means from the beginning, as did the Syrian branch of the Muslim Brotherhood in the 1970s, or by starting with legitimate political activity and supplementing this with violent demonstrations and attacks on the police. This was roughly the pattern of activities of the FIS in Algeria and An-Nahda in Tunisia.

The remainder of the Islamist political movement, which its leaders always claim is the mainstream, is outwardly and officially peaceful, though some of its members may sympathize with violent groups and periodically contribute money to them. This part of the movement is made up of linked political parties and Islamist societies. The parties may or may not be legal in any given state, but even where an organization is banned it is often known to exist unofficially, and people are aware of who are its principal members and sympathizers, and the tone of its political thinking. In these countries people will refer to there being a 'movement' reflecting the party's ideas, suggesting an amorphous group of sympathizers rather than a specific organization. The sympathizers will run various religious, charitable and cultural societies, each of which will quietly promote the party's views, without being overtly political.

How this system worked was well illustrated in Kuwait in the mid-1980s. Here there were three groups or movements: the Shia supporters of the ideas of Ayatollah Khomeini, who were represented by the Jam'iyat al-Takfir, the Cultural Society; the Salafiyyin, represented by the Islamic Heritage Society; and an unofficial body of Muslim Brotherhood sympathizers, who were members of the Jam'iyat al-Islah al-Ijtima'iya, the Social Reform Society. Of the two Sunni groups, the Salafiyyin was the more extreme. Its objective was to recreate the perfect Islamic society in which the first Muslims had lived in Medina, and its members were known for wearing an exaggerated form of dress with very long beards and their *dishdashas* ending half-way to their knees.

The Reform Society, which had equivalents in most Arab states, was concerned with much the same ends that prompted Hassan El-Banna to found the Muslim Brotherhood in 1929. It wanted to revive the vigour of Islam in Kuwait. This involved its members lobbying the government for the implementation of Islamic policies, preaching, whenever they were given the opportunity, and, above all, talking to the young in lectures and discussion groups, to draw them away from Western and secular values implanted by the international media and 'correct them morally'. To support these activities the Society carried out good works. It organized periodic Islamic book fairs, which it encouraged its young protégés to attend. An Islamic Word Committee gave financial support to preachers and societies doing missionary work (*dawa*) in the non-Muslim countries of south Asia and Africa, or in countries which were nominally Muslim but which followed a rather lax form of Islam. A particularly useful activity for the Society was the collection of *zakat*, the 2½ per cent tax on the annual increase in a person's assets, which Muslims are supposed to pay for the benefit of the needy.* This money the Society was able to distribute to what it considered were deserving causes, which in a small way helped increase its political influence.

In the poorer countries the charitable activities of Islamic societies – financed partly by bodies like the Kuwaiti Reform Society – are much more important and have a bigger political influence. In Egypt the Muslim Brotherhood, which is officially banned but is quite open in its activities, has been running its own schools and clinics, which are welcomed by the people because the services provided by the government are so bad. When an earthquake hit Cairo in October 1992 the Brotherhood and similar Islamic groups moved far more quickly than the government to provide relief centres in the poorest neighbourhoods, which had been the hardest hit. Within hours of the shock they were distributing food, providing money for those who needed it and finding accommodation for people who had been made homeless. The FIS was equally efficient in Algeria in October 1989, when it earned much goodwill by providing tents and blankets for the homeless after an earthquake near Tipaza. Its energy was in marked contrast to the performance of the local FLN authorities, whose first reaction to the disaster was to deploy riot police to protect government property from the protesting victims.

---

* *Zakat* is one of the five obligations of Muslims. The others are: to believe that 'there is no God but God and Mohammad is his messenger'; to pray five times a day; to go on the pilgrimage to Mecca once, if possible; and to fast during the month of Ramadan.

Some of the charitable clinics and schools are in or next to mosques
that are controlled by the Brotherhood or similar organizations. Even
nowadays, when most mosques are state controlled, there is nothing
to stop anybody building a private mosque, which need be only a very
rudimentary building, without even a roof. A Muslim may, after all,
pray wherever he likes and have whomever he likes lead the prayers.
In practice, though, the private endowment and ownership of mosques
is no longer common outside the Arabian Peninsula countries. In Egypt
and other poor countries the association of particular mosques with
charitable societies is most often achieved through the groups being
able to infiltrate their members, often as helpers, into the official mosque
establishments, or through their quietly recruiting the government
imams to their cause.

Although the groups have been quite successful in infiltrating the
'official' Islamic establishments, the majority of Islamist activists are
still laymen. They seem mostly to come from the professions. Some are
Western educated but reject Western values. They are teachers, lawyers,
doctors, civil servants, students – in general members of the intelligentsia, especially its poorer elements. Many of them have not been saying
their prayers all their lives. The process of their conversion has been
political. They have felt ideologically lost, have turned to search for
some principle to guide their lives, have found Islam and drawn out of
it ideas that correspond to their own needs and what they consider to
be the needs of society. It is because they attract this type of person
that one finds the movements have more support in the big, modern,
industrial towns than in the smaller, conservative provincial centres. In
Morocco, for example, there seem to be more Islamists in Casablanca
than there are in the old cities of Marrakesh, Meknes and Fez.

The activists draw support, and votes where there are elections, from
the poor, particularly the young and unemployed, and from a sprinkling
of the middle classes. Some of these have gone back to their religion
in a moderate way because they dislike the social changes they see
around them. Others are more seriously devout and learned in the
Shariah, and although opposed to violence and worried about the new
enthusiasts, support the Islamist parties out of anger at the greed and
corruption they see in the political establishments. And others, many
of them the impressionable young, support the movements because they
think that must be the morally right thing to do. A Saudi minister once
told me that one of his young nephews, whom he had not seen for
several months, had grown a beard down to his waist. When asked
why, the young man replied in a perfectly open and friendly fashion,
'I want to be like the Prophet', which caused the minister to explain,

no doubt with equal charm, that he was sure God would be more impressed by his deeds than by the length of his beard.

Among women there is a large proportion of the less well educated, particularly in lower-middle-class households in the poorer countries, who support Islamic movements because they are reassured by precisely the aspect of their policies that so upsets the Westernized and secular, intellectual part of the population. This is that women should be confined to their homes and do purely domestic work for their husbands and children. Such ideas threaten to destroy the lifestyles of the sophisticated bourgeoisie, but the uneducated and poor know no other vocation. Domestic work, they feel, gives them value, a purpose in life, whereas the prospect of their being liberated in some undefined way, pushed out into society and expected to perform a more 'modern' role fills them with fear. The Islamic parties play on this. The prospect of the women's vote being disproportionately Islamic came into the debate on political reform in Kuwait after the liberation of 1991. At that time the Ruler was being pressed, mainly by Westerners, to extend the franchise in parliamentary elections to women, and ministers and members of the Sabah family were saying, in private, that this might lead to more radical Islamist deputies being elected.

Younger elements of the female population, some of them university and high-school students, have turned to Islam for the same cultural reasons that influenced their fathers and brothers. In some of the Arab universities in the 1980s more than half of the female students could be seen wearing *hejab*, the Islamist uniform of a headscarf knotted under the chin, no make-up, a long, shapeless overall and flat shoes, often white trainers.* The appearance of the students *en masse* might have exaggerated the degree of Islamist commitment, however. There was a tendency, as elsewhere in the world, for girls to follow fashion and many wore *hejab* for this reason. The uniform had certain practical advantages. It was cheap, comfortable and simple, in that it did not require the wearer to spend time and money on make-up or on her hair. It was an effective means of signalling to young men that she was not interested in being chatted up or invited out. And, after university, girls from conservative families found that it helped calm their parents' fears and so enable them to go out to work.

---

* *Hejab* is to be distinguished from the traditional Saudi or Gulf style of dress, which is conservative but not overtly or aggressively Islamic. The latter includes a black shawl, often pulled over the head, sometimes a mask or veil, which might hide quite a lot of make-up, and a long dress, often brightly coloured.

As well as the types of people mentioned so far, all of whom might be said to have moved towards political Islam for idealistic or conservative reasons, there are some more unsavoury characters associated with the movement. Some of these are interested just in making money and gaining influence. In certain circles a beard, a pious look, some of the right Islamic talk and the regular and conspicuous saying of prayers can help a person win contracts or promote a business. An Islamist image and donations to charitable societies can also protect a business-man from criticism. They might even help him gain political office if and when an Islamist party gains political power. These sorts of people, who mix Islam and business, are thought of by the Westernized middle classes as 'Islamist spivs'.

A sub-category of the opportunists includes a few ex-convicts, reformed drug addicts and school dropouts. In Saudi Arabia some of these people have joined the Committee for the Commendation of Virtue and the Condemnation of Vice or are operating beside it on a freelance vigilante basis. The Committee is a long-established body, nominally under the control of the government, which devotes itself to combating public immorality. Its members are easily identifiable by their Islamist dress and facial expressions that run through the self-righteous, pious, surly and truculent. Which expression they adopt depends on the degree of vice they find themselves confronting.

The Committee members, who are known as *mutawa*, have awarded themselves a wide and flexible list of duties. They make sure that shops shut at prayer times, rattling their sticks on the doors and shouting '*salaat, salaat*' ('prayers, prayers'), and then looking inside ten minutes later to make sure that the owner has not kept back a Pakistani to do a little extra work on the accounts. They upbraid and occasionally beat Westerners, particularly women, whom they consider are showing too much of their bodies, which may mean just their arms and their legs below the knees. Saudi men may be stopped for wearing their *thobes* too long, so that they brush the ground in a dandified way.* Their wives may be told that their veils are too transparent or that high heels are visible below their dresses and *abayas* (black silk cloaks). Since the late 1980s the *mutawa* have become increasingly aggressive and have occasionally entered, or threatened to enter, people's homes, an idea which is very shocking to Saudis.

The leaders of the Islamist movements, in Saudi Arabia and else-

---

* A *thobe* is the same long white garment that Kuwaitis and Bahrainis call a *dishdasha*. *Thobe* is the correct classical Arabic term.

where, use the young vigilantes to increase their political weight and influence on their governments, but they are not at all like them in manner. Some are obviously idealistic, able and impressive; a widely respected person of this type is Rached Ghanouchi, the leader of An-Nahda in Tunisia, who has been in exile since 1989. A few are fiery and passionate, like Ali Belhadj, the deputy leader of the FIS. The majority give the impression of being more opportunistic. They are mild but faintly sinister, soft-spoken, smiling, and for much of a conversation totally reasonable. They explain that what they want to do is for the best of society and morally right. They are concerned, for example, to stamp out corruption because it is unfair to the poor. Preaching will instil better moral values into people and make them behave more generously towards their fellow men. They say that it must be right for any person who sees a wrong – adultery for example – to intervene to put it right. It is very difficult to disagree in theory, but in practice they are trying to justify such acts as the intimidation of a woman who is wearing high heels.

The leaders are likely to seem much less moderate when they talk about the West. They may be knowledgeable about Christianity and European history, and well armed with quotations and clichés, but their view of current events is extraordinary. Laith Eshbilath, the former spokesman for the Islamist members of the Jordanian parliament, began a conversation with me in 1992 in an urbane and charming manner, but when I asked him about international matters – making peace with Israel and Jordan's relations with the IMF – he began to rant. The Arab world, like other parts of the developing world, he declared, was entering a new era of slavery, of having the will of others imposed on it. 'I'm against this peace process,' he said. 'The West isn't looking for peace, it's looking to destroy itself and the world – it's not treating people as human beings. It wants to steal our resources . . . It doesn't even care about Christians – look at what is happening in South America – people are being crushed under the boots of the IMF.' His total lack of comprehension of the West and his bitterness towards it was typical of the Islamists.

The initial mildness of Eshbilath's manner cloaked not only his anti-Western views but a lack of scruple in the methods he was prepared to use to change the political system of his own country. Eight months after our conversation he was brought before the state security court on a charge of conspiracy to overthrow the government. He was convicted and sentenced to twenty years in prison, and then pardoned by King Hussein.

All of those members of the secular middle classes and the government establishments who oppose the Islamist movements are greatly concerned about the sources of their money. They feel, quite rightly, that if the movements' funds were cut off their political activity and preaching (and their charitable activity) would be stunted, and their more unscrupulous businessmen supporters would abandon them. If there were no Mercedes and large American cars available for the leading members there might even be a dampening of the enthusiasm of the politically ambitious.

In the Gulf and Saudi Arabia there is no secret about how the charitable and cultural societies raise their money. It is subscribed by businessmen and members of the ruling families, and by the governments, which traditionally have reasoned that if they pay these potentially difficult organizations they will be able to control them. As an extension of their patronage the ruling families of Bahrain, Qatar and Dubai in the 1980s managed to appoint some of their own members as presidents of the local reform societies, making the societies safer, richer and more comfortable.

The mystery and controversy surrounds the sources of funds of the political movements in the poor countries, where there are not many business contributors and probably relatively small amounts of money coming from expatriates working in the Gulf. Most of the money for groups in these countries must come from foreigners. Some groups are certainly financed by Iran, though given that the Islamic Republic is Shia and for most of the first ten years of its life was at war with an Arab country, Iraq, most Sunni movements prefer other sources. The Iranians' payments have been to Shia organizations, the government of Sudan and a few Sunni leaders who have been particularly impressed by the revolutionary thinking of Khomeini.

Much the biggest source of funds for Islamist movements all over the world has been Saudi Arabia, a conservative state which normally is expected to have an interest in maintaining the stability of the regimes around it. It is the support the Saudis give that so exasperates those who oppose the Islamists and is at the centre of many misunderstandings and conspiracy theories. Most of these stem from the fact that there is a difference in Saudi Arabia between the government, the *ulema* and the private sector, which in all financial matters, including overtly political ones, enjoys complete freedom.

The Saudi government for many years was very generous in its support for Islamic movements. As it ruled the country that was the home of Islam, was responsible for the holy cities of Mecca and Medina and for two hundred years had derived its legitimacy from its pledge to propagate a pure form of its religion, it felt obliged to help almost any Islamic good cause. The King, some of the senior princes and government departments, particularly the Ministry of Haj (Pilgrimage) and Awqaf were easily impressed by the people who came to them. The same went for the lawyers and scholars in the numerous government supported religious bodies, such as the Presidency for Religious Research, Iftah (the giving of *fatwas*, or legal opinions), Dawa and Guidance. Applicants for help might say that they were campaigning for the introduction of Shariah law in their country, or that they wanted to build mosques, found libraries or improve religious teaching in schools. They might back their requests by explaining that in, say, Tunisia the government would not allow a man to marry two wives and prevented newspapers publishing religious sections with long quotations from the Koran. The Saudi Crown Prince, Abdullah bin Abdel-Aziz, concerned by what he was told by Rached Ghanouchi, the leader of An-Nahda, more than once in the 1980s sent messages on these matters to the Tunisian presidents, Bourguiba and Ben Ali. In a similar way the Saudi *ulema* were stirred by explanations that in Tunisia and Algeria, as well as in Morocco, the people prayed at the tombs of saints (*marabouts*) and that local organizations needed money to teach them proper Islam. As well as giving money of their own, the *ulema* would provide the applicants with letters, which they would show to potential private donors, saying that the cause in question had their support.

The Saudi authorities were often naïve and complacent in making their disbursements. They did not check that money which was supposed to be being spent on mosques was not being used for political activities. Sometimes they were aware of what was happening, but either turned a blind eye to it or, unofficially, were quite pleased to discover what was going on. If a government had attacked Saudi Arabia in the past, the Saudis were not unhappy to see it being embarrassed by the religious right. In other cases when they gave money the authorities were worried that if they withheld support the applicants would turn to the Iranians. They also believed, naïvely, that if they supported moderate political organizations it would help draw support away from the extremists.

The government received a rude shock when the Gulf crisis erupted and almost all the Islamist groups rallied to the cause of Saddam Hussein. After this it stopped paying most of the groups, but it was unable to curb the *ulema* or the private sector. The *ulema*, who are not politically sophisticated, have continued since 1991 to give freely, as long as they have been satisfied that applicants are not Shias or members of what they would consider to be other fringe groups. Many private Saudi donors, particularly the older members of traditionally devout Nejdi families are similarly naïve. Among the young and middle generations there are also some who understand perfectly well how their money is being used but have been converted to the Islamist cause. Members of some of the major business families with assets of hundreds of millions of dollars have been paying for arms for groups in Afghanistan and for the Sudanese army, which is fighting a rebellion by the largely animist people in the south. They have also channelled money to An-Nahda, the FIS and militant Egyptian groups. Some of the private Saudi donations in the 1980s and early 1990s counted as *zakat*, which an individual used to be able to pay to any organization or poor person he chose.

The problem for the Saudi government since it changed its attitude towards Islamist groups has been that there is little it can do to influence the private sector. In March 1992, when the Basic Law for the Kingdom's government was announced it was seen that one of its provisions was for *zakat* to be levied by the government, which already collected corporate *zakat*, and disbursed to legitimate recipients. But this procedure could not be applied to any additional donations rich Saudis wished to make. The ironic fact is that although in Saudi Arabia people cannot vote, are not supposed to drink alcohol and, in the case of women, are restricted in their work and how they may appear in public, in most other respects they are freer from government regulations than the citizens of any other country. What a Saudi does in his own home and how he disposes of his property are regarded as sacrosanct. If he wants to give millions of dollars to a foreign organization that is working directly against the interests of his own government, that is his own affair.

13

Islamic Government

Evasiveness of Islamist politicians – Islamist social programmes – ideas on economic and constitutional reform – Sudan – terrorism in Egypt – social influence – fluctuations in support – prospects for Islamist parties in 1990s

Islamist politicians are carefully vague about the policies they would pursue if they came to power in an Arab country. When I talked to Abbassi Madani, the leader of the Front Islamique de Salut, at the end of 1989 about what he and his colleagues would do if they won the Algerian parliamentary election his answer to most of my questions was 'we shall consult'. After half an hour's pressure he went so far as to say: 'We shall put our ideas to the people to debate, and then work with them to find the appropriate Islamic solution to our problems'.

The idea of consultation is impeccably Islamic – it is at the centre of the Koran's teaching on government – and it has the modern political advantages of sounding democratic but being imprecise. It appears in all the Islamist leaders' speeches on constitutional matters and most of their replies to questions. The other stock element in their rhetoric, which emerged in Madani's brief replies, is that Islam has the 'solution' to everything. This idea ran through an interview that Roger Matthews, the Middle East editor of the *Financial Times*, had with Mustapha Mashour, a spokesman of the Muslim Brotherhood in Cairo, in 1993. Mashour stuck to pious generalities. Islam was the solution, he said, because the Koran was the word of God and God knew what was best for the people. On taking power an Islamic government's task would be to implement the simple and easily applied teachings of the Koran. Problems such as unemployment would be solved by members of the ulema being attached to government ministries. They would sit down with the officials and together apply the appropriate solutions provided by the Koran. 'We cannot provide a solution to just one of the country's problems in isolation,' Mashour concluded. 'Islam has to be fully applied and only then can everything be arranged to satisfy and please the people.'*

The main reason why the Islamists adopt this bland approach is that they have almost no definite ideas on the difficult economic questions that face their countries. Most of them do not understand the issues and they know that if they were drawn into discussing specifics their ignorance would be revealed. On political reform they know that some of their ideas, which would probably involve banning non-Islamic parties from elections, would not be popular, so on this too they keep quiet. They stick to referring to consultation and saying that 'Islam is the solution', in the hope that the people will pick up the slogan and vote for them because they represent something which has not been tried in their countries' recent history.

The issues on which the Islamists do have definite ideas are social ones. These they feel they understand. They do not require technical expertise and, more important, they can quite easily be related to Shariah law. The Koran's words on how women should conduct themselves in public can be applied as easily now as in the seventh century. Furthermore much of the Shariah law's teaching on these matters the politicians see would be popular with the poorer and less well-educated sections of the people who already live much of their lives in accordance with its provisions, in that they do not drink, borrow money at interest or allow their women to go out unveiled, and disapprove of the behaviour of the richer classes who copy the West. The consequence of this happy conjunction of understanding and political advantage is that Islamist politicians are always willing to discuss their social policies. They have no doubts about what social reforms they would introduce if they found themselves in government. How fast and radical these would be would depend on how they had come to power. There would be a big difference between an Islamic party swept to power by a revolution and one which had won a bare majority in an election in a stable state presided over by a strong legitimate monarch. Most probably a government that felt itself to be firmly in power would address the easier social issues, such as the banning of alcohol, in its first few weeks or months in office, and set in motion studies of the more difficult issues, such as

---

* Survey of Egypt in the *Financial Times*, 22 April 1993

banking reform, with the intention of bringing in reform within two or three years. The issues in question, together with the views of the Islamists and the types of changes – in theory and practice – that the application of the Shariah would bring about, are as follows:

Alcohol would be banned, as would gambling. In Iran, which under the Shah produced some wine and two excellent brands of vodka, alcohol was banned immediately after the Revolution, but it continued to be widely available.* To try to cut its consumption, as well as inhibit contact between the sexes and prevent dancing, patrols of the Iranian Committee for the Commendation of Virtue and the Condemnation of Vice used occasionally to raid private parties, but even in the early days of the Revolution this was regarded as a controversial intrusion into families' privacy. From time to time the practice was condemned by Ayatollah Khomeini.

In public women would be required by an Islamic government either to wear *hejab* or to dress modestly, in traditional or Western styles, with headscarfs. Polygamy would be made legal in any country where it had been banned, though this would make little practical difference to society because even in the most conservative countries it is now very rare for a person to take more than one wife. Whether women would be prevented from driving cars or working would depend on the previous customs of the country, rather than on the Shariah, which certainly does not say that women should not work and, naturally, is silent on the subject of women drivers. In Saudi Arabia the current restrictions in these areas come from traditional conservatism mixed with the idea that to give women the independence of being able to work or drive would be liable to weaken the family. In Iran, which had a large and *évolué* middle class before the Revolution, women still drive and work, and the occasional demands of the more conservative clerics that these practices be stopped have been ignored.

Western films showing what the authorities would regard as a permissive way of life would not be shown on television. An example of the type of film the Islamists particularly dislike is the American comedy series *Three's Company*, which was screened on Jordanian television

---

* The wine and vodka was supplemented in the mid-1980s by large amounts of Ballantyne's whisky, with a label stuck on the back of the bottles saying 'Imported for the Exclusive Use of the Iraqi Armed Forces'. It was understood that this was sold by officers of the Iraqi army to Iraqi Kurds, who transferred it to Kurds on the other side of the frontier, who, in turn, sold it to members of the Iranian clergy, who marketed it in Tehran.

in 1989 before the election of that year. It showed one man living with two beautiful women and it caused the Islamist parties great distress. In their eyes it represented promiscuous sex. It had nothing to do, of course, with a man being married to two women in a proper Islamic family devoted to bringing up children. Generally the Islamist view is that television should be used for educational purposes, particularly to make the people more aware of their own culture.

Islamist governments would increase the religious content of education, except in Saudi Arabia where it already occupies a third of the curriculum. Other changes would be directed to making people understand their Islamic identity and to producing more scientists and technicians. The Islamists attach great importance to science because they believe that it is through their countries developing their own inventive abilities and manufacturing capacity that they will become powerful.

The banking systems of Islamic states would be 'Islamized', which means that interest would be replaced by various types of profit-sharing arrangement. In practice the main difference between a conventional *riba* (interest) system and the Islamic system, as it has been introduced in Iran and Sudan and is operated by several Islamic banks in Europe, is in the documentation of transactions. All loan and deposit agreements are couched in Islamic terms but the rates of return on the banks' and depositors' money are predictable. In Iran in 1992 depositors were being paid a 'guaranteed profit rate' of 13 per cent, with half a per cent or so being credited to them every quarter as a 'bonus profit distribution'.

All the broader issues of constitutional reform and the construction of an Islamic economy, an Islamist government would address more slowly. What the Shariah says on these matters is not easy to relate to twentieth-century conditions, in which countries have populations of millions and complex economies, not to mention international debts and difficult relationships with the IMF and the World Bank. An Islamic regime would have to feel its way forward gradually, debating what weight to give the different and sometimes conflicting moral principles laid down in the law and trying to reconcile these with practical necessities.

On the economy the Shariah lays stress on the importance of people being productive; to illustrate the point the Islamists often quote from the Hadith in which the Prophet is recorded as saying: 'If you have a seedling on the last day of the world, you must still plant it'. In modern terms the emphasis on production is interpreted as meaning not only that governments should encourage agriculture and industry but, particularly, they should promote the development of science.

The main difficulty in applying the Shariah to modern economics lies in deciding whether it demands that an economy should be mainly private sector or public sector. The traditional view is that it supports the little man. It lays emphasis on the security of an individual's property, implying that businesses should not be nationalized, and, in encouraging the honest trade of merchants, it implies that the ideal economy is one composed of many small enterprises. The Islamist parties, particularly in Algeria and Iran, have drawn much of their support from small traders and in Algeria before the cancellation of the elections the FIS leaders, in their more specific statements on these matters, said that under their government there should be no monopolies and that small factories would be encouraged. Set against these ideas is the Shariah's stress on justice being done to the poor and dispossessed, the *mostazafin*. This implies high levels of taxation to redistribute wealth, land reform, and a substantial amount of direct state intervention to see that the bazaar merchants and manufacturers do not extract too much profit from their transactions, as, given the opportunity, they are all too likely to do.

In Iran after the Revolution the conflict between these two lines of thinking led to periodic modifications or reversals of policy. The cabinet, whose members were young and generally inclined to the left, favoured state intervention and promoted policies such as the control of prices and government ownership of industry and importing businesses. The parliament, which contained a wide spectrum of opinion, was more ambivalent in its views and generally worked to modify the radical measures put before it. At the final stage in the legislative process the Council of Guardians, a body of senior clerics established to vet legislation to ensure it did not go against the Shariah, quite often cancelled leftish-leaning laws altogether. The Ayatollah Khomeini, who withdrew from day-to-day politics after the Revolution, seemed generally to act in a traditional *bazaari* fashion, backing whichever side in the debate he thought was going to win. When he did make decisive interventions they were sometimes for the private sector and sometimes for the state. The result of the confusion was that Iran had no consistent economic philosophy in the Ayatollah's lifetime. Since his death, in 1989, the debate has been resolved in favour of the private sector, though more by the sheer necessity of stimulating production and the government's tacit acceptance of the thinking of the World Bank, than by anything in the Shariah.

The Islamists' views on forms of government, and in particular democracy, are rather less confused than their ideas on economics. It is accepted by everybody that there must be some consultation (*shura*) by a government of its people, but the consensus is that this must be carefully controlled.

There are a few Islamist politicians who say they would accept free elections in certain circumstances. They say that if an Islamist government were to come to power by elections it should continue to hold elections, though they would prefer to see the undemocratic Arab monarchies and one-party republics evolving in an Islamic consultative direction rather than copying Western democratic ideas. In effect they are saying that it would be better to be brought to power by a government instituting Islamic reforms than by its holding elections. The problem with a system of regular elections is that it might at some point involve an Islamist party being defeated, and then its leaders, the outgoing government, would have to pray and consult their consciences and decide whether the right course was really to accept the will of the misguided people, who had voted against God's law, or to remain true to the need to implement the Shariah, declare the election result void and continue in office. The question here is not just a matter of Islamic politicians wondering whether they should risk having their ambitions for power (and wealth) frustrated, there is also a serious philosophical question of whether Islamic rule can legally and morally tolerate democracy. In the eyes of most jurists it would be wrong for an Islamic government to allow the people to vote it out of office.*

The type of constitution most scholars and politicians would like to see built into an Islamic government would involve the executive, the leader and his ministers, looking for advice, or approval of their actions, to only the best qualified representatives of the people. This means that the representatives should be drawn from the best educated, most able and most morally upright and Godly members of society, those who, as a Saudi religious scholar once put it to me, 'are most aware of what society wants and needs'. The qualification for a person being able to judge society's wants, he added, was scholarship.

Naturally there are a great many views on what exact systems would best be constructed from these general principles, but there are two ideas which have wide support. One is for an appointed assembly (*majlis*), which would have a purely advisory role, and the other is for

---

* It was this logic that led to the famous remark of Edward Djerejian, an Assistant US Secretary of State, that Islamic government would be liable to mean 'One person, one vote, one time'.

a parliament (also *majlis* in Arabic and Persian), which would be able to give binding decisions but would not be allowed to debate or legislate on anything which ran against Shariah law. The second idea could imply elections in the Western sense, but it would restrict parties and candidates to those who agreed with the basic principle of a state having an Islamic government. Alternatively it could involve the people choosing representatives from the best qualified in their communities, in other words clerics or Islamist activists, and these people electing some of their own number to a parliament. The introduction of a parliament on either of these bases would necessitate the creation of a further body to vet its legislation.

Iran has adopted the parliamentary approach to consultation. Both its election campaigns and the debates in the Majlis are far more democratic, vigorous and interesting than they were in the Shah's day, but the spectrum of opinion allowed ranges only from the moderate Islamic left to the staunchly Islamic conservative. The Communists and the revolutionary Islamic left, the *mujahiddin* groups, were eliminated in the four years of internal fighting that followed the Revolution, and moderate and right-wing secular elements are, by the very nature of their views, excluded from public debate. The Iranian system is clearly very different from democracy as it is understood in the West, but it is less restrictive than people outside the country imagine. It produces much freer debate than is allowed in most Arab countries.

The only Arab country that has put into effect modern, republican, Islamist ideas has been Sudan. The political reorganization and social 'reforms' here have been imposed in rather unlikely circumstances, in which a regime which is superficially military has followed one which had good Islamic credentials and had itself inherited from its predecessors a legal system that contained elements of the Shariah.

The story of the evolution of modern Sudanese politics in an Islamist direction goes back to 1983. At that time the regime of Jafaar Nimeri, which had been in power since 1969, had become thoroughly discredited by its corruption, incompetence and the failure of its plans for economic development and, seeking for a way of rallying some support, it hit on the idea of adopting certain aspects of Shariah law. This was in spite of the fact that up to this point it had been thoroughly secular and in the early stages of its rule had brutally crushed the religious opposition. In September 1983 President Nimeri announced the banning of alcohol, which was accompanied by the conspicuous pouring of large numbers of bottles of whisky into the Nile, and, more seriously, the introduction of the capital and corporal punishments of the Shariah.

In practice these were implemented mainly with the purpose of frightening people. Beheadings and amputations were carried out in a random
fashion, which often ran contrary to Islamic Law. No attempt was
made by the regime to cut corruption or introduce the principle of
consultation.

In April 1985, eighteen months after beginning his experiment with
the Shariah, Nimeri was overthrown by the commander-in-chief of the
armed forces, who a year later organized elections and handed power
to a civilian government. The new Prime Minister was Sadiq Al-Mahdi,
the great-grandson of Mohammad Ahmed Abdullah, 'The Mahdi', who
had led the rebellion against Egyptian rule in the early 1880s and had
established an Islamic state, which had lasted until 1898 when his
successors had been defeated by General Kitchener at the battle of
Omdurman. Sadiq Al-Mahdi had not only the prestige of being
descended from this famous leader, by virtue of his ancestry he was
also the head of the Ansar, which is a major Sufi sect made up of
followers of the Mahdi's descendants.* The Ansar was represented in
politics by its own party, the Umma (Community), and after the 1986
election this was allied in government with the Democratic Unionist
Party, which represented another major Sufi sect, the Khatmiya.
Together the Ansar and the Khatmiya commanded the loyalties of a
majority of the Sudanese Muslim population. The effect of this inter-
locking of political and sectarian leadership was that Sadiq Al-Mahdi
and the leader of the DUP, Osman Al-Mirghani, had not only a democratic political legitimacy but a semi-tribal and religious legitimacy.
Sadiq Al-Mahdi, furthermore, was known as a scholar and an advocate
of Islamic principles in government. He therefore spoke and acted with
great authority when he opposed the continuation of Sudan's selective

---

* In the early Muslim period the emphasis in the new communities' observance was
on people living their lives in accordance with the Shariah. This rather legalistic
approach to religion did not satisfy the spiritual needs of all believers. There were some
Muslims who wanted a personal mystical relationship with God – who wanted to love
Him and feel inspired by Him. A century after the Prophet's death there began to
evolve groups in which people tried to achieve this through exotic techniques such as
dancing themselves into a state of trance, repeatedly chanting the names of God, and
singing hymns and litanies. The mystics became associated with storytellers who
appeared at this time, wandering from village to village and recounting tales of saints,
miracles and mysteries, which in many cases came from Judaism, Christianity and
eastern religions. The story tellers wore robes of wool (*suf*), which became the origin
of the words sufi and sufism. In due course various sufi orders appeared. Some of these
believed in saints and tended towards Shiism, others stressed the similarity of their
beliefs to the orthodox tradition. In the northern and central parts of modern Sudan
there are four Sufi orders, the Ansar and Khatmiya, and the smaller Gadria and Tigania.

version of Shariah law. He had said from the time it had been introduced that it was a distortion of Islamic principles and that it ran against the tradition of the Sudanese, who were devout, God-fearing Muslims, but had usually been known for a tolerant attitude towards their fellow men. He saw also that it was helping to prolong the war in the south which had been fought in two phases, the first from 1955 to 1972 and the second beginning in 1983, by rebel tribes, mainly animist but partly Christian and Muslim, who wanted either independence or a large measure of autonomy.

Slowly the ruling parties worked towards the repeal of the parts of the Shariah that Nimeri had put in place, though this was clearly not something which any Muslim government could do easily and it was made more difficult by the opposition of the Sudanese associate of the Muslim Brotherhood, the National Islamic Front. Two years after he had come to power Sadiq Al-Mahdi announced that some provisions of the Shariah were being suspended and that a new Islamic legal code was being prepared. Osman Al-Mirghani meanwhile had entered negotiations with the southern rebels for a settlement, which contained the suspension of Shariah law in all parts of the country as one of its main features. The southerners were particularly concerned that the Shariah should be set aside in the north, as well as in their own region, because they wanted to feel that in a federal Sudan they would be full citizens with access to all positions in central government, and not part of a legally separated minority in an Islamic state. For their part the northern politicians and senior army officers wanted to settle the war because it was unwinnable and sapped the resources of their bankrupt state. The idea of peace was popular among the ordinary troops because a large number were themselves southerners.

The people who were not pleased by any of this activity were members of the National Islamic Front, who were brought into the government in 1988 when a broader coalition cabinet was formed. This was supposed to be a means of promoting national unity as a step towards tackling corruption, famine, administrative chaos and the country's other appalling economic problems. Also displeased by the backtracking on the Shariah were what seems to have been quite a large number of middle-rank officers in the army, who were strong supporters of Muslim Brotherhood ideas. These people believed that if they pursued the war in the south vigorously they would be able to win it.

At the end of June 1989 a group of officers led by Brigadier Omar Hassan Bashir staged a *coup d'état*. They banned all political parties and detained their leaders, including the head of the National Islamic

Front, Dr Hassan Turabi, and his colleagues. It quickly emerged, however, that the coup leaders were closer to the NIF than they appeared. Turabi was released from prison within days and within a month it was becoming clear that the NIF and its leader were the inspiration of most of the new government's policies. The more knowledgeable Sudanese decided that the coup had probably been arranged by the Front from the beginning, and they have not changed their opinion since. Although, officially, the NIF remains banned, it is spoken of in Sudan as the *de facto* government.

In power the NIF and Lieutenant-General Bashir, who in the way of coup leaders promoted himself by two ranks after he became President, have behaved with a mixture of straightforward brutality and Islamic zeal. Their authoritarian face, which has been like that of any other Arab or African military dictatorship, has been seen in their continued ban on political parties and other civil institutions, such as independent trade unions, and their tight control on the press. The regime has been particularly brutal in its treatment of anyone it has seen as a threat to its security. Political opponents have been imprisoned or put under house arrest. Other people whom it is thought might be disloyal are arrested and given a few days or weeks in one of Khartoum's 'ghost houses'. These are apparently empty buildings that are actually used by the security police. Detainees are beaten up, tortured and thoroughly frightened, and then released. The advantage of the system from the government's point of view is that it is cheap – the police do not have to spend money on keeping prisoners alive for months or years – and it helps spread the detainees' fear, because when they are released they are bound to tell their friends what has happened to them.

A minor example of this system in operation concerned an employee of a contractor with whom I had lunch in 1992. In the middle of the meal the contractor was summoned to his building site by a messenger, and he reappeared half an hour later to say that one of his workmen had been given twenty lashes by the police. Apparently the man had been having a meal with friends, paying a pound or two (equivalent to one or two US cents) to share a pot of beans, and they had started to discuss rising prices, and then politics. One of the group, who must have been a government informer, slipped away and told his employers about the conversation, whereupon some policemen arrived, seized the most talkative of the workmen, took him away, beat him and released him, all within the space of two hours. This type of episode is not uncommon in Khartoum.

The regime's Islamic zeal has been seen in the reforms it has imposed on society. It has reintroduced the criminal provisions of the Shariah law, though in practice it does not make great use of them. It has Islamized banking and talked about Islamizing insurance, which is a sensitive business in Muslim countries because it can be seen as an impertinent attempt by man to provide against the consequences of God's will. Under an Islamized system insurance companies are made into co-operatives. The regime has also tried to discourage women from working and has asked them to wear veils, but neither of these initiatives has been effective. The country is too poor for anyone willingly to give up a job, if he or she has one, and it is too hot for women to want to cover their faces.

The curious feature of these innovations is that they have been running against the Sudanese tradition. The Islamic rule the government has been trying to impose is based on the fairly austere, orthodox attitudes of the Muslim Brotherhood, the intellectual discipline in which Turabi has been educated. The NIF has always had something of the character of a movement for the religious intellectual élite; its members are zealous, well organized and well grounded in the Shariah. They have gathered support from some of the middle classes and from small traders, to whom the party's sympathizers lent money when they were given permission to establish an Islamic bank during Nimeri's time in power. But the NIF has not had the same contact with the people that the big political parties related to the Sufi sects have had. The fact that Hassan Turabi is married to the sister of Sadiq Al-Mahdi has had no special effect in improving his populist credentials. The ordinary Sudanese are not greatly impressed by the NIF. They still prefer to look to the teachings and example of the leaders of their Sufi sects and to the various sheikhs who follow them.

It is difficult to say whether the Sudanese regime would be representative in this respect of other Islamist regimes, if such were to come to power in the Arab world. It is quite possible that it would be, at least in North Africa where popular superstitions and interest in saints are more important than they are in most of the eastern Arab world. It is not difficult to imagine the type of Islamist regime that might take power in Algeria or, conceivably, Egypt being of the same austere stamp as the NIF, in which case it would be out of harmony with local Islamic tradition.

Where the NIF would provide a model in a more formal sense for other Arab Islamist regimes would be in the system of 'consultation' it has introduced. This involves a chain of popular assemblies leading from the village to the parliament. It starts with the summoning of 'basic congresses', each made up, in theory, of all the citizens, men and women, living in a village or urban quarter. These congresses, or the citizens who come to participate in them, discuss whatever local business they like, and then each elects a 'popular committee' which puts into operation the decisions it has taken on local government and represents it at a 'council congress' at town or rural district level. The council congress, in turn, sends delegates to a 'province congress', which sends delegates to its 'state congress', which then is represented at the National Congress. At the state and national levels the congresses have added to them appointed representatives of various government controlled organizations including the police and armed forces, international friendship societies, the civil service and organizations for women and youth. In the final stage of the chain the National Congress provides two thirds of the members of the National Assembly, the other one third being directly elected from 'basic national constituencies'.

Officials of the government claim that this process is admirably democratic. When it is suggested to them that it is actually very like the system of 'democracy' that used to apply in the Soviet Union, they reply that the Soviet Union never had any members directly elected to its national parliament and that it did not have direct popular elections for the post of President, which Sudan intends to have. They also argue that the Sudanese system involves everybody in local government in the most democratic way possible. All of these points are technically true, but they ignore the fact that the only political organizations allowed to operate in the country are the government and, unofficially, the National Islamic Front, so it is bound to be the united (or identical) efforts of these two that dominate the electoral process at every stage.

Certainly it is the government's men – ostensibly just the most active members of each community – who control the voting at the basic congress level. At the meetings of these bodies there is much chanting, reciting of nationalistic poetry and whipping up of the crowds to a point where anybody who decided to vote against the motion being put forward by the activists would feel very uncomfortable, if not actually frightened. The government officials may be right in denying that their system is structurally entirely the same as the old Soviet one, but in its direction of people's emotions and methods of getting the 'right' results, Islamist democracy in Sudan is very much like Communism in many parts of the world in the 1950s and 1960s, and Fascism in Europe in the 1920s and 1930s.

In the last fifteen years, since they began to emerge as a political force, Islamist movements may have succeeded in gaining power in only one Arab country, but they have dominated politics everywhere. In some places – Jordan and Saudi Arabia – their challenge has been peaceful;

in others – Algeria and Tunisia – it has begun fairly peacefully but become violent. In several countries the Islamists have been violent from the beginning, as they were in Syria in the late 1970s and early 1980s and in Iraq in the 1980s. In neither of these particular countries did the Islamists ever have the option of entering politics peacefully. In Egypt there have been two stands in Islamist politics: the peaceful but not very effective Muslim Brotherhood, which has been mainly excluded from parliamentary politics by the law, and the terrorist groups, Islamic Jihad and the Gamaa Al-Islamiyya. Here and in all the other Arab countries the Islamist movements have been a constant threat to the regimes.

Since the cancellation of the Algerian elections the Islamist groups' most violent and publicized challenge has been to the government of Egypt. Islamist violence here has grown steadily since the late 1970s, when President Sadat, having initially encouraged the movement as a means of balancing the influence of the Nasserite left, offended his protégés by what they regarded as a betrayal of their country's Arab and Islamic integrity. He opened the Egyptian economy to foreign investment and encouraged its development in a Western capitalist and materialist direction, and then, worse still, he made peace with Israel, which in the eyes of Islamists is a symbol of the intrusion of the West into the Arab and Islamic world and the source of Arab humiliation.

In 1981 some young officers, who turned out to be members of Islamic Jihad, assassinated Sadat. They broke out of the ranks of a military parade and machine-gunned the steps on which the President and his guests were standing. During the next ten years the Islamists carried out random and increasingly frequent killings of policemen and attacks on Copts, their churches, shops and houses, particularly in Upper Egypt. In this area the Copts were more numerous than else-where, and they were visibly better off than the Muslims. At the same time the general standard of living among Muslims and the prospects of employment for young men were lower than in other parts of the country, which gave the Islamists a particularly large number of recruits willing to risk their lives in terrorist action. In the minds of these young men the Copts were quite easily associated with the malign influence of the West, America and Israel, and they were an accessible target. As a former minister put it, 'instead of fighting Mr Bush the youths could attack the Copt jeweller or pharmacist in their own street.' The purpose of these attacks was to create a rift between Copts and Muslims, in the hope that this might lead to more generalized violence and split society, but in fact it succeeded only in creating a malaise in the normally tranquil relations of the two communities in a few parts of Upper Egypt.

In the early 1990s the extremists switched to attacking political figures, including the Speaker of the Majlis As-Shaab (People's Assembly) whom they killed, and tourist targets, through which they hoped to destroy one of the country's major sources of foreign exchange, damage the economy and undermine people's confidence in the government. They had some success with this strategy. No more than a handful of foreign tourists were killed, but the result was that in the 1992–3 season tourist revenues fell to about half the level of the previous year. Early in 1993 the Gamaa al-Islamiyya announced that it might extend its attacks to foreign investments, and there were signs that this was causing a few firms to hold back from committing their capital to the country. The government was forced to respond with massive raids on suspected Gamaa strongholds. In the town of Asyut in Upper Egypt in March the security forces, armed with machine-guns and rocket-propelled grenades, fought militants for nine hours before they surrendered. In Cairo they raided the suburb of Imbaba and arrested six hundred. In Aswan they stormed a mosque. These confrontations resulted in dozens of extremists being killed, which was clearly the security forces' intention. Thousands more were arrested and more than twenty in 1992 and early 1993 were tried by military courts and sentenced to death. The heavy-handedness of the government's policy itself attracted international publicity and prompted criticism by human rights groups.

The violence in Egypt and other countries, particularly Algeria in 1992–3, was only one aspect of the pressure the Islamists were putting on governments. It was what worried the governments most and what caught the headlines, but it was not necessarily what most affected the lives of the people. For the great majority of Arabs the effect of the rise of Islamism in the 1980s and early 1990s has been to change the tone of society. It has forced governments to adopt a pose of false piety as a means of appeasing the Islamists or, possibly, winning their support. Presidents and prime ministers have been peppering their speeches with verses from the Koran and other religious references. Even Saddam Hussein, who runs a regime that is as secular as any in the Middle East, has found it expedient to Islamize his rhetoric. The numbers of religious programmes on the television have been increased. They include readings from the Koran, sermons, religious discussions and the interruptions of normal broadcasting for 'prayer breaks'.* In

---

* There are five prayers in the Muslim day: *fajr* at dawn, *dohr* at midday, *asr* in the mid-afternoon, *mahgreb* at sunset and *ashr* at nightfall.

the long term the effect of these is only to increase the numbers of young recruits to the Islamist cause, which is what the political movements and charitable societies have intended when they have called for more religious programmes. The same logic of demand leading to appease-ment, leading to a further strengthening of the Islamists has applied to the expansion of the religious curriculum in schools and the building of mosques. When governments have been confronted by Islamists demanding 'reforms', or have wanted to reinforce their standing with the establishment *ulema*, the easiest concession has been to commit themselves to building more mosques. Mosque building has become such a normal response to Islamist pressure that in Jordan just after the 1989 elections a vivacious journalist declared that she did not see what more the government could do to make the country look Islamic, because, she said, 'between every mosque and the next mosque they've already built two more mosques'.

The false Islamist manner of the governments has spread to part of the populations and produced a form of Islamic cant or 'political correctness'. There are some angry, Westernized members of the middle classes who remain resolutely secular and have nothing to do with this. There are others, the conservative elements who are reacting against Western ways and returning to Arab tradition, who are outside the new trend because they have thought about what they are doing and believe in it. The people who have adopted the new cant are merely conforming to fashion. Some are Islamists, others have no strongly held views. They have adopted numerous little changes in their speech and behaviour. Many have turned to stressing unnecessarily how often they pray or how important Islam is in their lives. A few men have started to see that their wives are veiled in public. Some have taken to muttering the words 'peace be upon him' every time they mention the name of the Prophet and putting PBUH after his name when they write it. All of them have become earnest and pious about Islamic matters.

An example of this which I encountered in the late 1980s stemmed from a joke, apparently told by President Nasser, which I had used at the beginning of a *Financial Times* article on Yemen. God, accompanied by an angel, visited the earth for the first time since the creation. He looked down on a large, rich, populous country and asked his com-panion where it was. He was told it was the United States. 'How amazing,' said God, 'it has changed so much, I would never have recog-nized it.' He then moved 10,000 miles eastwards and beheld a fertile river valley. On being told it was Egypt He exclaimed how much pro-gress the people had made. Then He moved a few hundred miles to the south-east and looked down once more. 'Ah,' He said, 'Yemen'. A few weeks after this was published I met a Yemeni who said he had liked the article but did not approve of the joke – and the reason he gave was not that it embarrassed him by pointing to the backwardness of his country but that it belittled God. God, he said, knew everything – he would not have had to be told which country was the United States and which was Egypt – so the person with the angel must have been Adam.

None of this Islamic cant has done anything to make people better morally. It has merely made some of them more self-righteous. It has had the unhappy effect of producing a group of people who are becoming more narrow minded in their view of the world, less interested in foreign cultures and less tolerant. This intolerance embraces secular philosophical ideas, other religions, and Muslims who in one way or another choose not to take their religion seriously. The Islamists and the people who have been influenced by them are far less tolerant than were the societies of the great Arab empires in the Middle Ages. In the Baghdad of the Abbasid Caliph, Haroun Ar-Rashid (AD 786–809), there was a flourishing secular, and occasionally erotic, literature. It was even possible for a poet to put on his grave the blasphemous epitaph 'here lies the sin of my father', which a pious man would say abused God's gift of life. Nobody in the Arab world would dare write such a thing today.

The important question for the Arab governments, and for the West, is whether the tide of Islamism will continue to rise. Most of the events that are reported in the Western press give the impression that it will. This is not surprising because news media concentrate on dramatic, violent and shocking events rather than on less visible social trends. They are concerned with bombings, defiant speeches by the leaders of Iran and Sudan, and the two Islamic republics' backing for terrorist groups such as the Gamaa and the outlawed FIS. There are many more events which would strengthen the impression given by the media, but which are not widely reported. One such was the riot that occurred in the town of Qalyoub, near Cairo, in early 1993. This was sparked by the authorities transferring a teacher from a school and expelling four pupils who had been listening in the classroom to tapes of an extremist cleric. The violent reaction of the townspeople was immediate and spontaneous. A church was burned and police had to be called from Cairo to restore order. Then the rulings against the teacher and pupils were reversed.

Not all the signs, though, support the impression given by such events. From the early days of the modern movement, support for the

Islamists has seemed alternately to rise and fall, often growing in one area at the same time as it has been shrinking in another. In the Gulf the influence of Iran was strong in the early period of the Revolution, in 1979–80, but the people of the region, who are very pacific and moderate in their views, were alienated by the chaos and bloodshed of the Revolution and the intransigence with which it pursued its war with Iraq. Like the rest of the world they were horrified by the enormous casualties the Iranians suffered in their human wave attacks in 1983 and 1984 and disgusted by the 'fountain of blood' which was built in Tehran to commemorate the martyrs. Then in the later 1980s the Iranians lost further goodwill when, after they had driven the Iraqis off their territory but failed to win a decisive military victory, they refused to make peace. In the minds of people throughout the Arab world their behaviour helped establish the idea that Islamic revolutions do not care about human life.

There has been something of the same reaction by many Egyptians to the bombings of the Gamaa. Most Egyptians, like the Gulf Arabs and the Sudanese, are easygoing people who are not impressed by extremist violence, whether it is directed against Copts, tourists or, as happened, inexplicably, with some bombings in mid-1993, poor Muslim Egyptians. There is also an important body of Egyptians – small traders, hotel staff, taxi drivers and people in similar service industries – who have been injured in a direct financial sense by the fall in tourism that the bombings have caused. A slightly more prosperous group of small businessmen was hurt when a number of Islamic investment companies were liquidated in the later 1980s. In some cases there had been obvious fraud on the part of the managements, in others the companies had just been incompetently run. When their problems became known the authorities insisted that the companies should make their operations conform to the normal provisions of the commercial laws (such as they were), and when they were unable to do this they were obliged to return as much money as they could to depositors. Some of the owners and managers were put on trial. In different ways both the bombing campaign and the failure of the Islamic investment companies must have cost the Islamists support, though how much is difficult to quantify.

This is one of the major problems faced by anyone who is trying to assess the prospects of the Islamist movement: there is no way of making any accurate assessment of its fluctuating support. There are few national elections in which Islamist parties are allowed to stand, there are no opinion polls, and the views of the people who are interested in the subject, ranging from social scientists to taxi drivers, are by their nature imprecise. There is, however, one interesting but rather random indicator, which is the results of the elections that are held in the less tightly controlled Arab countries for the officers of professional associations. These elections are fought on party lines and the results are much discussed. They were regarded as sufficiently important in Egypt in 1993 for the government to intervene to change the voting rules of its doctors', dentists', engineers' and lawyers' associations, to prevent the Islamists packing the meetings at which the votes were held. In Sudan in August 1991 the NIF took more drastic steps to help its cause. When it believed that the secular left was going to win the elections of the Khartoum University students' union, it closed the entire university for six months.

What the results, of those elections that *are* held, show is that support for the Islamists is unpredictable and prone to surprising fluctuations. In a period of seven months between November 1991 and May 1992 the voting of Palestinians and Jordanians in the West Bank and Jordan produced the following results: at Yarmouk University in November the Islamists lost badly, even though a year earlier they had won almost every seat on the student council; a month later an Islamist candidate won the presidency of the Jordanian doctors' association; then in Hebron the Islamists swept to power in the elections for the chamber of commerce committee; in February they lost elections held by the West Bank lawyers' association; in May they lost the Nablus chamber of commerce elections; and again in May, when all the secular parties co-operated, they were massively defeated in elections at the Bethlehem University students' union. In those elections that were held on the West Bank the contests were between candidates known to sympathize with different secular groups associated with the Palestine Liberation Organization and supporters of the Islamic Resistance Movement, known by its Arabic acronym, Hamas, which is associated with the Muslim Brotherhood.

From the point of view of secular Arab governments, and their Western friends, the chequered pattern of results, which has been seen in similar elections in other countries in the last four or five years, is reassuring. It shows that there is no inexorable rise in Islamist sentiment and, most significantly, that when secular parties work together the Islamists can be defeated quite decisively. But it also shows that the Islamists are on occasion able to sweep the board. It is anybody's guess what would happen if totally free elections were held across the Arab world. Much would depend on the competence of the secular opposition and the electoral systems employed; those used in most Arab countries that hold elections have tended to favour a single strong, well-organized party, such as an Islamist group, at the expense of a multitude of disunited parties which might, collectively, have more than half of the vote. In their informal estimates the people who discuss these issues suggest that Islamists might command anything up to half of the vote, which would mean that after free elections they would dominate most parliaments.

Governments, consequently, are being extremely careful about how they hold elections. Most – among those that have fairly regular elections that they would maintain were fair – are banning Islamist parties from competing. This is what has been done in Egypt, Morocco, Tunisia and, since the débâcle of January 1992, Algeria. Where parliaments are being reintroduced after long periods in which they have been suspended, in effect what happened in Jordan between 1967 and 1989, their powers are being carefully limited. If, in a country such as Jordan or Kuwait, an Islamist faction were to establish a dominant position in a parliament the head of state or his executive would probably try to outmanoeuver it.* It would probably be allowed to introduce only those of its policies that would prove most unpopular, great attention would be paid to its failures and to any cases of corruption that could be pinned on its members, and it would be blamed for whatever went wrong. In an extreme situation, in which an Islamist parliamentary majority challenged a government and demanded constitutional reform so that it could be allowed to take over the running of a country, most Arab kings and presidents would probably dissolve the parliament. In short, since the Islamists nearly took control of Algeria, it has been very unlikely that any other Arab government would let itself get into a position in which Islamists might oust it from power through elections.

If, for practical purposes, elections are closed to the Islamists as a means of coming to power, it is always possible that they will take over a government by *coup d'état*. In the wake of, say, serious bread riots an army officer might overthrow a government and then, wanting to cultivate popular support, turn to an Islamist party and bring it into his regime. Alternatively an Islamist party might persuade an officer to seize power on its behalf. There was, of course, just such a coup in Sudan in 1989, but elsewhere in the Arab world there has been no successful *coup d'état*, secular or Islamist, since 1970.

---

* In Arab countries government ministers do not have to be members of the parliaments. A majority for a particular party in a parliament, therefore, would not necessarily be reflected in a head of state's choice of prime minister, or in a prime minister's choice of ministers.

This leaves the possibility of a revolution, such as occurred in Iran. The sequence of events, if they followed the Iranian pattern, would be popular disenchantment with a government's economic policies and the corruption of its senior officials leading to mass demonstrations and strikes, followed by the government gradually losing its self-confidence and realizing that it had no options but surrender or flight. It is just possible to imagine this sequence of events happening in Egypt. The mass of the Egyptian people are very poor and many are sympathetic to the Islamists. They undoubtedly feel that their government is ineffective, uninspiring and corrupt, even though some acknowledge that Hosni Mubarak is a decent, well-meaning president. The main reason why the government is probably secure in spite of its short-comings is that the Egyptians, unlike the Iranians in the 1970s, have never had their material expectations raised, so even in the recent difficult years they have not been dashed. At the same time it does not seem that the Egyptian middle classes, particularly the civil servants, are losing confidence in their government to the extent that they would throw in their lot with an Islamist revolution, and while a modern government has control of its civil service, police and army it remains a powerful institution. A further consideration that makes Egypt a difficult candidate for an Islamic revolution is that in Sunni societies there is no independent established clergy, which means that there is no potential Islamist revolutionary leadership in being.

It is easier to imagine an Islamic revolution in Algeria, mainly because in that country expectations have been raised and then crushed. This has made the people that much more disenchanted with their leaders than the Egyptians have been.

In the long term Egypt is hoping that the economic reforms it is slowly putting in place will give its people jobs and raise their standard of living, and so lessen the despair that feeds the Islamist cause. In Algeria, once it decides on a definite and plausible programme of economic reforms, the government will presumably be hoping the same. In the short term in both countries the governments' policy towards the extremists is one of straightforward repression. They have been co-operating in this strategy and the Westernized and more prosperous middle classes in both countries have been behind them, as have been the foreign companies that have invested in Egypt.

The policy sounds crude but in Egypt it has been quite effective. By the late summer of 1993 the authorities thought they had arrested enough people to have destroyed the leadership and organization of the Gamaa. The Algerian campaign against the terrorists was less advanced and the country was still losing some of its best government servants, the heads of educational bodies and similar non-political institutions, to gunmen. It seemed that the terrorists were trying to isolate the government by frightening the intelligentsia away from working for it.

The two countries were regarded in the Middle East as the critical battlegrounds between established governments and revolutionary Islam. If the Islamists did succeed in overthrowing either government they might go on to spread their influence and take over other Arab countries, unless they were shown very quickly to be totally economically incompetent. If on the other hand the Egyptian and Algerian governments managed to subdue the Islamist challenge, it was thought that might mark the beginning of the decline of political Islam in the Arab world as a whole.

14

Steps Towards Democracy

The continued pressure for democratic reform – politics and reform in Morocco, Tunisia, Egypt, Jordan, Kuwait, Yemen

Much as they fear the Islamists, the Arab governments are still under pressure to reform. They know that they have to manage the process carefully, but they cannot stop it. Any government that abolished its parliament altogether, or reintroduced a single-party system and reimposed rigid controls on the press and on all unofficial political activity, would be able to pretend for a few months, or maybe a year, that it had returned to the happy authoritarian days of the 1970s and early 1980s, but quite quickly the people's demand for change and the need to compensate them for economic austerity would reassert themselves. The challenge for the governments, therefore, is to maintain some momentum towards greater freedom and democracy, enough to give their people a feeling of gradual improvement, yet at the same time keep control of the Islamists so that they and the entire secular political system of their countries are not swept away.

The whole logic of the governments' reforms, of course, is practical. The Arab heads of state have not been reading the work of the great political thinkers and been converted to the principle of democracy. They are reforming because they have to. Yet in the minds of all of them to different degrees there is also an acceptance that moves towards democracy are in keeping with the spirit of the times, that they are right and that they are unavoidable. Their pragmatism is blended with a genuine but cautious interest in managing the evolution of a new form of government for their countries.

This type of thinking has been reflected in the last few years in the policies of King Hassan of Morocco, who in the early 1990s began to show that he wanted slowly to increase the authority of his parliament, the traditionally bland and powerless Chamber of Representatives. In doing this he was altering the habits of three decades of virtually absolute rule. The first signs of a change came in late 1991 when the representatives of five left-wing parties presented to him a memorandum asking for some modest reforms. They requested that a general election, which had been due in 1990, be held the following year, that a new electoral roll be compiled (to include young voters and remove thousands of double registrations), that the voting age be lowered from twenty-one to eighteen, and that governments be answerable to the parliament and not just to the King. Slightly to the surprise of the five parties, the King in due course agreed to some of these proposals. He had the voting age lowered, though only to twenty, accepted the request for a new electoral roll and instituted an electoral commission which was charged with seeing that all elections (local and national), previously notoriously corrupt, should in future be free and fair. He also agreed that some changes to the constitution be drawn up and put to the people in a referendum. This was duly held in September 1992. The changes were undoubtedly popular and there would almost certainly have been a big majority vote in their favour, but because the opposition parties were not completely happy with them and were calling on their supporters to boycott the poll, it seems that the Ministry of the Interior became worried and, reverting to its old habits, provided the King with an endorsement of 99.96 per cent, rising to a more reassuring 100 per cent in the main cities.

Whatever the shortcomings of the referendum itself, the reforms it approved were quite important. They provided that future governments should reflect the balance of parties in the parliament and that the prime minister, who would continue to be chosen by the King, would have to submit his government's programme, and each annual budget, to votes of confidence. They also provided for new laws to be promulgated automatically a month after they had been passed by the parliament, rather than having to wait for the approval of the monarch, which in the past had sometimes been given belatedly and sometimes never given at all. They left the King with the right to dismiss a government.

Together these changes went a long way towards meeting the opposition parties' request that governments should be responsible to the parliament rather than the King. It was clear to everybody that if the King objected to a measure, or particularly wanted a measure passed, his counsellors would be able to find ways of obliging him, but it was equally clear that the sorts of parliament that would exist under the new constitution would be different from what had gone before. For most of the previous thirty years parliaments had been dominated by coalitions of centre-right place seekers, all loyal to the King, all happy to vote for whatever measures were put before them and none expecting to exercise any power.

In June 1993 the first general election for nine years was held. It had some traditional Moroccan characteristics. There was a case of a successful candidate discovering that his votes had been thrown away so that a former minister could be given a seat, and there were certainly many cases of vote buying. In some town squares polling cards were being openly offered for sale. The most active buyers were various types of *nouveaux riches* candidates: speculators, drug traders who had made fortunes from selling hashish from the Rif mountains, and smugglers (*trabendos*) who had been operating the Moroccan end of the contraband traffic with Algeria. Yet in spite of these abuses the election was reckoned to be much fairer than any previous contest and its outcome reflected roughly the true strength of the parties. Sixty-three per cent of the electorate – a plausible proportion – was said to have voted. The biggest blocks of seats were won by two of the opposition parties, the Union Socialiste des Forces Populaires (USFP) and the nationalist Istiqlal, but a coalition of 'government' parties, which were just groupings formed around powerful individuals, managed to gain a small overall majority.* These results applied only to the two-thirds of parliamentary seats which were chosen by direct voting; three months later the voting took place in the professional associations, trade unions, chambers of commerce and various other bodies, such as the employers' federation and the veterans' association, which fill the remaining one-third of the seats. The outcome of the election in these bodies, in which there was considerable intervention by the Ministry of the Interior, increased the overall majority of the 'government' parties.

It was accepted, in the period between the two elections, that the USFP, as the biggest single party, would be entitled to form the next government, but after the associations' elections the King decided that it did not have a big enough representation to warrant the prime minis-

---

* No Islamist group was represented in the new parliament because none was allowed to contest the election. The biggest of the Moroccan groups, *Al Adl wal Ishan* (Justice and Charity), was made illegal in 1990 and its leader, Cheikh Abdesalem Yassine, put under house arrest.

tership, and the USFP and its allies refused to accept his offer of all the minor ministries in a government in which the most important offices would be filled by his own appointees. The traditional 'pro-government' factions felt they lacked the moral authority to form a government, and so eventually, in November, the King appointed a veteran prime minister, Karim Lamrani, to head an administration composed of technocrats who had no party affiliations. He said at this time that he expected that in the next few years there would be a 'bipolarization' in the parliament in which two definite blocs or parties of left versus centre-right would emerge. A commonly expressed view in Morocco was that in two or three years' time one of these might be strong and confident enough to form a government.

It was easy enough for Western newspapers at the time of the elections to point to the shortcomings of Moroccan democracy and suggest that little in the country's politics had changed. Several journalists made much of cases of cheating they found on polling day in June. But the opinion of most of the Moroccan middle classes was that the reforms of the previous two years had been important. They felt that there was a new tone to the way the country was being run, and that the King wanted the change to be permanent and, perhaps, to be the basis for further changes in the future. The assumption was that the King was influenced not only by the expectation of change that was spreading through the Arab world but also by thoughts of his own mortality. In 1993 he was sixty-four and he was aware that he had lived longer than either his father or his brother. It was believed he was thinking about how his kingdom might be run after him by his son, Moulay Mohammad, then aged thirty, and had decided that the early years of his successor's reign would be easier if more of the responsibility for government were to lie with the parliament. There was speculation that while the King himself did not feel able to hand much of his power to an elected government, he envisaged his son introducing a genuine constitutional monarchy. He was also influenced, undoubtedly, by his desire to bring Morocco into as close as possible an association with the European Community, and for this free elections and a better record on human rights were essential.

In all the changes he allowed to be introduced in 1992 and 1993, King Hassan made sure that he did not surrender any of his ultimate authority; he kept the prerogative of choosing a prime minister and dismissing his government. What he was doing was withdrawing from the day-to-day management of government and letting parliament run that on his behalf. If, by any chance, the new system ran out of control and produced a parliament that demanded radical reform or the admission of Islamist parties, there was no doubt that the King would re-establish his old style of rule.

There are five other countries in the Arab world which have introduced democratic reforms in recent years. In one of them, Tunisia, the process has not been as successful as was originally hoped, and in another, Egypt, the pace of change has been so slow that it has become almost imperceptible. In Jordan and Kuwait parliaments have been reintroduced after periods in which the countries' rulers had governed without them, and in both places the reform has been a success, in the eyes of both governments and people. In Yemen there have been elections – the first ever in that country – though in practical terms there has been little change in the way the government has been run.

The story of reforms in each of these countries tells much of the difficulties governments face, of what types of government find reform easiest and of the benefit that societies receive even when reform moves slowly. It goes without saying that it shows that even the slowest reform is better than the well-intentioned but too complete and precipitate type carried out in Algeria in 1989–91.

In Tunisia the reforms begun by President Zine El-Abidine Ben Ali, after he came to power in November 1987, were designed to reunite the country. They followed an unhappy decade of violence and increasing social division in which a worn-out government had seemed incapable of addressing the country's problems.

The President's predecessor, Habib Bourguiba, was a staunch socialist, whose ideas were very much in keeping with the times in the twenty years or so after he led Tunisia to independence in 1956. The major features of his policy were the implementation of state control of the economy, an independent stance in foreign affairs, which led him long before other Arab heads of state to accept that one day the Arab world would have to make peace with Israel, and a thorough programme of social reform. For some fifteen years his policies worked well and in the late 1960s Tunisia seemed to be a model for other Arab states. It presented a picture of an enlightened government presiding over a well-educated, prosperous labour force working in quite efficient industries and services and enjoying nearly full employment.

One of the cornerstones of the government's social programme was the Statute of Women and the Family, which banned polygamy and changed the traditional laws on divorce. Instead of allowing a man to divorce himself by the simple process of renouncing his wife in front of a Shariah judge, it introduced procedures based on European law and allowed wives as well as husbands to petition for divorce. The

government took a firmly secular approach to many other less fundamental matters. It kept the French weekend of Saturday and Sunday,
rather than changing to Friday as the Algerians did. It permitted its
citizens to eat in public during Ramadan. The famous religious university of El-Zeitouna was shut because it was felt that in a secular state
there would be little need for imams or Islamic scholars. The President
missed no opportunity to promote secular ideas. It is said that whenever
he was told of the establishment of a new committee he would ask,
'does it have a Jew and a woman?'.

The government's secular policies impressed Europeans and were
popular with the educated Tunisian middle classes, but the almost
aggressive nature of some of them, such as the closure of El-Zeitouna,
upset the more conservative elements. This did not matter very much
while Tunisia continued to prosper, but by the early 1980s the country
found itself in difficulties. It had reaped the initial rewards of its education programme, in that its people were working in relatively sophisticated jobs, and it had benefited in the previous decade from the
beginning of some modest oil revenues, but it seemed to have reached
an awkward point at which its population was increasing fast while its
planners could see no obvious direction for its further development. Its
problems were made worse by the obvious corruption of the officials
who surrounded the President and his forceful wife, Wassila, and by
the President's increasingly tenuous grasp on affairs. Unemployment
and cynicism pushed young people towards various opposition 'movements' – the rebellious official trade union, the Union Générale des
Travailleurs Tunisiens (UGTT), the Communists, some socialist splinter
groups and, most significantly, the Movement de la Tendance Islamique
(MTI). These organizations were referred to as movements rather than
parties because for most of Bourguiba's period in power all parties other
than his own Destourian Socialist Party and its affiliate, the UGTT, were
illegal. For much of the early 1980s both of the leaders of the MTI,
Rached Ghanouchi, a high-school teacher, and Abdel-Fatha Mourou,
a lawyer, were in prison.

Starting in the late 1970s the tranquillity of Tunisian life was disturbed by strikes and demonstrations, and then by riots and increasingly
violent confrontations between students and unemployed youths and
the police. From January 1984, when cuts in food subsidies sparked
seven days of rioting, the principal force of opposition was the *intégriste*
(fundamentalist) MTI. The government responded to the disturbances
with mass arrests and imprisonments. In 1986 the President appointed
a general with a reputation for toughness, Zine El-Abidine Ben Ali,
to the post of Minister of the Interior, and then, in September 1987,

made him Prime Minister. Ben Ali found that Bourguiba's behaviour was becoming increasingly erratic, in particular in his decision in October to press for the execution of ninety *intégristes* who had been found guilty of threatening the security of the state. He therefore arranged to have him deposed. Acting with other senior members of the government he had seven doctors declare Bourguiba senile, which since the great man had declared himself President for Life in 1974 had become the only legitimate grounds for his replacement. On 7 November, in accordance with the constitution, Ben Ali himself became President.

As soon as Ben Ali came to power the tension seemed to go out of Tunisian society. The confrontations between students and the police, which had been taking place almost daily, stopped. The President announced a policy of reconciliation. In the eighteen months after he took office some 6,000 prisoners, including Rached Ghanouchi, were released. Political leaders from both the left and the Islamic movement who had gone abroad were let back into the country and allowed to speak publicly. Newspapers that had been suspended were allowed to be published again, and modifications to the press code gave publishers the right to prove the truth of 'defamatory' statements they might make about public figures – although the President and members of the cabinet continued to receive special protection.

Ben Ali realized that he needed to build himself a new power base made up of the support of as broad a cross-section of the population as possible. He had never been active in the Destourian Socialist Party and on coming to power he had pushed out of office a large number of its functionaries. Partly to compensate for this he sought the goodwill of the *intégristes*. One of his early acts was to go to Mecca on pilgrimage. He had El-Zeitouna reopened, allowed television programmes to be interrupted at prayer times, and ordered that the beginning of Ramadan, which depends on a sighting of the new moon, should be declared by the *ulema* and not by the state.

In April 1988 a law was passed to legalize political parties in addition to the Destour, whose name was changed to the Rassemblement Constitutionel Democratique (RCD). The law contained a provision which banned any party which had a purely linguistic, regional or religious character, but it was still hoped that the MTI would accept enough of the country's secular constitution for it to be registered. The government was hoping that in pursuing this idea it would divide the *intégristes*, splitting the extremists from those who would be prepared to work within the system. The President and Ghanouchi met and found they respected each other, and the *intégriste* leader said in general terms that he accepted the constitution. His movement turned itself into a political party, the Hizb An-Nahda (Renaissance Party). Yet Ghanouchi did not find he could compromise quite far enough. His party refused to spell out its principles and policies and the new Prime Minister, Hedi Baccouche, who was strongly against the *intégristes* and had declared that mixing religion and politics was 'the work of the Devil', refused to allow An-Nahda to register.

The government had further problems with the newly legalized secular parties. Six opposition parties had registered and it was the government's hope that in the general election of April 1989 they would return some members, so that the population would be shown that Tunisia really was no longer a one-party state. Accordingly it suggested that the opposition should enter a coalition with the RCD which would result in a few of its candidates being allowed to run unopposed. The opposition thought about the idea, but discovered that the government was not offering it any say in forming its policies, and eventually declined the offer. Its members went into what was generally considered to be an honest election representing little-known parties and having virtually no financial backing. They took about 1 per cent of the vote and none of them was elected. The Islamists hardly did better. They were not allowed to run under the banner of An-Nahda, but they fielded various independent candidates whose sympathies were known. They collected 18 per cent of the vote, but because of the electoral system, which worked on a 'first-past-the-post' basis, they took no seats in the National Assembly.

The election marked a parting of the ways. The *intégristes* turned against the whole system. They did things which made it impossible for the government to make further concessions to them. Most of their leaders, including Ghanouchi, left the country and from the safety of Europe began sending to their followers cassette tapes full of abuse of the government. Two of the senior figures who remained behind wrote articles libelling the President and were sent to prison. At the end of 1989 the government closed the theological faculty of El-Zeitouna, which it had come to regard as a hotbed of subversion. Then the old cycle of demonstrations, protests, riots and attacks on the police began again. In February 1991 the *intégristes* carried out an attack on an office of the RCD. They sent in two teams. One was supposed to make sure that the building was empty and the other was to set fire to it, but the first team failed in its job and the result was that two night-watchmen were burned to death. The government, naturally, gave great publicity to the event, displaying the bodies on television.

Then, in May, came the discovery of what appeared to be a plot to overthrow the regime. The police found arms caches on the university campuses in Tunis and Sfax, with lists of people who were to be assassinated and plans for a missile attack on the President's aircraft. Three hundred people were arrested – some clearly dangerous but many unimportant. Once again great publicity was given to the affair and the Tunisian people, it seemed, were impressed. Sympathy for An-Nahda had already weakened and after the fire and the plot, and the humiliation of Saddam Hussein, whom the *intégristes* had supported, it seemed to fade to a point where much of the population lost interest in the movement. Among foreigners in Tunis it was judged that the government had probably exaggerated the gravity of the May plot, presenting what may have been quite a minor conspiracy as a serious threat to the state.

While these events were unfolding the secular opposition parties were once more engaged in talks with the government on how they might enter the Assembly. Their discussions were concerned mainly with the modification of the voting system for the 1994 elections, and they led eventually to the government agreeing that some seats should be contested on the basis of proportional representation. It appeared to have in mind arranging things so that the opposition would win between ten and twenty seats out of 141.

The fact that the secular opposition parties had done so badly in the previous elections and now felt that they had to make a deal with the government needs some explanation. Given the country's recent history one would have expected them to have been more popular than the other parties. In 1989 they were competing on one side against a government party which was no more than a renamed version of the Destourian Socialist Party, which had been thoroughly discredited in the latter days of Bourguiba, and on the other against Islamists who were able to win only 18 per cent of the vote. (It is possible that if An-Nahda had been allowed to register for those elections, and had been able to throw its organizational weight behind its candidates, the Islamists would have picked up a bigger vote, but not even the highest estimates put their potential backing above 30 per cent.)

The prospects of the secular parties seemed to become better still after 1989. Support for the *intégristes* was undermined by their own violence, and at the same time there appeared to be a deepening well of potential support for parties that might combine respect for Islam, as part of their country's tradition and a rule for personal morality, with basically secular economic and social policies. The evidence for this came partly from things that were not related to politics. Each summer there was striking popular enthusiasm for the Festival of

Carthage, which included African music and dancing which made the audience aware of the links between Tunisia and the culture south of the Sahara. The dances had little to do with the austere Islamic society that was represented by the politics of An-Nahda. Similar indications of latent secularism were seen in a pageant that was held to celebrate the fifth anniversary of Ben Ali's presidency in November 1992. In this Tunisians were treated to a remarkably honest *son et lumière*, the like of which had not been seen since the country became independent. It showed the people that a majority of their countrymen had been Christians until just over a thousand years ago and that in the ninth and tenth centuries they had been ruled by the Fatimid dynasty, which had been Shia. The festival included a parade of the menorah candlestick, which reminded them that since Roman times Tunisia had had a Jewish community, which in the early 1990s numbered about two thousand.* The festival was particularly interesting as a sign of a government reaction against a conventional Arab nationalist representation of history, which had dominated teaching, television drama and the historical references in politicians' speeches for the previous forty years. Like the Festival of Carthage it aroused great and politically significant popular interest.

The reception given to the festivals reflected something which was beginning to be apparent across the Arab world at this time: that the Islamist tide was provoking a growing interest in secular culture and secular political ideas. People were becoming tired of the self-righteousness, bullying and cant of the Islamists. A lady in Saudi Arabia told the *Guardian*'s Middle East correspondent that in Europe she prayed regularly five times a day, but back in the Kingdom, in an atmosphere of religious coercion, she would not think of praying.† It was noticeable, also in Saudi Arabia, that people were flocking from Riyadh to Jeddah at weekends because they liked the more relaxed atmosphere, the seaside and the long corniche with its funfairs and modern abstract statues. Dubai and Abu Dhabi were popular with the Saudis and other Gulf Arabs for much the same reasons: they were green, attractive and, by Arabian standards, socially and politically free. Members of the secular intelligentsia of the Arab world were saying they could see a demand for new secular political parties. The likely

---

* See the article on the Jewish community in Tunisia by Francis Ghilès in the *Financial Times* survey of Tunisia, 14 June 1993
† See the series of features on Saudi Arabia by David Hirst in the *Guardian* of 14, 16 and 17 August 1993

backers were not only the speakers themselves, but a mass of people, above all members of the young generation, who had turned to the Islamists not out of true religious zeal but from disenchantment with the failed establishment. It was often said that most of the 'protest vote' would leave the Islamists if only a credible secular alternative could be found.

The new mood should have provided a perfect opportunity for the development of secular political parties, not only in Tunisia but in Algeria, Egypt, Jordan and the other Arab countries in which new parties had been founded in the previous five years. The parties should, in theory, have been winning elections, or at least gaining large numbers of seats in the parliaments. The main reason for their failing to do this was that none of them had any strong image. They lacked a single big idea, such as Communism or nationalism. Most of them represented just the half-thought-out ideas of small groups of intellectuals and former ministers, which, at their most definite, amounted to no more than modified versions of old ideas, most often socialism and Nasserism.

They also suffered from several other disadvantages which came from their being in countries that were still dominated by single government parties, which controlled not only the parliaments but also most other institutions of the state. In this the experience of the newly legalized parties in Tunisia was typical. The party leaders found that the ministers and other senior officials with whom they dealt failed to distinguish between their own party, the RCD, and the state. This meant that they tended to see the new parties as being in a small way subversive — against the state rather than against the state party. Although the President seemed to want the opposition to be given time on the radio and television for party political broadcasts, the officials below him created enough objections to block the idea. When the politicians talked to the state broadcasting organization about their being interviewed they would encounter the same response. The more senior officials would see them as being opponents of their own party and the journalists, many of whom were not members of the RCD, could not see any purpose in interviewing them. Having worked in a socialist economy, they did not see themselves as being paid to find out and report interesting new events or opinions, let alone generate controversy; they were simply state functionaries who waited to be told what to do and say. In the backs of the minds of all the employees of every state organization was the thought that if an opposition party was ever to come to power that might in some way jeopardize their jobs.

The opposition parties were unable to run major billboard advertising campaigns, publish daily newspapers, buy time on foreign satellite television stations, or promote themselves in most other ways used by Western political parties, because they had very little money. The biggest of the Tunisian parties, the Mouvement des Democrates Socialistes, could afford a staff of only three in its headquarters and had no representatives in the regions.

A general conclusion drawn by the opposition politicians a few years after their parties had been legalized was that in countries such as Tunisia it was difficult for new parties to make progress without there being a revolution which would actually overthrow the establishment party – as had happened in eastern Europe. They were not advocating a revolution, they were saying simply that political liberalization without revolution took a long time to come about. In their less philosophical moments they firmly blamed the government for their problems. They said that the President and Prime Minister should coerce the RCD into sharing the political life of the country with other elements of civil society. Specifically, they suggested, the media should be ordered to publicize their parties and state companies should be told to advertise in their journals. In putting forward these ideas they were reckoning without the great powers of resistance of the government party functionaries.

A comment often made outside Tunisia after May 1991 was that the process of reform had been abandoned and that the government had gone back to the authoritarian ways of the Bourguiba period. That judgement was too harsh. The reality was that Tunisian politics was changing but that the change was very slow. Under Ben Ali opposition parties had been made legal and it was clearly the government's intention that they should play a role in politics. It may have been that the President and his colleagues did not really understand that an opposition which had influence, and fulfilled the role of an opposition in a democracy, might be inconvenient. They appeared to believe that it should be possible for them to create an opposition which looked credible but was still controllable. Even so, the fact that the government was prepared to give some small help to rival parties was an important development. It opened the possibility of ministers and the public becoming used to the idea that an opposition was not something by definition subversive, but an institution that might occasionally have something useful to say. Governments have to cease to be frightened of oppositions before they can accept them as legitimate alternatives to themselves – and legalizing them, while trying to control them, is a first stage in this process. It is almost inevitable that at first middle-rank government officials will do what they can to frustrate the new organizations.

There were other important changes in the first five years of Ben Ali's presidency. The press became much freer and civil society revived. New, independent professional associations, and a consumers' association, were established. Debates on political issues, involving academics and journalists, and even leaders of opposition parties, were occasionally held on television. People felt freer to talk about politics, to criticize the government and lobby on behalf of their professions and businesses. They began to regard as normal a freedom and openness of discussion, and a sense of social and political evolution, which had not existed in the ten years before Ben Ali came to power.

In Egypt there was no single event which marked the beginning of democratic change. The liberalization of the one-party system created by Nasser proceeded slowly through the 1970s and 1980s. It was begun by President Sadat, who in 1976 allowed the formation of 'tendencies' within Nasser's Arab Socialist Union. In June 1977 he approved a law legalizing new political parties, but a few months later, disturbed by the criticism of the opposition, particularly a revived version of the liberal middle-class Wafd Party, he organized a referendum which gave him powers to control the new and difficult institutions.* The opposition parties promptly disbanded themselves. In 1978 Sadat founded his own National Democratic Party (NDP), which in effect replaced the Arab Socialist Union, and later in the same year an official opposition, the Socialist Labour Party, came into being. During the remaining three years of his government Sadat kept a tight rein on his country's politics, because while he was regaining the Sinai peninsula in stages from Israel he was anxious that there should be no domestic disturbances which might worry the Israelis and halt the process. He put in prison nearly 1,500 political activists, many of them from the Muslim Brotherhood, along with hostile journalists and other critics whom he felt were trying to undermine his policies.

After Sadat was assassinated in October 1981, Mubarak released

---

* The Wafd (Delegation) was a party formed after the end of the First World War. It took its name from the delegation headed by Saad Zaghloul, a nationalist politician and former minister, which in November 1918 went to the British High Commissioner and asked for independence. For their pains the four leaders of the delegation were deported. They were allowed back into Egypt in 1919 and they then organized the Wafd Party, which became the principal Egyptian nationalist party of the 1920s and 1930s.

many of the detainees and gradually went back to the stage of liberalization that his predecessor had reached in 1976. This did not allow
great political freedom. As in other countries, the law banned parties
based on religion and, to limit the numbers of parties that might appear
and to give the government a flexible pretext for refusing registration,
it also stated that new parties had to be significantly different from each
other in their ideologies and programmes. New parties were established
rather slowly. The Wafd reappeared and a group of left-wingers from
the Nasser era founded Tagammu, meaning Rally or Union.

The Socialist Labour Party (Amal) was allowed informally to take
the Muslim Brotherhood under its wing and run its members as its own
candidates. This had the advantage of keeping the Brotherhood above
ground and giving it a strange semi-legal status. Officially it was
banned, but the authorities calculated that its political appeal would
be weakened and its image blurred if it were invited into the world of
legal politics and associated with an unimportant 'official' opposition
party. It easily dominated its partner. It determined its policies and,
before it obliged it to boycott elections, it accounted for most of its
small representation in the People's Assembly. It would no doubt have
had more members had it been allowed to mobilize all its sympathizers
in the mosques and charitable societies to campaign for its candidates,
but that was precisely the type of activity that the government was
making sure it avoided by keeping religious parties officially illegal.

In April 1992 another potentially important opposition party was
established. Some former ministers and moderate socialists and nationalists were able to found the Arab Democratic Nasserite Party, which
it was hoped would have a much wider appeal than any of its secular
competitors and might eventually absorb some of them. By this time
there were twelve legal parties, eight of which had come into being
through court rulings. In each of these cases the government's Political
Parties' Committee had rejected the founders' original applications, and
the parties had only been able to obtain their licences by appealing to
the Supreme Administrative Court. This process had taken the Nasserite
Party eight years. It attributed the long delay to the government wanting
to block the foundation of a party which might be a serious rival.

In elections the new parties did not do much better than the parties
in Tunisia. They were short of money and they did not have access to
the media. The government refused to give them television airtime.
Their publications could not compete with the national press, and the
major newspapers, although at times quite critical of government policies and individual politicians, supported the National Democratic
Party in elections. The provincial governors, who were appointed by

the President, gave the NDP candidates practical assistance with their electioneering and appeared with them in public, which helped give the people the feeling that the men with influence – who would be able to help them and their villages – were the government candidates. The results in the election of 1987 were that out of 454 seats in the People's Assembly, opposition parties won 95. The next election, in December 1990, was boycotted by the Wafd and the Amal/Brotherhood alliance because they disagreed with the introduction of the 'first-past-the-post' system which they felt discriminated against them. They left Tagammu to win six seats and independents, many of them former members of the government party, to win more than a hundred. The advantage of the controversial new system was that it was simple for the public to understand. List systems and proportional representation sometimes lead to popular candidates failing to win seats and unknown candidates being elected, and in Egypt and other Arab countries this is liable to arouse the suspicions of electorates who are predisposed to accuse their governments of manipulation.

The concerns of the opposition politicians in Egypt were not that the government was manipulating election results in the sense of falsifying ballots, but that in delaying the licensing of parties, hindering their campaigns and altering the voting system it was not helping the development of democracy. Many members of the intelligentsia shared these concerns. There was a widespread feeling in the later 1980s that the country had come to the threshold of democracy, and that there its political development had stopped. Everybody conceded that it was far freer than it had been in the later days of Nasser, when it had been a police state, or during most of Sadat's rule. People were no longer frightened of their government. The opposition press was free to write anything it liked, and frequently abused ministers in an uninhibited and scurrilous way which in Europe would have laid it open to libel proceedings. In the entire time since Mubarak came to power there had been not one case of a newspaper being banned, closed or censored. Journalists, politicians, academics and anyone else who had opinions about the state of the country and its leaders felt free to say exactly what they liked, in public or in private. The judiciary was independent, which it had not been in the 1960s. Its willingness to defy the government was shown in the judgements which legalized the new political parties.

Together these improvements were having the same effect that Ben Ali's more modest liberalization was having in Tunisia. They were slowly making Egypt a freer, more democratic society, in which people were becoming used to exercising the types of freedom they would have enjoyed in the West. The idea of journalists being imprisoned, as some had been under Sadat, would have seemed extraordinary in the 1990s, and if President Mubarak had tried to do such a thing (which nobody was suggesting he would) there would have been an outcry. This sense that the meaning of freedom was becoming more deeply rooted in Egyptian society was reassuring to the political classes. A university lecturer and publisher reflected the feeling in some remarks he made to me in 1992: 'In spite of what I write criticising the government and saying we must go faster,' he said, 'I'm really quite impressed by what we have achieved. I know we are going slowly, but sometimes I am not unhappy about this. I think it helps us consolidate.'

It has to be said that this speaker was more patient than most of the Egyptian intelligentsia; as well as pleasure with the progress that has been achieved there is disappointment with the apparent inability of the Mubarak government to advance further. It is often suggested that it has managed to give Egyptians – or in effect the Egyptian middle classes, and particularly the intelligentsia – many basic freedoms, but is refusing to let them enjoy their fruits. The people have the freedom of simple human rights, which is important, but they cannot use them to influence public policy. As a former minister of the Sadat era put it to me: 'The government has been saying, in effect, "you are free to say what you like, but we shall still do what we like", and that makes the people frustrated, because they are left talking to themselves.'

To change this situation would require radical reform to the constitution and the whole structure of Egyptian politics. It would not be just a matter of seeing that elections were conducted more fairly. The government would have to stop its sponsorship of the NDP; in effect it would have to privatize the ruling party, by removing its official funding. This idea would be anathema to nearly the whole political establishment, because its members belong to the party and rely on its support for their seats in the Assembly or, in many cases, their positions in government. Ministers rely on a pliant Assembly to pass their measures. There would also have to be a change in the method used to elect the President, which is still very undemocratic and is linked to there being a large and secure majority of NDP members in the People's Assembly. Any candidate for the Presidency has to be nominated by a third of the Assembly members, endorsed by two thirds and then approved by the people in a referendum. The second stage of the process makes it impossible for there ever to be more than one candidate put to the people. Hosni Mubarak has been in the happy position of being the single candidate on three occasions, in 1981, 1987 and 1993. In spite of his approval being virtually assured – over half of the people would have to bother to register a 'no' vote to have him removed from the Presidency – his ministers of the interior have found it necessary on the last two occasions to give him approval votes of more than 95 per cent. In October 1993 a BBC correspondent who went to a polling station in the Cairo district of Imbaba, an Islamist stronghold, discovered at lunchtime that only twenty people had voted; but when he went back in the evening he discovered that, miraculously, the entire electorate of the district had turned out to vote in the afternoon.

It goes without saying that the initiative for the types of changes that the Egyptian intelligentsia would like to see would have to come from the top of the government – from a president who was confident of his own popularity and who was prepared occasionally to gamble. Anwar Sadat was this sort of personality, and although he was the author of the present Egyptian constitution, it is not impossible to imagine him, in the circumstances of the 1990s, taking a chance and suddenly introducing a democratic structure into Egyptian politics. Hosni Mubarak, though, is a much more cautious character. He is a *status quo* man. Like several other Arab leaders he believes that those who are demanding change are only doing so because they want to be in government themselves. He is also worried about what might be the consequences of attempts to reform. He is very conscious of what happened to the former USSR and the eastern European countries when they started to reform, and of what nearly happened in Algeria, and he fears that if he tried to introduce radical change in Egypt, it too might be swept up in some uncontrollable revolutionary tide, especially at a time when the government is being challenged by militant Islamist groups.

The near immobility of the political system and the disenchantment this caused among the middle classes was becoming a problem in Egypt in the early 1990s. It was widely acknowledged that basically the President was a decent man, that the country had become freer during his two terms in office and that the economic reforms he was having to impose were necessary; yet his government did not command respect or confidence. It was led by a long-serving and very uninspiring Prime Minister, Atef Sidki, and it contained many equally long-serving ministers who, in the popular view, were dull and incompetent. They were clearly incapable of commanding the sort of public support that would have reduced the appeal of the Islamic extremists and enabled them to fight the Gamaa by any method other than repression. Both the government and the ruling party were seen as havens for opportunists and profiteers; they were wreathed in the smell of corruption. The contempt that many well-educated people felt for the political establishment could be seen in the way members of the professional associations had been voting for Islamist candidates in the late 1980s and early 1990s. The Islamists may have been making sure that their committed supporters in the associations were attending the voting meetings, but they must also have been getting the support of some doctors, engineers and other professionals who would not have backed their candidates had they not wanted to register a protest against the government.

Most seriously the government was failing to give its people any sense of their country having a national dream, a social and political goal of prosperity or equality or power. This was something which Nasser had certainly given Egyptians and which Sadat had given them at the best moments of his presidency, but which Mubarak could not provide. It was in this context that the immobility of the system was important. The lack of either a national goal or a sense of evolution towards liberal democracy was making the Egyptian middle classes increasingly frustrated and uncertain about their country's future. They did not believe that the government would take a bold step forward and introduce further political reform – though that was what they were urging it to do. Without further change they feared there would be increased instability and that the government would respond with further repressive measures and, later maybe, the removal of some of the freedoms they had slowly been coming to take for granted. The stagnation of the process of political change, combined with the terrorism of the Gamaa, was producing greater anxiety and malaise than the country had known at any time since Hosni Mubarak succeeded Anwar Sadat in 1981.

The government of Jordan has been more decisive than the other Arab governments in the steps it has taken towards democracy. In 1989 it reintroduced a parliament which had been suspended for twenty-two years, since the Six Day War in June 1967. It has legalized political parties, both secular and Islamic, held two free elections, and lifted most of its censorship of the press. These changes have made a bigger difference to the country's political life than reforms have made in Tunisia and Egypt, not only because they have been bolder, but also because Jordan, being a monarchy, has not burdened itself with a single socialist political party. It lacks the institution which in the Arab republics is doing most to hinder change.

King Hussein's decision to re-establish his parliament was made in the immediate aftermath of the riots that took place in the south of the country when food subsidies were reduced in April 1989. This made it look as if he was thinking in a purely defensive fashion, which he was not. He had reached the age of fifty-three and had been reigning for thirty-seven years, and for some time he had been thinking of the political future of his country and of what form its government might take after him. Eight months earlier he had announced that he was relinquishing his claim to the West Bank, which his grandfather had annexed in 1950. For the rest of his kingdom he was developing the idea of writing a new constitution, or national charter, which would confirm the role of the monarchy but bring back the parliament, and allow that institution gradually to develop a role for itself in government.

An announcement that there would be elections was made within a few days of the riots, and the polling date was set for six months later, on 8 November 1989. Parties were still illegal at this time, but the authorities were unable or unwilling to stop the activities of the Muslim Brotherhood, which was registered as a charity and had had a role in the background of the country's politics since the 1950s, when the King had quietly encouraged it as a counter to the socialist propaganda of Gamal Abdel-Nasser. Since the early 1980s the informal links between the palace and the Brotherhood had been broken as the King had become alarmed by the growth of religious fundamentalism in all parts of the Middle East; he had in mind the religious and far right-wing parties in Israel as well as Islamist movements in the Arab world. Yet nothing had been done to curb the Brotherhood. In the months before the election it was therefore able to organize a group of sympathetic candidates and run a campaign for them. The main issue it addressed was the corruption that was linked to the economic mismanagement of the country, which had been revealed so dramatically a year earlier, when the government had announced that it was going to have to reschedule its debts. Its candidates talked about the extravagance of the people in and around the government, their Mercedes, and their wives' smart clothes and expensive perfumes. For good measure they inveighed against alcohol, which in all Arab countries is drunk mainly by the rich and sophisticated. The other candidates, of course, were not organized at all and had no special theme to their campaign. Most of them were concerned with nationalist issues: Palestine and the peace process.

The outcome of the election was that out of eighty seats the Brotherhood won twenty-three, independent Islamist sympathizers some ten or twelve — in some cases it was difficult to say exactly who sympathized with the Islamists and who did not — and secular nationalist and tribal candidates the rest. There was some debate as to whether this result left the Brotherhood and its allies over or under represented. In some of the bigger towns, Amman, Zerqa and Irbid, they took more than

40 per cent of the vote and won crushing victories over their opponents. In these places they might have won still more seats if they had fielded more candidates. But in the south it was thought that they did better than they deserved because the voting system worked in their favour. The system used in Jordan gave voters as many votes as there were seats for their electoral districts; in Irbid, for example, there were nine seats, so each voter had nine votes to spread among several dozen candidates. The result of this in tribal areas was that people cast their first votes for candidates connected with their families or tribes but then gave their remaining one or two votes to Islamist candidates whom they considered would be safe and conservative but whom they did not know personally.

After the election a new government was formed under Mudar Badran, who had already served as Prime Minister twice in his career, and five ministerial portfolios, including those for agriculture and education, went to the Islamists. The new government brought in some major reforms. It began by announcing the suspension of martial law, which had been imposed at the same time as the parliament had been suspended in June 1967. It was true that the main provisions of the law had not often been invoked and that it had not had much effect on the lives of the general public; but its existence had weakened the authority of the judiciary and had allowed abuses of civil rights by the security forces, and its removal was an essential first step towards a freer society. As soon as the law was suspended – it was not actually repealed until July 1991 – the government returned many of the passports its predecessors had seized and lifted the travel bans they had imposed on some of their opponents. At the same time it stopped trying to direct the press. Before the elections newspaper editors who had published stories that a government particularly disliked, either because they had been criticizing it or were likely to upset other Arab governments, had received telephone calls from the Minister of Information telling them that their stories had been noted and that similar stories ought to be avoided in the future. Immediately after the election the government declared that it would not interfere with the press in this way, and in the main it has kept its promise. The only exceptions have concerned articles which have directly criticized the King; when these have been published there has always been retribution, and it is difficult to imagine that policy changing. There is still a degree of instinctive self-censorship on the part of journalists, and most of the newspaper owners and editors are pro-government, so in practice the question of whether or not to publish an article criticizing the monarch does not often arise.

The Islamists, interestingly, were rather cautious in their new responsible positions. The members of the parliament said much on the rather unimportant issue of banning alcohol, and although in the early months after the election their campaign succeeded in worrying foreigners and the middle classes, in the end it failed. On women being required to wear veils or scarves, they confined themselves to a few mutterings, and on the comprehensive introduction of Shariah law and the creation of an Islamic state they said nothing at all. They seemed anxious to soothe the fears of the Christians, who make up about 4 per cent of the population but have nine seats reserved for them in parliament.

The most noticeable impact of the Islamists was on the running of the ministries they controlled. Their actions here were summed up by a notably outspoken secular member of parliament in 1992. 'They were fools,' he said. 'They concentrated on separating men from women in the ministries, sacking their beautiful girl secretaries and bringing in dirty men with beads. They put away their shoes and started telling people to wear sandals. The Minister of Education did away with the morning song, which had been sung in schools since 1921, and replaced it with long and silly verses from the Koran.' Even members of the public who were less aggressively secular than this MP were unimpressed by the ministers' performance. They wrote to the newspapers and organized demonstrations, and the Islamists, who were much less good at defending policies than attacking the government, found the poverty of their political thinking being exposed. In office they could no longer seek refuge in vague and pious phrases; they found themselves confronted with all the large and small policy issues that ministers have to tackle, and it became evident that if they were not allowed to institute a complete revolution their only ideas were for trivial, cosmetic adjustments to people's routines. When Mudar Badran was dismissed as Prime Minister in June 1991 the Islamists too lost their portfolios. The new Prime Minister, Taher Masri, did not offer them any further positions, and they did not ask for any.

While the Islamists were losing their credibility in government, the independent secular MPs were slowly organizing themselves. They formed small, semi-legal political groups, some with their names on the doors of irregularly manned offices and a few with their own magazines. In the twelve months after July 1992, when the King approved a law which legalized political parties, there was much negotiation between the MPs and a few mergers, and eventually sixteen of the groups were given licences and declared themselves parties. The new bodies were not of any substance. Like new parties elsewhere in the Arab world they were no more than groups of aspiring politicians formed around one or two individuals. They lacked distinctive ideologies. One of the MPs to whom I spoke said that he thought that for the next ten years 'the mosque, tribes or bribes' would be far more important than parties as a means of getting into parliament.

As matters turned out, it was tribal connections that were most important in the next Jordanian election on 8 November 1993. The Islamists by this time had formed themselves into the Islamic Action Front, dominated by the Brotherhood, but they were not the force they had been four years earlier. People remembered the poor performance of their ministers, and several of their MPs were known to have been corrupted by money or sex, which meant that those individuals could no longer be thought of as an independent force in parliament. Ultimately they could be faced down by the palace. To weaken the Islamists further, in August 1993 the government changed the electoral system to one person one vote. As it had calculated, when the election was held the people in tribal areas gave their single votes to the candidates they knew and trusted. In the new parliament the Islamists had twenty-one seats, thirteen fewer than before. The secular parties of left and centre, the tribal leaders and their sons and other loyal elements, including former ministers, had fifty seats. An interesting feature of this election was that more women than men voted, which suggested that both the parliament, which included its first woman member, and the candidates in future elections would be showing more interest in women's issues.

In both elections and the period in between, the whole Jordanian democratic experiment was counted a success by the people and the government. It helped unite the different parts of the population, giving East Bankers, bedouin and West Bankers, and Muslims and Christians, something of the feeling of being citizens of an emerging democracy rather than separate communities each represented by unelected leaders manœuvring for influence and the King's ear. People felt freer, and, as freedom does, that made them proud. They knew that their parliament did not have great authority and that the King would dissolve it if it became a serious obstruction to his governments, but they saw also that it allowed genuine debate and was not just an instrument of the government, controlled through a single party, as the People's Assembly was in Egypt.

The strength and confidence the parliament gave to Jordan was shown very well during the Gulf crisis. At that time the King and the government were under great pressure from the Western powers to abandon their support for Iraq and join the anti-Saddam Hussein coalition. Potentially their position was not very strong. The King himself had a good working relationship with Saddam but was not a great admirer of the man. He felt that Iraq had been wrong to invade Kuwait, but that the crisis was a purely inter-Arab affair and that the Saudis should not have invited the West to become involved. His people were much more fervently pro-Saddam; many of them had lived or worked in Kuwait and resented the arrogance of their hosts. The difference in attitude of the King and his people, and the King's traditional good relations with the West, might have divided them, but the existence of a parliament blurred the distinction and provided the King with an excuse for his independent policy. In the previous twenty years the Western powers would have known that he was his own master, and they would have expected him to have acted in what he and they might have felt were the long-term interests of his Kingdom; but in 1990–1 the Western powers, as supporters of democracy, could hardly bully a monarch who was trying to reflect the views of his people's elected representatives. Likewise, if there had been no parliament the people would have suspected that whatever the King did he was being manipulated by his Western friends, and then the most angry and militant elements might have resorted to terrorism or, at least, to organizing mass anti-government demonstrations. As it was, the existence of the parliament gave an openness to the King's policies. He let the members make fiery pro-Iraqi speeches and did not suppress them. At the same time he explained to the members why on certain issues he was having to compromise, and both members and their constituents were willing to accept that in dealing with other world leaders compromise was sometimes inevitable.

The King clearly hopes that the parliament will become more important in his country's government in the future. This was clear in the autumn of 1992 after he had been diagnosed as having cancer. He underwent an operation in America which was believed to be completely successful, but afterwards he seemed to become more concerned than before about strengthening the growth of democracy. On 5 November 1992 he made a speech to the nation in which he said he recognized that 'every living soul will meet its destined end', and that 'when the time comes no hour can be postponed or brought forward'. In later interviews he spoke of how he wanted Jordan to evolve as a model democratic state in the Middle East: 'Whatever remains of my life has to be dedicated towards consolidating more of the foundations, the grounds for democracy, for human rights, for sharing responsibility and for pluralism . . . I think there is a great need in the region for an example to be made, and I believe that Jordan can be that example.'*

---

* See 'The Monday Interview' by Mark Nicholson and Hugh Carnegy, *Financial Times*, 16 November 1992

What makes it possible for Jordan to be an example to other Arab countries is simply that its government is legitimate. Its monarch can transfer some of his powers to a parliament knowing that he has the moral authority to control that body, or dissolve it, and have his people accept his decision. He can regulate the pace of change, prevent a single-interest group, such as the Islamists, taking control, and let the members of the parliament become slowly accustomed to exercising power and to the complexities of government. The King of Morocco, if he continues with his more cautious steps in a democratic direction, will enjoy the same advantages. Most of the republics are in a less happy position. Given their past failures and the limited moral authority of their governments, the presidents and single parties cannot start to give away power without being afraid that they will lose the initiative in controlling the pace of reform to some opposition group. Then they fear that neither the opposition nor the people will accept any peaceful attempt they make to slow the change and that they will be left with an unhappy choice between allowing themselves to be swept away, and organizing a *coup d'état* against their own parliaments.

Kuwait, like Jordan, reinstated its parliament in the early 1980s. The country's rulers had made do without it for only six years, a much shorter time than King Hussein had ruled without his parliament, but because of the Gulf crisis much international attention had been focused on their undemocratic behaviour. In 1990 and 1991 the Western media came to see the Al-Sabah family as representing arbitrary government in the Arabian Peninsula and the Arab world as a whole, and journalists and politicians questioned whether the West ought to be sacrificing the lives of its young men to help such a regime. This was ironic and unfair, because for most of the time since its independence in 1961 Kuwait had been one of the freest and most democratic Arab countries. It had had a vigorous, freely elected parliament, the National Assembly, for twenty out of the previous twenty-nine years, which could be said to have made it more democratic than any other Arab state, bar Lebanon.

The Ruler of Kuwait, who was then Sheikh Abdullah Salem Al-Sabah, set in motion the establishment of the Assembly within a few months of the termination in June 1961 of the treaty of protection, under which the British had been responsible for his country's defence and foreign relations. In doing this Sheikh Abdullah was not only responding to the revolutionary climate of the time, which would have made it embarrassing and dangerous for him to have been a totally undemocratic ruler of a small rich state in a turbulent Arab world. He was influenced as much by the traditionally egalitarian relations between his own family and the leading merchant families of the country. The seven oldest Kuwaiti families had arrived together on the southern shore of the bay of Kuwait (meaning 'little fort') in the early eighteenth century, and Sheikh Abdullah's family had only begun its rise to prominence after 1756, when a certain Sabah, who gave it its name, had been chosen by the community to go as its ambassador to the Ottoman governor of Basra to persuade him not to tax it. The settlement by this time had become quite large and prosperous, certainly worth taxing. It contained some 10,000 inhabitants and 800 vessels, engaged in fishing, pearling and trade between the date gardens of Basra and the Malabar coast of India, where the merchants bought timber, cloth and rice, which was then sold into southern Mesopotamia and the northern Nejd. After Sabah's embassy to Basra it had become customary for the leader of the community always to be chosen from his descendants, but this did not raise the family as a whole above the rest of the community. Many of the merchants were much richer than the Al-Sabah and lent its members money. They were consulted on all important matters of state.

In 1899 the Sheikh's status was considerably enhanced when he concluded the treaty of protection with the British, which gave him direct relations with the Government of India and enabled him to draw on British help against any threat from the Turks, Persians or other foreign forces. In 1946 the power of the Sheikh, and the members of his family, was further increased when oil came on-stream. This made the Al-Sabah financially independent. In the next fifteen years many of the family became extremely rich, particularly through seizing, or being given, plots of land which were then bought by the Public Works Department for development projects. The merchant families became similarly rich, through contracting and importing, as well as land dealings. The increase in their prestige and independence made the members of the Al-Sabah, as a family, accepted as the leaders of the government, but the other families still expected to be consulted, to be given ministerial portfolios and to be, in effect, the Al-Sabahs' junior partners. It was in this context after independence that the Ruler (as the Sheikh became) called elections for a Constituent Assembly. During the next year this body drew up a constitution which restricted the succession to the position of Amir (Ruler) to successors of Sheikh Mubarak the Great (1896–1915), vested executive power in the Amir and a Council of Ministers, and provided for an elected National Assembly of fifty members, with the power to introduce and pass legislation and force the resignation of ministers. Up to twenty-five ministers were to be *ex officio* members of the Assembly, in addition to the elected deputies.

The constitution reflected traditions which were quite different from those of Saudi Arabia, the lower Gulf states and Oman. In most of these countries the rulers were available to their people and in some cases they consulted them, but nowhere was there any form of long-standing partnership between them. Qatar, Abu Dhabi and Dubai had only emerged as stable communities in the previous fifty years. Bahrain and Oman were older, but like Saudi Arabia they had been taken by conquest by their ruling families. All of these countries except Saudi Arabia at this time were under British protection and remained so until 1971. In only two places, Bahrain and the Saudi port of Jeddah, were there well-established trading communities whose members had travelled and been educated abroad.

Kuwait's first National Assembly began sitting in 1963. Both it and its three successors, of 1967, 1971 and 1975, were independent and outspoken. Their membership was made up of a handful of representatives of the big merchant families, some tribal leaders, who could be relied upon to support the government, a few committed leftists and a number of deputies who for want of a better word were described as nationalists. In the early 1970s the assemblies devoted themselves to the obstruction and radicalization of the government's oil policy. In 1972 deputies forced the government to put a ceiling of 3 million barrels a day on the state's oil production. They believed, in common with all other radicals of the day, that the Arab nation's oil, which they spoke of as its non-renewable birthright, was being sold too cheaply and that the concessionaire companies, which then ran production, were depleting the reservoirs too fast. In fact, even on the basis of the most conservative estimates, Kuwait in the early 1970s was reckoned to have a reserves to production ratio of sixty to seventy years, which was far above normal international levels.

A year after they had imposed the ceiling the deputies rejected the 'participation' agreement, negotiated on the Gulf states' behalf by the Saudi oil minister Ahmed Zaki Yamani, which was to have given the country a 25 per cent stake in the operations of its concessionaire, the Kuwait Oil Company, owned by BP and Gulf Oil. The Assembly demanded that the company be taken over completely, and after further protracted negotiations this is what was agreed two years later. The take-over did not necessarily work to Kuwait's advantage, in that when a surplus appeared in the market in the 1980s it made the sale of the country's oil more difficult.

Other matters to which the members devoted their energies were the government's foreign policy, which they wanted to be more strongly Arab nationalist and pro-Palestinian, and various domestic liberal issues. These included the granting of permission for political parties, which the government claimed were irrelevant in a state where 'everybody' knew each other, votes for women and the better treatment of non-Kuwaitis who made up a majority of the population. There was some question as to how sincere the members were on the last two of these issues. They seemed to be motivated as much by a desire to embarrass the government as to achieve reforms. By August 1976 the government had become so frustrated by the members' campaigns and their obstruction of what it considered to be more important legislation that the Ruler, then Sheikh Sabah Salem, had the Assembly suspended.

Four and a half years later, in response to popular pressure and hoping that it would have been chastened and made more obliging by the period of dissolution, a new Ruler, Sheikh Jaber Ahmed, brought back the Assembly. His hopes were disappointed. The 1980s proved to be a very difficult decade for Kuwait, and the series of trials it faced brought its government and legislature once more into conflict. The state's neighbours, Iran and Iraq, were at war; the sound of the bombardments on the most southerly sector of the front could often be heard in Kuwait City. The government's support for Iraq led the Iranians to sponsor terrorist attacks on the state. The conflict stopped a large part of the Kuwaiti merchants' re-export business, which had been a big source of income. In early 1986 their economic problems were increased by the fall in the price of oil, which led to the government cutting back its spending. By far the worst of the state's problems, however, was the collapse in September 1982 of the country's unofficial stock exchange, the Souk al-Manakh, on which Kuwaitis had been trading in the shares of insubstantial offshore companies, registered in the lower Gulf, many of them having no assets except shares in other offshore companies. The trading was financed by post-dated cheques, and when the crash occurred there was the equivalent of $92 billion outstanding.

The disaster was a typically Kuwaiti one. In the forty years since its oil production had begun the state had been remarkably uncorrupt – partly thanks to the existence of the National Assembly – but its citizens had been exceptionally greedy, many of them losing touch with what might be considered an adequate (or enormous) personal fortune elsewhere in the world. They had come to think of riches as a natural personal right, which they relied on the government to guarantee. Seeing that the government had been so generous to them, through buying companies that had got into difficulties and supporting the domestic stock market after a crash in 1977, as well as pumping billions of dollars into their hands through land purchases, they imagined that whatever foolhardy investment they entered into they could probably rely on the state to rescue them.

The speculators were not altogether wrong in their assumption. After the crash the government promptly put together a scheme to help small investors and later it was to find itself forced to provide much more extensive assistance. But it would never have had to provide the longer-term assistance if in the first two years after the crash it had not failed totally to work out the necessary comprehensive solution, which should have involved the writing off of a certain percentage of everybody's debts and the bankruptcy of those individuals who could not honour the balance. Solutions of this type were proposed but the Ruler would not accept them. Sheikh Jaber had reached his early sixties, he had been the driving force in his state's government since he had taken over the Finance Department several years before independence, and he was tired. The Manakh crash faced him with the prospect of having, in effect, to authorize the bankruptcy of several of his close relations, who were among the biggest debtors, and he came under great pressure not to do this. In this way the crash exposed what is the greatest weakness of the traditional Arabian Peninsula form of government: that in a crisis the rulers find it extremely difficult to act against the interests of their own families. The thought of embarrassing or humiliating a son, nephew, or even a more distant relation, runs against the whole framework of loyalties that has been the cornerstone of their lives from childhood.

While Sheikh Jaber and the other senior members of the Sabah family tried to implement piecemeal solutions designed to resolve the debts of a few individuals, in the hope that the crisis would become easier when the most sensitive cases were out of the way, the Kuwaiti economy ground to a halt. People stopped trading because they did not know whether or not they or the people they were doing business with were bankrupt. Nobody knew who was good for credit. The price of shares on the domestic stock market collapsed. Land and buildings, in many cases pledged as collateral for bank loans, became unsaleable. The banks found themselves with a quarter of their loan portfolios not performing. By 1986 what had begun as a stock market crash had ruined the country's economy and caused a banking crisis.

The National Assembly, as these events unfolded, devoted itself to demanding that the government use some of its reserves to stimulate the economy, while it did what it could to embarrass those members of the ruling family who had received help from public funds. It managed to force the resignation of one of the better Al-Sabah ministers, who had been involved in 'the Manakh' on a relatively small scale. The tone of debate was soured by the steady decline there had been during the previous decade in popular goodwill towards the Al-Sabah. The merchant families felt that they were being consulted less and that some of the younger Al-Sabahs were taking undue advantage of their position to win contracts, sell their land and generally promote their own interests at the expense of everybody else. As the attacks of the Assembly members became angrier and the prospect arose of more ministers having to resign, the government once again lost patience with the Assembly, and in August 1986 the Ruler dissolved it. At the same time he imposed censorship on the press, which was Kuwaiti owned but run almost entirely by Palestinians.

A month after these events the government finally produced a comprehensive rescue package which guaranteed the banks' capital and reserves while forcing them to extract what money they could from their debtors. The Finance Ministry had already pumped some billions of dollars into the economy, much of the money going, once again, to support the domestic stock market, and the new package, coming on top of the aid already given, only strengthened Kuwaitis' hopes that if they held out for long enough, resisting the banks' attempts to reach a settlement with them, they would have their debts paid for them. The general public comment, of course, was that the government had introduced the package to compensate Kuwaitis for the loss of their parliament. The whole arrangement was seen as a classic example of a government buying, and a people selling, a nation's freedom. This certainly was the view of most of the foreigners in the state, particularly the Palestinians, who were more radical than their hosts. Much of the Kuwaiti establishment was not sure that it had sold anything very valuable. Although the debates in the Assembly had been addressed nominally to important national issues, and had been presented to the outside world in this way, most Kuwaitis knew that the main concerns of the deputies were with gaining publicity and advancing their own power and prestige *vis à vis* the over-powerful Al-Sabah. The debates were more a matter of small-town rivalries than a noble confrontation of democrats and tyrants.

In most important respects Kuwaiti society was no less free after the dissolution. Kuwaitis continued to have access to members of the Al-Sabah and if anyone cared enough about an issue he could go to see the Prime Minister, Sheikh Saad Abdullah, in his *diwan* (the Kuwaiti expression for *majlis* or reception chamber) where there was normally a lively and uninhibited debate – a very much more open debate than could be found in the *majles* of the lower Gulf and Saudi Arabia. No Kuwaiti hesitated to speak freely in public or private. From the point of view of foreign visitors the country remained the intellectually stimulating place it had been before. It had many amusing and intelligent citizens and it was taken for granted that they would see whomever they wanted and say whatever they liked.

For three years after the dissolution Kuwaiti politics were quiet. The government continued to push the banks to implement its debt settlement programme and the big debtors continued to be evasive. The former deputies and their supporters, the radicals, nationalists and Islamists who make up the country's political classes, meanwhile got together a succession of petitions demanding the return of the Assembly, and in due course the government felt it had to respond. In 1989 it announced that it planned to revise the Constitution, obviously with the intention of making the Assembly less powerful. Much play was made of the Prime Minister and his advisers consulting the people on this. They toured the *diwaniyyas* (smaller, less formal *diwans*) to canvass opinion. The opposition summoned its friends to the *diwaniyyas* in its own houses. Inflammatory speeches were made, some of the meetings spilled out on to the streets and on more than one occasion the police dispersed crowds of rowdy supporters, using water cannon, truncheons and tear gas. This type of behaviour, involving Kuwaitis using violence on fellow Kuwaitis, was regarded as most improper and very much against the peaceful traditions of the state.

The outcome of the Prime Minister's consultations, or the rather unoriginal product of his discussions with his advisers, was an announcement by the Ruler in April 1990 that the revision of the Constitution would be entrusted to a National Council which would sit for four years – an extraordinary length of time – and contain fifty elected and twenty-five appointed members. Elections were set for 10 June. The whole idea of this body was unpopular with Kuwaitis. The population may not have had much respect for the individuals in the previous Assembly, but it was still very much attached to the principle of there being a National Assembly and it did not want to see its Constitution changed. The campaign for elections to the National Council, therefore, was marked by a mixture of public hostility and indifference. There were several more violent incidents, including one in which the police stormed the *diwan* of a politician who had been urging his supporters to boycott the poll. When the election was held there was a rather low turnout, but the government got the type of Council it wanted because virtually the only people who had been prepared to stand were its own trusties, the 'backwoods' tribal sheikhs.

Less than two months later everything in Kuwaiti politics, and temporarily every other aspect of Kuwaiti life, was changed by the Iraqi invasion. The catastrophe immediately united the whole population. The Iraqis found not a single Kuwaiti to co-operate with their government; they even had to dress up one of their own officials in a *dishdasha* and *ghotra* and *agal* headdress, so that they could have somebody who looked like a Kuwaiti reading the television news. Among those who most vigorously resisted the occupiers were the Kuwaiti shias, who had traditionally been the least privileged section of society. Outside Kuwait, in the other Arabian Peninsula countries and in London, where many Kuwaitis were taking their holidays, there was a powerful rallying of the people to the ruling family. The Amir became the symbol of the nation, of Kuwaitis' determination to have their whole country back and not to have foreigners impose political change on them. The idea put forward by President Mitterand, among others, that after liberation the people might be invited to choose their own form of government without the Al-Sabah being present, was much resented. It was also totally impracticable because the Al-Sabah, which numbers more than a thousand, is as much part of the population as any other family. In a very Arabian fashion, without much being said formally, there quickly emerged a consensus that what the Kuwaiti people wanted and what the leaders of the Al-Sabah had to give, and would give, after liberation was nothing more or less than the 1962 Constitution. There was some talk of the vote being given to women, who have the vote in Jordan and the North African countries, but it was accepted that this could be debated once the Kuwaitis were back in their country and a new parliament was sitting.

After the liberation in February 1991 there was a period of shock and considerable malaise. Kuwaitis were extremely upset about what had happened to their country – particularly the blowing up of their oil wells and vandalizing of some of their public buildings – and for more than a year they were haunted by all their deeply rooted feelings of the impermanence and vulnerability of their state. They showed greater interest than ever in foreign investment. They were also uneasy about the behaviour of the Al-Sabah. Soon after the Ruler returned to the country it was announced that because so many Kuwaitis were abroad, and because new identity cards would have to be issued, it would be impracticable for elections to be held before October 1992. This gave the people the impression that the ruling family was having second thoughts about the Constitution. Suspicions were reinforced by the government giving some $2000 compensation to every person who had been in Kuwait during the occupation and, much more importantly, repaying everybody's consumer loans – the loans people had taken to buy cars and finance other big household items. Half of the country's cars had been stolen by the Iraqis, and most of the rest had had their tyres removed. The government also cancelled the housing loans citizens had taken from the Credit and Savings Bank and compensated those few people whose homes had been destroyed by the occupiers. It is true that these gifts helped mainly the poorer Kuwaitis, not a very big or influential part of the population, but their overall effect was to implant the idea that once again the Al-Sabah was seeking to bribe the people into abandoning their Constitution. This interpretation was too cynical. The compensation was given because it seemed fair in the circumstances, and part of the reason why the Ruler was delaying the elections was because he was much beholden to Saudi Arabia, which was firmly against the idea, regarding elections in its neighbours as a bad influence on its own people. The Saudis had not only given the Ruler, the Kuwaiti government and many of its citizens hospitality during the crisis, they had invited on to their territory the foreign armies that liberated Kuwait and paid the biggest share of the cost of the operation.

In October 1992 elections were held as promised. The campaign was unusually civilized and the candidates' speeches were of a higher intellectual standard than they had been in the past. The government behaved well. It had previously organized constituency boundaries to give the Assembly a disproportionate number of deputies from sparsely populated conservative areas, but during the campaign itself it did not break up meetings, raid *diwaniyyas* or do anything else to obstruct the opposition. The result, in spite of the gerrymandering, was that almost all of the candidates it favoured, the backwoods sheikhs and the others who had stood for the National Council, were defeated. Most of the leading radicals of previous parliaments were returned along with some Islamists from the Salafiyyin and the Reform Society. These and a number of independent 'nationalist' members made the Assembly by far the best educated the country had ever had. In previous bodies it had often been said there were a few members who had scarcely been able to write their names.*

---

* The members of the Kuwaiti Assembly are elected on a narrow franchise. The state's population in 1992 was estimated to be about 1.5 million; before the invasion and the exodus of Palestinians and other Arab expatriates it had been about 2.4 million. Of these totals about 600,000 were Kuwaiti nationals, three-quarters of them being what were known as 'first class' or 'Article 1' Kuwaitis, that is Kuwaitis who were members of families established in the state by 1921. Adult male members of these families – a total of about 90,000 persons – were entitled to vote and hold ministerial office. Other junior categories of Kuwaitis, who included a few naturalized Palestinians, had restricted rights. They were not allowed to vote but most could own property and shares in Kuwaiti companies.

The government continued to earn its people's goodwill after the election by making six of the Assembly members ministers. This pleased the deputies – it had been one of their long-standing demands that more of them should hold office – and it indicated a degree of trust in the Assembly because it reduced the numbers of ministers who were not elected deputies. These, *ex officio*, were given seats and voting rights, and often in the past it had been only its ministers who had enabled the government to sustain a majority in the Assembly.

For their part the members of the Assembly were, at first, careful not to antagonize the government. The radicals and Islamists remembered the previous dissolutions and said openly that they wanted to avoid any further crisis in relations. But in the months that followed the Assembly seemed, almost by instinct, to drift towards a confrontation. It delayed the implementation of a 'final' debt settlement programme, which was to involve the state taking over the banks' bad loans and giving itself responsibility for recovering money from debtors. It demanded, and was given, the right to look into the accounts of the Kuwait Investment Office, the organization that managed most of the government's foreign investments. In itself this seemed sensible enough, but it raised the possibility of the Assembly embarking on another endless witch hunt – like the one it was already conducting to discover who was responsible for mishandling the country's foreign policy before the invasion. Some very intemperate speeches were made against the managers of the Kuwait Investment Office and on one occasion the Speaker of the Assembly became so carried away that he joined in. A member of the Kuwaiti business community, who said he was already bored by the Assembly's behaviour, told me that he expected that the outcome of the witch hunt would be the same as it had been in the mid-1980s: that the people who would be hurt most would be some of the best members of the Al-Sabah.

The deputies went back to their old habit of taking stands on issues for the sake of publicity. One of the radicals, pandering to the suspicions of the least intelligent element of the electorate, made a speech in which he said that the Iraqi invasion, of Kuwait was part of an American plot. The left and the Islamists later condemned the Palestinian-Israeli peace accord of September 1993, arguing that Yasser Arafat should not have compromised on his nation's sacred cause. They seemed to forget, in the heat of the moment, that three years earlier, when the PLO had supported Saddam's invasion, they and the rest of the population had regretted their previous uncritical support of Palestinian nationalism. Then, with further inconsistency, the deputies condemned meetings between the Kuwaiti Foreign Minister, Sheikh Sabah Ahmed, and the foreign ministers of Tunisia and Yemen because, they said, those two countries had been pro-Iraqi during the crisis.

The performance of the Kuwaiti Assembly in 1993 and in earlier years showed many of the worst features of democracy, but the conclusion to be drawn from this is not that democracy is an inappropriate form of government for Kuwait. The Assembly, rather, illustrated the old adage that democracy is 'the least bad form of government'. It may often have been irresponsible, but that is only to be expected in the early stages of the development of democracy, and on balance it is more popular, or less unpopular, with the people than direct rule by the Al-Sabah.

Whether or not the Al-Sabah realizes it, direct rule is no longer fair or practicable in Kuwait. As the Kuwaiti population grows and society becomes more diverse, the *diwaniyyas* are becoming less useful as a means of giving the Al-Sabah contact with its people. The increasing education of the population, and its considerable social mobility means that the groups in society which traditionally have rallied to the support of the ruling family cannot be relied upon to back it in future. What the Kuwaiti people are wanting, increasingly, is not just to be consulted, or heard, as they can be in a *diwan*, but to have some control over their government. This means having an Assembly which, in accordance with the Constitution, will itself propose and pass laws and will be able to look in detail into the running of the government. This is what the Assembly was trying to do, in an imperfect and often irresponsible way in the 1970s, 1980s and early 1990s. The process may have been inefficient, in that important legislation was delayed while the deputies' own proposals were impracticable, but it was part of a necessary and unavoidable evolution away from traditional personal rule. Most of the older members of the Al-Sabah, who have been in government for twenty years or more and who remember what Kuwaiti society was like before oil, understand this process. They realize that their family is very slowly losing its executive role and that they will in future be looked to by the people as leaders who will be above politics, guarantors of the Constitution and symbols of the nation's sovereignty. It is some of the younger, less able members of the family who feel threatened by the change and who urge their elders to resist it. It is they who make the family so grudging in accepting that it has to share its power.

There was one other Arab country, Yemen, which held democratic elections in the early 1990s. The changes here were popular with the people, they received much international publicity and they were often said by the Yemenis and by the many foreign admirers of that beautiful country to be having a powerful influence in Saudi Arabia and the Gulf oil states. The truth, however, was that the character and purpose of the reform in Yemen was different from that of the reforms elsewhere, and the influence they had on the country's neighbours was small.

The reforms stemmed from the unification of the Yemen Arab Republic (YAR) and its southern neighbour, the Popular Democratic Republic of Yemen (PDRY), in May 1990. This was not at all a union of equals. The southern leaders, who were nominally Communist, had seen their domestic political stability shattered four years earlier by an extremely bloody power struggle within the regime. Attempts to develop the country's economy along socialist lines had failed and during the previous few months the financial and military support they had been receiving from East Germany and the Soviet Union had been abruptly halted. They had been totally dependent on this support and without it they faced bankruptcy and, most likely, further domestic chaos. They were therefore happy to accept an offer of union from the President of North Yemen, Ali Abdullah Saleh, which held out not only the prospect of survival but half the cabinet seats in a united government. North Yemen was itself one of the poorest Arab countries, but it was in a much happier state than its neighbour. It was producing a small amount of oil, and was expecting to produce more, and its government had been in power for twelve years and seemed to be more firmly in control of its country than any government had been since the overthrow of the Imamate in 1962. The country also had a far bigger population than southern Yemen: a very vaguely estimated eleven million, compared with about two million.

The union was popular on both sides of the border. The Yemenis felt themselves to be one people. In so far as there is a cultural division in the country it is between the rough tribal people, mostly settled on smallholdings, who live on the mountain plateau of the north and centre of the former YAR, and the softer, more peaceful townsmen, farmers and fishermen who live in all areas to the south and south-east. The division is reflected in a religious difference: the tribesmen are Zaidis, members of a moderate Shia sect with strong Sunni leanings, and the southerners are Sunnis, following the interpretation of the Shariah law propounded in the ninth century by Mohammad bin Idris Al-Shafi. This has led to their being known always as Shafis. In both parts of the country most people still favour the national dress, made up of sandals, long, brightly coloured kilts, shirts and jackets and small turbans, though some of the southern middle classes wear Western dress, which reflects the influence of more than a century of British rule, from 1839 to 1967, and twenty-three years of Communism. Many of the northerners wear daggers in their belts, a custom which the southerners consider slightly uncivilized. In both the north and the south the people have the distinctive habit of chewing the mildly narcotic leaf, *qat*, after lunch. This leaf, which looks very much like privet, is by far the most widely grown crop in the country and, to the disappointment of the World Bank and other aid agencies, accounts for a large part of the country's agricultural GDP.*

Even though almost all Yemenis were delighted in a nationalistic and emotional sense with the union of their people, there were many who had practical reasons to be wary. Some of the more conservative elements of the tribal population in the north regarded the southerners as Godless and Communist and likely to bring bad habits to their people. In their own country alcohol was not actually illegal, though it was little consumed and seldom available to foreigners; but in Aden there was a brewery (producing excellent East German beer), which suggested that the southerners actually approved of the evil substance. Many of the tribal leaders had memories of the expulsion of their fellows in the south after the British left in 1967, and although they did not fear the same happening to them after unification, they viewed anyone who had been connected with Communist politics with distaste. Their doubts were strengthened by the Saudi Arabian salaries they were receiving. These were intended to make them independent of their own government precisely so they could resist leftish ideas or unification schemes.

Parts of the southern population had fears that were the mirror image of the northerners'. They had grown used to their secular way of life, and particularly the freedom it allowed to women, and they did not

---

* Visitors to Yemen will notice that soon after noon every day a large part of the male population starts to drift away from shops and offices, heading for their houses, or friends' houses, carrying large bundles of what look like hedge clippings. These bundles are *qat*. It is bought fresh in the markets and is normally consumed with friends. The chewers take the *qat* leaf by leaf, swallowing the juices and pushing the fibrous material into one of their cheeks, which gets bigger and bigger as the afternoon progresses. Yemenis find that *qat* makes them wide awake and talkative; it stimulates ideas. Almost the entire population, from the President down, chews the leaf. Much of the country's business and politics is transacted over *qat*. In July 1984 in Sanaa there was even an attempt at a coup during a *qat* session. According to the stories that circulated afterwards, the conspirators brought into the President's *majlis* guns concealed in *qat* bundles. Ali Abdullah Saleh, however, had been warned of their evil intentions and said to them, in the words of my informant: 'My friends, before we sit together and discuss, I have something important to say to you, so let us retire to a room and talk in secret'. The plotters were obliged to go with him, whereupon the guards gathered up the bundles and found the guns.

like the idea of having imposed upon them the conservative social regime of the YAR.

There was one way in which Ali Saleh too was not totally happy with the union. In 1990, seeing the need to achieve union quickly, before the Saudis could intervene and turn the northern tribes against it, he had generously given the southern leadership half of all senior positions in the civil service and the new government, including the post of vice-president, and more than a third of the seats in a newly appointed parliament, the Council of Deputies. This distribution of offices did not reflect the balance of population or power between the two states − except in so far as it acknowledged that the south had a better trained and equipped army − and it was obviously something which in due course the President would want to correct. It occurred to him that the best way of doing this would be to hold elections, in which the balance of population would give him a natural advantage. The promise of elections had the further attraction of gaining for him the acquiescence of the doubters among his tribes and showing the small Yemeni intelligentsia and the outside world (and above all the Saudis) that Yemen was a sophisticated modern state, fully abreast of the political ideas of the times.

Elections were eventually promised for 22 November 1992, after a new constitution had been endorsed by a referendum in May 1991, but manœuvring by the politicians had begun virtually from the date of the union. The main parties involved were the General People's Congress, which was a supporting front for Ali Saleh, the Yemen Social-ist Party, which was the former ruling party of the south, and the Yemeni Grouping for Reform, which was a conservative religious and tribal party led by the redoubtable Sheikh Abdullah bin Hussein Al-Ahmar, the chief of the powerful Hashid tribal confederation. The debate between these parties and the various minor factions and inde-pendent candidates was freer than any debate had been before in Yemen. Controls on the press were lifted, except for criticism of the President. More than fifty new newspapers and journals were launched. In the Council of Deputies members were able to ask questions which they would never have dreamed of asking before, such as why a minister receiving a relatively modest government salary had been able to build himself four houses. It was this freedom of debate and the exposure of corruption, rather than the fact of there being an election, which struck a chord with the public in Saudi Arabia.

Typically, the debate was accompanied by violence. This was part of the political culture of Yemen, derived from the division of the north between warring tribes, the civil war of 1962−9, and the weakness of the central government in the fifteen years or so after the end of the war. Anyone who travelled in Yemen in the 1970s and early 1980s noticed that government writ did not run for much more than thirty miles outside Sanaa. Beyond this point most people carried guns, as well as daggers, hardly anybody bothered to pay any tax or buy registration plates for his vehicle, and in Saada, in the wild north, there was a regular weekly arms market at which it was said there were tanks for sale.* Given this background, it is not surprising that bombings and assassinations became part of the election campaign of 1991–2. Among the incidents were the attempted killing of the Minister of Justice, a bomb blast at the Prime Minister's house, and an attack on the Saudi embassy in which the ambassador was held hostage. The last of these incidents turned out to be the work of a mentally deranged man who had merely been caught up in the violent atmosphere of the moment; for most of the others no culprits were ever found. For each bombing or assassination Yemenis could think of five or six plausible perpetrators, and usually they embraced the whole spectrum of the country's political parties.

Not surprisingly, it was assumed by many from the start that the result of the election was being negotiated between the major parties and that the violence was simply a means of politicians putting pressure on their rivals. When I was in Sanaa in the spring of 1992 a retired minister, who was a supporter of the Reform party, told me that the government was afraid that in a fair election his party would win a majority and that therefore it was trying to persuade it to accept in advance an allocation of 30 per cent of the seats. He added that the other main parties each wanted the same proportion, leaving 10 per cent for independents.

When the election was held in April 1993, after a five-month postponement made necessary by the general state of turmoil, it seemed to be something half-way between a political deal and an election in a democracy. There were allegations of vote buying and the pre-marking

---

* When I went to Saada in 1984, with Paul Adams of the BBC, I asked an arms agent in the souk if he could show us some tanks, but he refused, possibly because he thought we were not serious buyers. It was a testimony to the remoteness of the town at this time that a tribesman, whom we met a few minutes later and who claimed to be able to tell the nationality of any foreigner on sight, swore that we were both Japanese, even though Paul is well over six foot tall and has curly fair hair. There were no remotely civilized hotels in the town, so we spent the night at the Saudi-financed hospital. It had a notice at the entrance telling visitors that 'all guns and daggers should be deposited at Reception'.

of soldiers' ballot papers, and there was a serious case of intimidation in which soldiers fired on a polling booth. Most unusually, voters were required to write the name of their chosen candidate on their ballot papers, instead of simply marking a name with a cross. Some three-quarters of the Yemeni population is illiterate, which meant that on election day most people had to have the polling station officials write their vote for them, thus adding to the government's ability to control the outcome. One of the American observers who went to Yemen to monitor the election said a few days before the poll that he reckoned there was 'some major fancy footwork going on'.

After polling day, however, the observers' conclusion was that the election may have been fairer than it appeared. It produced a result which was both plausible and convenient for Ali Saleh. As he must have calculated his own General People's Congress and the Reform Party accounted for a large majority of the seats in the north, while the Yemen Socialist Party won all the seats in the south. This reduced the southerners from having a third of the seats in the Council of Deputies to having only a sixth, which reminded their leaders and everybody else in the country that the south was very much the smaller partner in the union and legitimized the more dominant role which Ali Saleh was clearly planning for himself. Once again the President invited the southerners into a coalition, but he also gave some posts to members of the Reform Party, whose conservatism helped balance the southerners' socialism, and he redoubled his efforts to control the parts of the southern administration that were still in the hands of the Yemen Socialist Party.

This was a highly contentious matter. After May 1990 the frontier posts between the two parts of the country had been immediately demolished, but in many important administrative respects there had been no union. The two regions – or their two political leaderships – kept their own armies and security forces. They also kept two separate airlines, separate currencies and separate car registration offices. The parts of the government machine that were unified were those that affected the development of the economy, and here it was quickly noticed that the system was dominated by the northern bureaucracy and the influence of northern businessmen. The government seemed to be biased in favour of the development of the north, even though the south badly needed an injection of capital and had great development potential and a more sophisticated population. The southerners were promised that property seized by their government after 1967 would be handed back to them and that Aden would be redeveloped as a free port, but neither of these things happened. It was believed that the big northern traders, realizing the potential of Aden, were anxious to stop its development. The southerners were angered by the inefficiency of the northern bureaucracy and its corruption. They had said in the early days of the union that even though their government had been brutal it had at least been honest, but after a few months they began to notice that their officials were being infected by their partners' corruption.

It was all these points of friction, combined with attempts by the President and his supporters to extend their influence over the southern security forces, which led to a steady deterioration of relations between northerners and southerners at the top of the government in the months after the election. It seemed possible that this would lead to a new division of the country, in spite of the union being popular with the people. If that happened it was suggested that Yemen's new freedom and its democracy, if that is what it had, would not survive.

15

Society and Democracy

*Need for political change to be slow – fear of social
disintegration – scepticism about parliaments – lack of
understanding of democracy – people's view of rights
and obligations* vis-à-vis *governments – need for recreation
of civil society – need for democracy to fit Arab and Islamic
traditions*

The idea that democratic change in the Arab world should come
slowly is the cornerstone of the policies of all the reforming governments at present. It is widely accepted that not only is slow change
better than fast change, but virtually the only possibility if there is to
be any successful political evolution at all in the region.

Many Arabs do not trust their societies with democracy. Although
most people are in favour of it, they feel they do not deserve it, would
not be able to make it work and, therefore, are frightened of it. They
look at all the religious and ethnic tensions in their societies, and the
ruthlessness and selfishness with which both groups and individuals
pursue their own interests, and reckon democracy would be a formula
for chaos. These ideas are not confined to a relatively small number of
intellectuals, they are part of the conventional wisdom of the Middle
East. When one asks Saudis what would happen if democracy were
introduced to their country, almost every one of them replies that it
would immediately recreate tribalism, that nobody would vote for anyone except a member of his own tribe, or somebody from his own
town, and that the different parts of society would soon be at each
other's throats. Similarly the Iraqis say that one reason why they have
tolerated Saddam Hussein for the last twenty-five years is that their

country would fall apart under democracy. The Syrians say the same about their acceptance of President Assad.

Yet it is not just fear of social disintegration that makes the Arabs wary of democracy. They have a more positive idea, derived from historical experience and the teaching of the Koran, that firm rule, based on consensus rather than elections, is a good form of government. In traditional Arabian society a tribe or a town accepts as its leader a person, normally from a well-established family, who is regarded by the members of that family and the other important people in the community as being best fitted for the job. In effect the leader is chosen by consensus and then in his government he consults advisers who reflect the views of the different sections of his people, which ideally means that his actions too represent a consensus. In practice, in both historical and modern times, there has tended to be less consultation than there ought, which has meant that good government has come to be seen as the rule of a person who is in touch with the opinions of society and governs firmly and effectively in its interests, even if most of what he does reflects his own instincts. A small step from respecting this type of government has been to associate strong government with competent government, which means that many people now admire strong government unthinkingly, as a matter of course. They are impressed by Saddam Hussein and Hafez Assad because they are strong, and they often admit only grudgingly that those leaders ought to have better respect for the human rights of their subjects. The reason why Mrs Thatcher was widely admired in the Arab world, even though she was not particularly sympathetic to the cause of the Palestinians, was that she was seen to be strong.

It is easy to appreciate that a society which admires the ruler who does what he thinks is best and does not tolerate too much debate or argument, may not be impressed by parliaments. It is noticeable in the Arab world that when people talk about 'democracy' (which they do a great deal), they are indicating their disapproval of incompetent government and demanding change, rather than admiring democratic government as it is organized in Europe and America.

One aspect of parliaments that Arabs dislike is their lack of dignity, which runs directly against the Arab ideal of civilized society. The Arabs in general are a very polite and formal people. They abhor confrontation. Great emphasis is placed on compromise, on saving face and on not embarrassing the losers of an argument, which is often best done by pretending that an argument never took place. Regrettably, in Arab eyes, parliaments do not encourage any of these virtues, and, worse still, in the Arab world when parliaments are introduced they tend to be even rowdier, more undignified and more unprincipled than they are in the West. The explanation may be that the members, working in institutions which run against the traditions of their society, find themselves with no social experience that has equipped them to indulge in public confrontation in a controlled manner. One finds a similar lack of discipline in the board meetings of Arab public companies, particularly in Saudi Arabia and the Gulf states, which in other respects are the most dignified of Arab societies. Here, as in the parliaments, the debate, or argument, may quickly become personal.

Not only is the Arab public put off by the tone of parliaments, it feels, with justification, that most of their members are guided even less than Western politicians by moral or political principles. Part of the reason for this is that outside the Islamic movement there are no proper political parties, standing for specific ideals and with defined sets of policies that are designed to introduce these ideals into the running of society. This leaves politicians voting sometimes according to their consciences but more often according to what they think is their own or their leader's political advantage. They make short-term, totally unprincipled alliances with their enemies, so that on any given issue in one of the freer parliaments – in Jordan or Kuwait – it is often impossible for an outsider, especially a foreigner, to analyse the outcome of a debate in terms of left or right or any other broad political biases. To all but the members of the parliament themselves the outcome may be incomprehensible. The major stable concerns of the members are no more than the promotion of their own careers (and financial advantage) and their re-election. All of these ends are best achieved by their cajoling or blackmailing their governments into making them ministers. The members either try to ingratiate themselves with the Prime Minister, or make such a nuisance of themselves, by tabling censure motions or organizing coalitions against his bills, that, in effect, he bribes them to be quiet.

This type of behaviour either encourages the electorate to turn to the Islamists, who at least have policies, or makes people not vote at all in general elections. The cynicism of the electorate was summed up by some remarks made to me by a member of one of the leading Kuwaiti business families, a few days after elections had been held for his country's new parliament in October 1992. 'The National Assembly will be fine if it behaves properly,' he said. 'But if it goes back to the publicity seeking, the personal abuse and the attempts to embarrass the government for its own sake that we saw in the last Assembly, we might as well turn the building into a theatre or a discotheque.'

Implied in this comment is another reason for the Arab public's sceptical view of parliaments, which is that they are not sufficiently constructive. People say they spend too much time attacking the executive – the ministers and their departments – and not enough working with them, trying to find solutions to the countries' problems. The criticism is valid – it could also be applied to Western parliaments – and it takes the argument back to the Arab instinct for consensus politics. In their hearts a great many Arabs feel that it is right and natural for them to be asked to support a born or appointed leader, but that there is something vulgar and improper in the spectacle of people distinguished by talent or money, but with no traditional claim to leadership, being elevated above others by a democratic system and competing with their equally vulgar peers. This prejudice belongs most obviously in the monarchies, but it also operates in a different form in the semi-democratic republics, where it benefits the government parties. Voters in Egypt and Tunisia back the government parties not only because they think their candidates are more likely to bring some benefit to their villages or their town quarters, they think there is something not quite respectable about supporting a member of an opposition party, who is probably only 'out for himself' and belongs to an organization which, because it is anti-government, seems faintly unpatriotic. In these countries the government parties, in spite of their corruption and incompetence, find themselves the 'right' parties for which to vote.

The Arab view of parliaments is part of a general view of society which is very different from that of people in the European and American democracies. The Arabs are different in their understanding of their place in society, in their loyalties and in their view of their rights and obligations.

Most fundamentally they do not see themselves as being free and independent individuals in the way that people in the West see themselves as being. They do not suppose that they are free to live their lives exactly as they like, within the law, supported in their independence by various rights and claims on their governments. Rather, they feel strong and definite obligations to their extended families, and lesser obligations to their tribe, village or whatever other community they come from. They accept, for example, that if one of their relations kills a person in a traffic accident they will be expected to help him pay compensation to the family of the victim. They understand that on many matters, including whom they marry and possibly what career they follow, they must accept the authority of their father or the head of their family. In their general conduct they must conform to the norms of society and not do anything to bring shame or dishonour on their families. The advantage of this system is that although it deprives the individual of much of his independence it gives him the comfort of a ready-made group of friends, as well as much moral and material support. Arabs coming to the West for the first time say they are struck and rather perplexed by the freedom and independence they see people enjoying, and horrified by the low level of support that individuals expect from their families and the community around them.

In effect, families in the Arab world fulfil much of the role of Western governments' social security departments. It is to their families that people turn if they are unemployed, disabled, retired or, in the poorer countries, in need of medical treatment. Because governments have not provided these things people are unused to going to government offices, filling in forms and demanding help as a right. When they approach their governments it is as supplicants asking for favours, and they make their approaches to important individuals rather than to ministries. One of the advisers of King Hussein told me that people come to his house and stand outside his gate so that they can speak to him as he leaves for his office in the morning. Often they make requests for employment. They say something along the lines of, 'Sir, my son has been unable to get a job in the civil service, but he is a good lad, he works hard and he has qualifications – can you speak on his behalf?' He says that the petitioners have never thought of approaching their MPs, and when he has explained to them what they should do they have been amazed at the idea and, in most cases, have seemed hardly to understand it. They have no idea that it is a member's job – his duty – to try to help a constituent who has a reasonable request or grievance. There is neither the knowledge of an MP's role nor any understanding that the constituent has rights in his dealings with his MP.

It is fair to say that these petitioners represent the workings of Jordanian and other Arab societies at their most traditional. Many people in Jordan, for instance, are beginning to look to their government in some of the ways that Westerners look to theirs. The better educated have made complaints to ministers and members of parliament about the general high level of unemployment in the country, and have demanded that the government does something to create jobs. And the government has been putting the beginnings of a social security system in place; for example, it has started paying a benefit to people on their retirement. Both the people's expectations and the government's response, therefore, have been moving in a Western direction. The reality is that the attitudes of society are at a point somewhere between the traditional and the Western.

Just as the Arabs have a limited view of their rights *vis à vis* their governments, so they have a limited view of their obligations. If a person looks to his family rather than to his government for his security he will not feel that he has to pay much in tax to his government. The more authoritarian his government is, the less he will feel he has a duty to support it. This is not necessarily because he dislikes it, but because authoritarian rule has the effect of absolving people from social responsibility. It excludes them from government, takes away their civil rights and, in effect, tells them that the running of their country is none of their business. It leaves them free in one area alone, the pursuit of business, either mainly legitimate private sector business in the capitalist economies or murky dealings on the fringes of government contracts in the socialist economies. Because there is no freedom of speech, no free press and no parliament, nobody exposes greed or corruption. People do not have to explain or justify their transactions, honest or dishonest, to journalists or parliamentary committees.

Self-restraint is not encouraged. When people are not given responsibility, they develop a defensive view of their lives, in which they keep away from matters that are the concern of their governments but grab and selfishly guard whatever advantage, of commercial profit, a job, or the advancement of their careers, that is allocated to them. Their selfishness is held back to some extent by social convention and a feeling that everyone is accountable to his village or tribe, but it is unaffected by any sense of moral obligation to society as a whole. People do not believe that they ought to abide by the law because that is what society expects of them. They do not have the attitude that most people have in Western countries, that they ought to declare their taxable income and pay the right amount of tax, because that is the right thing to do and ultimately benefits themselves as well as the rest of society.

This defensive and selfish view of the individual's relationship with society is not confined to financial matters. In Arab countries people do not feel the same need they do in the West to contribute to the discussion of government policies and the state of society. In some countries they are simply not allowed to do this, but in the semi-free countries, such as the Gulf states, Saudi Arabia, Jordan, Tunisia and Morocco, they tend to feel that speaking out on matters on which they hold definite views is not the right thing to do. Public political discussion lies within the province of government; entering an open debate would suggest that one had some commercial interest in its outcome. So people continue to talk in private, and if they are themselves important they may speak to somebody influential in government, but they do not make public speeches, talk on the radio or television or write articles for the newspapers. Because of their inhibitions, society is deprived of

the ideas of many able and experienced people, particularly members
of the leading families, who might be expected to carry most influence.
The public is mostly very aware of what it is losing. One often hears
it said that the reticence of these people is leaving the political and
social debate to governments, which are partly discredited, and Islamic
militants, whose policies are more extreme than most people want.
When in 1992 Dr Ghazi Algosaibi, a former Saudi minister who was
then his country's ambassador in Bahrain, wrote a long newspaper
article in which he took issue with the views of the Islamic extremists,
the favourable public reaction in the Gulf and Saudi Arabia was
striking.

If democracy is to be introduced successfully into Arab countries,
many more people will have to be prepared to stimulate public debate
in the way Ghazi Algosaibi did. Likewise people will have to become
aware that they have financial obligations to society, and they will have
to start to think that there are some freedoms and some types of material
help which they are entitled to demand from their governments. None
of these changes can begin without some liberal reforms by the governments to start the process. Reform and changes in people's behaviour
have to move forward together. Ideally one feeds the other: reform
leads to a change in public attitude and that in turn makes possible
further reform. This idea was summed up in the comment of a Moroccan university professor and publisher, who told me: 'You cannot
simply give freedom to people who do not know what to do with it.'*

The reforms and social changes, of course, are not just matters of
governments reintroducing parliaments, legalizing political parties and
allowing free elections, and the public responding with a gradually

---

* The professor's remark reminded me of the passage with which the French historian
Georges Lefebvre finished his famous work *Quatre-Vingt Neuf*. Referring to the importance of the Declaration of the Rights of Man, not only for France but for the whole
world, he wrote: 'The Declaration in proclaiming the rights of man appeals at the same
time to discipline freely consented to, to sacrifice if need be, to cultivation of character
and to the mind. Liberty is by no means an invitation to indifference or to irresponsible
power; nor is it the promise of unlimited well-being without a counterpart of toil and
effort. It supposes application, perpetual effort, strict government of self, sacrifice in
contingencies, civic and private virtues. It is therefore more difficult to live as a free
man than to live as a slave, and that is why men so often renounce their freedom; for
freedom is in its way an invitation to a life of courage, and sometimes of heroism, as
the freedom of the Christian is an invitation to a life of sainthood.' See *Quatre-Vingt
Neuf*, University of Paris, 1939, and English editions by Princeton University and
Vintage under the title *The Coming of the French Revolution*. The final passage of the
book might be used not only by the citizens of the emerging Arab democracies but by
the electorates of all the Western democracies.

growing civic consciousness. Governments have to allow the re-emergence of an independent judiciary and a free media, which eventually might include private television networks. They also have to see that trade unions, businessmen's organizations and professional associations are not supervised by the state in any way and are allowed to voice their ideas in public, criticize government policies and lobby on behalf of their members. A private enterprise economy has to develop, and this, like democratic society itself, is both stimulated by reform and generates pressures for further reform. Private sector companies, particularly the bigger types of quoted companies that think as institutions and plan their investments, need for their operations a proper framework of commercial law; and as their businesses develop they generate a need for further commercial legislation, to regulate them and define their rights *vis à vis* consumers and governments. The legislation itself helps institutionalize and democratize government, limiting the powers of personalities and preventing governments behaving in a capricious and unpredictable manner. It goes without saying that the directors of successful companies expect to be free to give their views on what further changes there should be in their countries' commercial law and what improvements their governments might make in economic policy. In these ways the development of a successful private sector economy is a powerful agency for political change.

As the Arab governments slowly introduce liberal reforms they should not look for their models only to the laws and institutions of the West. They should especially avoid doing this when they are reforming, or introducing, parliaments, which are at the centre of the process of change. It is often suggested in the Middle East that Arab democracy could never be like Western democracy, a totally secular process in which each individual casts his vote according to his view of a party's policies. In order to fit the social traditions of the region, it should incorporate elements of tribal and family loyalties, Islam and pan-Arabism. In this context it is noted that the 'new' societies that have succeeded best in this century, particularly those in the Far East, have been ones that have copied the pattern of some Western institutions but at the same time have remained true to their own cultures.

The problem is that although these principles sound right and logical in theory, it is not easy to see how they can be translated into practical new institutions. The two main theories that exist apply more to countries that might be introducing parliaments than to countries, such as Egypt and Tunisia, which have well-established parliaments that need to be reformed.

First, it is suggested, that regardless of the criticism they would encounter from the West, the ruling families of the Arabian Peninsula, which traditionally run enlightened, relatively liberal autocracies, would be wise to begin by introducing appointed assemblies. They should see, it is said, that the members of the assemblies are chosen wisely and that they faithfully reflect all the different religious sects and ethnic groups in society. Assuming this is done, appointed assemblies would have the advantage of not dividing societies in the way governments, and many other people, fear election campaigns would do. They would be consistent with the tradition of consultation, and they would enable the public and the members themselves gradually to get used to the idea of political issues being openly debated. Members of appointed assemblies are much more likely than elected members to argue about issues from the point of view of principle and the public good, rather than selfish, short-term political gain. They will probably be polite to their opponents and they may well try to think of ways of helping their government, instead of just criticizing it. All of these attitudes would appeal to an Arab public. The disadvantage of appointed assemblies is that their members are often not encouraged to debate freely and, even if they are allowed to be as outspoken as they like, they know that they owe their positions to their governments, and are likely to be unduly respectful towards them.

Even when appointed assemblies evolve towards the democratic election of members – as they are bound to do – it may be best for them still to have some of their members appointed. It might also be a good idea for this principle to be introduced to the parliaments of Iraq, Syria and Libya when eventually these countries' one-party dictatorships crumble and they too begin to reform. It is through some members being appointed that governments can best make sure that their parliaments reflect the importance of community loyalties in their societies and see that minorities are not overwhelmed by a tide of Islamic or pan-Arab sentiment. There are several Arab parliaments which have appointed members or seats reserved for particular sections of their populations, and the people of the countries concerned generally approve of this idea. In Jordan there are eighteen seats (out of eighty) which are set aside for candidates from three minorities. The Christians are given nine seats, the bedouin six and the Circassians three. In Egypt there is an arrangement under which the President considers which parts of the population may be under-represented after elections to the People's Assembly and compensates them by giving them some of the ten seats he has at his own disposal. He normally looks to see whether women or Copts are under represented, or whether the Assembly could profitably have more people of ability from, say, a legal or an academic background.

The second idea one hears is that in designing reforms and explaining them to the people the governments should look as much as possible to Islamic models. They should study the Shariah law and see which of its principles can be introduced into the structure and procedures of modern parliaments. In doing this governments would be bound to find that a certain amount of reinterpretation of the Shariah would be necessary. In this context it is sometimes suggested that there should be a revival of the concept of *ijtihad* (interpretation) which in the early centuries of Islam gave judges some flexibility and even allowed them to develop the law. The concept was never popular with the more conservative scholars, who regarded it as dangerous and subversive, and there was a steady narrowing of its scope. Eventually, in early Ottoman times, a group of scholars declared that the *bab al ijtihad* (the gate of interpretation) was closed, and it has been since then that the Shariah law has acquired its reputation for inflexibility. In recent years, as Islam has developed again as a political movement and, in the view of Islamist politicians, an alternative to secular government, there has been new interest in the idea of reopening the 'gate'. It is this concept that secular reformers are now suggesting might be used to help harmonize the institutions of Shariah law with modern parliamentary practice.

16

The Problems of Saudi Arabia

Private sector boom – increasing competitiveness of Saudi industry – government overspending – mounting debt – rise of Islamist opposition and attempts to control it – reforming the system of government

While the economies of most of the poor Arab countries have been becoming stronger, or at least better managed in the last five years, Saudi Arabia, the richest of all the countries in the region, has been sliding into debt. Both within the Kingdom and outside it in the early 1990s people were putting forward the extraordinary idea that its government was heading for bankruptcy. Its problem was not that its oil production was falling or, until late 1993, that prices were weakening; it was simply that it seemed unable to control its spending.

The crisis in the public finances was disguised by a boom in the private sector which gave the cities an atmosphere of bustle, made the people feel rich and provided a steady flow of contracts for foreign business. The boom began quite suddenly, a week after Saddam Hussein invaded Kuwait on 2nd August 1990. Wanting to bolster the confidence of its people, the government, which for the previous seven years had been delaying payments to contractors, wheat producers and all other private sector firms with which it did business, quickly paid off its arrears and in so doing injected several billion dollars into the economy. Then, as American troops began pouring into the country there was a surge in demand for all the goods and services that went with a military campaign. The army and the huge press corps that accompanied it needed trucks, cars for hire and purchase, construction equipment, building materials, catering services, packaged food, bottled water and every sort of accommodation. Demand was increased by the tens of thousands of Kuwaitis who escaped from the country and were invited by the Saudi government to stay in the Kingdom. Within a month every spare housing compound, hotel room and warehouse in the Eastern Province had been filled. Rents doubled. This should not have been of immediate benefit to those people whose buildings were already let, because rents in the Kingdom are supposed to be reviewed no more than once a year, but the more energetic landlords found they were able to extract from many of their tenants an immediate increase of 25 per cent. As a businessman in Alkhobar remarked to me at the time, 'If you're talking about a free market, there's no place like Saudi Arabia'.

A further huge stimulus to the economy, and one which gathered momentum during the following twelve months, came from the government starting a programme to bring its oil production capacity back to 10 million barrels a day, the level of output it had been able to sustain in 1980 and 1981. The programme involved not only the 'demothballing' of facilities and the replacement of a large amount of pipe and well equipment, but also the installation of an immensely expensive gas recovery system in the 'new' oil fields which were about to come on-stream for the first time. Previously the Kingdom had been producing oil from no more than half of its fields. In the view of the government, the market's need for some 4 million barrels a day to replace lost Kuwaiti and Iraqi production provided an excellent opportunity for it to restore its output to something close to the level at which it had been running before the oil market collapse of the mid-1980s, and keep it there. Since the crisis Saudi oil production has been maintained at between 8 million and 8.5 million barrels a day.

When the war ended at the beginning of March 1991 the economic growth continued. It was soon realized that part of the reason was that during the years of recession the Saudi private sector had restructured itself to do business in a new, slightly poorer economy that was at a more advanced stage of development than the one it had been used to during the great oil boom of 1974–83. At the same time the rapid growth of population, the need for people to replace items they had bought during the 1970s, and the general shaking off of debt and economic inertia which occurs at the end of recessions everywhere, led to a surge in consumer demand. The Saudi economy, in other words, was entering a period of cyclical upturn.

The most interesting aspect of this, which boded well for the country's future, was the reorganization within Saudi private companies. In the 1970s and early 1980s these companies had been geared almost entirely to doing business with the government, or, in cases where they were not actually winning government contracts, they were importing goods that were related to the first, construction, stage in their country's development. They were building roads, ports, schools and hospitals, sometimes with foreign partners, or representing foreign equipment and machinery manufacturers. Those firms that diversified into industry were making relatively simple products such as steel mesh, bricks, tiles, plastic and concrete pipes and aluminium door frames, often on a large and extremely profitable scale. Then, when the building boom came to an end, not only because oil revenues were falling but also because the biggest projects were finished, companies had to find new types of business. Many went into operations and maintenance. Others turned from looking to the government as their client to looking to other private sector companies and individual consumers. They developed business in office equipment, supermarkets, fast food and luxury goods. In many cases the big 'merchant' houses, which were highly diversified, already had a small presence in the new areas. Some firms moved into more sophisticated types of manufacturing, and found they were able to produce goods which ten years earlier nobody would have dreamed of making in Saudi Arabia. Then the high level of government spending and shortages and bottlenecks in all parts of the economy had raised manufacturing costs to a point where the only goods which could be produced profitably were those which were simple and bulky, or which needed a very high level of capital and energy input. In effect this meant cement, building materials and petrochemicals.

It was not just the return to economic normality that was making new types of business profitable. There had been an unexpected fall in the cost of labour – seen mainly at the bottom end of the market. The deterioration of some of the Asian economies, combined with slackening demand in the oil states for foreign workers led to wage rates falling by half. In the late 1980s Filipino and Indian drivers and factory workers, who had been being paid around $800 a month, were accepting $300–400, which was only double what they would have been getting at home. The labour contractors, who supply Asian workers on block visas for Saudi employers, were also discovering new, even cheaper sources of supply. In Bangladesh and Sri Lanka they were able to find workers who were happy to accept as little as $150–200 a month.

It was also found that the foreign workers were staying longer. They did not exactly enjoy the austere life they lived, but they appreciated the security and the supplementary material benefits it offered them. Their work and wages were not disrupted by political disturbances and strikes; safety standards in their factories were higher than at home. They were able to get proper medical care, and those who had their families with them found they could send their children to good schools. All the labourers were able to buy, very cheaply, the modern electronic goods they had dreamed of having at home, and every time they went back on leave they were able to take with them a video cassette recorder or a television. If they wished, they could import these items into their countries as personal effects, which exempted them from tax, and then sell them at a profit. The consequence of the workers being lured into staying longer was that they were becoming much more productive. In the 1970s most had gone home at the end of their first three-year contract, but in the 1980s many were staying for ten years or longer. They were becoming more used to the Saudi environment, happier and more experienced in operating the state of the art machinery of Saudi factories.

A parallel change was taking place at the middle-management level in Saudi companies. Traditionally here the employees had been Indians, Egyptians, Palestinians or Westerners – the Saudi staff of most organizations had been confined to the owners and messengers – but in the 1980s there emerged a new class of Saudi executive. The Saudi managers' salaries were the same as Palestinians' and lower than Westerners', but the advantage they gave their employers was not in their cost. They were effective because they spoke Arabic, understood Saudi customs and learnt quickly how to deal with the government. The appearance of 'nationals' doing middle-rank and even quite junior and menial jobs was a striking feature of Saudi business at this time. Employers were saying that as the population continued to grow and young Saudis found themselves unemployed, they could foresee a day when they would be prepared to take literally any job. That idea would have been unthinkable in the 1970s and early 1980s.

It was not only improvements in the labour market that were changing the shape of the private sector economy. Companies were finding that most of the special difficulties they had encountered during the 1970s had gone. There was no longer a shortage of housing. Companies did not have to build their own compounds for labourers and managers. They were able to go to the open market and pick whatever accommodation suited them best, at a cost that was far below the cost of similar housing in Europe. Back-up facilities in the form of companies that repaired machinery or manufactured parts remained few, though the shortage was not nearly as serious as it had been ten years earlier.

There had been a change in people's mentality, brought about by better education and lower incomes. People were looking after equipment more carefully and if it broke wanted it repaired. The average life of a car in the Kingdom had increased from two to five years.

The Kingdom's infrastructure had improved beyond recognition. The country had magnificent roads, ports, airports and industrial parks. Its hotels were excellent, quite cheap and seldom full. Telecommunications were as good as anywhere in the world. In the late 1970s very few new houses had telephones and office buildings had perhaps one per floor. Telexes at that time were equally rare. In 1973, when the oil boom began, there had been two in the Kingdom, one in the Saudi Arabian Monetary Agency and one in the Foreign Ministry. By the mid-1980s telexes had come and gone and fax machines, word processors and computers were as common as they were in Europe. Internal flights were cheap and plentiful, whereas ten years earlier travellers had had to waste the better part of a day to get a confirmed reservation and boarding pass. In those days the two came together, to discourage people from booking seats but then not taking their flights.

Saudi entrepreneurs continued to command large sums of capital. They were helped by there being no personal income tax and virtually no company taxes in the Kingdom. They had the further benefit of being entitled to half the capital they needed in the form of loans from the Saudi Industrial Development Fund – though in the later 1980s, when the government was short of money, these loans were being disbursed slowly and many businessmen decided they could do without them. They continued to benefit from highly subsidized water, electricity and fuel.

Equally important as a stimulus to industrial development was the enthusiasm for business of young Saudis. Many of these people had been educated in America. They spoke good English, travelled regularly, had been exposed to Western business ideas and had been taught much by the European and American corporations their fathers represented. Business had become their main interest in life. They were far more exposed to modern business ideas than entrepreneurs in the poor Arab countries, and much more receptive to them.

Taken together, the effect of the changes in the Saudi business environment was to turn the Kingdom into a healthy manufacturing base, to the surprise, not least, of the Saudis themselves. The government's plan of the 1970s, which had been to build a good infrastructure, provide financial incentives, and trust that these would encourage a diversified economy, had worked better than anybody expected.

Most of the new industries have aimed their products at the domestic market. The main source of their business has been the Kingdom's very fast-expanding population, now growing at 3.5 or 4 per cent a year. It was estimated in the early 1990s that 20 per cent of Saudis were under the age of five, 40 per cent under thirteen and 60 per cent under twenty-one. This extraordinarily young population structure has created a large market for any product associated with children, from nappies and baby food to video games. It is also leading to a very high rate of household formation. Saudis get married young and they have children soon after they are married. Young couples are moving into their own apartments, whereas fifteen years ago many of them would have stayed with their parents or, in the case of richer families, taken a small house in the family compound. The independence of the new young couples has produced an expanding market for furniture, house-hold electrical goods, and all sorts of packaged foods, as opposed to the bulk foodstuffs that the older generation used to buy. Much of the packet food that Saudis consume is now produced in the Kingdom and manufacturers expect that by the end of the century practically all of it will be home produced. Saudi-produced packet food is generally sweeter, juicier, more brightly coloured, and comes in bigger containers.

More surprising has been Saudi manufacturers' penetration of export markets. By far the most successful exporters have been the petrochemical companies in Jubail and Yanbu, which are partly owned by international companies and have become major forces in the world markets. Most of the rest of the Kingdom's exports, covering the whole range of its newer industries, have been to the other Middle Eastern countries. The owners of the new foods and consumer goods plants that are being established take it for granted that their markets will include the Gulf states, Yemen, Jordan, Egypt and probably several other Arab countries as well. Outside these areas there have been some striking successes, which Saudis hope point the way to the future, though the total value of goods involved so far has been small. Companies have sold steel pipe to the United States and steel factory buildings to Malaysia and other countries in southern Asia. A company in Jeddah has taken a significant share of the European market for can ends, the parts of aluminium drink cans with the ring pull openings. Two of the biggest and most diversified industrial groups, owned by the Juffali and Zamil families, are running large, well-established air conditioner plants. These began in the late 1970s as assembly operations, but they have gradually become more integrated, to a point where the local content of their products is now more than 70 per cent.

They have won export orders from Italy, Greece, Japan and China. With other investors the companies are building a plant to manufacture refrigerator compressors, a product, like vehicle tyres, which has to be made on a very large scale if it is to be economic. The venture's sponsors say that the opening of this plant, which will be one of only a dozen or so of its type in the world, will mark a coming of age for Saudi industry.

For the future the more successful Saudi companies are talking of investing in neighbouring Arab countries, particularly Egypt, in order to be closer to their export markets and take advantage of even lower costs. Their input would be their capital and their manufacturing and marketing expertise. In many cases the people who would be running the new plants would be nationals of the countries where they were located, who had gained their exposure to Western business methods in the Kingdom.

Encouraging as all these developments, in domestic and export markets, have been, they are only part of the reason for the continuation of the 1990–1 boom. The major reason has been that the government has maintained the high level of spending it began then. As well as expanding its oil production capacity it has embarked on a new phase of spending on infrastructure. It has signed contracts for some of the maintenance work it postponed during the austere days of the later 1980s and has started some new building which it is being forced to undertake by its growing population. This work will continue for the foreseeable future. As the population gets bigger – it is now 13 million, including 3 million expatriates, and is expected to reach nearly 17 million by the end of the century – the government will have to install new telephone lines, which are currently not paid for by realistic call charges, lay more electricity cables and water and sewerage mains, and build more telephone exchanges, power stations and sea water desalination plants. These last, which now provide the drinking water of all Saudi cities, even those furthest inland, are immensely expensive, and the consumers are hardly charged for their output. At the same time the government, like governments in the industrialized countries, is paying steadily increasing bills for education and its health service. It is also disbursing large amounts of subsidy to its people, not only on utilities but on basic foodstuffs and gasoline, housing loans, industrial and agricultural investment and wheat and barley production.

Further vast sums have been being spent since the mid-1980s on the two great mosques at Mecca and Medina, to further beautify them and expand their facilities to a point where they will be able to handle 2 million or more pilgrims in a day. Since the beginning of the 1990s spending on religious projects has been running at $200–400 million a month.

Most demanding of all is the government's military spending, which has been going towards huge and palatial bases as well as widely publicized purchases of hardware. Excluding the costs of Desert Storm, the operation to liberate Kuwait, in the last six or seven years the military budget has been consuming between 35 and 45 per cent of total spending. The exact figures, which are complicated by payment for some weapons being made in crude oil, are not published. The government has justified its spending by saying that it is surrounded by poor, envious, potentially aggressive neighbours with bigger populations than it has itself; and points to the Iraqi invasion of Kuwait as a case in point. Where it is unquestionably wasting money is in its tolerance of corruption, which on some weapons systems is estimated to account for up to 30 per cent of the purchase and back-up costs. It is accepted by Saudis in the private sector and in government that many of the people at the top of the defence establishment and the agents and middlemen who surround them have become pathologically greedy. There are important Saudis, including young princes, ministers and people of equivalent rank, who talk freely about this and say that the only way for the vice to be curbed is for it to be publicized abroad.

The overall effect of the government's uninhibited spending since 1991 has been to push its finances into serious and unsustainable deficit. Its oil revenues in this period have been $45 billion a year and it has had a few billions of dollars of income on top of this from petrochemicals sales, tariffs and some minor taxes, but it has admitted running deficits of the equivalent of $10 billion a year. That is the official figure given in the Kingdom's notoriously uninformative budgets; the real deficits are reported by officials to be up to twice as big. The government has been unable to draw on reserves because these have already been spent. In the early 1980s the Kingdom was reckoned to have official reserves of some $150 billion, the biggest of any country in the world at that time, but in the latter part of the decade this colossal sum was gradually reduced by budget deficits and the payment of $23 billion to help Iraq in its war with Iran. By 1990–1 there was under $50 billion left and this sum and more was consumed by the cost of Desert Storm and aid to Egypt, Syria, Morocco and other Muslim countries that supported the Kingdom. The final bill for the campaign was $52 billion, most of which went to the Western allies, whom the Saudis say were generous to themselves in calculating the cost of the operation.

To finance its deficits since 1990 and maintain its reserves at a level where it has $12–15 billion of liquid cash to draw on, the government has been forced to borrow. During 1990–3 the Ministry of Finance and government-owned corporations such as Aramco accumulated nearly $20 billion of foreign currency debt, and the Ministry borrowed the equivalent of $60–65 billion by issuing bonds and bills on domestic markets. Most of the borrowings in Saudi riyals were funded by the Kingdom's commercial banks, various state pension funds and the General Organization for Social Insurance drawing on their cash deposits, which, given the lack of significant money markets within the Kingdom, had been held mainly in dollars in Europe. In the process of buying the government's riyal-denominated securities, the banks and funds used their foreign currencies to buy riyals from the Saudi Arabian Monetary Agency, the central bank, and this meant that while borrowing, ostensibly, in its domestic market the government was conveniently accumulating foreign currency. By the end of 1993 the combined foreign and domestic debts of the Saudi government were estimated to be some $70 billion – excluding $10 billion owed by state agencies. The Government debt was equivalent to about 60 per cent of gross domestic product.

This debt was not enormous by international standards. As the Saudi authorities pointed out, in terms of its relation to GDP it was no bigger than the debts of the Italian and Belgian governments. What was alarming was the fact that it had been built up very fast, and that in 1993 the government seemed unable to stop it increasing further. The idea of it imposing income, corporation or value added tax on its citizens was unthinkable, and even the obvious preliminary step, the elimination of subsidies for individuals and businesses, was fraught with difficulties. The government had already flirted disastrously with the idea of tax in 1988. In that year, apparently without there having been any detailed consultation with the business community or government agencies, the Finance Ministry introduced income tax for foreigners in the budget announced by the King on 1 January. The measure produced such an outcry from employers, who anticipated their wage bills rising, that it was withdrawn within days. At around the same time the government did manage, in small stages, to increase the prices of electricity, fuel and some other subsidized items, but in March 1992, when there was public muttering about the amount being paid to the Americans for their military help, the King felt obliged to put back some of the fuel and water subsidy, at a cost to the budget of $1.5 billion.

Since then there has been a modest attempt by the government to reduce the sums it has been paying to wheat producers, whose crop it buys at three times the world market price. The subsidy was introduced in the 1970s, at an even higher level, as a means of spreading some of the benefits of the oil boom into the provinces, but within a few years it was enriching a much wider section of society. At the end of the 1970s word spread that there were huge amounts of water under the Kingdom and that, with the help of a little fertilizer, growing wheat on Saudi 'soil' was easy. Princes and businessmen from the big cities rushed to acquire the free land that the government was offering, and then borrowed half of the capital they needed for their centre pivot sprinkler systems interest free from the Agricultural Bank. During the 1980s wheat production steadily expanded to 4.5 million tonnes a year, a quantity which gave the Kingdom a surplus of 3 million tonnes and by 1993 had turned it into the world's sixth biggest grain exporter. Given the popularity of wheat production, which yields some 'farmers' profits of more than 100 per cent on their costs, and the importance of many of the people involved, it has been extremely difficult for the government to cut its guaranteed price of 2,000 riyals (about $570) a tonne. It reduced it in 1984, from 3,500 riyals a tonne, but since then it has been stable. In the later 1980s it let its payments to producers fall into arrears by up to a year – a typical Saudi government money-saving tactic – and then during the 1992–3 season the Grain Silos and Flour Mills Organization, without any warning, refused to buy some farmers' crops. It was, naturally, the smaller and less important farmers who suffered. Before the beginning of the 1993–4 season the Organization made its policy official by announcing that in future it would be taking only a certain proportion of the last year's production. The savings from this new policy were expected to be modest, perhaps no more than 10 or 20 per cent of the $2 billion the government had been spending on wheat purchase. What made the case of the wheat purchases interesting was that it showed the extreme difficulty the government had in reducing a subsidy, even when it was being obviously and shamelessly exploited.

The problem for the Saudi government, and also for the Gulf governments, which have periodically faced their own budget difficulties in the last ten years, is that their people have come to see them as the great providers. This attitude developed to some extent in most Arab countries during the 1970s, but in the oil states it exists in a particularly extreme form. It is manifest in Saudis' expectation of subsidies as a right, in Kuwaitis hoping that the state will repay their Souk al Manakh debts, and in Abu Dhabians expecting not only the usual array of subsidies but also the income of apartment and office buildings that are given to them and managed on their behalf by the state's Department for Social Services and Buildings.*

The governments should have been working slowly to change these attitudes since their incomes fell in the mid-1980s, but they have often done the opposite. King Fahd more than once has referred to the Saudi welfare state as his people's 'just entitlement' and 'privilege' and promised that it will continue. Both the King and the rulers of the Gulf states fear that if they lessen their generosity they will lose their people's goodwill. They are afraid of telling their people that they cannot have everything they have had in the past – even though they ought to have been informed by their advisers that the people's material expectations, like their attitude towards the types of jobs they will take, have become less ambitious in recent years. It is even said in the region that the rulers' fear has been the major stimulus to the high level of development spending, which has been a feature of the Gulf as well as Saudi Arabia since 1990. The suggestion is that the governments believe they can buy their people's approval by stimulating a boom.

There are two reasons why the Saudi and Gulf rulers think in these ways. One is that, in typically Arab fashion, they find it difficult to live with imperfection. They hate the idea of admitting that they cannot create the perfect state. In 1987, when King Fahd told his people that

---

* Abu Dhabians receive money from their government through two main channels. One is the 'compensation system', through which tribes, families and individuals who have sold land to the government in the past periodically have their 'compensation' updated to reflect increased market prices. Payments are made every five to seven years and average $150,000 per family. The general intention is that families should use the money to build a house (or houses) for themselves, on land which has been given to them by the Ruler.

The other income comes from the Department for Social Services and Buildings, known as the Khalifa Committee, after the Crown Prince, who is its chairman. The Committee works with land which, once again, has been given to Abu Dhabians by the Ruler, with the specific intention of its being developed commercially. The Committee, in effect, takes the land from the owner, determines the right height, size and use for a building in accordance with the state's strict planning regulations, provides 100 per cent of the finance, oversees construction, collects the rent and pays 20 per cent to the 'owner' while keeping 80 per cent for itself. When the building gets old the Municipality decides that it should be demolished and the 'owner' goes back to the Committee and starts the process over again. The effect of the Committee's work has not only been to give most Abu Dhabians a private income. It has produced a city that is much better planned, greener and more attractive than other Gulf cities, and has prevented the periodic speculative manias that have been seen elsewhere. It has also spread property fortunes more evenly among the population than they have been in Saudi Arabia and Kuwait.

the oil market was so unpredictable that his government could not prepare a budget for the year, there were tears in his eyes.

The other, much more important, reason for the rulers' fears is that their families are under attack. They are already being accused of having wasted their countries' revenues by tolerating corruption, and they know that if they reduce what they give their people the criticism will increase. In Saudi Arabia the Islamists have been talking openly about the greed, or 'robbery', of a few senior members of the royal family. They refer to the 'taxes' that are levied by the government – these being the tiny sums that are charged for utilities – and declare them 'unjust'. They claim that if the princes were not lining their own pockets there would be no need for any tax at all. It was in the face of Islamist criticism of this sort in March 1992 that King Fahd reduced the 'taxes' on fuel and water.

Even more than the Gulf rulers King Fahd is sensitive to the criticism of the Islamists – and to the criticism of anybody else who attacks his government, in Saudi Arabia or in the press abroad. In many respects he is an able ruler; he has been the guiding force in planning his country's development since 1973, he has a good grasp of oil policy and finance and he is an exceptionally good diplomat. But, by temperament rather than intellect, he is not well equipped to take the difficult decisions that are needed to deal with his country's financial problems. He dislikes having to say no to people and hates confrontations. He is too reasonable a person for the tougher aspects of politics. Ideally he would like to deal only with people who are as polite and civilized as he is himself. It is significant that he much prefers the relatively soft, cosmopolitan culture of Jeddah to the blunt, direct manners of the Nejd. He has built himself a palace on a well-forested artificial peninsula jutting into the sea off the Jeddah corniche, and this is where he spends most of his time.

The King, in short, is not the sort of person who will respond to his country's difficulties by introducing a comprehensive programme of welfare and subsidy cuts, or who will take on the Islamists and defend his family against them and tell them and his people that the complaints they are making, for instance about the cost of water and electricity, are absurd. Nor is he the person to cut back on his government's spending on Mecca and Medina. It has been suggested, no doubt out of his hearing, by some of the more secular members of his government that he might reduce spending on the two holy cities by accepting that they will never be able to accommodate more than 2 million pilgrims at a time. It is said that the government could try to make it possible for more Muslims to perform the *haj* by placing some restriction on

Saudis making 'repeat' pilgrimages. These people account for a quarter of the *hajis* in any one year. The King might tell them that the Prophet himself made only one pilgrimage to Mecca. But the reality is that there is not the slightest chance of King Fahd saying these things. He lacks the religious learning of King Faisal (1964–75) or the simple piety of King Khaled (1975–82), which prevents him making pronouncements with authority on religious matters. He is personally very interested in the projects in the holy cities, and no doubt hopes to commend his soul to God through his interest. And he believes his spending must be reducing the hostility of the Islamists.

Another suggestion was that the King might order a five-year freeze on arms procurements, but here he would run into the professional opposition of his brother, Prince Sultan, the Minister of Defence, and the rest of the defence establishment. Similarly it is said that he could act to curb the profits that princes and the people around them have been making from arms contracts and other business, but as this would involve a confrontation with members of his own family, including some of those to whom he is closest, he would no doubt find this the most distasteful option of all.

The type of criticism being levelled at the Saudi government has changed in recent years. It used to come from liberal, Western-educated members of the middle classes, who wanted the Saud family to introduce a range of 'modern' reforms. They were much concerned about the media. They wanted to be allowed to read more independent newspapers and watch less boring television, on which the first and longest item of the news bulletins would not always be the arrivals and departures at the airports of members of the royal family. They were angered by the censorship of foreign newspapers and books, which led to anything objective being banned, not necessarily because it was critical, but because if it was not presenting a bland and utterly uncontroversial picture of the Kingdom it might conceivably offend somebody in authority somewhere. The critics came to despise the Ministry of Information for its timidity.

Further complaints concerned the restrictions placed on women, whom liberals wanted to be allowed to drive cars and work more freely, and what they said was the excessive influence of the *ulema*. The government's close relationship with the United States was criticized, just as the Kuwait National Assembly used to complain about its government's relationship with America. Before the collapse of Saudi oil production and prices in the mid-1980s, when the great cry was that oil in the ground was a better investment than dollars in the bank, it used to be said that the government was overproducing its priceless asset to please the Americans. Another criticism was that princes were exploiting their positions to win representation of the best contractors and generally encroaching on commerce to the disadvantage of the traditional trading classes.

Above all the liberals said they wanted to be able to participate in politics not just as government servants or petitioners in the *majles* of princes, but in a policy-making role. They said, quite rightly, that the *majles* were useful for uneducated Saudis of the messenger or taxi driver class, but were irrelevant to the steadily increasing numbers of the foreign-educated intelligentsia. Likewise, those successful, able and well-regarded businessmen who were asked to have dinner with the King on Wednesday nights said that, while they appreciated the invitations, they were pointless because the nature of the occasion and the formal character of Saudi society made any controversial political discussion impossible. What the middle classes wanted instead of these traditional forms of political contact was some body, a parliament, in which they could engage in real debate. On all of these topics the criticism of the Saudi system was very polite. The people making the criticism, after all, were rich and far from revolutionary.

The classic reply of the princes was that Saudi society was very conservative and that it would be foolhardy to try to change it too fast. This dealt with the middle-class complaints about the role of women, the power of the *ulema*, the censorship of the media (in so far as it could be claimed that restrictions on foreign publications kept permissive ideas out of the Kingdom) and the lack of formal democratic consultation. The princes said, truthfully, that they had much more contact with the ordinary Saudis than did the middle classes and knew how the people thought. They added that if they liberalized their government too fast the religious leaders would call the people out on to the streets, as they had done when the government had introduced television and education for girls in the 1960s. To criticism from abroad the princes would say that the Saudis whom Westerners met – themselves, senior government officials and businessmen – were much more liberal than society as a whole. Some of these ideas, in the 1980s, seemed debatable, but at least it seemed to foreigners that the caution of the Al-Saud would keep the Kingdom free from the threat of radical Islam. The austere character of the country gave the Islamists little on which they could focus their indignation.

The Islamists became more prominent at the beginning of the 1990s. There had for many years been some criticism coming from the Islamic right in the Kingdom, but this burst forth in a completely uninhibited way during the Gulf crisis. At that time the government relaxed its censorship of foreign newspapers and signalled to Saudi editors by the informal but highly effective system of private conversation and comments made in *majles*, that the domestic press could be more outspoken. It felt that with thousands of foreign journalists coming into the country it would have to show itself to be a bit more liberal than it had been hitherto, and having been genuinely shocked by the Iraqi action it was happy for its people to say what they liked about other Arab countries.

The people who took best advantage of the new dispensation, predictably, were the Islamists. They promptly condemned the arrival of foreign, Christian forces in the Kingdom, and the Western journalists, many of whom were looking for a story and were only too eager to hear anything which would comply with their readers' fears about the onward march of militant Islam, happily wrote down what they said. None of the speakers had any alternative ideas for how their country might be protected from the Iraqis, but they said that if Saudi Arabia had had a proper army of its own – which they claimed it would have had if there had been less corruption in the Ministry of Defence – it would not have needed to ask for foreign help. This line of argument provided a convenient means of attacking the Al-Saud, but it is uncertain how much it impressed the Saudi people. Although the Saudis are in the main devout and did not enjoy having Christian soldiers on their soil, they are also interested in making money – and there was no question that the arrival of the foreign armies was good for business.

During the later stages of the crisis, and afterwards, the Islamists broadened their attacks. Much of what they said was personal and unpleasant. They insulted the King and the royal family – the first time that anybody had been able to do this and get away with it in the history of Saudi Arabia – and they wrote ridiculous, libellous articles, abusing ministers and other senior government servants, most of whom were honest, hard-working and as much opposed to corruption as the Islamists themselves. They made further attacks in sermons, in lectures and classes at schools and universities and, above all, in recordings on cassette tape, these last the main propaganda weapon of militants since Ayatollah Khomeini used them against the Shah in 1978. The tapes were extremely popular, less because the Saudis necessarily agreed with what they said than because they were a novelty after the blandness of the media they were used to. Some of them achieved as big a distribution as popular songs. Abroad, the Islamist sympathizers established propaganda offices, putting terms such as 'human rights' and 'justice' in their names, which helped them get sympathetic treatment from the Western press.

The Islamists concentrated their attention on corruption and princely greed because they sensed that these were what concerned the people. Some of their ideas were quite specific. They proposed that nobody in government should be able to spend money in ministry budgets except in the proper course of state business, which they calculated would be a means of correcting the blurred relationship that existed at the top of the government between state and royal family finances. They acknowledged that some of the senior princes were extremely generous with their money, giving away millions of dollars in their *majles* in the course of a year, but they wanted it made plain whether this was really their own money or their ministries'. Demands such as this were supported by various populist ideas, including the abolition of 'taxes' and customs duties, which were said to be 'un-Islamic', and jobs for everybody. These were simply a means of focusing people's attention again on the unduly large share of the nation's wealth that was being taken by some members of the royal family.

One demand the Islamists did not make, however, was for the removal of the Al-Saud. They said they wanted the family to reform itself and to lead the people in the creation of a proper Islamic state in which they envisaged, no doubt, having greatly increased power and prestige. In the document known as the 'Advice', which 109 of their leaders sent to the King in 1992, they called for 'the reinforcement of the role of the *ulema*, who are not sufficiently consulted by the government'. It said that every government department should employ Islamic scholars to vet its actions for religious orthodoxy. Privately, the more extreme Islamists would have liked to expand their role to the point of creating an Islamic republic; they kept this quiet because they knew that it would divide the movement, lose them popular support and probably lead to their being thrown into prison for subversion.

The Islamists say, of course, that they have the support of a majority of the population. Dr Ali Namleh, a lecturer at the Imam Mohammad bin Saud University, near Riyadh, told me in 1992 that in his estimation 10 per cent of the population was happy with society as it was, 20 to 25 per cent was liberal and 65 per cent favoured the country being run on more Islamic lines. Within his 65 per cent, though he did not say this, is a significant, noisy and aggressive body of people, mostly young, who have become virtually professional Islamists. They are the product of the government's decision in the early 1960s to back the Muslim Brotherhood and install its supporters in the educational system. The teachers of that period produced a generation of graduates who clamoured for the establishment of Shariah colleges (religious high-schools) and more religious faculties in the universities, and the graduates of these institutions demanded yet more religious education, which eventually caused the government to build the vast Imam Mohammad bin Saud University, which has absorbed the Shariah colleges but spawned branches of its own in provincial cities. The people who are now coming out of this university have degrees and PhDs, often awarded for flimsy dissertations on such subjects as divorce under Islam, and, believing themselves to be both well educated and Godly, they feel important. Yet in reality many of them are of limited intelligence – the religious faculties have low academic standards – and on graduation they find themselves unemployable. They try to get minor jobs in the schools or universities or they join the *mutawa*, the members of the Committee for the Commendation of Virtue and the Condemnation of Vice, which has an even less well-educated delinquent element. In the 1980s some went to Afghanistan and joined the *mujahiddin*, who were fighting the Russians. Now the Saudi 'Afghans', as they are known, have returned and are talking of their experiences. They have not turned to violence, as have the Egyptian and Algerian 'Afghans', but they are openly subversive and with the other religious graduates they form a body of disaffected Islamist agitators.

The liberal middle classes are horrified by the emergence of these elements. They have joined in their disgust with many members of the Al-Saud, such as those who are in business in a relatively small way, in the professions or in important but low-profile positions at the top of the civil service, who are not particularly rich and have much the same views as the more successful members of the middle class. Together the liberals, royal and bourgeois, have the same feelings towards the Islamists as the Westernized middle classes in Algeria and Egypt, with the one difference that their underlying attitudes are less secular. Most Saudis believe in God. They see the Islamists as a threat to a style of life which, within their homes, is comfortable, Westernized and gives religion a private and not very conspicuous place. They are alarmed by the way the *mutawa* have broken into people's houses, disrupted parties, abused men and women in the streets and engaged in such trivial harassment as stopping girls going into video stores because they fear they might tap their toes to the music. They are particularly concerned about what the Islamists in the schools are doing to their children by giving them, from the age of six, four or five lessons a week on the Koran, and the same number on each of the Hadith, Tawhid, the oneness of God, and Feqh, which concerns how a person should behave in his everyday life. Parents say that these lessons, which they sat through themselves but regarded as reactionary in the 1950s and 1960s, are good for their children's Arabic, for their basic knowledge of history and their understanding of the difference between right and wrong, but they obviously reduce the amount of time they are able to spend on science subjects and tend to produce narrow, prejudiced attitudes towards the rest of society and particularly towards foreigners. A Saudi friend of mine told me that when he took his eight-year-old son to Rome and showed him St Peter's and the Vatican the boy announced dismissively that he 'would like to knock them down', because, he said, the Pope was 'a bad man'. It took his father two hours to make him realize that the Pope was 'good'.

The liberals maintain that although the Islamists are conspicuous and noisy they have much less support than they claim. According to their interpretation of society something between half and three-quarters of Saudis are conservative and broadly content with the tone of society as it has been for the last thirty years, 10 to 20 per cent are liberal, 10 to 15 per cent are Islamist and 15 to 20 per cent are mixed in their views. In a country in which there are no opinion polls – and where most people would regard polling as an intrusion into their privacy – nobody can be sure of these or any other figures and one is forced to rely on personal impressions and anecdotal evidence to back one's estimates. One of the major pieces of evidence the liberals use to support their case is the enthusiastic public response there was in January 1992 to the Riyad Bank's offering of shares to increase its capital. The Islamists preached against people having anything to do with the stock, because they said the bank dealt in usury, but in spite of their tirades the issue was oversubscribed three and a half times. Seven hundred thousand Saudis applied for shares, which suggested that at least 15 per cent of the adult population, male and female, was unimpressed by the Islamist arguments and eager to be shareholders in an openly un-Islamic bank.

It is a logical step from these calculations for the liberals to say that the government is being too timid in its response to the Islamists. Their view is that, on this issue, the government has more support than it realizes and that if it were firm the Islamists would be cowed. To back their argument they cite what happened in early 1989, when Saudi Arabia was host to the World Youth Football Championship. On that occasion the *mutawa* and their supporters first insisted that the emblem of the games should be changed, because they thought the face of the youth it incorporated would incite lust. Then, when the games started, they were shocked to see on their television sets female spectators at the matches – foreign nurses, air stewardesses working for Saudia, nannies and servants – bare-armed and smoking on the terraces. They planned a massive demonstration against this debauchery, but when Prince Faisal bin Fahd, the President of the Youth Welfare Organization, heard of this he told his father that it would be seen on television all over the world and would bring discredit on the Kingdom. The King said, quite simply, that the *mutawa*, whose regular members receive government salaries, should stay at home for the duration of the games – and this is exactly what they did.

The difficulty the royal family faces in broadening this type of action into a general policy of regulating the behaviour of the Islamists and reducing the numbers of religious students going through its educational system, is that it gets its legitimacy from upholding a government which has as its aim the creation of an Islamic state run in accordance with the Shariah. Nevertheless, in his quiet and cautious way, King Fahd has begun slowly to respond to the liberal outcry. His approach has been to enlist the senior members of the *ulema*, some of whom are well respected, conservative and traditionally part of the governing establishment, and persuade them to curb the wilder elements of their followers. The government is trying to isolate the militants and deny them pulpits and funds. Some of the more moderate *ulema* have conceded that the authorities might draw up formal regulations for the *mutawa*, to define their authority and give guidelines for their behaviour in dealing with the public.

In the view of the King and other senior members of the royal family the control of the Islamists will best be achieved as part of the gradual restructuring of the way Saudi Arabia is governed. This has been under discussion since Fahd succeeded King Khaled in 1982 and it has been being implemented since 1992. The process is an extremely slow one and is not just a matter of the King introducing a single package of reforms. It has been described as the Sauds gradually rewriting their social contract with their people, over a long period, without ever tearing up the old one.*

What this has entailed in the last few years has been the introduction of a Majlis as-Shura (Consultative Council), a Basic Law on the Kingdom's government and a Law on Regional Authorities. These were mentioned first by King Faisal in the 1960s and then they were proposed specifically by King Fahd in 1982. For the next ten years they were discussed within the royal family, while to show that the idea had not been abandoned the King had constructed a magnificent building to house the Majlis. There were some of his relations who did not see the

---

* See Robert Kaplan, 'Tales from the Bazaar', *Atlantic Monthly*, August 1992

need for change, who believed that all was well in the Kingdom, that there was a happy, family-like bond between the Al-Saud and its people, and that those individuals who were demanding reforms were just troublemakers. Other princes, and the King, worried about what powers the Majlis should have and who exactly should be in it. There were still deeper concerns about the provisions for the succession in the Basic Law. It was sometimes said in foreign newspaper articles and other analyses written on Saudi Arabia that the King had to consult all the senior members of his family on these matters, but this was not the case. The Saudi monarch is entitled to take whatever decision he likes on his own, and even on constitutional matters it would not be neces- sary for him to talk to more than a handful of his brothers. The reason for the long delay was the King's reluctance to hurt or offend people, let alone cause a split in his family, which led to him listening to the views of a great many princes and letting those who opposed change slowly become reconciled to it.

The Majlis as-Shura was finally 'announced' in a royal decree in March 1992. The decree stated that its sixty members were to be chosen by the King from among 'scholars and men of knowledge and expertise'. They were not to have other government posts or to be managing companies, unless the King chose to make exceptions, and they were to sit for four years, after which time a new Council would be appointed containing no more than half of the old members. For a 'consultative' body the Council was given quite extensive powers. It was authorized to give its opinions on all government policies, form special committees, summon ministers and junior officials to discuss their ministries' per- formance in front of the committees, interpret legislation and propose new laws.

After this outline was published there was a further delay of six months before the King appointed a Speaker in September 1992, and then in August 1993, when the public was wondering whether the project had been forgotten again, the King published a list of the Coun- cil's members. Much to the surprise and delight of the liberal middle classes it contained many extremely able people. A majority of the Council members had doctorates, there were many more people with technical qualifications than had been expected, there were soldiers, doctors and businessmen as well as lawyers, and there were even several representatives of the neglected Shia community. There were some lawyers and academics of an Islamist inclination, but fewer than expected. It seemed that the King had decided that a fairly secular Council, made up of people whom society respected, might be a power- ful agent for curbing rampant Islamism. The questions that remained were when the Council would be inaugurated, how much notice the King would take of it, and how bold it would be.

As well as the Majlis as-Shura the decrees of March 1992 included two new laws. One was a Law on Regional Authorities, which defined the system of provincial government in accordance with established practice and provided for the institution of regional councils similar to the national one. The other, which was much more important, was the Basic Law, which was a form of secular constitution for the Kingdom, supplementing the Shariah, which has to be the official constitution. Like the Majlis as-Shura, the Law was directed, to some extent, against unruly Islamic militants. It stated that people's houses were sacrosanct and could not be entered except with the permission of the owners, that *zakat* would be levied by the government and paid to legitimate recipients, and that the media were to employ courteous language. The sensitive part of the Law, from the point of view of the Al-Saud, concerned the rules for the appointment of a crown prince. The problem during the 1980s had been that although it was accepted that Fahd would be succeeded by Crown Prince Abdullah, the Commander of the National Guard, and then by Prince Sultan, there was no consensus on who would succeed them, or on how a successor should be chosen, and the disagreement on this score contained obvious potential for family division, which in Saudi Arabia and the Gulf states has long been seen as the most serious threat to the continuation of traditional rule. What Fahd finally decided, or agreed, was that from Sultan onwards (assuming he outlived his older brothers) the King would choose his own successor. It was taken for granted that there would still be consultation, but with a law in the background the potential for disagreement and division would be reduced.

The law also stated that the succession was to be confined to the heirs of King Abdel-Aziz (1902–53). It had long been taken for granted that this would be the case, but the fact that the exclusion of other members of the family was made formal was seen as a step towards the family redefining its membership. The gradual pushing away from the centre of those princes not descended from Abdel-Aziz was intended, in part, to limit the demands that the princes made on the public purse. All of the Sauds were receiving stipends from the treasury, though in most case the amounts were small. Their incomes were supplemented by a mixture of gifts of land, grants from richer relations, the profit of business, and salaries from jobs in government and the armed forces.

It was suggested in the early 1990s, by people in the royal family and outside it, that the redefinition of the family's membership might in due course by supplemented by some unofficial redefinition of its role, of what types of business its members might undertake and what should be the division between the finances of senior princes and the state. New rules in this area would be part of an established process of evolution. In the days of King Abdel-Aziz and King Saud, and for much of the reign of King Faisal, it used to be accepted that members of the royal family should not enter business. It was their job to distribute money, not to compete with the trading classes. But as their numbers grew it was felt that for all of them to be maintained by the state in princely style would be too great a drain on revenues, and in the later 1960s it became the custom for only the leading members of the family to receive large stipends; the rest were left to earn an income in business or government. In the 1970s and 1980s many princes who were in government, some of them receiving large stipends and some drawing most of their regular income from salaries, went into business, and particularly into business that involved their managers bidding for government contracts. Now the feeling among many members of the royal family, as well as the business community, is that some further definition of the rules governing stipends and royal participation in business is needed. The obvious solution is that those princes who are in government should not be allowed to be in business in an active sense, though they might remain as investors in public companies or property. In practice it is most unlikely that in the immediate future there will be any hard rules laid down on these lines, but it is possible that over the next few years there will be a few quiet steps in this direction.

There are three important questions facing Saudi Arabia in the mid-1990s. They are whether the King, or his successor, will be able to regulate royal business activities, whether the Majlis as-Shura will be allowed to have a real influence on the way government is run, and whether the King and the Council of Ministers, assisted by the Majlis, will be able to control the country's budget deficit. On the last of these matters it is important that the government acts soon, otherwise it will face a serious and destabilizing financial crisis.

If the King is able to address the deficit, and the issue of royal finances, he will maintain the considerable goodwill that his family still enjoys in the Kingdom. The Saudis are fundamentally loyal to the royal family, as the Kuwaitis are loyal to the Al-Sabah. They have a surprisingly strong collective memory of the chaos that existed before King Abdel-Aziz brought their country under his firm rule. They are grateful to the royal family for the stability it has given them, and most of them attribute their present prosperity to that stability. They are, furthermore, a remarkably conservative and conformist people. They feel at ease with the system on which their country is run, strange and hostile as it often seems to Westerners. Part of the reason is that the country has never been a colony and has been able to evolve its own institutions, particularly the royal *majles*, its informal channels of communication, and its use of the Shariah in much of its legal system. Government and society have the appearance, and much of the substance, of being run on Islamic lines, which must limit the amount of support that the militants can attract. Equally important, society is still rich. Saudi Arabia is not, in short, fertile ground for revolution.

Yet the Saudis are certainly less happy with their government than they were ten years ago and their goodwill towards it is slowly weakening. Unless the Al-Saud can reform and improve its government, and do so more quickly than it has done in the past, the country will not look as stable in the later 1990s as it does in 1993.

17

Pressures for Peace

September 1993 – evolution of Palestinian attitudes from the 1920s – the intifadah *– anxieties of PLO in exile – evolution of Israeli attitudes from the 1940s – reaction to* intifadah *– pressures on Israel in 1991 – the bilateral talks and growth of Palestinian-Israeli contacts – Labour Party's election victory*

On 13 September 1993, on the White House lawn in Washington, the Israeli Foreign Minister, Shimon Peres, and one of the members of the Palestine Liberation Organization Executive Committee, Mahmoud Abbas, signed a peace agreement. In brilliant morning sunshine the two men were watched by President Clinton, former presidents and secretaries of state and the entire US Congress. When the signings were finished the Israeli Prime Minister, Yitzhak Rabin, made a short speech in which he said: 'We who have fought against you, the Palestinians, we say to you in a loud and clear voice, "enough of blood and tears, enough".' Then the Chairman of the PLO, Yasser Arafat, wearing his usual Palestinian headdress and neatly pressed khaki uniform, made a rather more prosaic speech in Arabic. Both men shook hands with the President, and then came the most famous moment of the ceremony. There had been much speculation in the previous week about whether Rabin and Arafat would shake hands. The Israeli Prime Minister had made it clear he would prefer not to do so. He had said he would shake hands only 'if necessary'. But Arafat, being more of a showman and opportunist, and having learnt in the past five years how to embarrass the Israelis, saw the chance of making a small piece of political capital. With a broad grin, he offered his hand to the grave-faced Rabin, who accepted it, to a cheer from the audience and the approval of the millions around the world who were watching the event on television.

The handshake was the culmination of an extraordinary fortnight, which began with the announcement that Palestinian and Israeli negotiators meeting in secret in Norway had agreed on the PLO's recognition of Israel and a form of autonomy for the Gaza Strip and the West Bank. In the context of the politics of the late 1980s and early 1990s the idea of the two sides reaching an agreement on these lines was logical enough, even predictable. The Arab countries had been edging towards accepting Israel for twenty years. Arafat had renounced terrorism and acknowledged Israel's right to exist in 1988 and since then the PLO had engaged in two series of negotiations with its enemy. The process of acceptance and negotiation was a reflection of the growing realism of the Arab world, which was seen also in the economic and political reforms of the period. What was surprising was the route by which the Palestinians and Israelis reached the 1993 agreement and the suddenness with which it was announced. To see how this happened, it is best to trace the two sides' attitudes to each other from the time Jewish settlement in Palestine was gathering momentum in the 1920s and 1930s.

The Palestinians in the inter-war years were worried about what was happening in their country, yet their response was inflexible and in some ways complacent. They felt threatened by the growing numbers of Jewish immigrants, by the vigorous and exclusive society they created and, above all, by their acquisition of land. They believed that what was happening was unjust, but it did not occur to them that the Zionist movement they faced would ultimately be so powerful, or the British government so powerless, that they ought to reach a settlement with the Jews. They complained continually to the authorities about immigration, but they could not bring themselves to accept the successive proposals the British put forward for a mixed legislative council, partition and a round-table conference. Their usual reply to royal commissions and the government in Jerusalem was that Palestine was their own land, that they were the descendants of people who had lived there from time immemorial, and that they saw no reason why they should live with, or share government with, immigrants they did not want. There was no compromise. Their attitude was the precise opposite of that of the Jews, and in particular of Chaim Weizmann, one of the founders of the Zionist movement and, later, the first President of Israel. The Jews always avoided confronting the imperial power. They agreed to every proposal it put to them. They worked on winning the support of influential figures in Britain and America and acquiring Palestine, as Weizmann put it, 'immigrant by immigrant, dunum by dunum and goat by goat'.

In 1947 the Palestinians, supported by the Arab governments, rejected the United Nations' partition plan for their territory, and when the British withdrew and the Arab armies failed to crush the new state of Israel, they lost not only the land the UN had designated for the Jewish state, but much of the area that had been allocated to an independent Palestine. Some 800,000, two-thirds of their people at the time, were forced into exile. For several years they remained supine, as if in a state of shock. They did not start a guerilla war against their enemy. The idea of a national liberation struggle was still new in the late 1940s, having been used by the Israelis but hardly anybody else. Those Palestinians who had not fled their country and were not pushed out later by economic pressure or Jewish attacks on their villages became second-class Israeli citizens. Those who left settled in United Nations' refugee camps or established themselves in the towns of the West Bank, Lebanon, Syria or Kuwait. Their leaders had no policies and no ideas about the future, except the assumption that at some point they would return to their land and that the return would be arranged for them by outside powers – the United Nations, America and Britain. Later, in the early 1950s, they began to put their faith in Gamal Abdel-Nasser.

In 1964 an Arab summit conference established the Palestine Liberation Organization, which was intended to organize the exiled Palestinians under the supervision of the Egyptian government. The new body was later given a National Charter, which contained a series of repetitive statements saying that Palestine was Arab land, that Israel would never be recognized and that the only way to liberation was through armed struggle. The document rejected compromise of any sort and said nothing specific about what should happen to the two million or so Jews who by this time were living in the country. In effect the PLO in its early days was less concerned with formulating policies than with self-deceiving, bombastic rhetoric, which was one of the worst features of the Nasser era. There is some question as to whether its first Chairman, Ahmed Shuqairy, actually said that he would 'drive the Israelis into the sea', but that phrase certainly summed up the tone of his speeches. It was seized upon by the Palestinians' enemies and haunted them for the next twenty years.

In February 1968 the PLO was taken over by the Palestinian guerilla groups and Yasser Arafat became its Chairman. A month later Al-Fatah won its extraordinary success at the battle of Karameh. The Palestinians began to believe in ideas of bringing about 'national liberation' through guerilla war. This caused the PLO leaders and intellectuals in Amman and Beirut to think about what 'liberation' might mean if it happened, and that led them to produce the formal objective of a 'multiracial, secular, democratic state in Palestine'. The policy had a pleasanter ring to it, but it was hardly more practicable than driving the Israelis into the sea. It would have involved the dismantling of the Jewish state as it had existed since 1948, and that would have required an outright military victory or the co-operation of a large part of the Jewish population. The most idealistic and impractical of the Palestinian thinkers did indeed believe that 'enlightened' Jews would join them in their struggle.

A 'multiracial' Palestine continued to be the PLO's aim for as long as its forces were able to confront Israel over the border of a neighbouring country. Then in 1982 and 1983 its leaders and most of its fighters were thrown out of Lebanon. The leadership was given a base in Tunis, which was then the headquarters of the Arab League, and the guerillas were dispersed to Tunisia, Yemen and Iraq. Those who managed to remain in Lebanon were kept under firm Syrian control. The new exile made the continuation of the armed struggle impossible. The Palestinians had no more opportunity to wear down the Israelis with their raids, which had never seemed likely to have much effect, and they had no hope of forcing another Arab state to fight on their behalf and causing an international crisis. The leadership could see that its official objective was futile, but it did not want to abandon it. There was no other attractive and obtainable substitute in prospect and there were strong domestic reasons for sticking with it. These derived from the very parochial nature of Palestinian patriotism. The ideal of a state in all Palestine, as opposed to a West Bank state, which since the early 1970s had been canvassed as a possible alternative, appealed most strongly to all those who had come from Jaffa, Haifa and Galilee. As it happened it was these people, the Palestinians whose families had left in 1948, rather than those who fled the territories the Israelis occupied in 1967, who made up most of the populations of the refugee camps and the other Palestinian communities in exile. It was they, naturally, who provided the PLO leadership and most of the guerilla fighters. They were not interested in a West Bank state, not only because that would have involved shameful compromise but also because their own homes were not there. With their views in mind, and knowing the fractious character of his organization, Yasser Arafat in Tunis had to adopt a safe policy, and he opted for the lowest common denominator of Palestinian belief, which was the National Charter's insistence that there should be no recognition of Israel. On other ideas, possible compromises which might have got his people out of their desperate predicament, he was flexible. He sniffed at them, talked about them but saw no reason to commit himself to any of them.

While the Palestinians in exile were living through the high point of Karameh to the disaster of Beirut, the rest of their people were enduring a different but equally unhappy life under Israeli occupation in the West Bank and Gaza Strip. In the early stages of their rule the Israelis seized much property, particularly in the quarter near the Wailing Wall in Jerusalem and in the desolate country areas near the Jordan river and the Dead Sea. There were regular house demolitions, which the army used as a means of inflicting collective punishment on villages whose young men helped the guerillas. Then, from the mid-1970s, the territories settled down to an occupation which was unpleasant, unjust and onerous, but not particularly brutal. From time to time there were further house demolitions, and there were quite frequent arrests and curfews. Occasionally the 'Civil Administration', as the Israeli military government was called, expelled people whom it considered to be actively subversive.

Much of the unpleasantness of the occupation derived from the way it seemed designed to impoverish the population, with the obvious intention of encouraging it to leave. For instance, the Palestinians were restricted in what they could import or export. If a merchant wanted to buy foreign goods he would only be given a licence if he was acting through an Israeli agent and bringing the goods in through an Israeli port. Exporters of fruit and vegetables, which were the main internationally saleable goods that the territories produced, had their trucks unnecessarily delayed at Israeli checkpoints and customs posts, often for long enough to have their loads go bad. The population was restricted in building and in its consumption of water. Existing wells had meters put on them, and generally the authorities refused the Palestinians permission to drill new wells. Not knowing whether they would be able to irrigate their land, or whether it might be confiscated, farmers were reluctant to invest capital and effort in developing their land. By the early 1990s it was reckoned that the 100,000 Jewish settlers on the West Bank, who were not restricted in their drilling (even if the purpose was to fill swimming pools) were using as much water as 1.1 million Palestinians.*

---

* In 1993 the total Palestinian population was estimated to be about 6 million. It was divided between 1.1 million on the West Bank, 800,000 in the Gaza Strip, 800,000 in Israel (the Israeli Arabs, holding Israeli passports), 2.2 million in Jordan, 400,000 in Lebanon and some 700,000 dispersed through the other Arab countries and the rest of the world. About 900,000 of the Palestinians lived in sixty refugee camps in Gaza, the West Bank, Jordan, Lebanon and Syria. The Israeli population in 1993 was nearly 5 million – made up of about 4 million Jews and 800,000 Israeli Arabs. The Jewish population included 120,000 settlers in the West Bank and Gaza and 400,000 immigrants from the former Soviet Union, who had arrived since 1989.

As well as the legal and administrative obstruction, the Palestinians faced countless small humiliations. Their houses could be entered and searched by soldiers. They were stopped and searched at checkpoints, and if a man did not have the right documents on him he might be abused or hit by soldiers in front of his children. All the time, say the Palestinians who endured the occupation, they had the worst and most frustrating humiliation of not being in control of their own lives. They did not know what was going to happen to them. They could not plan for the future. Their unhappiness gave rise to what a Palestinian journalist described to me as 'extremism, tension and high emotions'.

Yet there were ways in which the occupation was less bad than it might have been. The Palestinian press was freer than the press in most Arab countries. Photographs of Arafat certainly appeared on the front pages more often than they did elsewhere in the Arab world. The press was able to criticize the Israelis, discuss the policies of the PLO and attack Arab governments. It was only matters that were regarded by the Civil Administration as affecting security, which could be very broadly defined, that were censored. Palestinians were able to travel on Israeli-issued documents. They could establish trade unions, theatre groups, journalists' associations and students' unions, as long as they were not overtly political.

The Palestinians, therefore, tolerated the occupation, and even co-operated with it. Many of them went daily to work in Israel. Contractors helped build Israeli settlements on the West Bank and carried out jobs for the armed forces. Some food manufacturers obtained kosher certificates for their products. The population obediently paid its taxes and carried its identity cards. The Civil Administration found it could control the territories with 1,200 soldiers, and a few hundred border guards and Shin Bet internal security agents. By the mid-1980s the Israelis were making a profit from the occupation. They were investing nothing in the territories and benefiting from a captive supply of cheap labour and a small flow of taxes.

In retrospect, many of the Palestinians in the territories are rather embarrassed by their failure to have done more to resist the Israelis than mount the odd strike or demonstration in the twenty years after 1967. They say that resistance was made difficult by their being watched by the occupiers, who promptly arrested and deported anyone who looked like a leader. More reluctantly they admit that they were not willing to endure the economic and personal hardship that would have gone with civil disobedience and non-cooperation. If they had refused to pay taxes the Administration would have prevented them from working in Israel and obtaining driving licences, travel permits and all the other routine authorizations they needed. Part of their difficulty was that their economy in the West Bank and Gaza Strip was too small and undiversified to sustain them if they cut themselves off from contact with Israel. What the Palestinians less often say is that, as they had always done, they tended to look to other people to help them. Some pinned their faith in the PLO's liberation struggle, or on its mobilizing international pressure on Israel. Others had become unconsciously Jordanianized or, in the case of the Gazans, Egyptianized during the years between 1948 and 1967 and looked instinctively to their former governments for help.

These were the typical attitudes of people who were in their twenties and thirties at the time of the occupation and who led their community during the next twenty years. By the mid-1980s, however, a new generation was emerging. Those who by then were in their teens and twenties, who with younger Palestinians constituted two-thirds of the population, knew nothing but the Israeli occupation. They had a much stronger Palestinian identity than their elders. They did not associate themselves with any Arab government and they were affected by the growth in consciousness of Palestinian nationality, in all parts of the world, that had been brought about by the PLO and the guerillas in the late 1960s and 1970s. Their sense of being Palestinian, ironically, had been allowed to mature by their living in a relatively free society in which there were few restrictions on political discussion. It was these young Palestinians who became the force behind the *intifadah*, the uprising, which began suddenly in December 1987.

The *intifadah* was not planned by any group. It stemmed from a series of relatively small incidents. On 6 December a Palestinian stabbed and killed an Israeli shopper in Gaza, a type of attack which was neither common nor completely out of the ordinary. Two days later an Israeli truck driver killed four Palestinians in a road accident, which local rumour immediately had it was an act of revenge. Then, on the following day, Israeli soldiers on patrol in the Jabaliya refugee camp in the Gaza Strip were pelted with stones by Palestinian youths, and in the confrontation which followed, when the youths surrounded the soldiers' vehicle and threw Molotov cocktails at it, the patrol commander fired at one of the crowd and killed him. Later in the day the authorities were unable to take the teenager's body from the local hospital mortuary for the usual quiet night-time burial they gave Palestinians they had killed. Instead a large crowd held a funeral procession of its own which quickly turned into a riot. The next day the rioting spread to the nearby town of Khan Younis, and then to refugee camps and small towns and villages on the West Bank. Israeli guard posts were attacked, streets were barricaded with burning tyres. There were strikes, shops shut, and workers stopped going to their jobs in Israel. Most worrying for the authorities, on 21 December the Palestinian community in Israel mounted its own general strike in sympathy with its compatriots in the territories.

In the weeks and months that followed the start of the *intifadah* it looked as if the Palestinians might be going to separate themselves, socially and economically, from Israel, through a campaign of non-cooperation and minor violence which would deprive the Israelis of their taxes and labour and increase the costs of the occupation. Apart from the hit-and-run stoning of Israeli patrols, the part of the *intifadah* seen on Western television screens, their weapons were strikes and shop closures. These obviously hurt and inconvenienced themselves more than the Israelis, but they were an important means of encouraging the beginning of what their leaders hoped would be a self-sufficient Palestinian economy, which would enable the people to stop paying their taxes with impunity. In 1988 there were signs that these hopes were being fulfilled. Palestinians boycotted Israeli goods. New distribution channels for their own goods were created. People discovered they could be more self-sufficient in foods and manufactured goods than they had realized. There were a few attempts to organize tax boycotts. But in the end the economic separation was not pushed far enough. The Palestinians could not bring themselves to face the pain it would have involved. Too many of them were dependent on their jobs in Israel, and they had no local substitutes for Israeli electricity, gas and kerosene. Realizing that ultimately they could be hurt more than they could hurt the Israelis, they slowly went back to economic life as usual.

Had there been a strong central direction of the *intifadah* some of the difficulties of economic separation might have been overcome, but whatever the Palestinians said about the 'internal' and 'external' leaderships of the PLO working together, the reality was that there was no co-ordinated control. The PLO in Tunis was taken by surprise when the *intifadah* began and although in the next twelve months it was able to establish co-operation with many of the organizers in the territories, and frequently was able to direct them, there was always some tension between it and those who were nominally its representatives. The situation was complicated by the emergence from the beginning of the *intifadah* of the Islamist group Hamas, an acronym of Islamic Resistance Movement, as the most militant organizer. Hamas, which reflected the thinking of the Muslim Brotherhood, was not affiliated to the PLO, which was a traditional socialist and secular institution. The rivalries between the three elements of the leadership did not produce a serious split in Palestinian ranks, but they did prevent the careful organization of the *intifadah*. They stopped the leaders from working out methods of compensating the people for economic distress, and made it impossible for anyone to control the level of violence and direct it in a way which would hurt the Israelis most.

The lack of central control became very obvious in 1991 and 1992 when there was a wave of killings of alleged 'informers', not by any group, but by individuals who had had friends arrested by the Israelis and who suspected they had been betrayed. The killings divided and embarrassed the Palestinians. Yasser Arafat and the PLO leaders in the territories frequently ordered that they should stop, but having no links with the killers their orders were ignored.

The organization of the uprising was made more difficult by the Israelis introducing a policy of mass arrests. They started this in the spring of 1988 and continued it, releasing one batch of leaders and then seizing another, until the end of 1991. Gradually the violent aspect of the *intifadah*, like the economic separation, faded. There were still occasional stabbings and shootings, but in the early 1990s the big strikes, demonstrations and confrontations between youths and the army, which had occurred almost daily at the beginning of the uprising, only happened if there was some special event that aroused the Palestinians' anger.

None of this meant that the *intifadah* was a failure, or that the Israelis were steadily suppressing it. The position was, rather, that the uprising had changed the relationship between the Palestinians and Israelis, the character of the occupation and the pattern of life in the territories, but no more succeeded in developing a momentum towards liberation, than the Israelis succeeded in crushing it. The Israelis kept control of the land – the border, the roads, the major towns or wherever else their forces were – but they lost control of the people. They found that whereas in the early 1980s when they summoned a person to appear at a police station he would present himself as requested and ask what he had done wrong, in the early 1990s he would disappear, and a large number of soldiers would have to be deployed to look for him. An Israeli journalist told me that if he visited a refugee camp he had not only to tell the army but also inform the local leadership of the *intifadah*, because otherwise, if his car was not actually in sight of an army patrol, it would be burned. In effect, this journalist said, the *intifadah* had given the Palestinians 'informal autonomy'. He likened the new situation to a football match 'in which the game stays drawn no matter how long you go on playing'.

The *intifadah* further strengthened the Palestinians' identity, through giving them pride and bringing them still more to the attention of the outside world. And it put the West Bankers and Gazans at the centre of Palestinian politics. This was of great significance for the future. It brought to the fore the difference in priorities between the exiles, who wanted to return to their homes in Israel proper, and the people of the territories, most of whom simply wanted the Israelis off their land. Although they did not say it openly – neither the leaders of the *intifadah* nor the demonstrators ever made any specific demands of the Israelis – it was clear that for them a state made up of the West Bank and Gaza, rather than a 'multiracial, secular, democratic' state in all Palestine, would be a practicable and perfectly acceptable solution.

The *intifadah* put Yasser Arafat in a difficult position. It had not been started by him or his guerillas, and it was obvious from reports he received from the territories and the fact that the demonstrators did not seem to be carrying his picture, that the people did not regard him and the PLO in exile as their inspiration. The *intifadah* took the limelight from him, both in the Arab world and in Europe and America. There were comments in the Arab countries that it was being far more effective in putting pressure on Israel and winning goodwill for the Palestinians than the PLO guerillas had ever been. In this way it carried an obvious threat to Arafat's leadership. The danger came not only from Hamas but from the increasing prominence of the well-established, respected, secular leaders of the Palestinians in the territories, people who were nominally loyal to the PLO but were bound to have ambitions of their own.

There were other difficulties facing Arafat. After five years in Tunis he and the other PLO leaders were beginning to despair of ever re-establishing themselves in a state near Palestine, let alone returning to their homes. There were the beginnings in Palestinian ranks of the idea that the PLO should accept what it could get rather than hold out for what it claimed as its right. And it had long gone without saying that the Palestinians could not rely on the active support of other Arab countries. The Arab governments had been aware since the mid-1970s that they were moving slowly towards making peace with Israel. The war of 1973 had been frighteningly big and bloody, and hugely expensive, and that alone had made the idea of another round of full-scale fighting unthinkable. Then at the end of the 1970s Egypt had made peace with Israel, which made war impossible. At this point it had become clear to all the Arab governments that the Palestinians' aspirations were hopeless, though none of them could make peace with

Israel before the Palestinians did, without being accused of betraying the national cause. What developed instead was an increasing amount of contact between senior people in the Israeli government and Arab leaders. Both King Hassan and King Hussein met Israeli ministers, and at a less exalted level contacts were established between various Israeli politicians, Foreign Ministry officials, academics and the directors of research institutes, and Arab politicians, many of them former ministers or members of ruling families.

All of these developments put pressure on Arafat to change his policies. He was also being pushed in this direction by the United States, which he knew was the one power which might be able to force Israel to make concessions. What he had to do was move away from his demand for a state in all Palestine and towards acceptance of a state in the West Bank and Gaza, not only so that he would be able to deal with the United States and Israel but also so that he could align himself with the *intifadah* and more easily represent himself as its leader. The manœuvrings he had to perform were not easy. The PLO was permeated with unpleasant and occasionally violent internal politics. It had a few idealistic rejectionists who honestly thought that the Palestinians should continue to demand the state that was their right, and it had many more who were pragmatic in their private views but were only too ready to accuse their leader of treachery if he compromised, and to try to take his place.

Arafat therefore moved slowly and cautiously. In November 1988, eleven months after the beginning of the *intifadah*, he persuaded the Palestine National Council, his people's parliament in exile, to declare an independent Palestinian state, without specifying its borders. At the same time, in very convoluted language, the PNC conditionally accepted the United Nations' partition plan of 1947 and Resolutions 242 and 338, which set out principles for the solution of the conflict. After the announcement he evaded questions on whether this meant that the PLO had recognized Israel. Under pressure from Arab governments and Palestinian leaders in the territories there followed a series of statements 'clarifying' the PNC's resolutions, and finally on 13 December Arafat addressed a special session of the United Nations General Assembly in Geneva – he could not go to New York because he was denied a US visa – and appeared almost to recognize Israel. The next day at a press conference he was more specific. He spoke of 'the right of all parties concerned in the Middle East conflict to exist in peace and security', and then added the words, 'and, as I have mentioned, including the state of Palestine, Israel and other neighbours'. At the same press conference he announced that the PLO 'totally and absolutely renounced all forms of terrorism'. In the view of the United States government this finally opened the way to its negotiating with the Organization. Immediately after the Geneva statements the State Department established contact with the PLO through its embassy in Tunis and began, in effect, to act as a go-between in trying to stimulate negotiations between the PLO and the Israeli government. The Israelis were not particularly enthusiastic about the exchanges and in June 1990, after PLO guerillas from Lebanon had been intercepted carrying out a raid on the Israeli coast and Arafat had found himself unable to condemn the attack, both the Israelis and the Americans broke off the talks.

For Arafat events then moved from bad to worse. The PLO backed Iraq in the Gulf crisis, which further alienated the Americans and led to a prompt, total and lasting cut-off of the funds it had been getting from the Arabian oil producers. This was a major blow to Arafat because he was heavily dependent on the oil states for his income – he got some other money from well-off Palestinian exiles – and like all Arab leaders his prestige and influence depended on his ability to pay his supporters. At the same time the gradual collapse of the Soviet Union was removing from the PLO and its radical Arab backers a source of arms and the major international source of moral and political support. And throughout this period the Israelis were founding new settlements in the occupied territories. From 1989 there had been a steady flow of Russian Jews into Israel, which decisively reversed the previous trickle of Jewish emigration from the state, and although few of the newcomers went to the settlements the fact that Israel's population was growing again seemed to make it inevitable that there would be more pressure for new settlements in the future. By the middle of 1991 the Palestinians were beginning to see that if they did not get back to negotiations and make some decisive compromises soon, they would risk losing their whole country for ever.

As it happens, the evolution of the Palestinians' thinking on recognizing Israel has been paralleled by the development of the Israelis' thinking on accepting that they have to live with the Palestinians.

In the early years of their state the Israelis liked to think that the Palestinians as a nation simply did not exist. Their official view was that there were some Arab refugees who had left their land but that these people in no sense constituted a community with a claim to nationhood. Their attitude was summed up in the famous words of Levi Eshkol, the Prime Minister from 1963 to 1969, who asked a correspondent of *Newsweek*, 'What are Palestinians? When I came here there were 250,000 non-Jews, mainly Arabs and bedouins'. His successor, Golda Meir, was even more blunt. She told *The Sunday Times*: 'It was not as though there was a Palestinian people and we came and threw them out and took their country away from them. They did not exist.'* Both prime ministers and most of the rest of the Israeli population in the 1940s, 1950s and 1960s hoped and believed that the people they had displaced (whoever they were) would quite quickly be absorbed into the countries to which they had fled and would soon cease to think about their old homes. Their expectations were shared by the United States and most of the other countries at the United Nations. The assumption was that some appropriate regional development projects would help the Palestinians' disappearance.

The Israelis' doubts about the existence of the people they had displaced were matched by a very flexible attitude to the borders of their own state. They agreed to the UN partition plan of 1947, knowing that the Arabs were not going to accept it, and when the fighting that followed the Arab armies' invasion ended in 1949 they found themselves with more territory than the partition had given them. Because none of their Arab enemies was willing to recognize their state they signed only armistice agreements with them, which meant that they did not have to accept in treaties any limitation on how much of Palestine they might aspire to gain in the future. Many Israelis continued to hope that eventually their state might expand into the whole of Eretz Israel, which included the West Bank and Gaza. The West Bank was particularly important to them because it contained the old cities of Jerusalem, Hebron, Bethlehem and most of the other towns and sites that had been at the centre of their ancestors' lives in Biblical times. In 1967 Israel took these territories. It promptly incorporated East Jerusalem into its state, but it was not politically possible or socially feasible for it immediately to absorb the rest of the West Bank and Gaza. It began to settle the areas and encouraged the Palestinians to leave, and it was the hope of the mainly right-wing governments that ran the country from 1977 to 1992 that eventually an opportunity would arise which would enable Israel to seize them. There were extremists who spoke of their taking much bigger areas, in southern Lebanon and to the east of the Jordan river.

Both of the Israelis' policies, of encouraging the disappearance of the Palestinians and expanding their state, were pursued with violence. In the spring and summer of 1948 they waged a highly successful terrorist

---

* *Newsweek*, February 1969 and *The Sunday Times*, 15 June 1969

campaign to persuade as many as possible of the Palestinians to leave their homes. They vigorously opposed the ideas of the United Nations' Mediator, Count Folke Bernadotte, who proposed that along with a ceasefire and some boundary revisions, a precondition for a peaceful settlement should be that the refugees be given an unconditional right of return. In September 1948, four months after his appointment, Count Bernadotte was murdered by the Stern Gang. In the years that followed their victory in the 1948–9 war of independence the Israelis periodically continued their terrorist campaign, with the general purpose of spreading fear and securing the evacuation of villages near their *de facto* frontiers. One of the last of their attacks took place in October 1956 when the army imposed a curfew on the village of Kafr Qasem near the then border with Jordan. It informed the *mukhtar* (headman) only half an hour before the measure was due to go into effect, and then shot forty-seven of the villagers as they returned home after the deadline. Because this was regarded as an unduly brutal interpretation of their orders, the soldiers involved were put on trial, but there was little moral outrage in the courtroom, the accused all received 50 per cent increases in their salaries during the proceedings, and in the end they were either pardoned straight away, or pardoned almost immediately after they had begun their sentences. The brigadier who had commanded the operation was reprimanded for a 'merely technical error' and fined one piastre.* The trial was well reported in Israel, but at a time when television was not common in the West and the foreign coverage of the networks rather sparse and slow, it went unnoticed in Europe and America. Also at that time, soon after the Second World War and the Holocaust, the industrialized countries had more sympathy for Israel than they had later. The Middle East seemed further away and the fates of former colonial peoples less important. The massacre of Kafr Qasem, like those at Dier Yassin in 1948 and Qibya in 1953, was the type of act which the Israeli army could carry out with impunity in the 1950s, but which would have attracted huge international publicity in the 1980s and 1990s and which, then, the Israelis would never have contemplated.

From the 1960s onwards the Israelis continued their policy of violence in dealing with the Palestinians, though by now they were less often trying to drive them off their land than punishing them for guerilla or terrorist attacks and hoping that by retaliating on a massive scale they would not only prevent further attacks but destroy the guerilla

---

* See David Hirst, *The Gun and the Olive Branch*, Faber, 1977, pp. 185–7

groups altogether. In 1982, when they invaded Lebanon, they partly succeeded in this aim in that they drove most of the guerillas out of the country and reduced the numbers of Palestinian attacks on their northern frontier. (In the later 1980s and 1990s most of the fighting in and around Israel's security zone in southern Lebanon involved Lebanese Shia militias.) Yet the Israelis did not succeed in their deeper objective of destroying the Palestinians as a nation. Throughout the period of massive retaliation they spoke of wanting peace, but what they meant as far as the Palestinians (and other Arabs) were concerned was the unconditional acceptance of their state, rather than the type of peace negotiations which would have involved their sitting down with the Palestinians, making concessions and having finally to make decisions about what land was going to be included in Israel. Whenever it was involved in military action against PLO forces the Israeli government spoke of them as 'terrorists', rather than dignifying them with the name Palestinians. Even as late as the mid-1980s its instinct was to pretend that as a distinct people the Palestinians did not exist.

What gradually forced the Israelis to change their attitude was, first, the cumulative effect of a change in the international view of the Palestinians. This began in the late 1960s at the start of the Palestinian terrorist campaign of 1969–73. The world may have been disgusted by the actions of the terrorist groups, but it was forced to acknowledge that there was such a people as the Palestinians. Then gradually, as it learnt more about their plight, the sympathies of the European intelligentsia began to move towards the Palestinians, and the harder the Israelis pounded the guerillas in Lebanon the more pronounced the shift became. In 1982, when the Israeli army invaded Lebanon and watched over the massacre of refugees in the Sabra and Chatilla camps by the Phalange militia, opinion in America began to shift slightly away from uncritical support of Israel. During all of this period the Palestinian national identity grew steadily more distinct. It seemed to thrive on the non-absorption of the people by other Arab countries, the actions of the guerillas and international publicity.

Then came the *intifadah*. This was a major embarrassment to Israel. It showed to the Israelis in the most unmistakable way that there were Palestinians living under their occupation who wanted a state of their own. And it showed the occupiers in a very bad light internationally. Instead of seeming to be a brave citizens' army confronting the Arab hordes, the Israeli Defence Force was shown as a powerful bully confronting Palestinian youths armed only with stones. In February 1988 there was, from the Israeli point of view, a particularly unfortunate episode when an American television crew filmed some soldiers systematically breaking the limbs of two Palestinian youths. This sort of cruelty not only lost the Israelis friends abroad, it was demoralizing for them at home. When Thomas Friedman, the *New York Times* correspondent in Jerusalem, asked an official of the Labour Party in the summer of that year what sort of moral challenge the *intifadah* was posing for the army, the reply was: 'If you ask me, the sooner the Palestinians return to terrorism the better it will be for us'.

The *intifadah* also turned the occupation of the West Bank and Gaza from a minorly profitable enterprise into a cost for Israel, albeit a small one. In its first year the uprising virtually killed the tourist business, caused the army to double the period of reserve duty required of men from thirty to sixty days, and helped lower the growth in the country's GDP from more than 5 per cent in 1987 to between 1 and 2 per cent. It did not, however, cause many Israeli deaths. In 1988 only eleven Israelis were killed, the equivalent of two weeks' deaths on the roads.

More important than the immediate, quantifiable cost was the effect the *intifadah* had in making Israelis reconsider whether the occupation of the territories would be of material or military benefit to them in the long term. From 1990 onwards they began to see that the money they were spending on policing the territories and building settlements was at the expense of investment in the domestic economy, which would stimulate growth and enable them profitably to absorb the Jews who were arriving from the Soviet Union. The immigrants were being provided with the usual basic welfare benefits given to new arrivals – temporary accommodation, a living allowance and training in Hebrew; but it was felt that at the next stage, when they were moving into Jewish society, their abilities were being wasted because the government did not have the money to invest in major new projects, particularly of a scientific nature. There were reports in the newspapers of physicists, some of them the best brains of the Soviet Union, only being able to find jobs serving tea. The government was also unable to provide the newcomers with good long-term housing. This led people to compare the benefits of building houses in Israel proper with building settlements on the West Bank, which seemed to appeal mainly to Jews with a 'Wild West' mentality (many of them American); these were occupied in many cases for only part of the time and were internationally controversial.

Once they had begun to consider the relative benefits of the West Bank settlements and the absorption of Russian Jews, the Israelis started to think about the broader advantages and disadvantages of holding the occupied territories. This raised the general question of whether Israel saw its future as a democratic state, living in only part of its Biblical territories but able to provide a home and a decent standard of living for Jews of the diaspora, or whether it was to dedicate itself to holding every bit of Eretz Israel, knowing that the population of the occupied territories was not going to leave – in fact was expanding fast – and had to be ruled by methods which ran against Jewish democratic tradition. It would be wrong to suggest that between 1990 and 1992 the thinking of the mass of the Israeli population swung decisively to the former scenario – even in 1993 there were many who felt uneasy at the prospect of giving up any territory – but there was certainly a drift of opinion in that direction. The change was reinforced by periodic episodes in which workers from the occupied territories, particularly Gaza, shot or stabbed Israeli citizens when they came across the border to work. After each killing there were popular demands for the government to 'kick the Arabs out of here', as rioters shouted when a fifteen-year-old girl was stabbed in May 1992. There was a big fall in the employment of Palestinians in Israel; the numbers of Gazans crossing the borders each day dropped from 100,000 before the *intifadah* to only 15,000 in 1993. And once people saw that they did not want, and were no longer getting, the benefit of cheap Arab labour, they inevitably found themselves having further doubts about keeping the land where the workers lived.

All these thoughts were made thinkable by a general lessening in the late 1980s and early 1990s of Israelis' fear of other Arab countries. By this time the peace agreement with Egypt had remained solid for a decade and the public had become aware that its government and King Hussein had agreed a framework for peace between their countries, which made the West Bank much less important as a buffer between Israel and potential enemies to the east. Just as the Palestinian leadership realized at this time that the Arab governments as a group had long given up on the idea of going to war with Israel, so in spite of its engrained insecurity, did the Israeli public. An idea was emerging that for the first time in the country's history there was a chance of virtually all the Arabs, including the Palestinians, accepting peace on Israeli terms, and that the country ought to seize it rather than subject another generation to the inevitability of war.

In 1991 the Israelis received another push in the direction of compromise from the American reaction to the Gulf crisis and the collapse of the Soviet Union. The Gulf crisis showed the Western world, and particularly the Americans, that there was a link between the unresolved problem of Palestine and the popular support that was given to bad, aggressive, anti-Western governments. Americans were struck by seeing on their televisions in August and September 1990 pictures of Palestinians in Amman and the West Bank demonstrating in support of Saddam

Hussein, particularly after the Iraqi leader linked the possibility of his pulling out of Kuwait to Israel's withdrawal from the occupied territories. The idea spread beyond specialist foreign affairs circles that the issue of Palestine helped give a form of legitimacy to regimes such as Saddam's. Then, in January 1991, when the crisis reached the stage of war, the Americans learnt another lesson. They and their Arab allies, particularly Saudi Arabia, were anxious that when Saddam launched missiles at Israel, which he seemed bound to do, the Israelis should not retaliate, thus making it appear that America and Saudi Arabia were associated with them in a campaign to destroy a 'patriotic' Arab leader. The American government therefore sent batteries of Patriot anti-missile missiles to Israel and undertook to protect it from whatever the Iraqis fired at it. They also sent, just before the 'air war' began, the Deputy Secretary of State, Lawrence Eagleburger, reasoning that his presence would make it doubly difficult for the Israelis to ignore their wishes. This constituted very heavy pressure on Israel, and it worked. The Israelis left the attacks on the Iraqi Scud batteries entirely to the coalition forces. Looking back on their diplomacy after the crisis the Americans saw that for the first time since the Eisenhower presidency they had employed the leverage they had on Israel, and the Israelis had taken notice.

Later in 1991 the collapse of the Soviet Union altered America's perception of the usefulness of Israel as a strategic ally in the Middle East. This idea had developed during the periods of the Nixon and Reagan administrations, when America had found it necessary to have spread around the world allies and bases which it would be able to use in the event of a confrontation with the Soviet Union. In Israel's case it was seen that the state could provide an important port for the Sixth Fleet, in Haifa, and might be useful in gathering intelligence and providing a link in America's communications network. With this there went some rather unclear thinking on how Israel might prevent Soviet subversion of pro-Western regimes in the Middle East and even help the spread of democracy. These were not valid ideas. The reality was that Israel, as the national enemy, had no positive influence at all on the Arabs. Its example was more likely to prevent them from moving towards democracy than encourage it. Even on the purely strategic and military levels the American-Israeli alliance was not as logical as it appeared. The Americans looked at it in the context of confrontation with the Soviet Union, which imposed on the Israelis a role with which they never felt easy, while the Israelis tried to portray it as a front against radical Arab regimes, which was not what the Americans intended. Both sides wanted the alliance but each was embarrassed by the other's interpretation of it. In practice it tended to work more to Israel's advantage than America's. The conflicts which arose in the 1980s and early 1990s, in Lebanon and the Gulf, were not global but regional, and in these the link with Israel was a hindrance to American diplomacy.

The practical result of the collapse of the Soviet Union and the American government's gradual reappraisal of its relationship with Israel, was that the US became less willing to give its ally financial help. There was no question of its reducing the $3 billion a year that it regularly gave, but it became reluctant to give supplementary assistance. In 1990 President Bush and his Secretary of State, James Baker, had been very annoyed to see that $400 million that had been given to Israel on the understanding that it would not be used for the construction of settlements had been used quite shamelessly for this purpose, and so in 1991 the President used his powers to veto a Congressional proposal that the US government provide Israel with a further $10 billion of loan guarantees for housing projects. Significantly, the America-Israel Public Affairs Committee (AIPAC), which had once been one of the most powerful lobby groups in Washington, did relatively little to try to influence the President, and opinion polls showed that a large majority of the American public approved of his decision.

The argument over the loan guarantees and the obvious change in America's strategic interests was much analysed in Israel. The conclusion that was drawn, as the adviser of a senior Israeli politician put it to me in 1992, was that 'the price of defying the US' was going to be higher than before. It seemed likely that in future more of America's aid, and possibly its willingness to provide the arms Israel wanted, would be made conditional on Israel pursuing policies of which America approved. Both the adviser and other political figures suggested that the American-Israeli relationship would have to go back to the more balanced cultural and strategic form it had taken in the 1950s and 1960s, when America's goodwill towards Israel was based as much on its being a democracy, and on its (apparent) observance of human rights, as on a perceived identity of strategic interests. If the relationship was to move back in this direction, it was suggested, Israel would probably have to show itself more responsive to America's peace proposals.

It was clear to the Americans in the spring of 1991, after the end of the Gulf war, that there was an opportunity for peace negotiations. In different ways both the Palestinians and Israelis were feeling vulnerable, and in this mood it was thought they might be persuaded to compromise. Nor was it only they whose attitudes had changed. The war had altered the politics of the region. The extremists, led by Iraq, had been humiliated, and Syria, the one hard-line regime that had joined the anti-Iraq coalition, mainly because Hafez Assad loathed Saddam Hussein, had been neutralized by the mere fact that it had done this. The Arab moderates had found themselves on the same side as the Israelis, which is where the Americans had always thought, rather naïvely, they ought to be. Many of the moderate governments, and many of their people, had never had any direct quarrel with Israel and the war made it possible for them to acknowledge this. I heard views of this sort put forward during and soon after the war in Saudi Arabia, the United Arab Emirates, Kuwait and Tunisia. The crisis certainly made the peoples of the Arabian peninsula oil states realize that Iraq was a much greater threat to them than Israel had ever been. Its effect was to make it possible for moderate Arab governments to talk to the Israelis without being frightened of the extremists.

Encouraged by these developments, James Baker undertook a series of trips to the Middle East to try to arrange a peace conference. He received some early encouragement in April, when the Saudis and the Gulf states said they would participate, and during the next few months he managed to persuade the Syrians to attend. This, in turn, forced the hands of the Israelis, who initially had rejected the idea. By the late summer the Americans were proposing two parallel series of negotiations. One, which came to be known as the 'Multilateral' talks, involved the moderate Arab states, together with the Palestinians and, in most cases, the Israelis, meeting in specialist groups to discuss five issues which were of obvious importance to the whole region: the environment, water, regional security and arms control, economic development and refugees. The groups discussing the last two of these topics the Israelis at first boycotted, because they held that the Palestinian delegates to them were too overtly connected with the PLO. The purpose of the talks, which were to take place in different capitals around the world, was not only to promote co-operation on the matters they were addressing directly, but to show both sides that 'the other people didn't have horns', as a Western diplomat put it, and to give cover and legitimacy to the talks that the front-line states would be holding on making peace. It was reasoned that if almost all the Arab countries could be involved in the 'multilaterals' – as they were, with the exceptions of Sudan, Iraq and Libya – they would not be able to criticize the combatants for talking to Israel.

The other series of meetings, which was more immediately important, was to be conducted on a bilateral Israeli-Arab basis. It involved Israel negotiating with Syria, Lebanon (whose delegation was under the close supervision of the Syrians) and a joint Jordanian-Palestinian delegation, which had two separate and independent components. It was, predictably, the composition of the last of these delegations that caused most problems in the months before the meetings began. Neither the Israelis, nor the Americans since the terrorist operation on the Israeli coast in June 1990, would talk directly to the PLO in Tunis, which meant that the Palestinian delegation had to be made up of people who lived in the occupied territories. The Israelis insisted, further, that it should attend the conference under the auspices of Jordan, because they did not want to imply at the start that they accepted the Palestinians as a distinct people. And in the early stages of their bargaining with the Americans they insisted that the delegation should include nobody in east Jerusalem, which they had annexed in 1967. Later they relented, unofficially, and allowed four Jerusalemites to be included in the 'Executive Office', which was formed to support and guide the delegation. The four were Faisal Husseini, whose father had been one of the principal Palestinian leaders in 1948, Hanan Ashrawi, Sari Nusseibeh and Zahira Kamal. They became prominent members of the Palestinian team and spoke on its behalf to the international media.

The main part of the Palestinian delegation, which was to sit opposite the Israelis in talks, was made up of fourteen permanent 'negotiators', led by a doctor from Gaza, Haidar Abdel-Shafi. With it came several dozen other delegates, who did not take part in negotiations and had no useful supporting expertise. They were included in the delegation, and changed in every round of negotiations, simply so that every village could be satisfied that it had been represented.

The loyalties of the delegation were ambiguous. The more important members were local notables who had been chosen by a process of consultation among the community leaders in the occupied territories. They all came from major families and they represented a careful balance between regions, Muslims and Christians and the sympathizers of different PLO factions. Officially they were not 'members' of the PLO but everybody knew they had connections with it. They were all approved by it and claimed to be taking their instructions from it. They proclaimed their loyalty to it in order to win themselves the backing of their people in the territories and abroad and to show they had been able to defy one of the Israelis' conditions for holding the conference. But from the beginning there was speculation as to whether they might not have ambitions of their own to supplant the PLO. It was because they were as aware as anybody else of this that the Israelis were happy

to negotiate with people who made such a point of emphasising
their connections with the Organization. They hoped, and believed,
that the delegates were protesting too much their loyalty to the
PLO.

The bilateral talks were finally begun in Madrid in late October 1991,
and further rounds later that year and in 1992 were held in Washington.
They made slow progress. In some important ways the Palestinians
proved themselves to be shrewd. In dealing with the media they kept their
connections with the PLO in the background and pushed forward the
extremely articulate Hanan Ashrawi as their spokeswoman. At an early
stage they introduced what for the Israelis was the embarrassing issue
of the 'right of return' of the refugees, which was encapsulated in UN
Resolution 194 of 1948. They were good at wrong-footing the Israelis in
front of international public opinion, which was something the PLO in
the 1970s and early 1980s had never been able to do.

Yet in the negotiations themselves the Palestinian delegation was
ineffective. It looked to the Americans to work on its behalf. Its
members felt, as their people had always done, that they were powerless
before the Israelis, and they thought that their enemy would only give
ground if it was forced to by the Americans. It therefore seemed to
them pointless to argue about agendas or forms of interim self-
government, when they believed that the eventual aim of the negotiations was to agree the outline of some form of Palestinian state or
Jordanian-Palestinian confederation, which is what the Americans had
envisaged since the time of the Camp David accords in 1978.* It seemed
to them most sensible that America, the country which in their view
controlled the region, should work out what it wanted and then impose
it on all the parties.

In so far as the Palestinians were willing to negotiate at all they
referred immediately to two preconditions, which were that there
should be a freeze on settlements in the territories and a military with-

---

* The Camp David Framework for Peace in the Middle East, which accompanied the
Egyptian-Israeli peace treaty, specified the following: the governments of Egypt, Jordan
and Israel should negotiate the establishment of an elected self-governing Palestinian
authority for the West Bank and Gaza. Once the authority was in place Israeli armed
forces and the military administration would be withdrawn and a five-year transitional
period would begin. Within the next three years negotiations between Israel, Egypt,
Jordan and the elected Palestinian representatives should begin to determine the final
status of the territories. What the Americans envisaged coming out of these negotiations
was either a form of Palestinian state, with restricted sovereignty as far as security
matters were concerned, or a Palestinian-Jordanian confederation. These principles
have guided American peace initiatives in the Middle East from 1978 onwards.

drawal from the centres of population, and once these were granted, they said, they would talk about more detailed questions. They were deaf to American suggestions that their most effective tactic would be to engage the other side on small practical matters of self-government and through winning 'a point here and a point there' build their own self-confidence, weaken the Israelis' stand and gradually force them to make some important concessions. They had several opportunities to adopt this approach. At one stage the Israelis proposed that as an initial step towards self-government they might turn over to the Palestinians authority for collecting taxes in the occupied territories. This might have been of considerable benefit to the people living there because the tax burden on them was heavy and unfair, in that they started to be taxed at lower income levels than the Israelis. The system had long been a major cause of Palestinian resentment. The Israeli delegation was not actually suggesting that the Palestinians should be empowered to set new tax rates, but it should have been obvious to all parties that once they got authority for collection they would be in a good position to bargain over rate adjustments. The Palestinians, however, refused to discuss the matter at all, until their preconditions were met.

The reason for the Palestinians' inability to negotiate was not just a combination of temperament and ignorance of the ways of international conferences, it was also that they were disorganized. Their leaders could not delegate. It is not part of Arab culture for leaders to delegate. They do not trust their subordinates and they have a compulsive need to maintain control of whatever is happening around them. Their habits are part of the Arab tendency to think of personalities as being 'real' and important and institutions, such as committees and sub-groups in negotiating teams, as being unimportant. In this case their instincts made the Palestinians incapable of working out detailed policies or producing position papers on the various subjects that were raised by the Israelis and the Americans. The leaders of their delegation said that they were establishing committees to do this work – they could draw members from the vast PLO bureaucracy in Tunis and the thirty-seven academic societies in Jerusalem – but the only document they actually produced in the first six months of negotiations was a fifteen-page blueprint for a Palestinian Interim Self-Government Arrangement, which outlined how they might eventually achieve an independent administration. When they saw that the paper and their inflexible approach to the negotiations were not producing results they became even more stubborn. They went back to hoping that they would be saved by some external event, such as the Labour Party winning the

Israeli elections in June 1992 or President Bush being re-elected in November.

The most useful product of the negotiations was that, together with the multilateral talks which began early in 1992, they broke the psychological barrier that separated the Arabs and Israelis. The two sides seemed surprised to find themselves talking to each other, but on a personal level they got on remarkably well, far better than the Israelis and the normally easygoing Egyptians had got on in the early months of the Sadat initiative in 1977 and 1978. Part of the reason must have been simply that because the Palestinians in the occupied territories had been living under Israeli administration for more than twenty years they had come to know their rulers and their way of thinking quite well. Some of the academics on both sides had already met many times at small conferences and seminars in Jerusalem. The multilateral talks, in particular, increased these types of contacts. Palestinians from the occupied territories and Western universities, where some were teaching, went away from the meetings to write papers and then found themselves discussing them with their Israeli opposite numbers when they met at the next round of talks. A number of parallel conferences were held outside the official series of meetings. In the autumn of 1992 a conference of Arab and Israeli women took place in Madrid. Arabs and Israelis met again at international academic conferences which had nothing to do with the peace process but were concerned with the Middle East in general. There were even the beginnings of Arab-Israeli friendships. An American official told me that he was ushering a Syrian out of his office in Washington in the summer of 1992 when they met an Israeli who had just arrived for his next appointment. The two turned out to know each other from a parallel conference that had been held a few weeks earlier, and they stood in the official's door and talked for twenty minutes. The outcome of the whole mass of contacts, official and unofficial, was to produce what a British diplomat referred to as 'a complex architecture of Arab-Israeli connections: a structure that will not easily be demolished'.

In June 1992 one of the events for which the Palestinians had been hoping happened. The Labour Party won the Israeli election. The main reason for this lay in changes in the internal social politics of Israel, which caused the right-wing Likud Party, which had formed most of the country's governments since 1977, to lose the votes of some of the working and lower middle classes. These people, or their parents, were mostly Oriental and Sephardic Jews who had come to Israel from Egypt, Yemen, Iraq and Morocco in the big 'in-gathering' that followed the foundation of the state, in the late 1940s and early 1950s.* They were different from the Ashkenazi Jews, who had come from Europe to work on the early kibbutzim and establish the independent state. They were less educated and they did not share the Ashkenazis' European culture or their pioneering European socialism. When they arrived they were put in camps and then sent to development towns on the northern frontier and the Negev desert, places which the government wanted to be settled but where most of the European Jews did not wish to go. The development towns acquired something of the character of working-class ghettos. Their inhabitants, many of whom worked on kibbutzim as day labourers, did not feel a great affinity for what was seen in the 1950s and 1960s as the European, liberal, Labour Party establishment. They were a potentially powerful body of voters waiting to be won over to an opposition party. In the elections of 1977 the Likud, then led by Menachem Begin, realized their potential, courted them, won the election and became the dominant government for the next sixteen years.

What happened in 1992 was that a proportion of the Oriental and Sephardic Jews switched their loyalties to the Labour Party, which from the point of view of its economic philosophy should have been their natural party from the beginning. The economy was in a bad recession, unemployment was at a record high and a connection had become established in people's minds between the money that Likud was spending in the occupied territories and the lack of stimulus being given to the economy in Israel proper. The *intifadah* was making people start to think of the territories as a cost. The Labour Party wisely put forward Yitzhak Rabin, who had been Chief of Staff during the Six Day War, as its candidate for Prime Minister, which calmed the fears of all parts of the electorate that it might not be as sound on security matters as Likud. Given the perception that the country was under pressure from America, for instance in President Bush's refusal to agree the loan guarantees, and that the Arab nations were becoming less of a threat, the electorate was slightly more inclined than it had been four years earlier to vote for a party that was prepared to be flexible in searching for peace. The Labour Party was putting forward a policy on the occupied territories that was based on the Camp David accords, though it was being carefully vague about what arrangements it envisaged for the eventual form of a West Bank state. Likud, in contrast, was proposing

---

* Sephardic Jews are those who were expelled from southern Spain by the Castilians in 1492 and settled in Morocco. The name is often used loosely to refer to all North African and Middle Eastern Jews.

very limited self-rule for the Palestinians, the continuation of Israeli settlement, and no firm definition of the territory that might be included in the autonomous Palestinian area. Yitzhak Shamir, the Prime Minister, was emotionally unable to compromise on these issues. He believed in Eretz Israel and in the strength of the national will, embodied in his office, and he felt that if he surrendered any of the homeland he would be betraying the trust his people had put in him.

In the event the greater flexibility and more credible economic policies of Labour were enough to make it the biggest single party in the Knesset. It won 44 seats. The left-wing Meretz group won twelve, the Israeli Arabs five, and the religious parties, which generally have to ally themselves with governments because their colleges depend on state funding, sixteen. With these 'allies' Labour was able to form a coalition government, though given the permanently shifting nature of Israeli politics, on difficult issues it could not be sure of commanding more than a small majority of the 120 members of the Knesset.

Yitzhak Rabin clearly wanted to move towards a peace settlement for the same reasons that had caused Israelis to vote for him, and because he feared that if he waited the resurgence of the Islamic right, represented by Hamas, would make the Arabs less flexible. At an early stage in his government, in August, he agreed to talk officially and openly to the PLO, because he saw that the old rule banning talks, which had been made into a law in 1986, was obviously being disregarded and had become an embarrassment. But then the Prime Minister became very cautious, and extremely tough in all dealings with the Palestinians. In December, after a spate of killings of Israeli soldiers, he deported 418 Islamic militants, dumped them on the northern side of the Lebanese border and refused to allow them to return. His action caused a four-month break in the bilateral talks. In March 1993, in response to a series of stabbings, he sealed off the occupied territories. In July, provoked by attacks on Israel's security zone, he bombarded southern Lebanon for a week. The reaction to his policies of those diplomats and academics, American, European and Arab, who were involved in the bilateral and multilateral meetings was one of disappointment. There was much talk, and many newspaper articles were written, about how Israel had 'voted Labour' but still 'thought Likud'. It was suggested that Rabin was not the de Gaulle or de Klerk it had been hoped he would be. But, in view of what later became known had been happening in the government's contacts with the PLO, it may have been, during the spring and summer of 1993, that Rabin was showing toughness in order later to be able to compromise.

18

Peace

*Isolation of Arafat – Norway talks – peace framework –
problems of implementation – divisions among the Palestinians
– fear of 'insiders' – prospects for peace with Jordan and Syria
– multilateral talks – Israel's hopes of integrating itself in the
Middle East*

During 1992, as the bilateral and multilateral talks slowly progressed, Yasser Arafat in Tunis felt isolated and worried. Faisal Husseini and the other leading figures in the Palestinian negotiating team were becoming increasingly prominent in both Arab and international eyes. They had the advantage of knowing the Israelis and the people of the occupied territories at first hand. They were more articulate than the old exiled PLO leadership and they had no association with terrorism. For the American and Israeli governments they represented a thoroughly desirable new type of Palestinian politician. There was no doubt that these and other foreign governments hoped to be able to promote them, and from occasional remarks they themselves made to diplomats involved on the fringes of the talks, it seemed they had ambitions of their own. For the time being they did not question that they needed Arafat's endorsement to make them legitimate as representatives of the Palestinian people, but if in the end it was to be they who won autonomy and independence for the occupied territories, and the terms of that independence were accepted by the people, it would be they who would become the legitimate leaders. In that case they would most probably replace the PLO Chairman and run the new Palestinian government themselves.

Arafat's lack of money put further pressure on him. Since August

1990 he had had no income from the Gulf and for ten years his followers had gone without the pickings from bribery and extortion they
had enjoyed in Beirut. Like any other Arab leader, Arafat had to be
able to reward the people around him, and when he could not do this
he found that his less committed followers in the PLO bureaucracy
were beginning to drift away. The Organization as a political force was
fading.

In January 1993, therefore, Arafat leapt at an opportunity for beginning his own talks with the Israelis. It came about through the efforts
of Terje Rød Larsen, a member of a Norwegian labour institute, who
was working in Gaza and had been struck by the obvious desire for
peace of most of the Arabs and Israelis he met. Larsen had introduced
some of his Arab and Israeli friends to each other and managed to
establish a good personal rapport, and trust, between them. He and
his friends had contacted people in their own governments and the PLO
to bring more senior people into the discussions and in due course these
contacts led to members of the Israeli Foreign Ministry arranging to
meet some PLO officials in Norway, under the auspices of the Norwegian Foreign Ministry. On the Israeli side were a handful of officials
close to the Foreign Minister, Shimon Peres, including his deputy, Yossi
Beilin, and his personal adviser, Nimrod Novik. The Palestinians were
represented by Mahmoud Abbas, the head of the PLO's Pan-Arab and
International Section, and Abu Ala, the head of its Economics Section,
both of whom were known as moderates and staunch Arafat loyalists.
A small group of Norwegian officials was led by the country's Foreign
Minister, Johan Joergen Holst. Between January and August 1993 the
team held fourteen rounds of meetings on Norwegian farms and in
private houses. The process was kept extremely secret. In Israel only a
handful of people at the top of the government were aware of it. Yitzhak
Rabin in the early stages was not very interested in it, because he did
not expect it to yield results. The people involved on both sides in the
bilateral talks in Washington were kept completely in the dark. What
proved to be the decisive point for the secret talks came after the end
of the tenth round of the bilaterals in June, when Rabin began to realize
that the PLO in Tunis might be more anxious to strike a deal than
the leaders from inside the territories. At this point his attention
became focused on the Norwegian talks, though he decided to keep the
bilateral negotiations going, in case the new initiative failed or was
exposed.

By the end of August the two sides had the outline of an agreement
and announced their achievement to the world. On 9 September they
formally recognized each other. Rabin sent a letter to Arafat in which

he said that 'the government of Israel has decided to recognize the PLO as the representative of the Palestinian people', and Arafat sent two letters to Rabin. One committed the PLO to recognizing Israel's right to exist in peace and security, to the peaceful settlement of all future conflicts and to the renunciation of terrorism and violence; the other pledged that he would call on the Palestinians in the occupied territories to suspend the *intifadah*. Then on 13 September in Washington Shimon Peres and Mahmoud Abbas, watched by the two leaders, signed the famous 'Declaration of Principles', which outlined the sequence of steps for concluding a formal settlement.

The Declaration was modelled very closely on the framework that had been incorporated in the Camp David accords fifteen years earlier. It provided for an interim five-year period of Palestinian self-rule and then a permanent settlement between Israel and a Palestinian state in the West Bank and Gaza. The first practical step towards implementing the agreement was to be a withdrawal of Israeli troops from the Gaza Strip and a small area of about a 100 square kilometres around Jericho, which is the Palestinian town closest to the Jordan river. This was to begin on 13 December, three months after the signing, and be completed exactly four months later, in April 1994, when Israel would transfer powers of government in these areas from its Civil Administration to a 'nominated Palestinian authority'. The protocol to be negotiated by 13 December, in order to make the withdrawal possible, had to include arrangements for: the assumption of responsibility for internal security and public order by a Palestinian police force, which would include Egyptian and Jordanian passport holders; a temporary international or foreign presence; co-operation at border posts between Gaza and Egypt, and Jericho and Jordan; and an economic development and stabilization programme, which would incorporate an emergency fund and plans for foreign development assistance.

After the first, quite ambitious, steps had been negotiated and completed, it was agreed that there would be 'free and general' elections for a Palestinian Council, to be held on 13 July 1994, and that by the eve of these elections Israeli forces would have withdrawn from populated areas in all the occupied territories. Once elected the Council would take over from the 'nominated Palestinian authority' responsibility for education, culture, health, social welfare, direct taxation, tourism and the police force. It would establish a Palestinian electricity company, a Gaza port authority, a development bank, an export promotion board and agencies for the environment, land and water. Specifically excluded from the Council's remit were jurisdiction over east Jerusalem, though it was agreed that Palestinians from the city would be allowed to vote in the elections. Also excluded were authority over Israeli settlements in the territories, defence and foreign relations with neighbouring states. As the Palestinian Council took over the administration of its region the Civil Administration was to be disbanded.

The last stages set out in the 'Declaration of Principles' were to begin not later than 13 February 1996, by which date Israel and the Palestinians had to have started negotiations on a permanent settlement. This was to resolve all the remaining issues concerned with Palestinian statehood, including the status of east Jerusalem, refugees, the Israeli settlements, defence and borders. The final settlement was to come into force by 13 February 1999.

The signing of the Declaration of Principles did not in itself end the Arab-Israeli conflict, but, as several writers and politicians said at the time, it marked the beginning of the end game. The new phase in the story seemed likely to be as difficult and eventful as every previous one had been.

The implementation of the Principles was clearly going to lead to much tough bargaining and even bloodshed, and many temporary reverses. It seemed probable that there would be violence between the PLO and Hamas, possibly leading to the PLO, in co-operation with the Israelis and aided by Arab governments, trying to eliminate Hamas. There was also the prospect of an upheaval within the PLO, stemming from tension between the 'insider' and 'outsider' leaderships and quite likely involving the replacement of Yasser Arafat and the exiled leaders by people who lived in the territories. And at some point it was taken for granted that the other Arab countries, led by Jordan and, when the right moment came, Syria, would make their own peace agreements with Israel. Then Israel would redouble its efforts to do what it had been trying to do through the multilateral talks, which was to integrate itself into what it imagined was 'the Middle Eastern economy' and have itself accepted as a natural part of the region.

The different parties began manœuvrings in all these areas as soon as the Declaration was made public. Within days Palestinian and Israeli officials were striking negotiating poses to define their positions on a permanent settlement. The three obviously difficult issues concerned Jerusalem, the Israeli settlements in the West Bank and Gaza and the Palestinian refugees' rights of return.

On the first of these matters the Israelis' position was that Jerusalem had to remain their capital and be entirely under their sovereignty, the reasons being that the Jewish, as well as the Christian and Muslim, holy places were in east Jerusalem and that through a rigorous process of building (and demolition) and settlement since 1967 they had managed to make east as well as west Jerusalem predominantly Jewish. Within these limits they said they would be happy to discuss some form of connection between the city and the eventual Palestinian state. This would be made necessary by the fact that east Jerusalem contained the Al-Aqsa Mosque, which is the third holiest place in the Muslim world, and was the home of a substantial Palestinian population which included a large part of the West Bank leadership. It had also been the capital of Palestine. The likely area of difficulty in negotiations over the city concerned the potential for the Israelis feeling that the proposed links between Jerusalem and a Palestinian state would impinge on their sovereignty.

On the issue of settlements in the territories the Israelis' initial stance was more uncompromising. On the very day the Declaration of Principles was signed, Yitzhak Rabin in Washington stated that no settlements would be uprooted and that the settlers would remain under Israeli and not Palestinian authority. He had to adopt this position because he needed to reduce the opposition of his own right wingers to the peace deal. In the longer term, though, it looked as if the Israelis would have to compromise. They understandably did not want to cede authority over their settlements to the Palestinians, and the settlers themselves said they would never leave; yet once the government had decided to withdraw from the occupation and abandon the idea of creating Eretz Israel, much of the purpose of the settlements disappeared. Some of them might still be strategically useful, but they were no longer important to the state in a religious or cultural sense. For the Palestinians, the idea of their having on their territory a large number of foreign settlements that were outside their jurisdiction was obviously unacceptable. A plausible way out of this deadlock, it was suggested, would be for the settlers, or most of them, to leave their new homes in return for a substantial sum in compensation, which no doubt all parties would expect to be provided by America, Europe and the Arabian Peninsula oil states.

The third foreseeable problem, concerning the right of return of the Palestinian refugees, was the one that lay furthest in the future. During 1992, with the intention of embarrassing the Israelis, the Palestinian negotiators had raised the issue of all the people who had left the country since 1948 being given the right to return, as Count Bernadotte had proposed a few months after the creation of Israel, but for practical purposes it was accepted by all sides that in the short term the individuals who might be allowed back would only be those who had been evicted relatively recently. It seemed possible that the two sides would agree that during the five-year period of autonomy permission would be given for the return of people who had fled the West Bank when the Israeli army occupied it in 1967 or been deported during the occupation. What looked much more difficult, for either the interim period or later, was the return of the 1948 refugees, both those in camps and those integrated into other Arab populations. One problem, from the Israelis' point of view, was that the return of a large number of Palestinians to the West Bank and Gaza would increase the potential military threat they might face from those areas. A large population of returnees might enable a Palestinian state – if it were to ignore the demilitarization clauses that would certainly be built into its constitution – to build a bigger army. It would also be bound to create tension between Israel and its new neighbour by producing a demand by the returnees that they be allowed to take one further step back to their original homes in Israel. Officials said informally that their fears on these matters would be much reduced if the new Palestinian state were linked in a confederation with Jordan. Then the movement of Palestinians, from whatever towns or villages they originally came, would naturally be permitted between the west and east banks of the river, but it was assumed that the Jordanians would be able to control any aggressive instincts the new state had. And the fact that the Palestinians would have a relatively large state as a home would limit the force of their demand to be allowed back into Israel.

At every stage in negotiations the Israelis were utterly determined to oppose any idea of Palestinians being allowed to return to their state, but, equally, it was difficult to imagine the Palestinians at some point in the interim period not raising this possibility. And even if they did not raise it, or it was raised in negotiations and brushed aside, it was hard to see them not raising it again in the future, as a demand for the accepted right of a person to live in the home where he was, or his parents were, born.

On every one of these issues it seemed certain that negotiations would be long and difficult and that the Israelis would only give ground with great reluctance. The Israelis have always been extremely careful and unyielding negotiators. The reason has been partly that in spite of their military victories they always feel threatened. Over the last two decades, as they have discussed the Holocaust more openly and been less preoccupied with the immediate challenges of building a new state, their consciousness of their tragic past has not faded. If anything, it has become more acute. Reinforcing their reluctance to make concessions in the early 1990s was the knowledge that they were in an extremely strong negotiating position, that the Palestinians were supplicants and that they did not have to give very much. Yitzhak Rabin in particular was made more intransigent by his belief that the tougher he was in the implementation talks the more he would win over the hardliners in his population to the general idea of a peace based on compromise.

It seemed inevitable that most of the deadlines for the different stages of implementation set in the Declaration of Principles would be missed, because, as the Israeli Deputy Foreign Minister remarked in December, it simply would not always be possible for both sides to agree on all the issues that had to be negotiated by each specified date. This is exactly what happened in the first three months of implementation, when the Israelis missed the target date, 13 December 1993, for beginning the withdrawal of their forces from Gaza and Jericho. In this case negotiations had been bedevilled by arguments over the control of roads used by the 5,000 Israeli settlers in the Gaza Strip, the joint policing of the border crossing into Egypt, and the Israelis insisting on only 'redeploying' some of their troops in the area rather than withdrawing them.

In further rounds of negotiations there was potential for matters being equally obstructed by the Palestinians. It seemed likely that when under pressure, and finding themselves lacking bargaining counters of their own, the Palestinians would simply refuse to compromise and, as so often before, turn to the United States for help. They also seemed bound to be hampered by their own internal divisions, which would prevent Arafat being able to make what he might consider worthwhile concessions, for fear of exposing himself to attack from his enemies. The problem for the PLO leader was that the Palestinian opponents of the peace agreement were much more vociferous, powerful and violent than the Israeli opponents.

Most of the people of Gaza and the West Bank – about 60–65 per cent – were jubilant in early September when they heard news of the talks in Norway and discovered that in the near future they were going to be given a degree of independence. The Palestinian flag, which the Israelis had banned, suddenly appeared everywhere. Cheering crowds came out on to the streets, posters of Arafat were carried through east Jerusalem and journalists were able to report, completely truthfully, that people were 'dancing on the rooftops'. But not everybody was happy. There were riots in some of the towns and camps in the West Bank from which the Israeli army was not to be withdrawn straight away. In Damascus ten Palestinian factions, from both the left and the Islamic right, formally declared themselves against the deal. In Sidon and other towns in Lebanon, where Palestinians at last had proof that

Arafat was abandoning their claim to their homes in Israel, the Chairman's picture was publicly burned.

The most dangerous opposition came from Hamas, the one dissenting group which was in a position to try to destroy the peace agreement by force. As soon as it heard the news of the deal it said that Arafat had no right to concede to the Israelis any part of Palestine, because the land belonged to all Muslims. This was a reference to its containing the Al-Aqsa Mosque. It had two further reasons for wanting to continue the struggle. One was ideological, in that it saw the Zionist state as a Western intrusion into the Arab world and a source of Arab humiliation. The other was a matter of realpolitik. Hamas was the rival of the PLO and it was aware that any success for the Organization would be a blow to its own prospects of expanding its support in the territories and, ultimately, according to the dreams of its leaders, bringing about an Islamic revolution there. It guessed, further, that if the peace settlement held it would lead to the PLO and the Israelis cooperating to crush it, which would be a disaster not only for its own leaders but for the prospects of the Islamic revolutionary movement as a whole. A peaceful Palestine, accepted by the majority of its people, would remove one of the principal causes of the Arabs' sense of failure and, therefore, of their rallying to Islamic political parties. Hamas's reaction to the signing of the Declaration in Washington, therefore, was prompt and callous. It quickly shot and killed three Israeli soldiers in Gaza and organized some of the worst riots and tyre burnings that had been seen since the early days of the *intifadah*. In November the Israelis killed two of the principal Hamas leaders in Gaza, which must have been convenient for the PLO as well as themselves. It was expected that the campaign against Hamas would be continued.

Just as Hamas was waiting to exploit any mistakes or over-generous concessions that Arafat made, so, it seemed, was the 'insider' leadership. By mid-December several of the people who had been prominent in the Palestinian team at the bilateral talks, including Dr Haidar Abdel-Shafi and Hanan Ashrawi, were making quite open and direct criticisms of the PLO Chairman. Their remarks reflected not only their irritation at his having failed to negotiate the beginning of the Israeli withdrawal by 13 December, but a general tension that existed between the insiders and the external representatives of the PLO.

The PLO officials and the community leaders of the Palestinians inside the territories represented different political worlds. The PLO had very much the character of one of the less attractive Arab governments. Many of its officials were corrupt and rich. Arab and foreign businessmen who dealt with them in the months after the Declaration found that their ideas on how ministries of finance and central banks were run were primitive and dubious. In their conversations with potential European aid donors they seemed to think that governments financing the development projects they needed, for a port and electricity supply, would simply pay their money into an account controlled by Yasser Arafat and allow him and his supporters to use it as they liked. Some of the well-educated, honest, young Palestinian economists in Jerusalem were equally surprised by the Organization's approach to money and government.

There was further nervousness about what appeared to be the PLO's political attitudes. Its officials claimed they were democratic, because they had to deal with so many factions in their organization, but in reality they were not so much democrats as accomplished political wheeler-dealers. Even this apparent talent for compromise was marred from time to time by their resorting to violence to settle their internal disputes. The prospect of their arriving to administer the occupied territories caused many of the people there to think more carefully than they had done before about their liberators and realize that their natural instinct might be to crush all opposition, whether it came from Hamas, the radical left or any embarrassing and argumentative liberals they encountered. As early as October there were threats from the PLO that radicals obstructing its government in Jericho and Gaza might have to be imprisoned, and this caused some people in the territories to say that if these statements were representative of PLO policy they might be happier living under the Israelis.

To set against these doubts and criticisms, Arafat still had the prestige of having led the PLO and been the symbol of the Palestinians' hopes of independence for a quarter of a century. He also seemed to have just enough money to pay the people who were really important to him. In the autumn of 1993 it appeared that those people in the West Bank and Gaza – mayors and other community leaders – who supported Arafat and the Declaration of Principles still had PLO incomes and even a little money to distribute. This was important, because although people commonly spoke of there being two groups of Palestinians, insiders and outsiders, the reality was that society in the territories was infinitely fragmented, which gave Arafat an opportunity to influence people's loyalty with money. Many Palestinians said that even those who appeared to foreigners to be the most honest and idealistic leaders of the insiders were in the pay of either Arafat or the Israelis. They were saying that it was quite likely that Arafat would be able to buy his way into his new state.

People with less cynical views – or the same commentators in differ-

ent moods – were suggesting that Arafat's days were numbered. It
was observed that in the months after the signing of the Principles in
Washington he was holding on to all the reins of organization himself,
just as a guerilla leader might, but in a way which was completely
inappropriate for a person engaged in a complex series of negotiations
and the establishment of an autonomous government. Even more than
other Arab leaders he had a horror of giving away authority. He was
criticized for having given a lot for his peace deal and getting little in
return. There were further murmurings that he was getting quite old;
he was in his mid-sixties. Even though he had married, for the first
time, less than two years earlier – he had previously claimed that his
bride was Palestine – he had the manner and appearance of a man of
his age and was beginning to be classed with all the other ageing Arab
leaders whom the people felt they had known for too long. It seemed
quite possible, therefore, that within the next two or three years he
would be eased aside. Then he would be seen as the guerilla leader
who had kept the Palestinian flag flying during his people's blackest
days but who, sadly but inevitably, had not been the man to lead the
independent state.

There were further series of difficulties to be overcome in Israel making
peace with its Arab neighbours, Jordan and Syria. In Jordan's case the
conclusion of a treaty, on its own, seemed to be straightforward. A
draft deal, sometimes referred to as an 'agenda' for final discussions,
was agreed in October 1992, at the seventh round of the bilateral talks,
and initialled on 14 September 1993, one day after the Declaration of
Principles was signed in Washington. It was understood that apart from
formally making peace between the two countries, it concerned water
rights, minor border issues south of the Dead Sea and the entitlement
of refugees to Jordanian passports. Its final signature awaited only
substantial progress in the implementation of the Israeli-Palestinian
Declaration, so that Jordan would not appear to be making a peace of
its own too hastily.

   What was more complicated was the question that might arise when
the Israelis and Palestinians began talks on a final settlement, of whether
Jordan might be linked to an eventual Palestinian state in some form
of confederation. This idea was very much part of the thinking of all
the protagonists in the late 1980s. It was made possible, paradoxically,
by King Hussein on 31 July 1988 declaring that he no longer claimed
the West Bank as part of his own territory. In effect he was saying that
he recognized the right of the PLO to have its own state there, and this
made it possible thereafter for Jordan and the Organization to deal

with each other without having a sense of conflicting aspirations. It made the PLO leaders feel that if they were ever to achieve a West Bank state they would be able to enjoy some of the practical advantages that a link with Jordan might bring without surrendering their sovereignty. The assumed benefits of a confederation were that it would reassure the Israelis, on the issues of security and the return of refugees, and that it would stimulate the West Bank economy by giving it a bigger domestic market and helping its exports.

After the 1991 peace initiative and the emergence of the insider leaderships the idea of a confederation faded, though none of the parties involved made any formal statement against it. The reasons were simply that the Palestinians seemed to be making progress in concluding a settlement with Israel on their own, and in recent years had become less well disposed towards Jordan because it had been obstructing any West Bank exports that competed with its own produce. The one influence which it was thought might revive the confederation plan would be pressure from the United States, and whether or not that would be brought to bear would depend on how the talks on a final settlement progressed.

The conclusion of a peace with Syria was a more serious and politically sensitive issue for the Israelis. Syria had been their most implacable enemy and, after the end of the Gulf crisis, was the one Arab country which remained in a state of war with them and had armed forces which were both large and intact. Yet in spite of their bitter and engrained hostility, in the spring of 1992, nearly a year after President Assad had accepted President Bush's invitation to the bilateral talks, the two sides were getting near to doing a deal. The Israeli government had long pursued a policy of dividing the Arabs whenever possible, and in the view of Yitzhak Shamir's administration at this time it seemed that its interests might best be served by its making peace with Syria and so isolating and weakening the PLO. Much as it hated Syria it could see that removing that state from the conflict would allow a better chance of keeping the West Bank and creating Eretz Israel. The Syrian government likewise had reasons for concluding peace. It had lost the support of its military backer when the Soviet Union collapsed at the end of 1991 and it was under pressure from the United States, which had become the predominant power in the region. In President Assad's view, if the PLO was being drawn into negotiations and the political climate in the Arab world was swinging in favour of peace with Israel, there was no major issue of principle to prevent him making a peace of his own and getting back the Golan Heights.

Accordingly the Israelis and Syrians, assisted by the Americans, mapped out a peace agreement. It specified that Israel would withdraw from Golan, though that area would be demilitarized and the Israelis would be allowed to keep their listening facilities there, possibly being manned by Americans. Israel would also withdraw from its self-declared security zone in Lebanon, provided the PLO and Syria undertook to curtail attacks on its northern border areas by the Shia militia, Hizbollah. This framework for a deal was not affected by the victory of Labour in the June 1992 election. In the early summer of the following year it was still thought that all that stood in the way of a peace agreement being completed were some relatively small and technical matters concerning what for Syria would constitute full Israeli withdrawal along its northern borders and what for Israel would be the substance of a full Syrian commitment to peace.

Then at the beginning of September the Israeli-Palestinian agreement took the Syrians by surprise. President Assad was embarrassed and angry to discover what had been happening without his having been consulted. He made several hardline statements saying that 'in his opinion' the Palestinians and the Arabs had 'lost' from the agreement, and he called for the Arab boycott of Israel to be strengthened.* He did not, however, say that he was opposed to the deal or that he would work against it. Part of the reason was that he could see that if the Palestinians were making peace with their enemy, in due course it would be easier for Syria to do likewise. So he simply withdrew from the scene of political activity to watch the progress of the detailed Israeli-Palestinian negotiations.

Assad's response was mirrored by the Israelis. Having taken the bold and extraordinary steps of recognizing the PLO and agreeing to withdraw from the occupied territories, the Israelis in the autumn of 1993 were suffering from what was described as 'peace fatigue'. They, like the Syrians, wanted to see how discussions with the Palestinians went before making another leap forward.

Assuming that the Israeli-Palestinian negotiations made gradual progress it was taken for granted by both sides that eventually they would

---

* The boycott, which was established after the 1948–9 war, banned Arab states from all economic contact with Israel. It also banned governments and companies from doing business with foreign corporations which invested in Israel or had other commercial relationships which were deemed to strengthen the Israeli economy. These relationships included the export of strategically valuable goods (an area in which many exceptions were made), the licensing of patents and the sale of technological processes, and lending to the state. The boycott was run by a head office in Damascus, with branches in the other Arab capitals.

revive discussion of their agreement. Syria wanted the Israelis out of Golan and southern Lebanon, and Israel wanted peace and had an interest in seeing the Syrians controlling the Palestinian rejectionists and Shia militants in Lebanon. It was their ability to influence the level of attacks that guerilla groups made on Israel from southern Lebanon that gave the Syrians their one strong card in negotiations with Israel. Whenever in the previous few years they had wanted to make their presence felt by the Israelis they had allowed the guerilla groups a fairly free hand. The Israelis had then retaliated, either attacking the guerillas in the south or, if they had wanted to send an angrier message to the Syrians, bombing positions near the Syrian forces. This harassment by proxy had been an easily read form of diplomacy, but from the point of view of both governments a peace agreement, if that were politically feasible, would have been better. The ideal solution in Lebanon for both sides was for the Syrians and a reconstructed Lebanese army to be given authority to crush or disarm all militias (including Israel's allies) that had survived the Syrian clean-up operation of 1990–1, and for the Syrians to have a motive to complete the job.

When the Syrians and Israelis would resume their discussions depended on what happened on the West Bank and on the political strength and self-confidence of President Assad. The President had not only to consider the attitudes of other Arab countries to his making peace – which was particularly important for him because of Syria's role as the keeper of the Arab conscience on Palestine – but also his own domestic position. Without the war against Israel Assad would not be able to justify his authoritarian rule. Pressures for greater personal freedom and some steps towards democracy would emerge. The government would not need to spend so much on defence, which would damage the financial interests and power bases of the Alawite generals who were Assad's principal supporters. There would be demands for the further liberalization of the economy. In short, there would be pressure for change in the system that had been constructed since the Baathists came to power in 1963, and if these pressures were not controlled they could lead to the collapse of the regime. For Assad, therefore, making peace with Israel was a complex challenge. It was much more difficult for him than it would be for King Hussein or any other more liberal Arab head of state. He had to win credit for regaining lost territory, give Syrians some material benefit and a greater sense of freedom, and yet keep his government in power.

While the American government in 1991 was arranging talks between Israel, its neighbours and the Palestinians, it was also working to reinforce the mood of acceptance of Israel that had been developing in the Arab world for more than a decade. This was an area in which America's ideas were the same as Israel's. Both countries in the 1970s and 1980s had seen advantage in Israel trying to develop small, practical links with Arab states. The Israelis believed these would help undermine the famous Arab consensus, agreed at the Khartoum summit in August 1967, of 'no talks, no recognition and no peace'. The aim was to divide the Arab world, win the *de facto* recognition of a few countries and put themselves in a stronger position when they came to negotiate directly with the front-line states and the Palestinians. They wrapped their strategy in the plausible general proposition that peace would more easily be built by small steps than by a single grand series of negotiations. The Arabs were not impressed by this idea. Their view was that once the Israelis had agreed a proper, comprehensive solution to the Palestine problem, they could have all the minor, detailed benefits of normal relations with their neighbours.

As well as spotting a political advantage in the indirect approach to peace, the Israelis had an eye on what they hoped would be its long-term economic benefits. These were important to them. They were very aware in the late 1980s that their standard of living was supported by a $3 billion subsidy from the United States – the biggest American subsidy paid to any country – and although they knew that this figure was probably sacrosanct, in that no administration or congress would court the embarrassment that would come from trying to cut it, they could see that it was unlikely to be increased and would gradually have its practical value eroded by inflation and the growth of the country's population. At the same time the country's links with Jews in the United States were slowly weakening. In 1948, when Israel was founded, many Jews in America had been in that country for hardly forty years; the big period of Jewish immigration had been at the beginning of the twentieth century. They still spoke central and eastern European languages and they thought of themselves as being as much Jews as Americans. They therefore associated themselves closely with the fate of Israel, visited it and willingly gave it large sums of money. By the early 1990s the Jews in the United States were feeling more American and more secular. They felt less close to Israel and the Israelis' fear was that in future they would be less active in supporting it.

The prospect of a reduction in both official and unofficial help from America was making the Israeli government aware that it had to do more to make its economy efficient and competitive. It was pushed in the same direction by the knowledge that in the decade before the wave of immigration from the former Soviet Union began in 1990 there had been a small net emigration of Jews from Israel. One of the long-term strategies available to it was the gradual reduction of the very big subsidies it had always given to its agriculture; but this was politically sensitive when the idea of honest toil on the land producing a healthy, self-sufficient, secure community had been part of the ethos of the Zionist movement from the beginning. The other obvious strategy was for Israel to try to develop economic links with its neighbours, which appeared to be ideal markets for its industrial products. The Arab countries relied mainly on imports for the more sophisticated manufactured goods they needed, and Israel, being on their borders, seemed to be in a position where it could be a competitive supplier.

The Israelis, and Americans, saw a perfect means of promoting steps towards peace and economic integration in 1991 in the multilateral talks. These were made possible by Israel and several of the Arab states having been on the same side in the Gulf crisis. The crisis had crystallized new political ideas in the Arab world. For many years the Arab countries had known they could not fight Israel but the Iraqi invasion of Kuwait and the split this had caused in Arab ranks had made them realize that they were fundamentally divided in their political interests. They were shown, in effect, not only that they could not fight Israel but that many of them had no interest in doing so. It suddenly became possible for each to take cautious steps towards making its own peace with Israel.

The result was the launching of the multilateral talks in Moscow in February 1992. During the following twelve months these came to involve, in an active or nominal role, every Arab country except Iraq, Libya and Sudan. In a direct sense in the short term they produced rather limited results. The talks on arms control were hampered by what the Israelis considered to be the greed and opportunism of Europe and the former members of the Soviet Union in competing to do business with the Arabs; and the discussions on refugees were made difficult by the Palestinians demanding a right of return. The best that could be said for these negotiations was that they helped the two sides get to know each other. The groups addressing water, the environment and regional economic development, however, made better progress. Various studies on environmental issues were put in hand and the participants in the development groups began drawing up a list of possible joint projects. The Israelis were delighted to find that many of the Arab delegates seemed perfectly relaxed in talking to them. Senior Israeli officials made a point of talking to their opposite numbers informally in the corridors and dining rooms, and the Arabs made no attempt to avoid them. The mere fact that the two sides were meeting in these talks broke the partial diplomatic quarantine that the Arabs had succeeded in imposing on Israel. In the three months that followed the Moscow meeting Israel opened or renewed diplomatic relations with China, India and Nigeria.

Israel's and America's expectations of the meetings were initially that they would 'build confidence' between the two sides. The idea of how this could be done and what benefits it would yield had been developed by the Americans almost into a science during the Conference on Security and Co-operation in Europe, which had started in 1970 and ended with the Final Declaration in Helsinki in 1990. The Conference, which involved the United States, Western Europe and the Soviet bloc, had been concerned with security, human rights and economic co-operation, subjects not so different from those being addressed by the Arabs and Israelis. During its long life the Americans and Europeans had found that there were dividends to be won from a non-confrontational approach, in which they tried not necessarily to address the most important issues but to discuss smaller matters on which progress seemed easier and to look for the major benefit coming from a growing sense of trust between the two sides. They found that the talks, the studies they generated, the follow-up contacts and the commercial and cultural exchanges they produced 'de-demonized' the opponents and in every country created constituencies which had a vested interest in peaceful co-operation. It was this type of evolution that the Americans wanted to stimulate in relations between the Arabs and Israelis.

It was thought that in the Middle East the improvement in relations might begin with the installation of 'hotlines' between the heads of government, in order to prevent misunderstandings leading to crises and, possibly, military exchanges. The Israelis believed strongly in this idea. In 1967 they had sent messages to King Hussein through various indirect channels, including the United Nations, telling him that if he stayed out of the fighting he would not be attacked. They knew he had received the messages, yet he had still entered a defence agreement with Egypt and sent his troops into action when the war began. They have said since that they assume he did not completely trust the messages, and they believe that if they had been able to communicate with him directly he might have been reassured. More recently, in April 1989, the Israelis proposed a 'hotline' to Iraq via Egypt, but they were rebuffed. Through the multilateral talks their hope is that they will establish lines to all Arab governments with which they might possibly come into confrontation. These are not only their immediate neighbours but other countries that have large airforces and arsenals of missiles.

It was suggested that a major area of economic contact between the two sides might be the encouragement of tourism. This would involve apparently simple matters, such as the opening of roads and the introduction of direct flights between Israel and Arab countries, so that tourists could take a holiday that included in one ticket, say, Egypt, Israel and Yemen. In the Israeli view this sort of innovation would be less important in the short-term financial sense than in the long-term political and indirect economic benefits it would bring. Tourism may damage the fabric and character of historical sites, but it has the benefit of bringing peoples together. It introduces to underdeveloped and tightly controlled countries Western standards of service, expectations of assistance rather than obstruction from government, demands for foreign newspapers and prompt (and private) international telecommunications, and the necessity of permanently open frontiers. From their own point of view, the Israelis say, the development of tourism between their country and Egypt after 1979 helped greatly to de-demonize the Arabs in Israeli eyes. Some 450,000 Israelis visited Egypt in the thirteen years after the Camp David accords, and although there were three unhappy incidents in which visitors were murdered, the general impression they gained of their hosts was good. They were disappointed that only 3,000 Egyptian tourists travelled in the other direction. The Egyptians' lack of interest in Israel, compared to Israel's interest in them, was typical of Arab attitudes generally. It was noticeable that although their delegations at the multilateral conference were happy to talk to the Israelis, the Arab governments were much less enthusiastic about the substance of the meetings. The driving force behind the talks was very much Israeli and American, rather than Arab.

A secondary area of economic interest for the Israelis was in co-operation on water and the environment. This, they suggested, was less important than tourism because it did not produce the same continuity of contact. Once two countries had co-operated on the construction of, say, a dam or built two pumping stations, they could operate the facilities without ever again speaking to each other. Nevertheless in a purely material sense the Israelis could see benefits – for the Arabs as much as themselves – in their co-operating on these types of projects. The Arab neighbours of Israel were receiving fewer grants from the Arabian Peninsula countries, which used to give without strings attached, and the European countries and America were making some of their aid conditional on environmental good behaviour. Such behaviour might involve the Syrians, for example, stopping the dumping of raw sewage and rubbish into the Mediterranean and the Lebanese preventing their people from fishing with dynamite. In some cases it was thought there would be advantages in the Arab countries obtaining advice or technology from Israel. Areas in which the Israelis proposed co-operation were the cleaning of the Mediterranean and the elimination of malaria-spreading mosquitoes.

Regardless of the cautious Arab response in the multilateral talks, the Israelis may succeed in bringing about some contact between themselves and the economies of the Arab countries in the later 1990s by means of the hoped-for peace agreement with a Palestinian state. It is accepted by all parties involved in the peace talks that the West Bank of Palestine will need to be able to sell its products freely in both Israel and Jordan and be given unrestricted access to Israeli ports, Gaza and Aqaba so that it can reach foreign markets. In return for facilitating the trade of this area (which hitherto they have carefully obstructed), the Israelis will certainly demand access to the West Bank's own market and, whether or not the Palestinian state is linked in a confederation to Jordan, they will want access to the Jordanian market as well. Shimon Peres has already suggested that there might be a form of economic union between these states, along the lines of Benelux.

The Jordanians, and the businessmen of other Arab countries, are rather afraid of these ideas. They think that the Israelis will want to use the West Bank as a Trojan horse through which they will get their goods into Arab markets, and their anxiety is that this will damage their own rather uncompetitive fledgling industries. They have become aware that Israel, despite its worries about the absorption of Russian immigrants and the maintenance of what it considers a reasonable standard of living, has a much bigger and more efficient economy than most of their own countries. Its GDP in 1992 was $60 billion, produced by a population of 5 million. By comparison, in Jordan 3.6 million people created a GDP of only $5 billion, and in Egypt 58 million people produced $50 billion, though this last figure excluded the output of the large black-market economy, or 'informal' sector. The GDP of Saudi Arabia, which has a population of 13 million, was roughly $110 billion.

There was some debate in Jordan and its neighbours about the implication of Israel's economic strength. Some people thought that an Israel at peace with its neighbours would dominate them commercially, though free traders suggested that even if some of their industries were driven out of business in the long term they would receive a much greater compensating benefit by being able to reduce their defence expenditure.

The true likelihood is that both the hopes of the Israelis and the fears of the Arabs are exaggerated. The prospects of Israel being able to 'integrate itself into the regional economy', the phrase used by its more optimistic economists, are limited by the Arab economies themselves having few links with each other. There is remarkably little trade and investment moving between Arab countries and much of what there is is managed on the basis of inter-governmental protocols. Most of the economies, even in the semi-reformed states, are heavily regulated and obstructed by bureaucracy, and their industries are still protected from foreign competition. In the Arabian Peninsula countries, where these generalizations apply least and there are flourishing private sectors, the public is rich enough to buy Western goods. Everywhere it seems certain that people will be suspicious of any product which comes from Israel. The Israelis claim they are aware of these problems and they say their aspirations to enter the regional economy are for the long term, but they probably do not realize just how long it will take for their hopes to be even moderately fulfilled.

19

A Pragmatic Arab World

Effect of the Gulf crisis in encouraging pragmatism – likely effect of Arab-Israeli peace undermining militancy – growing power of Turkey and Iran and their links with central Asia

The Arab world has become a more sober and realistic place since the mid-1980s. The influences acting upon it have been those described in this book: the economic crisis, peoples' loss of faith in their governments, the collapse of the USSR which had been the backer of the nominally socialist radicals, and the realization of both governments and peoples that they have to make peace with Israel. Most important of all has been the Gulf crisis, which has had more influence on the attitudes of individual Arabs and on relations between governments than any other event of the last ten years.

The crisis was a shock to the Arab world because it involved a conflict between peoples. Previous wars in the Arab world had been between governments or leaders fighting for political advantage and their own pride. When mediation had brought the fighting to a halt and everybody's face had been saved, the leaders kissed and made up and their citizens, accepting that life was cheap in their part of the world, shrugged, told themselves that war was a natural part of politics and went back to living their lives as normal. They continued to hold to the belief that they themselves, the Arab people, were one nation, united in interests and intentions. They persuaded themselves that they had been divided into separate states only by imperialist manipulation. They ignored the fact that they had different histories and different cultures. The appeal of these ideas was understandable among peoples who had only recently emerged from Ottoman and then British and French rule and were looking for an identity – especially one which held the promise of power – but it was sentimental and illogical.

The Gulf crisis destroyed these ideas of unity by pitting the peoples of the Arab countries against each other. It showed that the citizens of the Arabian Peninsula oil producers valued their sovereignty and wanted to keep their wealth for themselves. During the crisis various ideas were put forward in the poorer Arab capitals for funds which would take, say, 30 per cent of the region's oil revenues and distribute it to the other Arab countries, as a right. It was suggested that this would not only help the development of the Arab nation but also remove the envy which was at the root of the conflict. Rightly or wrongly, the Gulf Arabs failed totally to respond to these proposals.

The Egyptians at the same time were shown to be not at all unhappy at the humiliation of Iraq. It was not only their government, mindful of the advantages of debt forgiveness and getting the Arab League headquarters back to Cairo, that readily joined the anti-Iraq coalition; the campaign had the support of the people as well. Most of the population seemed to be influenced by basic Egyptian nationalism. If Saddam was allowed to keep Kuwait, Iraq would become the leading Arab power, while if he was expelled their own country would be back at the centre of Arab politics where they always knew it belonged.

The rest of the Arab peoples backed Iraq out of a mixture of motives: a naïve hope that Saddam might be able to defeat Israel, jealousy of Kuwaiti wealth and an old belief that they were more cultured and civilized and therefore more deserving than the Kuwaitis. The last of these ideas, closely connected to their jealousy, was deeply embedded in the psyche of the 'poor' Arabs. The people of Syria, Lebanon, Palestine and North Africa were very aware that their own regions had given birth to some of the earliest civilizations and then had experienced long and periodically glorious histories, and they were equally aware of how unsuccessful and uninfluential they had been in the last half century. This made them angry and jealous of the success of the Arabian Peninsula countries, especially when that success derived entirely from oil revenues which had come to the peoples through sheer good fortune. The prosperity of Saudi Arabia and the Gulf states compared to their own moderate poverty seemed to them unfair and against the proper order of things. The result was not only that they harboured a jealousy of the *nouveaux riches*, but that they refused to recognize the huge human and material development that had taken place in the oil states in the previous thirty years. They would frequently refer in conversation to the Saudis and Gulf Arabs as being 'primitive' and 'stupid'. This was in spite of many of them having been to the region to work and having seen the development with their own eyes. Whatever good impressions they may periodically have gained during their stays were nullified by their own prejudice and by the Gulf Arabs treating them as inferior on account of their being poorer. When Saddam Hussein invaded Kuwait it was their natural instinct to rejoice. They were pleased at the prospect of the Kuwaitis being humiliated and their wealth redistributed. Even the most thoughtful and best educated could not help but react in this way. Soon after the invasion a Palestinian friend of mine said that Saddam had 'done the right thing in the wrong way'. Although he was critical in the literal sense, he could not hide his secret satisfaction, and he told me that if the West attacked Iraq it would be hit by 'a wave of terrorism such as it had never known before'.

This revelation of the totally different attitudes and interests of governments and peoples in 1990–1 shattered the old idea that Arab policies towards the outside world (and especially Israel) ought to be based on consensus. This idea in the past had enabled the radicals, presenting themselves as patriotic, to exercise a veto over the conservatives pursuing pro-Western policies. The Gulf crisis destroyed this veto and made the Gulf states and Saudi Arabia feel that they were entitled to do whatever was in their own interests.

The immediate reaction of the oil states was to reconsider their policies towards the poor countries. They reminded themselves that in the past as a proportion of their GDP they had given more aid than any of the industrialized countries. On the day war broke out in January 1991 the Saudi government revealed for the first time that in the previous ten years it had given Iraq no less than $32 billion. This and many other billions transferred to other poor countries had been given partly out of a sense of moral obligation and partly in an attempt to win goodwill. For many years it had been clear that these gifts had not been as effective in buying friendship as had been hoped and the Iraqi invasion provided final proof of their failure. The Gulf and Saudi governments felt rather embarrassed by their misguided generosity and gullibility. The Saudi ambassador to Bahrain, Dr Ghazi Algosaibi, said in an interview with a Gulf magazine that it had become the governments' habit 'if somebody hits our right cheek' to 'show him our left pocket'. Recognizing that their whole approach to aid giving had been unhealthy – more a matter of paying protection money than giving serious development assistance – the Gulf governments decided individually and informally to reduce their donations and, in the case of money that was given for general budgetry assistance rather than specific projects, to give only to countries that were proven friends. Some of the first fruits of this policy were the writing off of the loans to

Egypt and Morocco and the cancellation of payments to the PLO.

At the same time the governments felt they could be more open in showing their goodwill towards the West. It was, after all, the West which was doing most to liberate Kuwait. On any practical analysis the governments could see that their countries were more involved commercially and politically, and had more interests in common, with the capitalist, industrialized world than with the poor countries. Seen in a cold light at the end of the crisis these interests seemed to balance the interests of race, culture and religion that joined the Gulf to the Arab poor.

The countries of the Levant and North Africa after the crisis turned in on themselves. The old ideas of Arab nationalism, that governments had a right to interfere in each other's internal politics, demand total unity of views and abuse countries that did not agree with them, had been fading since the mid-1970s and the shock of the Gulf crisis discredited them completely. What was emerging instead in the later 1980s and early 1990s was what an Egyptian university lecturer described as 'a functional relationship between states', in which countries 'promoted economic co-operation, put ideology on one side and accepted a degree of inter-dependence' – in other words accepted that if their internal and external policies were going to succeed they would have to have at least the acquiescence of other states. Governments were looking to their own interests in a pragmatic way, recognizing that others had different interests and discovering that when they respected those interests their relationships with their neighbours improved. In so far as they still felt a need to bind themselves to other Arab countries they were turning their attention to small regional groupings, such as the Gulf Co-operation Council and the Arab Maghreb Union, which were concerned with practical co-operation, mainly on economic matters, and not in promoting any particular ideology. It was suggested by politicians and academics that the Arabs might find a model for this type of co-operation in the Organization of Latin American States. The members of this Organization, with the exception of Brazil, spoke the same language, had, to some degree, a common culture, and could see an advantage in linking their economies, but they never thought of uniting their countries or promoting themselves as a political or military power.

The new type of thinking in the Arab world could be seen in the Maghreb. In the 1970s and early 1980s two of the countries in this region had been self-righteously expounding their own ideologies. Tunisia believed that it had won the battle for modernity and as a sophisticated, economically successful state could give a practical lesson to its neighbours and the rest of the Arab world; and Algeria was preaching its own austere brand of revolutionary socialism, which emphasised the development of heavy industry and promised its people that they were about to become citizens of a great industrial power. The third Maghreb country, Morocco, was ideologically on the defensive, but being engaged in the conquest of the former Spanish Sahara it was able to channel its people's energies to this patriotic end, which stimulated as much popular interest as the economic development programmes of the other states. None of the countries could see the slightest need to compromise with its neighbours on the various quarrels that arose between them. As a senior official of the Algerian government put it to me in 1992, 'We could all afford to indulge in external disputes that reflected little more than our own pride'. When they encountered problems that seemed to require the co-operation of other countries they would turn to the forum of the whole Arab world and persuade themselves that 'Arab unity' would enable them to pressure their rivals into doing what they wanted.

Since the mid-1980s, however, the Maghreb governments have all been humbled by their economic failure, and in Algeria's case by internal chaos as well. Now they have to concentrate on the very practical matters of providing food and jobs for their own people. And the Gulf crisis has shown them finally that there is no purpose in maintaining the illusion that their problems can be solved by some form of joint Arab action to crush Israel, bolster oil prices, bring about a new world economic order or redistribute the wealth of Kuwait. Instead they have to pursue as quickly as possible pragmatic policies that will generate wealth, and these are forcing them to co-operate with each other. Already one can see evidence of the change. Algeria is planning to build a gas export pipeline to Spain through Morocco, and neither of the Arab countries involved in this project is letting their differences over the Western Sahara and Algeria's (much reduced) support for the Polisario guerillas (the Western Sahara independence movement) stop them working together. Ten years ago Algeria would not have contemplated laying a pipeline through such a politically incorrect neighbour as Morocco. It has also been noticeable in the last few years that minor disputes have not been allowed to interfere with the flow of gas through a line from Algeria to Italy through Tunisia, as they would probably have done in the 1970s or early 1980s.

The more pragmatic politics of the three states have been accompanied by a change in people's view of their national identity. In the 1960s and 1970s the emphasis was on the Arabism of the region, but in the early 1990s people are recognizing that they belong to several places. They are part of the Arab world, but also part of Africa, of the Mediterranean basin and, they say, of Europe. The Tunisians and Algerians in particular are not happy with this complicated, ill-defined identity – the Moroccans are more satisfied with being simply Moroccan – but the change in emphasis away from Arabism may have the long-term practical benefit of discouraging dreaming and encouraging regional co-operation. Ironically it has occurred at the end of a period in which the use of the Arabic language in Algeria has developed fast. When the country became independent in 1962 its administration and most of its teaching was conducted in French and even among its best-educated people few spoke classical Arabic; by choice they spoke French, though they could manage poor colloquial Arabic. In recent years classical (or 'modern literary') Arabic has become sufficiently widespread for the government to have come close to making its use compulsory for all official purposes. It was about to put this into law in July 1992, but it decided that the change would be disruptive – it would certainly have angered the Kabyle population – and in the context of the country's reorientation of itself it seemed regressive, so at the last moment the implementation was suspended.

Many of the older members of the intelligentsia across the Arab world, the people who think of themselves as Nasser's generation, are unhappy about the changes of the last few years. They mourn the collapse of pan-Arab sentiment and the growth of purely pragmatic government. They regard the change as a defeat, which in a sense it is, and an abandonment of ideals in politics. There is another view, though, held by many of the young, the less politically minded members of the middle-aged generation and the Arabian Peninsula Arabs, that the change is good. These people maintain, first, that the new politics has a virtue in itself in that though it may involve the abandonment of an attractive ideal, it at least avoids bloodshed and produces tangible material benefits. Second, they say it is more honest. When there are differences in Arab ranks they are now accepted and perhaps discussed, in a limited practical way, if there is any chance of their being resolved. In earlier years Arab governments either fought each other over their differences or held a summit conference, in which, instead of talking pragmatic politics, they would paper over the cracks and pretend they were united.

Third, it is occasionally said that in the long term pragmatism might, paradoxically, be a road towards Arab unity. According to this line of thinking, the removal of ideology from politics and the pursuit by states of short-term practical goals will have an initial, useful effect in strengthening the nation state and the authority of governments. Strong confident governments, which are not worried by other Arab countries, should be more prepared to co-operate with their neighbours on economic programmes, including joint projects, the dismantling of trade barriers and the harmonization of commercial legislation. They would, in effect, find themselves starting down the path which may slowly be leading to economic and political union in Europe. This is a comparison that the ambassadors of the European countries make often in political discussions with Arab governments, particularly when they are urging a peaceful, co-operative approach to the region's problems or to its relations with outside powers.

It is also assumed that Arab governments which do not feel threatened by their neighbours will be more prepared slowly to move towards democracy, and democracy in turn is seen as a prerequisite for successful political unity. The benefit of democracy in this context is that it considerably weakens the vested interests that stand in the way of two states uniting. If two absolute monarchies or two authoritarian republican governments join their countries (in any genuine way) it goes without saying that one of them has to be dissolved or made subservient to the other – both options which the weaker government is bound to resist – but if two democracies unite, their parliaments can simply be merged. Unity as brought about through pragmatism and democracy, unlike the other benefits of the new-style Arab politics, remains very much in the realm of theory and a long way in the future, but it can act as a consolation to those Arabs who mourn the passing of the days of union by passionate political will, brief negotiation and decree.

The development of practical politics will be reinforced by the Palestinian-Israeli peace agreement, if it can be made to hold. This will probably happen, though the agreement will go through many crises and its implementation may be much delayed. The reasons for optimism are that both sides have an interest in concluding a settlement and the Americans, now that the Declaration of Principles has been signed, will be extremely concerned to see that it is not abandoned.

In the short term, even if there is a settlement, the region will remain in turmoil. The dissenters – some of the guerilla groups in Lebanon, Hamas and Islamic militants in other countries – will consider it a betrayal. They will try to disrupt it, the governments of the Palestinian state, other Arab countries and Israel will act to control them, no doubt brutally, and to the outside world it will look as if little has changed. But once the dissenters have been subdued and some form of peaceful normality is established in relations between Israel and a Palestinian state, the major cause of tension and violence in the Middle East in the last seventy years will have been removed. An end to the Arab-Israeli confrontation will also take away one of the causes of crises and wars between Arab countries. It will undermine republican militancy of the sort pursued by Saddam Hussein and Muammar Gaddafi. Without the background of 'the conflict', Saddam Hussein would not have had an angry nationalist constituency to which he could appeal, would not have had a cause by which he could promote himself as an Arab leader, and would have had less reason to arm his country and invade either Iran or Kuwait. The same logic applies to Islamic militancy. The humiliation of the Arabs by Israel has certainly not been the only cause of the growth of fundamentalism but it probably has been the most important. Without the conflict the Arab people will still suffer the poverty and much of the bad government and corruption on which political Islam feeds, but they will not feel quite the same frustration. Nor will they feel the same hostility to the political influence and secular culture of the West, which has been Israel's backer.

It may even be, in the long term, that peace will bring about an improvement in Arab government. It will take away from authoritarian regimes the old excuse for harsh rule: that they are in a state of war and that in these conditions normal freedoms can be suspended. In this its influence will be combined with the other pressures for reform that have been mentioned in this book: economic failure, the increase in people's expectations brought about by better knowledge of other countries, and the collapse of the USSR. The last of these changes has been important in depriving the harder regimes of a source of international moral support, arms and occasionally aid, and making them less confident as a result. It has also led to the further discrediting of socialism, which is a principle the republics have long abandoned in a militant idealistic sense, but which still serves to justify the rigid control they maintain of their economies, and hence of their people.

If there is to be a peaceful improvement in the quality of the more authoritarian Arab governments – and it has to be said that the conventional wisdom has been that these regimes can only be changed by force – it will probably begin in Syria. This is the one country in which the government will conceivably be shrewd enough to change on its own, and it is also the only country in which the government, if it wants, will be able to attempt change under normal political and economic conditions. The other two hardline republican regimes, in Iraq and Libya, have been cut off from normal contact with the outside world since 1990 and 1992 by various United Nations sanctions, which have put them in a state of crisis in which peaceful change is virtually impossible.

In Syria the government is being helped by a useful flow of oil revenues and the end of the civil war in Lebanon. It has had the confidence to undertake a very cautious and not very meaningful liberalization of its economy. If in the next few years it concludes a peace with Israel it is possible that it will feel obliged to undertake further economic, and political, reform. If it were to do this it would be responding to the expectations of its people and President Assad's increasing age and ill health. The process would be difficult and slow because whatever the President wanted – and he might have notions of creating some form of democracy as his legacy to his people – change would be against the instincts and interests of many of his supporters. The Alawite generals would find it very difficult to accustom themselves to a government in which they were not controlling all aspects of society and, equally important, they would find that many of the sources of their enrichment, the state-controlled companies over which individuals and parts of the armed forces had established control, would be taken from them. There is no question that the military would resist political reform.

Yet if one of the effects of a Palestinian-Israeli peace agreement and the other pressures for change in the region were to be the liberalization of Syria – and it remains an outside chance – the repercussions in the rest of the Arab world would be enormous. Syria is culturally and politically at the centre of the region – it was described by Nasser as 'the beating heart of Arabism' – and since the death of Nasser it has carried the torch for the Arabs in the struggle against Israel. Without its leading the way no Arab state, except Egypt, has been able to make peace with Israel. And while the Arab countries have been officially at war, they have been able to justify to themselves and their people their reluctance to make political and economic changes. Even in countries where there have been tentative reforms there is no doubt that the changes would have been faster and more thorough if the governments had considered themselves to be officially at peace. The acceptance of peace by Syria, therefore, and the beginning of change in that state would have a huge psychological liberating effect on both peoples and governments in other Arab countries. More than any other event it would act as a stimulus to change in the Arab world.

All of the changes in the Arab world have to be seen in a broader regional context in which the Arabs may be becoming less important and their relations with Israel less a focus of the world's attention. This, at least, is a view of the region that was popular in 1992 and 1993. It clearly appealed to the Israelis, because it suggested that the Arabs would be less useful as friends for Western powers and that anyone analysing the region should start to think less of a simple two-sided confrontation and more of a pattern of shifting alliances between Israelis, Arabs, Iranians, Turks and possibly even Armenians and Kurds. The Israelis went so far as to suggest that in the future they might find themselves allied with Arab countries against over-mighty neighbours to the north and east – this being an idea which fitted well with the regional co-operation they were trying to promote through the multilateral talks. The Israelis' ideas were regarded by the Western foreign policy establishments as being too radical, though it was accepted that a period of uncertainty and change was beginning.

The origin of the change has been the collapse of the Soviet Union at the end of 1991 and the emergence from it of six Muslim, or partly Muslim, independent republics. These were, to the west of the Caspian Sea, Azerbaijan, and to the east, Turkmenistan, Uzbekistan, Kyrgyzstan, Khazakstan and Tajikistan. The peoples of these countries are predominantly Turkish, though some countries have Persian minorities and Tajikistan is mainly Persian. Most of the people are Sunni Muslims, in so far as they have any religion, though in Azerbaijan there is a large Shia community. Together the six republics, if grouped with Turkey and Iran, have a bigger population than the entire Arab world. This might greatly alter the strategic balance in the Middle East and western Asia, if the ethnic and cultural bonds between the Persian and Turkish peoples were to lead to political and military alliances. The central Asian republics are militarily important not just because they have supplies of conventional arms but because they have, if not nuclear weapons themselves, access to nuclear technology. It has been lack of expertise and a scientific base, rather than a lack of capital, that has so far prevented any of the Middle Eastern countries, except Israel, producing a nuclear weapon.

Both Iran and Turkey have been interested in the prospect of making friends with their new neighbours. The Turks, in particular, have long felt a need to be part of some sort of international grouping and they have courted the new republics assiduously. In November 1992, at a summit meeting of the Turkish-speaking countries in Ankara, the then President, Turgut Özal, spoke of his guests as Turkey's 'relations and brothers' and declared that the 21st century would be 'the century of the Turks'. In saying this he was evoking the idea of Turanian nationalism – the nationalism of the Turks and the kindred Turkish-speaking peoples of the steppes and deserts of central Asia. This concept, which is totally different from the idea of a multiracial Islamic community represented by Ottoman rule, had emerged with the rise of the Young Turks before the First World War but had been little heard of since soon after the Russian Revolution. In the five years immediately after the Revolution there were several attempts by the central Asian peoples and their khans, helped by various refugee Turkish and central European commanders, to create their own independent states, but the Russians crushed the revolts, sacked the cities and massacred the inhabitants. In Bukhara the Red Army burnt what was believed to be the greatest library of Muslim manuscripts in the world.

For President Ozal in the early 1990s the revival of pan-Turanianism was a very attractive idea. It not only appealed to the strong nationalist feelings of his own people, but also gave his government an alternative to continuing its forlorn attempts to join the European Community. Suddenly the lands to the east, which had been shut off for seventy years, were open to Turkey, politically and commercially. In practical, material terms the Turks' reaction to the opportunity was to promote themselves as a link between the new republics and the Western industrialized world. They had good political, trading and financial connections with the industrialized countries, which were what the republics needed, and their own manufacturers and contractors were able to sell quite sophisticated but relatively inexpensive goods and services. They represented access to capital, consumer goods and the ideas and methods of private sector business.

The Iranians in 1992 found themselves in a less strong position and had more limited expectations of what they might achieve in central Asia. They had the advantage of being geographically closer to the region than Turkey and they were aware that in the seventeenth, eighteenth and early nineteenth centuries, until they managed to break away or were conquered by the Tsars, parts of the central Asian lands had been under their rule. The difficulties they faced were that most of the central Asian peoples were Turkish and Sunni, and that their own country, having recently emerged from an eight-year war and having no spare money and undeveloped or worn-out industries, had little to offer the new republics. Some of the few remaining optimistic and aggressive Iranian politicians dreamed of creating Islamic republics in central Asia but the more sober members of the government hoped merely that their neighbours would use Iran as a route for their trade with the outside world and give it some friendly diplomatic support. The government tried to begin this type of relationship by mediating in the dispute between Armenia and Azerbaijan over the enclave of Nagorno Karabakh.

The emergence of the new republics clearly represented a diplomatic opportunity for Iran, just as it did for Turkey, and it certainly made Western politicians and journalists worry about the export of the Islamic Revolution, but the impression gained by anybody who visited Tehran in 1992 was that on balance the Iranians would have been happier to have kept the Soviet Union as their neighbour. Even though it had been invaded by Tsarist Russia in 1915 and the Soviet Union in 1941 Iran had had an easy relationship with its super-power neighbour over the past forty years, during both the monarchy and the Islamic Republic. It had engaged in much trade and immediately after the Iran-Iraq war had bought some sophisticated Soviet arms. The break-up of the Union not only offered no obvious benefit, it raised the distant possibility of Iran's own minorities, who were as numerous as the Persian population in the heartland of the state, starting their own secessionist movements. The Iranian minorities included Turkomans, Baluchis, Arabs, Armenians, Kurds and Azerbaijanis, the last of whom were briefly incorporated into the Soviet republic of Azerbaijan after the end of the Second World War.

Both the Turks' diplomacy in 1992 and, less surprisingly, the Iranians', met with a cooler response from the central Asians than either the suitors themselves or the Western foreign ministries watching the process expected. In Tehran early in the year much anecdotal evidence was circulating on how government visitors to the new republics had met with either a general lack of Islamic enthusiasm or polite incomprehension. The Deputy Foreign Minister, who visited Tajikistan in February, was telling a story of how at the end of his meeting he had suggested that as a brotherly gesture the minutes should be written in Persian, which, in theory, was the two countries' common language. To his disappointment it had taken the Tajiks a day to find a Persian typewriter, and then nobody in their foreign ministry had known how to use it. Eventually he had had to type the minutes himself. Another story, from a good source close to the President, concerned a Turkish speaking *rohani* (the most junior rank of cleric, commonly known as a mullah) from Iranian Azerbaijan who went across the border to former Soviet Azerbaijan to give a lecture on Islam. His small audience listened politely to his talk and afterwards some of its members handed round vodka and sandwiches. The *rohani* explained that alcohol was prohibited by Islam, and then he was surprised and hurt to find not only that the audience was unaware of this but on being enlightened lost interest in the meeting and drifted away.

Later in the year, in October, there was a minor scandal on the north-eastern side of the border when the President of Kyrgyzstan, Askar Akaev, set out on a visit to Saudi Arabia and was reported at home as saying that 'for the sake of credit' he would be making a pilgrimage to Mecca. The Kyrgyz public was genuinely shocked by this abandonment of their secular principles, and by the idea of its leader currying favour with the Saudis, and Akaev was forced to change his plans. He went only as far as Medina before returning home.

The lesson that all the Middle Eastern countries have learnt from these and other episodes in the last two years is that the central Asian republics have become very different from them during seventy years of Communist rule. The people there talk of themselves as being Muslim but few know what this entails. The only way in which Islam might enter their politics would be through a revolutionary movement, exploiting broadly based discontent with economic difficulties, using it as a rallying cry that held out a vague promise of better times. (This would not be very different from how it is used by Islamist parties in the Arab world, though there the population knows more about the religion.) Most of the citizens of the central Asian republics are firmly secular in their views. In none of the countries do people feel particularly close to the Middle East and Khazakstan and Kyrgyzstan do not regard themselves as even remotely connected to that region. The language of government and business, and of most families in their homes, is Russian, and even when the people speak Turkish it is so impregnated with Russian words that it has become what the Turkish ambassador to Iran described in 1992 as 'only a form of Turkish'. Nor are the central Asians as impressed by the Turks' technology and their business links with the West as they were expected to be. Although they lack capital and factories making good-quality consumer goods, their scientific and technological institutes are in many cases superior to the Turks'. The overall impression one had during 1992 and 1993 was that in spite of Turkish and Iranian advances, the governments and people of these countries wanted to remain independently central Asian.

What was not in doubt, however, was that both Turkey and Iran on their own were going to become increasingly important in the Middle East. The two countries had large populations, estimated to be about 58 million in Turkey in 1993 and 57 million in Iran. Turkey had come through a long period of lack of interest in the Arab world which had followed the collapse of the Ottoman Empire and Ataturk's orientation of the republic towards Europe. In the 1980s Turkish companies had carried out a large number of construction contracts in Iran, Iraq, Libya and Saudi Arabia. Turkish workers and managers, who in earlier years had not liked going to Arab countries, were happier to live and work there. Since its approaches to the European Community had finally been rebuffed in 1989, the government had begun to take a more active political interest in the Arab countries. In the early 1990s it was concerned mainly with Syria's and Iraq's reaction to its use of the Euphrates waters, but speculation could be heard in Arab and Western foreign policy circles about how the Turks might become more involved if, for example, there was to be renewed fighting between Iran and Iraq, or between Iraq and Syria, or if Iraq fragmented in the process of a rebellion or *coup d'état* that overthrew Saddam Hussein. There were suggestions that Turkey might want to reabsorb the former Otto-man *wilayet* of Mosul, giving itself a large amount of oil, or that the country might be persuaded by internal revolt and international pres-sure to allow the creation of an independent Kurdistan from Mosul and its own south-eastern provinces. Neither of these possibilities seemed very likely, but in the aftermath of the fragmentation of the Soviet Union and the allies' creation of a safe haven for the Kurds in northern Iraq at the end of the Gulf war, they were worth discussing.

Iran's approach to its Middle Eastern neighbours was much more aggressive and disruptive. The country gave what backing it could to the Palestinian groups that rejected the Arab-Israeli peace accord, the Shia groups fighting the Israelis and their allies in south Lebanon, the Islamic regime in Sudan and the terrorists in Algeria. It was working hard on rebuilding its armed forces, which had lost almost all of what usable equipment they still had when they retreated at the end of their war with Iraq. It was particularly interested in acquiring technology to help it produce its own ballistic missiles. These policies worried Israel and the Western powers, particularly the Americans.

In the Gulf it was generally accepted, and explained fairly openly in Tehran, that the government's aim was to force itself into the region's councils. It was afraid of the Gulf becoming an American military base – the Iranians were just as neurotic about the Americans as the Ameri-cans were about them – and it did not like the idea of Egypt and Syria being involved in the region's security, as was intended after the end of the Gulf war. It wanted at least to be consulted about security arrangements in the area and, ideally, involved in a regional group with the Gulf states and, in the future, Iraq. Naturally it opposed the involvement of any powerful outsiders. It also said it wanted to develop a more co-operative relationship with Saudi Arabia and the Gulf states on oil production policy. In essence it wanted the role to which it felt its large population entitled it.

Dealing with Iran was made difficult for all foreign powers by the government of President Rafsanjani not being in complete control of its country. It ran the major ministries and state economic organizations but it had no authority over the office of the Imam, Ayatollah Khamenei

(Khomeini's successor), over a number of *bonyads* (foundations) for the dispossessed, war wounded, martyrs and other good (and bad) causes, or over two militant clerics' organizations and various missionary bodies. Its control over the Revolutionary Guards, which were supposed to be being integrated in the army, the revolutionary *komitehs* (committees), which were meant to be merged with the police, and the *hezbollahis*, militant local gangs which could still occasionally be brought on to the streets by angry clerics, seemed to be less complete than it should have been. All of these bodies had funds of their own — the Imam's office could dip into the budget at will — and had their own political agendas, which were invariably less pragmatic than Rafsanjani's. The result in the early 1990s was that the government had to pursue a more militant line abroad than it might have chosen, to protect itself from criticism and divert its opponents' attention from the economic reforms it was trying to introduce at home. It was, in part, this logic that made it virtually impossible for Rafsanjani to arrange the repeal of the *fatwa* (legal judgment) of Ayatollah Khomeini which sentenced to death Salman Rushdie, the author of *The Satanic Verses*. The same pressure was one of the causes of the government reopening a trivial dispute with the United Arab Emirates over the ownership of the tiny island of Abu Musa, which lay on the median line in the Gulf. On occasions when the government did try to improve its relations with foreign powers, particularly the industrialized countries, it was often frustrated by one or other of the independent revolutionary bodies performing some deed calculated to stop it. In 1991 an attempt to develop relations with France ended when assassins killed Shahpour Bakhtiar, the Shah's last prime minister, in Paris. In the next three years a further forty or fifty Iranian dissidents were murdered in Turkey, France, Germany and Italy.

Given that Iran is powerful on account of its sheer size and is intent on making its presence felt, it will inevitably be an important force in the politics of the region in the 1990s — unless it gets involved in another war such as the one that preoccupied it for most of the first ten years after its revolution. The consequence of this is that there is bound to be much manoeuvring by others — the Arab countries, some of the Western powers, Turkey and Israel — to contain it. The Turks are not only traditional rivals of the Iranians, they are competing with them for influence in central Asia and they have shown that they have an interest in preventing their rearmament. In March 1992 they seized a ship with a cargo of arms, on its way from Bulgaria to Iran, as it was sailing through the Bosporus. Israel in the foreseeable future is most likely to be involved in efforts to contain Iran in secret alliance with the Turks or Americans. It might also play a role in offsetting Iran's not very effective diplomacy in central Asia. Its main aims in this region will be to prevent the export of nuclear technology, ensure that the emigration of Jews is allowed to continue and win itself support as it pursues its final negotiations with the Arabs. What it hopes it can give the central Asians in return is technology, particularly in drip irrigation and the cultivation of crops in saline soils, a major problem in Uzbekistan and Turkmenistan.

Turkey's revived interest in the Middle East will likewise produce new manœuvrings and alliances. Initially these may be stimulated by its confrontation with Syria over the Euphrates waters, which it is taking to develop its South-Eastern Anatolia Project. The Syrians have reacted to what they see as a threat to their economic well-being by giving support to the Kurdish Workers' Party, a separatist terrorist group in eastern Turkey, and to the independent republic of Armenia in its war with Azerbaijan. They have also begun to talk again about their claim to the *sanjak* of Alexandretta, the small piece of territory on their northern coast which was incorporated into Turkey after the First World War. If the Syrian-Turkish confrontation is pursued it is quite possible that the Iranians will be called to support Syria, with which they have had an unholy alliance since the early days of their war with Iraq, and the Israelis will join an alliance with Turkey, with which they have traditionally good relations.

It is even suggested in the Arab capitals that if Turkey bears too heavily on the region, Iraq, the one potentially powerful country in the eastern Arab world, might be promoted by other Arab countries and Western powers as a counter to it. The assumption in this case is that the Iraqis would finally have liberated themselves from Saddam Hussein and might have introduced a form of democracy, which would make them acceptable, indeed desirable, Western allies. This idea, like the possibility of Saddam's regime disintegrating in chaos and the Turks taking Mosul, is utterly speculative. But the fact that all of these propositions are being discussed in the Middle East in the early/mid-1990s suggests that in a world in which the concept of an Arab consensus has been broken by the Gulf war, the Soviet Union fragmented, and a final settlement of the Arab-Israeli conflict set in motion, the old patterns of diplomacy will no longer operate. Even the post-First World War settlement of the region's frontiers may not be set in concrete.

20

The West and the Arabs

The West's involvement with the Arab world – oil – trade, investment, Arab emigration, relations with Europe – arms sales – new international order and Western pressure on radicals – hoped-for benefits of democratic reform – likelihood of relations remaining difficult

Whether they like it or not the Western industrialized nations have a great interest in the economic and political state of the Arab world. The public becomes most aware of this when Europe and the United States are drawn into the region's wars. In the last fifteen years this has happened on a number of occasions, these being: the despatch of forces to Lebanon in 1982, the US Navy's protection of reflagged Kuwaiti tankers in the mid-1980s and its skirmishes with the Iranian navy at this time, the Gulf war of 1991, and the operations mounted to protect the Kurds in northern Iraq and the Shias in the south after the end of that war. There have been several further occasions on which American forces, responding to provocation or what their government believed was terrorism sponsored by Colonel Gaddafi, have gone into action against Libya.

Until recently, when the Soviet Union collapsed and the Palestinians and Israelis began making peace, the West feared the possibility of its becoming involved in a full-scale Arab-Israeli war and, through that, in a confrontation with the Soviet Union. Even without this happening, Arab-Israeli wars have had serious consequences. They led to oil embargoes in 1967 and 1973, on the latter occasion helping to cause a huge increase in the price of oil. Another round of oil price rises was brought about by the Iranian Revolution, which was a further manifestation of the region's instability.

The West has considerable commercial interests in the Arab world; it does a great deal of trade and financial business with it. This is not just in oil and arms. The region is a major market for food and manufactured goods. It is Britain's third largest export market after the European Union and North America. The United States, Japan and all the major European countries have investments in the region, not only in oil and petrochemicals but in manufacturing and banking. They have huge outstanding loans to Arab governments – as well as significant sums to private companies and individuals – and they give billions of dollars of aid, in grants and soft loans, to the region every year. Periodically they become involved in major programmes of disaster or famine relief, such as that undertaken in Sudan in the mid-1980s. They are concerned with the reform and restructuring of the Arab economies. In the minds of the European governments there is always the fear that the collapse of an economy in North Africa might lead to a wave of emigration, in which desperate, hungry unemployed Arabs would pour into southern Europe.

The most fundamental interest of the West in the Arab world is in its supplies of oil. The Western economies are much less dependent on oil, and particularly Arab oil, than they were at the time of the first 'oil shock' of 1973–4. Their consumption has remained more or less static since the end of the 1970s while their gross domestic products have continued to expand. They have been able to achieve this change by becoming much more efficient in their use of energy and, to a smaller degree, developing alternative sources of energy, particularly electricity produced from gas. Even so, oil remains an extremely important and attractive fuel. It is relatively cheap to develop, easy to transport compared to coal or liquified gas, yields a large amount of energy from a given weight or volume, and therefore can usually be delivered to the consumer at a price which is competitive with any other source of energy. In short, it remains the fuel which companies and the public prefer to use.

During the next decade or so it seems likely that demand for oil in the industrialized world will remain static, but in the developing and newly industrialized countries it will continue to rise. At the time of the first oil shock demand in these countries was regarded as almost insignificant, but since 1984 it has been growing by about 1 million barrels a day every year and it seems set to continue to grow at this rate for the next twenty to twenty-five years. Given that world oil

demand in 1993 was running at some 67 million barrels a day, the
additional demand from the developing countries will represent an
annual increase of about 1.5 per cent during the later 1990s, which
does not seem very much. The potential problem for the oil market is
that unless there are some large and unexpected discoveries elsewhere,
virtually all of this additional demand will have to be met from just
one area, the Middle East. It is possible that if the economy of Russia
recovers from the confusion it was in as it tried to reconstruct itself in
1992–3, that country might make a contribution by doubling its
exports to some 3 million barrels per day. It is also possible that at the
beginning of the next century the developing countries will start to
become more efficient and more pollution-conscious in their use of fuel.
There is great scope for their doing both of these things, and if they
do act they will reduce the increase in their demand. Yet even with a
contribution from Russia and more efficient energy use, it is hard to
see the Middle East not being asked to produce an extra 15 million
barrels per day in the course of the next twenty years.

    The additional demand will fall on five countries: Iran, Iraq, Kuwait,
the United Arab Emirates, and specifically Abu Dhabi within the UAE,
and Saudi Arabia. In 1993, when Iraq's production was still shut down
by United Nations' sanctions, these countries were producing some 16–
17 million barrels per day, which means that for the group as a whole
the increase demanded will involve nearly a doubling of production.
Much the biggest share of the additional oil is expected to come from
Iraq, which before it invaded Kuwait was producing nearly 3 million
barrels per day. Iraq is known to have huge reserves, but they have
never been properly exploited. Part of the reason for this during the
early years of production, in the 1940s and 1950s, was that the first
fields to be discovered were in the north of the country, hundreds of
miles from any port. For the oil to be exported, pipelines had to be
laid to the Mediterranean, which made Iraqi production less profitable,
and less able to be expanded quickly in the event of a crisis, than
Kuwaiti and Saudi production. It also happened that the country's
concessionaire, the Iraq Petroleum Company, was owned by five principal shareholders, BP, Shell, Total, Exxon and Mobil, which meant that
no single company had a major stake in the country's reserves. Each
of the shareholders, except Compagnie Française des Petroles (Total),
had more interesting concessions to develop elsewhere in the Middle
East. The Iraqi government, naturally, complained that its resources
were being under-exploited, and almost from the time production began
its relations with its concessionaire were difficult. This, added to the
country's instability, only increased the companies' preference for

investing in production facilities elsewhere. Eventually, in 1972, the Baathist government, encouraged by Saddam Hussein, then Vice-President, nationalized IPC and vowed to develop the country's oil itself.

Iraq's problem since then has been that although it has had highly competent engineers capable of running a production operation, it has not had the expertise, personnel and back-up required to mount the massive exploration and development programme it needs, and for political reasons it has not wanted to employ major Western companies, and particularly American companies, as contractors. Most of the firms it has used as contractors and production-sharing partners have been small by world standards; some of them have come from other developing countries. Once the United Nations' sanctions have been lifted and production begins again, which presumably will be after Saddam has been removed, it is assumed in the oil industry that Iraq will invite back the big American and European companies to work for it, either as contractors, or, more likely, given its shortage of capital, on some form of production-sharing basis. If it does this it is estimated that it will be able to raise its production capacity to 8–10 million barrels per day.

The remaining four big Gulf producers should quite easily be able to provide the additional 5–7 million barrels per day that will be needed on top of the Iraqi output. All except Iran have reserves that are under-exploited at present and two of them, Saudi Arabia and Iran, will certainly be glad of the extra revenues that increased production will bring. Iran, like Iraq, will probably be forced to bring in Western companies, though in its case the purpose will be to help sustain and slightly increase production from complex and ageing fields that have been on-stream for many years.

As the production capacity of all these countries increases during the next twenty years there will always be a fairly delicate balance between supply and demand. In these conditions even quite small disruptions in supply in the Middle East or elsewhere in the world will be liable to lead to what oil analysts refer to as 'excursions into higher prices' – probably in the $40–60 per barrel range – but for the reasons explained in Chapter 1, the Gulf producers will try to see that these excursions do not last long. They will not want to encourage a movement by the consumers away from oil until their reserves are much more depleted than they will be by 2015. Nevertheless the fine balance of the market, and reminders of its fragility, will make Western consumers extremely concerned about the possibility of a major upheaval in the Middle East. Both governments and oil companies remember that it was an Arab-Israeli war that was one of the causes of the price rises of 1973–4, which were maintained without difficulty for five years, and that just as the market was beginning to weaken it was the revolution in Iran that pushed prices up again and kept them above $30 for a further seven years. Price rises of this duration lead to major transfers of wealth – goods and services – to the oil producers, rich and poor. They make the industrialized countries poorer, which from their own governments' and electorates' point of view is something to be avoided, and in the first two or three years after the initial shock they lead to recession and unemployment. For these reasons, as much as their wishing to avoid further military involvement in the area, the Western countries have a very strong interest in trying to make the Middle East more stable, or, at the very least, in seeing that it does not become more unstable than it is already.

The industrialized countries' other commercial concerns with the Arab world are in their exports of manufactured goods, imports of foodstuffs, raw materials and various unsophisticated industrial products, and their investments in the region. Much of this business involves the straightforward export of goods to Saudi Arabia and the Gulf states, which are much bigger markets than the numbers of their populations suggest. Their demand for consumer goods is inflated by the extravagant habits of their own people (which, admittedly, have been much curbed in recent years), by the re-exports of their traders and by the large quantities of goods bought by immigrant labourers and pilgrims from poorer countries. Their desirability as markets is increased by their lack of exchange controls and ability to pay cash. Unlike trade with many countries of the developing world, transactions with governments in the Arabian oil producers do not have to be linked to the exporters' or contractors' governments providing credit.

With the Arab countries around the Mediterranean the Western countries' commercial relations are extensive but more difficult. The volume of trade flowing in both directions is enormous. The European Union, which on the Western side is the biggest trading partner, does far more business with this area than it does with Japan, and it registers a large surplus in its dealings. The complications stem from some of the trade being restricted still, in both directions, by tariffs and quotas, and from the Arab countries' need for commercial credits. This in due course has involved the industrialized countries in negotiations on debt rescheduling and, hence, on the reform of the Arab economies. Relations are further complicated by the Arabs' fear that the Europeans may see them just as a market on which they can dump their goods, while they develop closer economic links with eastern Europe. For their part the Europeans fear Arab immigration.

The source of both sides' fears is the underdevelopment and high unemployment of the Arab countries, particularly in the Maghreb. The Arab governments and middle classes are frightened of their countries being overwhelmed by poverty and unemployment, leading to riots, the flight of the most able and best-qualified people, and ultimately Islamic revolution, as so nearly happened in Algeria. They argue that Europe too ought to be worried by this prospect. It already has a large population of North Africans on its territory which would be greatly increased if economic collapse led to unstoppable waves of emigration; and if revolution in the region were to be followed by civil war, it is very likely that the Europeans would be dragged in. The cries of the North African intelligentsia in the last five years, therefore, have been, '*La richesse et la misère ne peut pas cohabiter*', and 'Europe must help us find a solution'.

A specific plea is that Europe should not try to keep out Maghrebi workers, because the possibility of these people emigrating provides a safety valve for some of the region's unemployment and a potential source of foreign exchange remittances. A fear that is expressed in this context is that Europe is in the process of turning itself into a 'social fortress' in which its own relatively rich workers will be protected by a generous social security system while foreigners will be kept out, if possible, or in cases where a few are allowed in, given inferior benefits and treated with contempt. Moves towards closer European integration, such as the creation of the single market and the Maastricht Treaty, only reinforce such fears. Instead of looking inward, the North Africans say, Europe should do all it can to encourage the development of their countries, by allowing the free movement of their people, investing in them and buying their products. In general, when planning its own future it should bear in mind the importance of its having stable neighbours.

The officials of the European Commission, which maintains its own offices in the Arab countries, and European diplomats and other civil servants, are quite sympathetic to the Arabs' concerns, though they consider them slightly neurotic and say that they would do better to look more to themselves for a solution to their problems and less to Europe. European politicians are much less sympathetic. Since the beginning of the 1990s governments, and opposition parties, have been worried by Europe's own recession and unemployment, and, responding to the fears of their own electorates, they have been particularly concerned with the issue of immigration. There is anxiety about the growing numbers of immigrants. In 1993 it was estimated that there were some 7 million people from non-European Union Mediterranean countries resident in member states, the majority there legally, some, perhaps 20 per cent, illegally. In itself the number of these immigrants was not big, but it was substantial in relation to the numbers of EU unemployed. The Europeans' fear is that immigration will increase and that this will bring with it not only increased unemployment but lower wages and a lowering of the standards of social services as more non-Europeans paying relatively small amounts of tax compete for places in schools, hospital beds and welfare benefits. In France, in particular, there is a fear that Islamic religious extremism will take root among the immigrant population. The greatest anxiety of all is that there will be mass illegal immigration from North Africa to Europe, with hundreds of thousands arriving in Italy and Spain by boat.

Responding to these fears, in 1990 the European governments began demanding that all Arabs coming to their countries should have visas. The new rules came as a shock to the North African governments and, particularly, to their middle classes. The idea behind the change was that it would move the point of decision on whom should be allowed in, and on what terms, from European frontiers to the respective embassies in Arab countries, where the process would be easier and cheaper. It enabled the authorities to consider more carefully who might be liable to ignore the permitted period of stay, but, of course, it did nothing to prevent illegal immigration.

In the long term it will probably be necessary for Europe to liberalize its policies, because the birth rates of its own people are now so low that from about 2005 onwards it seems that it will need a steady flow of immigrants to maintain the size of its workforce. The irony is that by then it may be that the birth rates in North Africa will have fallen low enough for most of the young people coming on to the labour markets to be absorbed at home.

Meanwhile the European governments' response to the North Africans' cries of anguish over their immigration policies, and their other pleas for help, has been to urge them boldly to implement the reforms proposed by the IMF and the World Bank and to try to integrate their economies. They point out that the three Maghreb countries make up a market of some 60 million consumers and that their economies should to some extent be complementary, with Algeria producing energy, Morocco agricultural products, and Tunisia, potentially, industrial goods and services that will make use of its relatively skilled labour force. Half of the aid, made up of grants, project loans and technical assistance, which is now being given by the European Union to non-member Mediterranean countries, is for what is known as 'horizontal co-operation', which involves joint projects and regional environmental schemes.

In liberalizing trade the Europeans argue they have already done about as much as they reasonably can. Practically all manufactured goods from the Arab (and non-Arab) Mediterranean countries now enter the Union free of tariffs and quotas. If manufacturers are to increase their sales they have to improve the quality and packaging of their goods, while maintaining competitive prices. Given the very low cost of labour in the Arab countries – a quarter of the European average – this adjustment ought to be possible.

The Arab exports which are still subject to quotas are certain types of agricultural products – those which the European Mediterranean countries already produce in surplus. The problem for the Arabs – mainly the Tunisians and Moroccans – in this case comes from the Europeans' long-established policy of subsidizing their own farmers and so increasing their output. Changes in this area will only come through negotiations carried out under the General Agreement for Tariffs and Trade (GATT), or through a change in European social and economic policy.

The most important help, it is agreed, that the industrialized countries can give North Africa, will be through European and American companies increasing their investment there. There has already been considerable European investment in Tunisia and Morocco, but much of it has gone into garment manufacture, which from the host countries' point of view is not an ideal type of industry. It uses an almost entirely female workforce and very basic technology, and it is a type of business which local entrepreneurs are perfectly capable of launching and running on their own, as many of them have. The host countries would much prefer foreign investment to go into electrical and mechanical components production. There has already been substantial investment in this area – in Tunisia Alcatel, Siemens, BASF, L.M. Ericsson, Goldstar and Sony have established plants – though many of the components being produced are rather simple. The North African governments would like to see foreign companies transferring more complicated and higher-value types of work, particularly the production of car parts, to their territories. They argue, predictably, that by providing employment and so increasing the purchasing power of their people, the manufacturers will be expanding the markets for their products.

The reason why foreign companies have not been more active investors in the region has much to do with bureaucracy and/or the engrained socialist attitudes of the governments. They also find it difficult to recruit local managers who have a real understanding, or any experience, of doing business in a free market. Companies that have been looking for potential partners have run into the same problem – as was seen in the experience of the US government's Overseas Private Investment Corporation (OPIC), which organized exploratory visits by twelve American corporations to Tunisia in April 1992. OPIC and the American embassy publicized the visits well in advance and they were contacted by some hundreds of Tunisians who were interested in working with the corporations. Many of the potential partners were intelligent and well educated but they tended to assume that all they needed to put into a relationship was land or their good contacts in the government. Some, when asked what sort of business they wanted to go into, replied 'anything'. Even after the embassy and OPIC had weeded out most candidates of this type in their initial interviews, the corporations after their meetings said they were struck by the short-term mentality of the potential partners, by their failure to understand the need for planning and by their general lack of market-orientated entrepreneurial flair. It was noticed that they were totally unlike businessmen in the Far East. Most of the companies were disappointed at the end of their visit.

The moral of this tale for the North African governments, particularly in Tunisia and Egypt, is that the encouragement of foreign investment is not only a matter of giving investment incentives and signing protocols with industrialized countries' governments. It requires a change in the mentality of the local business classes that will best be brought about by the continued unravelling of socialism and the pursuit of structural reform.

A large part of the trade of Europe and America with the Arab countries, particularly in the eastern part of the Arab world, is in arms. Both of the two recent wars in the region have increased demand by showing how effective high-technology and weapons of mass destruction can be. At the end of the Iran-Iraq war in 1988 it was Iraq's use of poison gas and the Scud missiles it fired at Tehran that caused the Iranians' morale to crack. Then in the Gulf war both sides exploited sophisticated weapons. The Iraqis fired Scuds at Saudi Arabia and Israel and caused much alarm in both places, particularly in the early stages of the war when it was feared that they might be going to use warheads filled with poison gas. The allies used cruise missiles and laser-guided bombs, which for the most part avoided civilian casualties but left the Iraqis with a feeling of helplessness. Both the Iraqis' and the allies' weapons greatly impressed the world's television audiences and the governments of developing countries.

One lesson learned, mainly by governments ill-disposed to the West, was that if a developing country was ever to have a chance of standing up to the West it had to have weapons of mass destruction that would frighten its enemy's public and offset his superior conventional technology. The weapons that seemed by far the most desirable were long-range ballistic missiles and nuclear warheads. Another lesson, learned mainly by the West's friends, who would obviously not be provided with nuclear technology by their patrons, was that if they were going to win a regional war or resist aggression they would have to have the highest technology conventional weapons they could handle.

Since the end of the Gulf war the arms purchases of Middle Eastern countries have been further stimulated by the rearmament of Iran, which has worried the Saudis and Gulf Arabs. The peace between the Palestinians and Israelis, if it holds and leads to peace between Israel and Jordan and Syria, ought to have the opposite effect, in reducing demand for arms. It should lead fairly quickly to a cut in defence spending by the combatants, and in the longer term, through removing the prime cause of instability in the region, it should create a happier and less volatile Arab world, which would be less inclined to spend money on arms. But that is only in theory. The re-emergence of Iran as a military power and perhaps the greater involvement of Turkey in the region's politics, and the shifting alliances that the rise of these two powers may cause, are quite likely to offset the effects of the end of the Arab-Israeli conflict.

Whatever happens there is no doubt that there will be plenty of arms available for the governments to buy. Since the collapse of the eastern European Communist regimes the free market has been awash with arms, including the most sophisticated Soviet equipment, for sale at about a third of its production cost. The availability of arms has been increased by the break-up of the Soviet Union and the economic crisis in Russia. The Russians, as they took stock of their prospects in 1993, were quite open in saying that they had to sell (conventional) arms because these were the only products they made that could be exported, without a subsidy, for hard currency. It was feared that individuals, rather than governments, from some of the new independent states that used to make up the Soviet Union might be offering to help other countries develop nuclear weapons technology. They were joined in the market by North Korea, which was believed to be a possible seller of nuclear technology, and it was known that North Korea and Pakistan, using Chinese technology, were helping Iran develop ballistic missiles.

The West, meanwhile, has been happy to provide its own friends in the Middle East with almost any conventional weapon they have wanted to buy. In the eighteen months after the end of the Gulf war the United States committed itself to selling $28 billion of arms to Saudi Arabia alone. Further contracts were negotiated with Saudi Arabia and the Gulf states by Britain and France. The enthusiasm of the Western governments for selling arms led one of the members of a conference on the Middle East, held at Ditchley Park near Oxford, in December 1992, to remark that they were 'worse than the Bourbons', in that they had 'forgotten nothing and learnt nothing'.

The obvious effect of this was to increase the potential severity of any future conflict in the region. Less obviously, some of the Western sales were working against the stability of the very countries they were supposed to be helping. In Saudi Arabia in 1993 weapons purchases were one of the main causes of the government's budget deficit and, because they were well known to be accompanied by much corruption, they were also a cause of popular anger. Resentment of the pay-offs, made in the form of commission to the exporters' local representatives, was not confined to Islamist agitators and their supporters; it spread to almost the highest levels in the government. A very well regarded minister to whom I spoke in a London hotel in 1993 told me that 'the main fact determining who gets an arms contract is the corruption', and he then added with some passion: 'listen, the only thing that will stop this is you [the Western press] writing about it – embarrassing our government and your people who pay the bribes. And your government must stop allowing people to pay, if it wants us to remain a stable country'. Ten minutes after the end of this conversation, I met a young member of one of the Gulf ruling families who said much the same thing. It would have been possible and logical for me to have replied to both that if the Arab governments wanted to stamp out corruption they had it in their power to do so, but that would not have altered the fact that the speakers' views were that the West was partly responsible for their countries' problems. Right or wrong, their views contained a message for the Western governments.

The Western governments, of course, deplore both the build-up of weapons and the corruption they realize goes with it, but they cannot bring themselves to stop their sales. They are under pressure from several sources. They know that if they do not sell to their friends those countries will be at a disadvantage *vis à vis* their enemies. They have to worry about the expense of their own arms procurement programmes, which can be much reduced if part of the development costs can be spread over some export orders. They have to think of their balance of trade, the need to create jobs and the need to keep their arms manufacturers profitable.

Each Western government also knows that if it does not sell to its friends, its competitors will be only too happy to do so. This, in effect, is what happened when Britain in 1986 won the first of its series of huge Saudi contracts for Tornado bombers. The US Congress, under pressure from Zionist groups seeking to undermine America's relationship with Saudi Arabia, for many years had been delaying and modifying its own government's programmes for arms sales to the Kingdom, and the Saudis, tired of the humiliation this caused them, turned to another supplier.

In the case of the sales of arms and arms-making equipment to Iraq in the mid- and late-1980s, which have caused much controversy since the Gulf crisis, the Western governments came under a further series of pressures, some external and some generated by themselves. Their behaviour at that time raises the question of what should be the proper balance between commercial advantage and morality in Western countries' dealings with governments that are not obviously hostile but are clearly unpleasant and potentially dangerous.

The external pressures came from Iraq's then allies, Egypt, Jordan and Saudi Arabia, which were terrified that if Iraq were to lose its war with Iran an Islamic republic would be established in Baghdad and then the Islamic revolution would engulf them and spread across the Middle East. The Western governments subscribed to this theory themselves, with differing degrees of conviction; the most ardent believers were the French. They therefore decided to help Iraq. The French supplied it with aircraft, Exocet missiles and air defence equipment, the Americans with intelligence and the British with munitions and arms-making equipment. Western officials found the Iraqis with whom they dealt impressively business-like and they persuaded themselves that, though severe, their government was probably not as unpleasant as it had been made out to be. Many of the officials (outside the British and American foreign services) whom I met during the later stages of the war seemed remarkably ignorant of the record of Saddam's regime (and of previous Iraqi republican regimes) and much of that ignorance no doubt extended to the top of the governments.

After the end of the war the Western governments' inhibitions were further reduced by what they saw as the need to build relations with a country which seemed quite likely to become the leading Arab power. Both the British and American governments hesitated in their granting of credit facilities, and even talked of imposing restrictions on trade, in the early autumn of 1988 after the Iraqis had used poison gas against the Kurds, but neither of them pursued the matter. In striking a balance in their policies between promoting their trade in civilian and military goods, and trying to use their influence to make the Iraqi government more humane and less aggressive – it was already being asked why it was not demobilizing its forces – the emphasis was put on trade. Here, as in similar cases, it was much easier for the governments to concentrate on business, not just because it was more profitable, but because it yielded a more tangible, measurable benefit than a policy which tried to balance trade with attempts to exert moral influence, which might produce a country that would be more stable and potentially a better friend in the long term. In retrospect it is clear that the Western powers were much too ready to overlook the unpleasantness of the Iraqi regime and give up all but the mildest attempts to influence it. There is, of course, no certainty that a bolder, more moral policy would have prevented the invasion of Kuwait, but there is no doubt that the eagerness of the Western powers to do business with his regime in the later 1980s encouraged Saddam in his belief that if he invaded Kuwait nothing would be done to stop him.

Since the end of the Gulf war the Western powers have taken a slightly more moral (or in Arab eyes coercive) line in their dealings with unpleasant regimes in the Middle East, though this has not had any effect on their arms sales because the countries affected have been ones to which the West would not have sold arms anyway. For there to be a change in the level of arms sales there would have to be not just a huge change in the balance between morality and commercial advantage in their policies, but a number of other practical changes as well. The governments would have to agree with each other and with Russia not to compete in the arms market, and they would have to be prepared to see their arms manufacturing industries run down and many of their employees diverted into civil work, which would imply that they believed they were going to live at peace in the foreseeable future. It is very unlikely that any of these changes will ever happen.

The improvement in the West's bargaining position and ability to criticize unpleasant regimes brought about by its victory in the Gulf has been further strengthened by the collapse of Communism. Arab, and other African and Asian countries can no longer play off Western governments against the Soviet bloc, by implying that if they criticize their human-rights records, stop giving them aid or credits, or refuse to sell them arms they will turn to the other side. The Western governments' concern, when this type of manœuvring was still possible, was not so much commercial – trade rivalries are regularly exploited by developing countries playing Western states off against each other – it was that they would be giving the Soviets an opportunity to establish a presence in the countries whose policies they were hoping to change. Aid deals, after all, lead to construction contracts and further loans and contracts, and military sales need to be supported by instructors and maintenance crews. As a *quid pro quo* in a big arms contract the seller is often given the use of base facilities.

In the changed conditions of the early 1990s it was thought that the new international order might enable the West to be assertive in putting pressure on oppressive governments. There was talk of it being able to suppress terrorism and improve governments' treatment of their own people. In a speech in June 1990, Douglas Hurd, the British Foreign Secretary, stated bluntly: 'Countries which tend towards pluralism, public accountability, respect for the rule of law, human rights and market principles should be encouraged. Governments which persist with repressive policies, corrupt management and wasteful and discredited economic systems should not expect us to support their folly with scarce aid resources which can be better used elsewhere'. At about the same time President Mitterand, addressing a summit of Francophone African heads of state, announced that France would be less generous towards regimes that acted in an authoritarian manner, 'without accepting evolution towards democracy'. Similar criteria for aid were laid down by the United States and Germany, and Japan announced its intention of reducing aid to countries which spent too much on defence.

After the end of the Gulf war the Western powers began to talk, and act, even more firmly. When what remained of the Iraqi army was brutally suppressing a rebellion by the Kurds, they sent troops to establish a safe haven for the people on Iraqi territory and declared an air-exclusion zone covering a much bigger area of northern Iraq. A year earlier the idea of America, Britain and France intervening in the internal affairs of an Arab country, even to protect a people on whom the government had used poison gas on several occasions, would have been inconceivable.

In the mood of the moment it began to be suggested in the West, in the press and in government circles, that the major powers might redefine their international moral and political duties. For the previous forty-five years it had been accepted that countries could and should help other nation states defend their borders against aggression, but now it was being suggested that the international community might have an additional responsibility, to protect peoples, particularly minorities, inside their own countries. The established idea that the sovereignty of governments should be inviolable was being questioned.

The whole debate was conducted with reference to the United Nations, as the organization which would give legitimacy to groups of Western, and developing, countries intervening in other states' affairs. It was recognized that the operation in the Gulf had only been a success because it had been conducted entirely under the authority of UN resolutions, and had stuck scrupulously to the terms of those resolutions, particularly in ensuring that allied forces were withdrawn from southern Iraq within days of the end of the fighting. The intervention in Kurdistan, likewise, had taken place under a UN mandate.

As events turned out in the following two and a half years the implementation of the new ideas was difficult. The Western countries could not find a way of intervening to stop the succession of wars in former Yugoslavia, and when the United States, acting under a UN umbrella, sent troops to try to restore order in Somalia, so that food aid could be distributed, its expedition was a failure. In sponsoring resolutions at the United Nations on Bosnia and Libya in 1992 the United States and the European countries encountered resistance from China and from influential developing countries, including India, which were concerned about the infringement of countries' sovereignty. There was a noticeable growth of resentment in the Middle East of the power of the West in a 'uni-polar world', and this seemed to make some countries, notably Iran and Sudan, more inflexible. There were fears expressed that the dominance of the West might actually encourage confrontational policies, in countries which felt they no longer had the security of being able to play the Soviet card.

For all these difficulties, the influence the West could exert in 1992 and 1993 was greater than it had been a few years earlier. Most radical governments in the Middle East and other parts of the developing world had to make their peace with the United States, even if that meant no more than ceasing to attack it verbally and co-operating coolly with its diplomacy. It was noticeable that almost every Arab state agreed to take part in the multilateral talks with Israel. It was also noted in 1992 that Syria was persuaded to plough up the extensive fields of opium poppies in the Bekaa valley, which had been a useful source of income for its own senior officers as well as for Hizbollah. In Sudan the complete cut-off of Western government aid that followed the coup of 1989 and mounting human rights abuses did not lead to any obvious change in policies but it was assumed that it was restricting the government in its promotion of terrorism abroad.

The countries on which the West was putting most pressure in the early 1990s were Iraq and Libya. Iraq, since its defeat in 1991, had been the subject of a series of UN resolutions ordering it to demolish all its weapons of mass destruction and submit to UN supervision of the process, as well as random inspections intended to discover any stockpiles or manufacturing facilities it might be disguising. By the end of 1993 it had mainly complied with demands in this area, but it was still under UN instructions to pay compensation to Kuwait for the damage it had done during its occupation and accept a new demarcation of its border, where there had been a small adjustment in Kuwait's favour. It had also been instructed to cease all military action against the Kurds, and against the Shias in the southern marshes. Until it complied with these orders Iraq was to remain subject to comprehensive sanctions, banning all trade, freezing its assets abroad and stopping all flights to and from the country. Given that Saddam clearly had no intention of accepting these resolutions – and that if he did accept them there would be little chance of his staying in power – the UN position effectively put an indefinite embargo on Iraq. The government had turned down the United Nations' invitation for it to sell $1.6 billion worth of oil, under international supervision, so that it could buy essential foodstuffs and medical supplies to alleviate its people's suffering and pay the UN's costs in supervising the destruction of its weapons.

Libya likewise had sanctions imposed on it. These stemmed from the discovery by the American, British and French police and intelligence services that Libyan agents had been responsible for the bombing of a Pan Am flight over Lockerbie in December 1988, when 270 people had been killed, and for the bombing of a UTA flight over Niger a few months later. The agents involved had been identified and the three Western governments were demanding that they be handed over to stand trial. When the Libyans refused, the governments turned to the United Nations to impose sanctions. An initial resolution was passed in April 1992, stopping all flights into and out of the country, and a second resolution in November 1993 banned the sale to Libya of all equipment needed for oilfield production and maintenance, and froze the country's official assets abroad. It was assumed that if the Libyans remained obdurate further resolutions would be proposed, if support could be mustered, to embargo its oil exports and its import trade. As in the case of Iraq, it seemed that there was very little chance of the government doing what the United Nations and the Western powers wanted; if it handed over the agents they would implicate important people in the bombings, and that would lead to the country being subject to additional sanctions and demands for the surrender of these people.

In dealing with both the Iraqi and Libyan governments the Western powers knew that their sanctions were probably not going to make the regimes do what they wanted, but that was not their sole purpose. The powers' unstated intention was steadily to weaken and marginalize two thoroughly nasty regimes, to prevent them from making further international mischief – an aim which was being well fulfilled in 1992 and 1993 – and if possible bring about their downfall. While the process was going on the fate of the two countries served as a lesson to other unpleasant regimes, and if eventually Saddam Hussein and Muammar Gaddafi were replaced, it was assumed that their successors would behave more pleasantly, both to other countries and to their own people.

It was sometimes suggested in discussions on these countries' future in the West and the Arab world, that there was no guarantee that new regimes in Iraq and Libya would necessarily be any better than the ones they replaced. However, the Western powers calculated that there was a good chance of getting better replacements. They could see that in both countries any new government was going to be forced by its circumstances to be more moderate and responsible than its predecessor. It would have to make a clean break with the previous regime, in Libya's case by handing over the accused agents, and in Iraq's by reaching some sort of settlement with the Kurds, the Shias and Kuwait. It would also have to negotiate with the West to secure the assistance it would need for the reconstruction of its economy and the rescheduling of its debts. It was difficult to imagine any leader who did not think he could achieve these tasks having the self-confidence to take over, or try to take over, his country's government.

The West's hope is that in the next decade or so it will be dealing with an Arab world which will gradually become better disposed towards it, as the Arab-Israeli conflict recedes in people's memories and more of the governments move slowly towards democracy. Democratic, or semi-democratic, governments in the Arab world, if these emerge, will have roughly the same institutions as Western democracies, they will probably favour free-market economic policies and respect human rights, and they are likely to be more self-confident than one-party regimes. All these features, the Western powers feel, should make for a more natural rapport and better understanding between themselves and the Arabs. The benefits, though, are not guaranteed and they may be apparent only in the long term. It is very likely that in individual cases, particularly in the early years of change, steps towards democracy will make relations between Arab states and the West more difficult.

This is what happened in Jordan during the Gulf crisis, when King Hussein was obliged to be much more pro-Iraqi than he would have been had he not been answerable to a parliament. In Jordan and elsewhere democratic governments will be representing a populace which may not be pro-Western. The point was made by Mahdi Tajir, the former UAE ambassador in London, who told me during the crisis: 'They will reflect the views of the societies they govern, not necessarily the views of other democratic governments'.

The basic fact will remain that the Arab countries are part of the poor 'South' of the world, while the Western industrialized countries belong to the rich 'North'. This is a vital distinction between them. Now that Communism has collapsed, the separation between North and South will be the major division in the world during the rest of the 1990s and well into the next century. Before he became Secretary General of the UN, while he was still Egypt's Minister of State for Foreign Affairs, Boutros Boutros Ghali referred to the division as 'the new Iron Curtain', one which would be 'more difficult to destroy than the old one, because it is based not on ideology but on economic facts'.

Arab-West relations will be made more difficult by the Arabs being Muslim and the Westerners Christian or, and this is perhaps worse from the point of view of the two cultures' respect for each other, secular, having no faith at all. Westerners do not always realize it, but the hostility of many Muslims towards their society is not always based on a lack of understanding of it, or on an ancient hostility to Christianity, but on a reasoned rejection of its materialism and lack of clearly defined moral principles. This fundamental difference may not deepen in future – it may even become less pronounced if Islam recedes as a political force – but it will remain important.

A further strain in relations will come from what are perceived as the past wrongs of colonial rule inflicted on the Arab countries and from the cultural confusion the imperial powers have left behind them. This confusion exists in all former colonial countries but it is particularly strong in the Arab world. It has been reinforced by the frustrations that have come from the conflict with Israel. The Arabs feel that the West has humiliated them and made them weak by corrupting their culture. This idea was bluntly expressed by the Algerian novelist, Leila Hamoutene, who told me, 'We all feel our countries have been raped by you'. She and many other people have explained to me that in their view the West is still trying to dominate the Arab world, manipulate it and take away its independence. It was in part this feeling that led so many Arabs to support Saddam during the Gulf crisis. They saw him as the one Arab leader who was prepared to defy the West, and they believed that the West, in uniting to crush him, was trying to empty the Arab nation of the last vestige of its independence. This view may seem absurd to Westerners, who take the independence of the Arab countries for granted and are happy to deal with them on equal terms as long as they are not blatantly hostile to their interests. But in the minds of the Arabs the idea of the West's malevolence and of its conspiring against them is deeply rooted and will remain for many years.

These three divisions – between rich and poor, a Muslim and a chiefly secular society, and what are seen as a dominant and a weaker power – will not be removed by the Arab countries gradually introducing democracy or by the end of the confrontation with Israel, if that finally is the result of the Palestinian-Israeli accord of September 1993. Democracy and peace will help relations between the West and the Arabs, but they are not all that is needed to make them friends. From a Western point of view the Arab world will remain a difficult place for a long time. Most likely the words of a former British ambassador to the region will continue to apply. 'In the Middle East,' he said, 'you should always expect the worst. But remember three things: it will take longer to happen than you suppose, it won't be quite as bad as you fear, and it will be different from what you expect.'

INDEX

Sub-entries under major countries are not listed alphabetically but chronologically or in the order in which they are discussed in the text.